The Major Writings of
Nichiren Daishonin

The Major Writings of Nichiren Daishonin

Volume Two

Editor-Translator
The Gosho Translation Committee

NICHIREN SHOSHU INTERNATIONAL CENTER · *Tokyo*

Editor-Translator: The Gosho Translation Committee. Book design and typography; Rebecca M. Davis. Cover design: Nen Tanaka. Composition and printing: Komiyama Printing Co., Ltd., Tokyo. Binding: Maki Book Binding and Printing Co., Ltd., Tokyo. The typeface used is Bembo.

First Edition, 1981
Ninth Printing, 1988

Published by Nichiren Shoshu International Center, 1–33–11 Sendagaya, Shibuya-ku, Tokyo 151

Library of Congress Catalog Card Number: 79–313378

ISBN4–88872–012–6 C1315
Printed in Japan

Contents

Preface

THROUGHOUT two exiles, repeated attempts on his life, continual harassment by the authorities and the privation of his years at Minobu, Nichiren Daishonin continued to pour out encouragement to his followers in a succession of letters and treatises. The collection of doctrinal essays, recorded oral teachings and personal letters which we call the Gosho contains not only the doctrines, but the spirit, of his Buddhism. In it the timeless principles of Buddhism are clarified from the standpoint of the Daishonin's enlightenment, and the fearlessness and compassion of the man himself stand out vividly.

In response to a growing interest in Nichiren Daishonin's teachings among English-speaking people, volume one of *The Major Writings of Nichiren Daishonin* was published in 1979. This first volume contains thirty-six writings including the epochal treatise, "The True Object of Worship." The present volume is the second in a series designed to make available all the Daishonin's major works. It includes two of his most important essays—the "Risshō Ankoku Ron" (On Securing the Peace of the Land through the Propagation of True Buddhism) and "Kaimoku Shō" (The Opening of the Eyes)— as well as fifteen letters to individual believers. The Gosho in this volume are arranged chronologically. An explanation of format, historical background, the life of Nichiren Daishonin, etc. may be found in the introduction to volume one.

In publishing volume two, we are indebted to the editorial staffs of Nichiren Shoshu Soka Gakkai of America (NSA) and Yasuji Kirimura, chief of the Soka Gakkai Study Department. We especially wish to thank Burton Watson, adjunct professor of Columbia University, for his invaluable assistance in preparing the translations.

This year, 1981, the 700th anniversary of Nichiren Daishonin's passing will be commemorated. We are very happy to be publishing the present volume in honor of this significant event.

Nichiren Shoshu International Center
Editorial Department

The Major Writings of
Nichiren Daishonin

"The Risshō Ankoku Ron is the great mirror that reflects the reality of modern society"

[handwritten annotations:]

- wrote because the land was being attacked by 3 calamities and four derits disasters
- disease spread easily/no medicine
- for us airplane crashes, earthquake

3 calamities
- illness
- inflation } happening around the world
- warfare

it accords with the life condition of the people must change within it
- compassion is the prime pt. of our Buddhism
- nembutsu nothing but illusions kills the people's spirit. Teaches people how to die not live ex. drugs / escape

Risshō Ankoku Ron

O NCE there was a traveler who spoke these words in sorrow to his host:

In recent years, there are unusual disturbances in the heavens, strange occurrences on earth, famine and pestilence, all affecting every corner of the empire and spreading throughout the land. Oxen and horses lie dead in the streets, the bones of the stricken crowd the highways. Over half the population has already been carried off by death, and in every family someone grieves.

All the while some put their whole faith in the "sharp sword"[1] of the Buddha Amida and intone this name of the lord of the Western Paradise; others believe that the Buddha Yakushi will "heal all ills,"[2] and recite the sutra that describes him as the Tathagata of the Eastern Region. Some, putting their trust in the passage in the Lotus Sutra that says, "Illness will vanish immediately, and he will find perpetual youth and eternal life,"[3] pay homage to the wonderful words of that

1. Sharp sword: Reference to Shan-tao's *Hanju-san*, in which he says that calling on the name of Amida Buddha serves as a sword to cut off earthly desires, karma and suffering.

2. Heal all ills: One of the twelve vows of Yakushi Buddha, which appear in the *Hongan-yakushi* Sutra. This sutra also says that if one hears the name of Yakushi Buddha, he can be free from all desires.

3. Passage from the *Yakuō* (23rd) chapter. Here this is a reference to a practice of the Tendai sect.

3

sutra; others, citing the passage in the *Ninnō* Sutra that reads: "The seven difficulties vanish, the seven blessings at once appear,"[4] conduct ceremonies[5] at which a hundred preachers expound the sutra at a hundred places. There are those who follow the secret teachings of the Shingon sect and conduct rituals by filling five jars with water;[6] and others who devote themselves entirely to Zen-type meditation and perceive the emptiness of all phenomena as clearly as the moon. Some write out the names of the seven guardian spirits[7] and paste them on a thousand gates, others paint pictures of the five mighty bodhisattvas[8] and hang them over ten thousand thresholds, and still others pray to the gods of heaven and the deities of earth in ceremonies[9] conducted at the four corners of the capital and on the four boundaries of the nation; others, taking pity on the plight of the common people, make certain that government on the national and local levels is carried out in a benevolent manner.

But despite all these efforts, they merely exhaust themselves

4.   Another reference to the Tendai sect, which held a ritual of prayer based on this passage.

5.   Ceremonies: According to the *Ninnō* Sutra, a type of ceremony originally held by the god Taishaku to defeat the evil king Chōshō. The ceremony of the *Ninnō* Sutra was sometimes conducted to protect or bring about peace.

6.   Filling five jars with water: Ritual in which priests of the Shingon sect placed five jars, colored white, blue, red, yellow and black, on a platform, and put into them, respectively, gold, silver, lapis lazuli, pearls and crystal. In addition, they placed in these jars the five grains, five herbs, and five types of incense, and then filled them with water and set flowers in them. The ritual of filling the jars in this manner was believed to eliminate disasters.

7.   Seven guardian spirits: Spirits referred to in the *Kyakuon-shinju* Sutra.

8.   Five mighty bodhisattvas: Reference in the *Ninnō* Sutra. According to this sutra, if a ruler embraces the correct teachings of Buddhism, these five powerful bodhisattvas will protect him and the people in his country.

9.   Ceremonies: Ritual for protecting the country. The four corners of the capital mean the northeast, southeast, southwest and northwest. In these four corners of the capital, the god who eliminates epidemics and the god of medicine were enshrined as protection against the invasion of demons and evil spirits. These gods were also enshrined at the four boundaries of the country for similar reasons. This ritual was often held when an emperor became ill. In the Kamakura period (1185–1333) the gods were enshrined at the four corners of the site of the government buildings and at the four boundaries of Kamakura.

in vain. Famine and disease rage more fiercely than ever, beggars are everywhere in sight, and scenes of death fill our eyes. Cadavers pile up in mounds like observation platforms, dead bodies lie side by side like planks on a bridge.

If we look about, we find that the sun and moon continue to move in their accustomed orbits, and the five planets[10] follow the proper course. The three treasures of Buddhism[11] continue to exist, and the period of a hundred reigns [during which the Bodhisattva Hachiman vowed to protect the nation][12] has not yet expired. Then why is it that the world has already fallen into decline and that the laws of the state have come to an end? What is wrong? What error has been committed?

The host then spoke: I have been brooding alone upon this matter, indignant in my heart, but now that you have come, we can lament together. Let us discuss the question at length.

When a man leaves family life and enters the Buddhist way, it is because he hopes to attain Buddhahood through the teachings of the Dharma. But attempts now to move the gods fail to have any effect, and appeals to the power of the Buddhas produce no results. When I observe carefully the state of the world today, I see ignorant people who give way to doubts because of their naiveté. Therefore they look up at the heavens and mouth their resentment, or gaze down at the earth and sink deep into anxiety.

I have pondered the matter carefully with what limited resources I possess, and have searched rather widely in the scriptures for an answer. The people of today all turn their backs upon what is right; to a man, they give their allegiance to

10.   Five planets: Jupiter, Mars, Venus, Mercury and Saturn. The more distant planets remained undiscovered in thirteenth-century Japan.

11.   Three treasures of Buddhism: The Buddha, Law and Priesthood. The sentence indicates that various sects of Buddhism are still prospering. *See also* Three treasures in the Glossary.

12.   This refers to an oracle said to have been received from Bodhisattva Hachiman in the reign of the fifty-first sovereign, Emperor Heizei (774–824). The "Risshō Ankoku Ron" was written in the reign of the ninetieth sovereign, Emperor Kameyama (1249–1305).

fundamental cause of calamities and disasters
sending people into hell

when peoples life condition is weak devilish function take over and cause disharmony

evil. That is the reason why the benevolent deities have abandoned the nation, why sages leave and do not return. And in their stead come devils and demons, disasters and calamities that arise one after another. I cannot keep silent on this matter. I cannot suppress my fears.

The guest said: These disasters that befall the empire, these calamities of the nation—I am not the only one pained by them; the whole populace is weighed down with sorrow. Now I have been privileged to enter your home and to listen to these enlightening words of yours. You speak of the gods and sages taking leave and of disasters and calamities arising side by side—upon what sutras do you base your views? Could you describe for me the passages of proof?

The host said: There are numerous passages that could be cited and a wide variety of proofs. For example, in the *Konkōmyō* Sutra we read: "[The Four Heavenly Kings said to the Buddha,] 'Though this sutra exists in the nation, the rulers have never allowed it to be propagated. In their hearts they turn away from it, and they take no pleasure in hearing its teachings. They do not serve it, respect it, or sing its praises. Nor are they willing to respect . . . or give material support to the four kinds of Buddhists[13] who embrace the sutra. In the end, they have made it impossible for us and the countless other heavenly beings who are our followers to hear the teachings of this profound and wonderful Dharma. They have deprived us of the sweet dew of its words and cut us off from the flow of the True Law, so that our majesty and strength are drained away. Thus the number of beings who occupy the four evil paths increases and the number who enjoy the human and heavenly states decreases. People fall into the river of birth and death and turn their backs on the road to nirvana.

" 'World-Honored One, we, the Four Heavenly Kings, as

13. Four kinds of Buddhists: Also called four kinds of believers: priests, nuns, laymen and laywomen.

well as our various followers and the yakshas[14] and other beings, observing this state of affairs, have decided to abandon this nation, for we have no more heart to protect it. And it is not we alone who cast aside these rulers. All the great benevolent deities who guard and watch over the countless different regions of the country will also invariably reject them. And once we and the others have abandoned and deserted this nation, then many different types of disasters will occur in the country and the rulers will fall from power. Not a single person in the entire population will possess a heart of goodness; there will be nothing but binding and enslaving, killing and injuring, anger and contention. Men will slander each other or fawn upon one another, and the laws will be twisted until even the innocent are made to suffer. Pestilence will become rampant, comets will appear again and again, two suns will come forth side by side and eclipses will occur with unaccustomed frequency. Black arcs and white arcs will span the sky as harbingers of ill fortune, stars will fall, the earth will shake, and noises will issue from the wells. Torrential rains and violent winds will come out of season, there will be constant famine, and grains and fruits will not ripen. Marauders from many other regions will invade and plunder the nation, the people will suffer all manner of pain and affliction, and there will be no place where one may live in safety.'"

The *Daijuku* Sutra says: "When the principles of Buddhism truly become obscured and lost, then people will all let their beards, hair and fingernails grow long, and the laws of the world will be forgotten and ignored. At that time, loud noises will sound in the air and the earth will shake; everything in the world will begin to move as though it were a waterwheel. City

14. Yakshas: One of the eight kinds of lowly (nonhuman) beings who protect Buddhism. Originally Hindu demons, they were later incorporated into Buddhism as protectors of the True Law, under the command of Bishamonten, one of the Four Heavenly Kings. *See also* Eight kinds of lowly beings in the Glossary.

walls will split and tumble, and all houses and dwellings will collapse. Roots, branches, leaves, petals and fruits will lose their medicinal properties. With the exception of the five highest heavens in the world of form, all the regions of the worlds of form and desire[15] will become deprived of the seven flavors[16] and the three essences[17] that nourish life and human society, until nothing remains alive any more. All the good discourses that lead men to emancipation will at this time disappear. The flowers and fruits that grow in the earth will become few and will lose their flavor and sweetness. The wells, springs and ponds will all go dry, the land everywhere will turn brackish and will crack open and warp into hillocks and gullies. All the mountains will be swept by fire and the heavenly dragons will no longer send down rain. The crops will all wither and die, all living creatures will perish, and even the grass will cease to grow any more. Dust will rain down until all is darkness and the sun and the moon no longer shed their light.

"All the four directions will be afflicted by drought, and evil omens will appear again and again. The ten kinds of evil behavior[18] will increase greatly, particularly greed, anger and stupidity, and people will think no more of their fathers and mothers than does the roe deer. Living beings will decline in numbers, in longevity, physical power and enjoyment. They will become estranged from the pleasures of human and heavenly existence and all will fall into the evil states of existence. The wicked rulers and monks who perform these ten kinds of evil behavior will destroy the True Law of the Buddha and make it impossible for sentient beings to be born in the

15.   Worlds of form and desire: First two divisions of the threefold world, the world of unenlightened beings of the six paths. *See also* Threefold world in the Glossary.

16.   Seven flavors: Sweet, pungent, sour, bitter, salty, astringent, and faint flavors.

17.   Three essences: The power of earth, the power of worldly and Buddhist laws, and the power of human life and society.

18.   Ten kinds of evil behavior: Killing, stealing, committing adultery, lying, deceiving, defaming, engaging in duplicity, greed, anger and stupidity.

human and heavenly states of existence. At that time the various benevolent deities and heavenly rulers, who would ordinarily take pity on living beings, will abandon this nation of confusion and evil and all will make their way to other regions."

The *Ninnō* Sutra states: "When a nation becomes disordered, it is the spirits which first show signs of rampancy. Because these spirits become rampant, all the people of the nation become disordered. Invaders come to plunder the country and the common people face annihilation. The ruler, the high ministers, the heir apparent and the other princes and government officials all quarrel with each other over right and wrong. Heaven and earth manifest prodigies and strange occurrences; the twenty-eight constellations,[19] the stars, the sun and the moon appear at irregular times and in irregular positions, and numerous outlaws rise up."

The same sutra also states: "When I look at the three ages of past, present and future with the five types of vision, I see that all the rulers of nations were able to attain the position of emperor or king because in past existences they served five hundred Buddhas. And this is the reason that all the various sages and arhats are born in their nations and are assisting them to gain great advantage. But if a time should come when the good fortune of these rulers runs out, then all the sages will abandon them and depart. And once the sages have departed, then the seven disasters are certain to arise."

The *Yakushi* Sutra states: "If disasters and calamities should befall members of the ruling *kshatriya*[20] class and anointed kings,[21] such disasters will be as follows: the calamity of disease

19. Twenty-eight constellations: Celestial houses, divided into four houses of seven major heavenly bodies each, corresponding respectively to the four directions and four seasons of east, or spring; south, summer; west, autumn; and north, winter.

20. *Kshatriya*: Second of the four classes or castes in ancient India: the priestly class, military and ruling class (Skt kshatriya), farmers and traders, and serfs.

21. Anointed kings: Rulers of major kingdoms. In ancient India, when the

and pestilence among the populace; the calamity of invasion and plunder from foreign lands; the calamity of revolt within one's own domain; the calamity of irregularities and strange occurrences among the stars and constellations; the calamity of eclipses of the sun and moon; the calamity of unseasonable wind and rain; and the calamity of rain that fails to fall even when the season for it has come and gone."

In the *Ninnō* Sutra, the Buddha addresses [King Prasenajit][22] in these words: "Great King, the region where my teachings now hold sway consists of a hundred billion Sumeru worlds[23] with a hundred billion suns and moons. Each of these Sumeru worlds comprises four great continents. In the empire of the south, which is Jambudvipa, there are sixteen great nations, five hundred medium-sized nations, and ten thousand small nations. In these nations, there are seven types of fearful calamities that may occur. All the rulers of these nations agree that these are indeed calamities. What, then, are these calamities?

"When the sun and moon depart from their regular courses, when the seasons come in the wrong order, when a red sun or a black sun appears, when two, three, four or five suns appear at the same time,[24] when the sun is eclipsed and loses its light, or when one, two, three, four or five coronas appear around the sun, this is the first calamity.

"When the twenty-eight constellations do not move in their

---

ruler of a powerful kingdom ascended the throne, the rulers of smaller kingdoms and their ministers poured water on his head.

22.   Prasenajit: King of the country of Koshala. He converted to Buddhism at the urging of his wife and through Shakyamuni's instruction, and endeavored to protect and support the Buddhist order.

23.   Sumeru worlds: Planets. According to ancient Indian cosmology, each world had a sun, a moon, and a great Mt. Sumeru at its center, surrounded by four continents. The southern continent, Jambudvipa, was considered to be the land where Buddhism spread.

24.   Two, three, four or five suns appear at the same time: Reference to an unusual phenomenon when the sun is seen as a multiple image. Such illusions involving the sun have appeared in the form of many bright disks arcing outward from the sun. Scientists say that they are caused by reflection or refraction of light by ice crystals floating in the stratosphere.

regular courses, when the Metal Star,[25] the Broom Star, the Wheel Star, the Demon Star, the Fire Star, the Water Star, the Wind Star, the Ladle Star, the Southern Dipper, the Northern Dipper, the great stars of the Five Garrisons, and all the many stars that govern the ruler, the three high ministers and the hundred other officials—when each of these stars manifests some peculiar behavior, this is the second calamity.

"When huge fires consume the nation and the people are all burned to death, or when there are outbreaks of demon fire, dragon fire, heavenly fire, mountain god fire, human fire, tree fire or bandit fire[26]—when these prodigies appear, this is the third calamity.

"When huge floods drown the population, when the seasons come out of order and there is rain in winter, snow in summer, thunder and lightning in the winter season and ice, frost and hail in the sixth month, when red, black or green rain falls, when mountains of dirt and stones come raining down, or when it rains dust, sand or gravel, when the rivers and streams run backward, when mountains are afloat and boulders are washed away—when freakish happenings of this kind occur, this is the fourth calamity.

"When huge winds blow the people to their death and the lands, the mountains and rivers and the trees and forests are all at one time wiped out, when great winds come out of season or when black winds, red winds, green winds, heavenly winds, earthly winds, fire winds and water winds blow—when prod-

25. Metal Star: Venus. The Broom Star, the Fire Star and the Water Star respectively mean comets, Mars and Mercury.

26. Different types of disaster caused by fire. Demon fire refers to fires of unknown origin attributed to the anger of demons. Dragon fire means fires ascribed to the wrath of dragons, who were thought to be able to convert water to fire at will. This may have indicated fires caused by lightning. Heavenly fire was said to be caused by the wrath of Heaven, and mountain god fire—possibly a reference to volcanic eruptions—by the wrath of mountain gods. Human fire refers to fires caused by human error or negligence. Tree fire probably indicated forest fires caused by spontaneous combustion, and bandit fire meant fires set by invaders.

igies of this kind occur, this is the fifth calamity.

"When heaven and earth and the whole country are stricken by terrible heat so that the air seems to be on fire, when the hundred plants wither and the five grains[27] fail to ripen, when the earth is red and scorched and the inhabitants all perish—when prodigies of this kind occur, this is the sixth calamity.

"When enemies rise up on all four sides and invade the nation, when rebels appear both within the ruler's family and without, when there are fire bandits, water bandits, wind bandits and demon bandits[28] and the population is subjected to devastation and disorder, and fighting and plundering break out everywhere—when prodigies of this type occur, this is the seventh calamity."

The *Daijuku* Sutra says: "Though the ruler of a state may have for countless existences in the past practiced the giving of alms, observed the precepts and abided by the principles of wisdom, if he sees that my Law, the Dharma of the Buddha, is in danger of perishing and stands idly by without doing anything to protect it, then all the inestimable store of good causes that he has accumulated through the practices just mentioned will be entirely wiped out, and his country will become the scene of three inauspicious occurrences. The first is high grain prices, the second is warfare, and the third is pestilence. All the benevolent deities will abandon the country, and although the king may issue commands, the people will not obey them. The country will constantly be invaded and vexed by neighboring nations. Violent fires will rage out of control, evil winds and rains will abound, the waters will swell and overflow, and the inhabitants will be blown about by winds or swept away by floods. The paternal and maternal relatives of the ruler will join in plotting revolt. Before long,

27. Five grains: Wheat, rice, beans and two types of millet. Also generic term for all grains, which is its meaning here.
28. Fire bandits, water bandits, wind bandits and demon bandits: Bandits who do evil amid the confusion of disasters caused, respectively, by fire, water and wind. Demon bandits are said to be abductors.

the ruler will fall gravely ill, and after his life has come to an end, he will be reborn in one of the major hells. . . . And the same fate will befall the ruler's consort, his heir, the high ministers of the state, the lords of cities, the village heads and generals, the magistrates of districts, and the government officials."

The passages I have quoted from these four sutras are perfectly clear—what person in ten thousand could possibly doubt their meaning? And yet the blind and the deluded trust to heretical doctrines and fail to recognize the correct teachings. Therefore, throughout the empire these days people are inclined to turn away from the Buddhas and the sutras and no longer endeavor to protect them. In turn, the benevolent deities and sages abandon the nation and leave their accustomed places. As a result, demons and followers of heretical doctrines create disaster and inflict calamity upon the populace.

The guest thereupon flushed with anger and said: Emperor Ming of the Later Han dynasty, having comprehended the significance of his dream of a golden man, welcomed the teachings of Buddhism brought to China by missionaries leading white horses.[29] Prince Shōtoku,[30] having punished Mononobe no Moriya for his opposition to Buddhism, proceeded to construct temples and pagodas in Japan. Since that time, from the supreme ruler down to the numberless masses, people have worshiped the Buddhist statues and devoted their attention to the scriptures. As a result, in the monasteries of

29. This refers to the tradition that Emperor Ming (27–75) dreamt of a golden man levitating above the garden. He awakened from sleep and asked his ministers about his dream. One of them said that he had once heard of the birth of a sage in the western region during the reign of King Chao of the Chou dynasty and that this sage had been called the Buddha. The emperor sent eighteen missionaries in order to obtain the Buddha's teachings. They brought Buddhist scriptures and images of the Buddha to China in 67 A.D.

30. Shōtoku (574–622): The second son of the thirty-first emperor, Yōmei, famous for his application of the spirit of Buddhism to government. As the regent for Empress Suiko, he carried out various reforms. He revered the Lotus Sutra, Shrimala Sutra and Vimalakirti Sutra, writing commentaries on them.

Mount Hiei[31] and of the southern capital at Nara, at the great temples of Onjō-ji and Tō-ji,[32] throughout the land within the four seas, in the five areas adjacent to the capital[33] and the seven outlying regions, Buddhist scriptures have been ranged like stars in the sky and halls of worship have spread over the land like clouds. Those who belong to the lineage of Shariputra meditate on the moon atop Eagle Peak,[34] while those who adhere to the traditions of Haklenayasha transmit the teachings of Mount Kukkutapada.[35] How, then, can anyone say that the doctrines of Shakyamuni are despised or that the three treasures of Buddhism are neglected? If there is evidence to support such a contention, I would like to hear all the facts!

The host, anxious to clarify his words, replied: To be sure, Buddha halls stand rooftop to rooftop and sutra storehouses are ranged eave to eave. Priests are as numerous as bamboo plants and rushes, monks as common as rice and hemp seedlings. The temples and priests have been honored from centuries past, and every day respect is paid them anew. But the monks and priests today are fawning and devious, and they confuse the people and lead them astray. The ruler and his ministers lack understanding and fail to distinguish between truth and heresy.

The *Ninnō* Sutra, for example, says: "Evil monks, hoping to gain fame and profit, in many cases appear before the ruler, the

31. Mt. Hiei: Site of Enryaku-ji temple, head temple of the Sammon school of the Tendai sect. This school derives from Jikaku, the third high priest of the Tendai sect, who incorporated the esoteric teachings of the Shingon sect into the doctrine of his own sect, thereby causing confusion.

32. Onjō-ji and Tō-ji: Onjō-ji is also called Mii-dera, the head temple of the Jimon school of the Tendai sect. This school derives from Chishō, the fifth high priest of the Tendai sect. Tō-ji (Eastern Temple) is a principal temple of the Shingon sect, more properly called Kyō'ō-gokoku-ji.

33. Five areas adjacent to the capital: Areas under the direct control of the emperor.

34. This refers to those who set store by the practice of meditation.

35. This refers to those who attach greater importance to abiding by the teachings than to practicing meditation. Haklenayasha was the twenty-third of Shakyamuni's twenty-four successors. Kukkutapada is near Rajagriha, the capital of Magadha. Mahakashyapa transferred the teachings to Ananda and died on this mountain.

heir apparent or the other princes and take it upon themselves
to preach doctrines that lead to the violation of the Buddhist
Law and the destruction of the nation. The rulers, failing to
perceive the truth of the situation, listen to and put faith in such
doctrines, and proceed to create regulations that are perverse in
nature and do not accord with the rules of Buddhist discipline.
In this way they bring about the destruction of Buddhism and
of the nation."

The Nirvana Sutra states: "Bodhisattvas, have no fear in
your hearts because of such things as wild elephants. But evil
friends—they are what you should fear! If you are killed by a
wild elephant, you will not fall into any of the three evil paths.
But if evil friends lead you to your death, you are certain to fall
into one of them!"

The Lotus Sutra says: "There will be monks in that evil age
with perverse views and hearts that are fawning and crooked
who will say they have attained what they have not attained,
being proud and boastful in heart. Or there will be forest-
dwelling monks wearing clothing of patched rags and living in
retirement who will claim they are practicing the true Way,
despising and looking down on the rest of mankind. Greedy
for profit and nourishment, they will preach the Dharma to
white-robed laymen and will be respected and revered by the
world as though they were arhats who possess the six supernatural powers[36] . . . Constantly they will go about among
the populace, seeking in this way to slander us. They will
address the rulers, high ministers, Brahmans and great patrons
of Buddhism as well as the other monks, slandering and
speaking evil of us, saying, 'These are men of perverted views
who preach the doctrines of heretical sects!' . . . In a muddied
kalpa, in an evil age there will be many different things to fear.

36. Six supernatural powers: 1) The power of being anywhere at will; 2)
the power of seeing anything anywhere; 3) the power of hearing any sound
anywhere; 4) the power of knowing the thoughts of all other minds; 5) the
power of knowing past lives; and 6) the power of eradicating illusions.

Demons will take possession of others and through them curse, revile and heap shame on us . . . The evil monks of that muddied age, failing to understand the Buddha's expedient means, how he preaches the Dharma in accord with what is appropriate, will confront us with foul language and angry frowns; again and again we will be banished."

In the Nirvana Sutra, the Buddha says: "After I have passed away and countless hundreds of years have gone by, all the sages of the four stages[37] will also have passed away. After the Former Day of the Law has ended and the Middle Day of the Law has begun, there will be monks who will give the appearance of abiding by the rules of monastic discipline. But they will scarcely ever read or recite the sutras, and instead will crave all kinds of food and drink to nourish their bodies. Though they wear the robes of a monk, they will go about searching for alms like so many huntsmen, spying sharply and stalking softly. They will be like a cat on the prowl for mice. And constantly they will reiterate these words: 'I have attained the state of arhat!' Outwardly they will seem to be wise and good, but within they will harbor greed and jealousy. [And when they are asked to preach the Dharma,] they will conceal it, like Brahmans who have taken a vow of silence. They are not true monks—they merely have the appearance of monks. Consumed by their erroneous views, they slander the True Law."

When we look at the world in the light of these passages of scripture, we see that the situation is just as they describe it. If we do not admonish the evil monks, how can we hope to do good?

The guest, growing more indignant than ever, said: A wise monarch, by acting in accord with heaven and earth, perfects his rule; a sage, by distinguishing between right and wrong, brings order to the world. The monks and priests of the world

37. Four stages: The four stages which the people of *shōmon* (Learning) can attain. The highest of the four is arhat.

today enjoy the confidence of the entire empire. If they were in fact evil monks, then the wise ruler would put no trust in them. If they were not true sages, then men of worth and understanding would not look up to them. But now, since worthies and sages do in fact honor and respect them, they must be nothing less than paragons of their kind. Why then do you pour out these wild accusations and dare to slander them? To whom are you referring when you speak of "evil monks"? I would like an explanation!

The host said: In the reign of Emperor Gotoba there was a priest named Hōnen who wrote a work entitled the *Senchaku Shū*.[38] He contradicted the sacred teachings of Shakyamuni and brought confusion to people in every direction. The *Senchaku Shū* states: "The Chinese priest Tao-ch'o[39] distinguished between the *Shōdō* or Sacred Way teachings and the *Jōdo* or Pure Land teachings[40] and urged men to abandon the former and immediately embrace the latter. First of all, there are two kinds of Sacred Way teachings, [the Mahayana and the Hinayana]. Judging from this, we may assume that the esoteric Mahayana doctrines of Shingon and the true Mahayana teachings of the Lotus Sutra are both included in the Sacred Way. If that is so, then the present-day sects of Shingon, Zen, Tendai, Kegon, Sanron, Hossō, Jiron and Shōron[41]—all these eight schools are included in the Sacred Way that is to be abandoned.

38. *Senchaku Shū*: "The Sole Selection of Nembutsu," a two-fascicle work written in 1198 at the request of Kujō Kanezane, which is the fundamental justification of the Jōdo sect. In it Hōnen, basing himself on the three major sutras of the Jōdo sect, exhorted people to discard all teachings other than the Nembutsu teachings.

39. Tao-ch'o (562–645): The second patriarch of the Jōdo school in China.

40. Sacred Way teachings and Pure Land teachings: The former are the teachings which assert that one should practice in this real *saha* world and attain enlightenment through his own effort. In contrast, the Pure Land teachings define the *saha* world as a defiled world and assert that one should aspire to rebirth in the western Pure Land by relying on the power of Amida Buddha.

41. Sanron, Hossō, Jiron and Shōron: Sanron literally means three treatises and refers to the three treatises on which the Sanron sect is based. They are Nagarjuna's *Chū Ron* and *Jūnimon Ron* and Aryadeva's *Hyaku Ron*. This sect

"The priest T'an-luan[42] in his *Ōjō Ron Chū* states: 'I note that Nagarjuna's *Jūjūbibasha Ron* says: "There are two ways by which the bodhisattva may reach the state in which there is no retrogression. One is the Difficult-to-Practice Way, the other is the Easy-to-Practice Way."'

"The Difficult-to-Practice Way is the same as the Sacred Way, and the Easy-to-Practice Way is the Pure Land Way. Students of the Pure Land sect should first of all understand this point. Though they may previously have studied teachings belonging to the Sacred Way, if they wish to become followers of the Pure Land school, they must discard the Sacred Way and give their allegiance to the Pure Land teachings."

Hōnen also says: "The Chinese priest Shan-tao[43] distinguished between correct and incorrect practices and urged men to embrace the former and abandon the latter. Concerning the first of the incorrect practices, that of reading and reciting sutras, he states that, with the exception of the recitation of the

---

was founded by Chia-hsiang and introduced to Japan in 625. The Hossō sect aims at discovering the ultimate reality by examining the aspects and characteristics of all things. The sect's basic works are the *Gejimmitsu* Sutra, *Yuishiki Ron* and *Yuga Ron*. In the period of the T'ang dynasty Hsüan-tsang brought this teaching from India to China and his disciple Tz'u-en founded the sect. In 653, Dōshō brought this teaching to Japan after his study under Hsüan-tsang. The Jiron sect was founded in China by Hui-kuang with Vasubandhu's *Jūjikyō Ron* (Treatise on the Ten Stages Sutra) as its basic teaching. The sect prospered in the Liang dynasty but was later absorbed by the Kegon sect. The Shōron sect was based upon Asanga's *Shōdaijō Ron* (Collection of Mahayana Treatises). It prospered in the Ch'en and Sui dynasties but was later absorbed by the Hossō sect.

42. T'an-luan (476–542): The founder of the Jōdo school in China.

43. Shan-tao (613–681): Priest of the Jōdo teaching in China during the T'ang dynasty. In the *Ōjō Raisan* (Praise of Rebirth in the Pure Land) he classified Buddhist practices into the categories of correct and incorrect. According to him, the correct practices are those directed toward Amida Buddha. The correct practices are further divided into five, that is: 1) reading and reciting, 2) meditating, 3) worshiping, 4) calling on the name, and 5) praising and giving offerings. These five practices are directed toward Amida Buddha, the Pure Land sutras and the Pure Land. The incorrect practices are also divided into five, in the same manner. The latter part of the text discusses the incorrect practices.

Kammuryōju Sutra and the other Pure Land sutras, the embracing and recitation of all sutras, whether Mahayana or Hinayana, exoteric or esoteric, is to be regarded as an incorrect practice. Concerning the third of the incorrect practices, that of worshiping, he states that, with the exception of worshiping the Buddha Amida, the worshiping or honoring of any of the other Buddhas, bodhisattvas or deities of the heavenly and human worlds is to be regarded as an incorrect practice. In the light of this passage, it is clear that one should abandon such incorrect practices and concentrate upon the practice of the Pure Land teaching. What reason would we have to abandon the correct practices of the Pure Land teaching, which insure that, out of a hundred persons, all one hundred will be reborn in the Western Paradise, and cling instead to the various incorrect practices and procedures, which could not save even one person in a thousand? Followers of the Way should ponder this carefully!"

Hōnen further states: "In the *Jōgen Nyūzō Roku*[44] we find it recorded that, from the six hundred volumes of the *Daihannya* Sutra[45] to the *Hōjōju* Sutra,[46] the exoteric and esoteric sutras of Mahayana Buddhism total 637 works in 2,883 volumes. All of these should now be replaced by the recitation of the single Mahayana phrase, [the Nembutsu]. You should understand that, when the Buddha was preaching according to the capacity of his various listeners, he for a time taught the two methods of concentrated meditation and unconcentrated meditation.[47] But later, when he revealed his own enlightenment, he ceased

44. *Jōgen Nyūzō Roku*: A list of the sutras which the priest Yüan-chao selected at Emperor Te-tsung's command during the Cheng-yüan (Jap Jōgen) era (785–804).

45. *Daihannya* Sutra: "Great Wisdom Sutra" (Skt Mahaprajnaparamita-sutra). An extremely long sutra setting forth the doctrine of *kū*.

46. *Hōjōju* Sutra: One-volume Mahayana sutra expounding the eternity of the Law.

47. Two methods of concentrated meditation and unconcentrated meditation: In the *Kammuryōju* Sutra, sixteen types of meditation and three kinds of practices are described, which lead people to rebirth in the Pure Land. In the

to teach these two methods. The only teaching that, once revealed, shall never cease to be taught, is the single doctrine of the Nembutsu."

Again Hōnen states: "The passage which says that the practitioner of the Nembutsu must possess three kinds of mind[48] is found in the Kammuryōju Sutra. In the commentary on that sutra,[49] we read: 'Someone asked: "If there are those who differ in understanding and practice from the followers of the Nembutsu, persons of heretical and mistaken belief, how can one make certain that their perverse and differing views will not cause trouble?"' We also see that these persons of evil views with their different understanding and different practices are compared to a band of robbers who call back the travelers who have already gone one or two steps along their journey. In my opinion, when these passages speak of different understanding, different practices, varying doctrines and varying beliefs, they are referring to the teachings of the Sacred Way."

Finally, in a concluding passage, Hōnen says: "If one wishes to escape quickly from the sufferings of life and death, one should confront these two superior teachings and then proceed to put aside the teachings of the Sacred Way and choose those of the Pure Land. And if one wishes to follow the teachings of

first thirteen types of meditation, one concentrates his mind and meditates on the splendor of the Pure Land and the features of the Buddha and bodhisattvas. These types of meditation are regarded as "concentrated meditation." The other three types of meditation and the three kinds of practices can be carried out even if one's mind is not focused. Therefore, they are called "unconcentrated practice." Hōnen regarded both concentrated and unconcentrated practices as practices which the Buddha expounded in accordance with people's capacity. He asserted that only the practice of Nembutsu was the Buddha's true teaching as well as the sole teaching for the Latter Day of the Law. Nembutsu is interpreted in various ways though it literally means to meditate on Amida Buddha. Shan-tao and Hōnen took Nembutsu to mean calling on the name of Amida Buddha and emphasized this practice.

48.   Three kinds of mind: Three requisites for reaching the Pure Land: 1) the sincere mind, 2) the mind of deep faith and 3) the mind of resolve to attain the Pure Land.

49.   Commentary on that sutra: Shan-tao's commentary, the Kammuryōju-kyō Sho.

the Pure Land, one should confront the correct and incorrect practices and then proceed to abandon all those that are incorrect and devote one's entire attention to those that are correct."

When we examine these passages, we see that Hōnen quotes the erroneous explanations of T'an-luan, Tao-ch'o and Shan-tao and establishes the categories he calls Sacred Way and Pure Land, Difficult-to-Practice Way and Easy-to-Practice Way. He then takes all the 637 works in 2,883 volumes that comprise the Mahayana sutras of the Buddha's lifetime, including those of the Lotus Sutra and Shingon, along with all the Buddhas, bodhisattvas, and deities of the heavenly and human worlds, and assigns them all to the Sacred Way, the Difficult-to-Practice Way and the incorrect practices categories, and urges men to "discard, close, ignore and abandon" them. With these four injunctions, he leads all people astray. And on top of that, he groups together all the sage monks of the three countries[50] of India, China and Japan as well as the students of Buddhism of the ten directions, and calls them a "band of robbers," causing the people to insult them!

In doing so, he turns his back on the passages in the three Pure Land sutras,[51] the sutras of his own sect, which contain Amida's vow to save everyone "except those who commit the five cardinal sins or slander the True Law."[52] At the same time, he shows that he fails to understand the warning contained in the second volume of the Lotus Sutra, the most important sutra expounded in the five preaching periods[53] of the Buddha's life, which reads: "One who refuses to take faith in this sutra and

50. All the sage monks of the three countries: Those who propagated Buddhism correctly. Indicates Nagarjuna and Vasubandhu in India, T'ien-t'ai, Chang-an and Miao-lo in China, Dengyō and Gishin in Japan, and so on.

51. Three Pure Land sutras: The basic scriptures of the Japanese Jōdo (Pure Land) sect. The *Muryōju* Sutra, the *Kammuryōju* Sutra and the *Amida* Sutra.

52. This refers to the eighteenth of the forty-eight vows, described in the *Muryōju* Sutra, that Bodhisattva Hōzō (Skt Dharmakara), the name of Amida Buddha before his enlightenment, made to bring all people to the Pure Land.

53. Five preaching periods: *See* Five periods in the Glossary.

instead slanders it . . . . After he dies, he will fall into the hell of incessant suffering."[54]

And now we have come to this later age, when men are no longer sages. Each enters his own dark road, and all alike forget the direct way. How pitiful, that no one cures them of their blindness! How painful, to see them vainly lending encouragement to these false beliefs! And as a result, everyone from the ruler of the nation down to the humblest peasant believes that there are no true sutras outside the three Pure Land sutras, and no Buddhas other than the Buddha Amida with his two attendants.[55]

Once there were men like Dengyō, Gishin,[56] Jikaku and Chishō who journeyed ten thousand leagues across the waves to acquire the sacred teachings, or visited all the mountains and rivers of Japan to acquire Buddhist statues which they held in reverence. In some cases they built holy temples on the peaks of high mountains in which to preserve those scriptures and statues; in other cases they constructed sacred halls in the bottoms of deep valleys where such objects could be worshiped and honored. As a result, the Buddhas Shakyamuni and Yakushi[57] shone side by side, casting their influence upon present and future ages, while the Bodhisattvas Kokūzō and Jizō[58] brought benefit to the living and the dead. The rulers of

54. Lotus Sutra, chap. 3.
55. Two attendants: Bodhisattvas Kannon and Seishi. *See* Kannon in the Glossary.
56. Gishin (781–833): Dengyō's successor and the first chief priest of Enryaku-ji, the head temple of the Tendai sect.
57. Shakyamuni and Yakushi: Buddhas whose images were enshrined in the head temple of the Tendai sect on Mt. Hiei. It is said that the image of Yakushi was enshrined as well as that of Shakyamuni because Yakushi Buddha, having vowed to "heal all ills" (*see* footnote 2), represents the parable of the excellent physician in the *Juryō* (16th) chapter of the Lotus Sutra.
58. Kokūzō and Jizō: Kokūzō is a bodhisattva said to possess immeasurable wisdom and blessings. An image of Bodhisattva Kokūzō was enshrined on Mt. Hiei. Jizō is a bodhisattva entrusted by Shakyamuni Buddha with the mission of saving people. It is said that he will appear during the period from the death of Shakyamuni Buddha till the appearance of Miroku Buddha, in order to

the nation contributed counties or villages so that the lamps might continue to burn bright before the images, while the stewards of the great estates offered their fields and gardens [to provide for the upkeep of the temples].

But because of this book by Hōnen, this *Senchaku Shū*, the Lord Buddha Shakyamuni is forgotten and all honor is paid to Amida, the Buddha of the Western Land. The Lord Buddha's transmission of the Law is ignored, and Yakushi, the Buddha of the Eastern Region, is neglected.[59] All attention is paid to the three works in four volumes of the Pure Land scriptures,[60] and all the other wonderful teachings that Shakyamuni proclaimed throughout the five periods of his preaching life are cast aside. If temples are not dedicated to Amida, then people no longer have any desire to support them or pay honor to the Buddhas enshrined there; if monks do not chant the Nembutsu, then people quickly forget all about giving those monks alms. As a result, the halls of the Buddha fall into ruin, scarcely a wisp of smoke rises above their mossy tiles; and the monks' quarters stand empty and dilapidated, the dew deep on the grasses in their courtyards. And in spite of such conditions, no one gives a thought to protecting the Law or to restoring the temples. Hence the sage monks who once presided over the temples leave and do not return, and the benevolent deities who

---

instruct the people of the six worlds. This bodhisattva's image also was enshrined on Mt. Hiei, together with that of Kokūzō.

59.   At the ceremony of the Lotus Sutra, Shakyamuni Buddha transferred his teachings to the bodhisattvas of the theoretical teaching such as Yakuō and entrusted them with the mission of propagating them in the Middle Day of the Law. It is said that Bodhisattva Yakuō was later born as the Great Teacher T'ien-t'ai in China and as the Great Teacher Dengyō in Japan. Based on the Buddha's parable of the excellent physician in the *Juryō* (16th) chapter, T'ien-t'ai and Dengyō used Yakushi Buddha (the Buddha of Healing), lord of the Emerald World in the eastern part of the universe, as an object of worship for their sect. In this sense, to neglect the Buddha Yakushi and revere the Buddha Amida is to ignore the Lord Buddha's transmission.

60.   Three works in four volumes of the Pure Land scriptures: The two-volume *Muryōju* Sutra, one-volume *Kammuryōju* Sutra and one-volume *Amida* Sutra.

guarded the Buddhist teachings depart and no longer appear. This has all come about because of this *Senchaku Shū* of Hōnen. How pitiful to think that, in the space of a few decades, hundreds, thousands, tens of thousands of people have been deluded by these devilish teachings and in so many cases confused as to the true teachings of Buddhism. If people favor perverse doctrines and forget what is correct, can the benevolent deities be anything but angry? If people cast aside doctrines that are all-encompassing and take up those that are incomplete, can the world escape the plots of demons? Rather than offering up ten thousand prayers for remedy, it would be better simply to outlaw this one evil doctrine that is the source of all the trouble!

This time the guest was truly enraged and said: In the ages since our original teacher, the Buddha Shakyamuni, preached the three Pure Land sutras, the priest T'an-luan had originally studied the four treatises[61] but abandoned them and put all his faith in the Pure Land teachings. Similarly, the priest Tao-ch'o ceased to spread the multifarious doctrines of the Nirvana Sutra[62] and devoted all his attention to the practices of the Western Region. The priest Shan-tao discarded the incorrect practices and concentrated on the single practice of the Pure Land, and the priest Eshin[63] collected passages from various sutras to form his work,[64] stressing the importance of a single practice, the Nembutsu. Such was the manner in which these men honored and respected the Buddha Amida, and uncountable numbers of people as a result were able to gain rebirth in the Pure Land.

---

61. Four treatises: The *Chū Ron, Jūnimon Ron* and *Daichido Ron* by Nagarjuna as well as the *Hyaku Ron* by Aryadeva.

62. Nirvana Sutra: Sutra which expounds five bodhisattva deeds, as against the single practice of the Jōdo sect. *See also* Nirvana Sutra in the Glossary.

63. Eshin (942–1017): The eighteenth chief priest of Enryaku-ji temple. He put faith in the Pure Land teachings but later embraced the Lotus Sutra.

64. His work: *Ōjō Yōshū* written in 985, which influenced people not only in Japan but also in China.

Of particular note was the venerable Hōnen, who as a child entered the monastery on Mount Hiei. By the time he was seventeen, he had worked his way through all sixty volumes of Tendai literature[65] and had investigated all the eight sects[66] and mastered their essentials. In addition, he had read through the entire body of sutras and treatises seven times, and exhausted all the works of exegesis and biography. His wisdom shone like the sun and moon, and his virtue exceeded that of the earlier teachers.

In spite of all this, he was in doubt as to the proper path to salvation and could not make out the true meaning of nirvana. Therefore he read and examined all the texts he could, pondered deeply and considered every possibility, and in the end put aside all the sutras and concentrated on the single practice of the Nembutsu. In addition, he received confirmation of his decision when Shan-tao miraculously appeared to him in a dream,[67] and he proceeded to spread his doctrines among friends and strangers in all four corners of the land. Thereafter, he was hailed as a reincarnation of the Bodhisattva Seishi, or was revered as Shan-tao reborn. In every quarter people of eminent and lowly birth alike bowed their heads in respect, and men and women from all over Japan sought him.

Since that time, the springs and autumns have succeeded each other and the years have accumulated. And yet you insist upon putting aside the venerable teachings of Shakyamuni

65. Sixty volumes of Tendai literature: T'ien-t'ai's three major writings (the *Maka Shikan*, the *Hokke Mongu* and the *Hokke Gengi*) consisting of thirty volumes and Miao-lo's three commentaries on them which also consist of thirty volumes.

66. Eight sects: Eight major sects of Buddhism well established in Japan before the Kamakura period. Historically they fall into two categories: the Kusha, Jōjitsu, Ritsu, Hossō, Sanron and Kegon sects which prospered in the Nara period (710–784), and the Tendai and Shingon sects which appeared in the Heian period (794–1185).

67. Reference appearing in Hōnen's biography. According to this account, Hōnen in a dream received permission from Shan-tao to spread the practice of calling on the name of Amida Buddha and was entrusted with the Pure Land teaching.

Buddha contained in the Pure Land sutras and willfully speak evil of the writings concerning the Buddha Amida. Why do you try to blame the sacred age of Hōnen for the disasters of recent years, going out of your way to slander the former teachers of Pure Land doctrine[68] and to heap abuse on a sage like Hōnen? You are, as the saying goes, deliberately blowing back the fur and hunting for flaws in the leather, deliberately piercing the skin in hopes of drawing blood. From ancient times to the present, the world has never seen such a speaker of evil! You had better learn a little caution and restraint. When you pile up such grave offenses, how can you hope to escape punishment? I am afraid even to sit here in your company. I must take up my staff and be on my way!

The host, smiling, restrained his guest and said: Insects that live on smartweed forget how bitter it tastes; those who stay long in privies forget how foul the smell is. Here you listen to my good words and think them wicked, point to a slanderer like Hōnen and call him a sage, mistrust a true teacher and take him for an evil monk. Your confusion is great indeed, and your offense anything but light. Listen to my explanation of how this confusion arose and let us discuss the matter in detail.

The doctrines that Shakyamuni Buddha preached in the course of his lifetime can be assigned to five distinct preaching periods. The order in which they were preached can be established, and they can be divided into provisional and true teachings. But T'an-luan, Tao-ch'o and Shan-tao embraced the provisional teachings and forgot about the true ones, went by what had been taught in the earlier period of the Buddha's life and discarded what was taught later. They were not the kind of men who delve into the deep places of Buddhist doctrine.

Hōnen in particular, though he followed the practices advocated by these earlier men, was ignorant as to the source from

68.   Former teachers of Pure Land doctrine: T'an-luan, Tao-ch'o and Shan-tao.

whence they came. How do we know this? Because he lumped together all the 637 Mahayana scriptures with the 2,883 volumes of text, and along with them all the various Buddhas and bodhisattvas and the deities of the heavenly and human worlds, and urged people to "discard, close, ignore and abandon" them, with these four injunctions corrupting the hearts of all people. Thus he poured out perverted words of his own invention and took absolutely no cognizance of the explanations put forth in the Buddhist scriptures. His is the worst kind of baseless talk, a clear case of defamation. There are no words to describe it, no way to censure it that is not too mild. And yet men all put faith in this baseless talk of his, and without exception pay honor to his *Senchaku Shū*. As a consequence, they revere the three sutras of the Pure Land and cast all the other sutras aside; they look up to one Buddha alone, Amida of the Land of Bliss, and forget about the other Buddhas. A man such as Hōnen is in truth the archenemy of the Buddhas and the scriptures, and the foe of sage monks and ordinary men and women alike. And now his heretical teachings have spread throughout the eight regions of the country; they have penetrated every one of the ten directions.

You became quite horrified when I blamed an earlier period[69] for the disasters that have occurred in recent years. Perhaps I should cite a few examples from the past to show you that you are mistaken in your feelings.

The second volume of the *Maka Shikan* quotes a passage from the *Shih Chi*[70] or *Records of the Historian* which says: "In the closing years of the Chou dynasty, there were persons who let their hair hang down, went about naked to the waist, and did not observe the rites and regulations." The *Guketsu* com-

69. An earlier period: The age in which Hōnen propagated the Pure Land teaching.

70. *Shih Chi*: Work written by Ssu-ma Ch'ien of the Former Han dynasty, recording history from the time of the legendary Yellow Emperor of ancient China to that of Emperor Wu (140–87 B.C.) of the Former Han dynasty.

mentary on the *Maka Shikan*, in the second volume, explains this passage by quoting from the *Tso Chuan*[71] as follows: "When King P'ing of the Chou first moved his capital east to Lo-yang, he saw men by the Yi River who let their hair hang down and performed sacrifices in the fields. Someone who had great understanding said: 'In less than a hundred years the dynasty will fall, for the rites are already neglected.'" From this it is evident that the portent appears first, and later the disaster itself comes about.

The *Maka Shikan* passage goes on to say: "Juan Chi[72] of the Western Chin dynasty was a man of extraordinary talent, but he let his hair grow like a mass of brambles and left his belt undone. Later, the sons of the aristocracy all imitated him, until those who behaved in a churlish and insulting manner were thought to be acting quite naturally, and those who were restrained and proper in their behavior were ridiculed as mere peasants. This was a sign that the Ssu-ma family, the rulers of the Chin dynasty, would meet with their downfall."

Similarly, the *Nittō Junrei Ki* or *Record of a Pilgrimage to China in Search of the Law* by Jikaku Daishi records that in the first year of the Hui-ch'ang era (841), Emperor Wu-tsung of the T'ang dynasty commanded the priest Ching-shuang of Chang-ching temple to transmit the Nembutsu teachings of the Buddha Amida in the various temples. Ching-shuang spent three days in each temple, going about from one temple to another without ever ceasing.

In the second year of the same era, soldiers from the land of the Uighurs[73] invaded the borders of the T'ang empire. In the third year of the same era, the regional commander in the area

71.   *Tso Chuan*: Work attributed to Tso Ch'iu-ming of the Spring and Autumn period (c. 770–403 B.C.). It is a commentary on the *Ch'un Ch'iu* or *Spring and Autumn Annals*, a chronicle (722–481 B.C.) of twelve dukes of the state of Lu.

72.   Juan Chi (210–263): A Chinese poet.

73.   Uighurs: A Turkish people of Central Asia who prospered from the eighth through the mid-ninth century.

north of the Yellow River suddenly raised a revolt. Later, the kingdom of Tibet once more refused to obey orders from China, and the Uighurs repeatedly seized Chinese territory. On the whole, the conflicts and uprisings were like those that prevailed at the time when the Ch'in dynasty and the military leader Hsiang Yü were overthrown, and the towns and villages were devastated by fire and other disasters. What was even worse, Emperor Wu-tsung carried out a vast campaign to wipe out Buddhist teachings and destroyed a great many temples and monasteries. He was never able to put down the uprisings, and died in agony shortly after. (This is the essence of Jikaku's original passage.)

In view of these events, we should consider the fact that Hōnen was active during the reign of Emperor Gotoba, around the Kennin era (1201–1203). And, as everyone knows, in 1221 the Retired Emperor Gotoba was thwarted in his attempt to assert the authority of the throne, and he and two other retired emperors were forced into exile.[74] Thus China provided an earlier example of how the Pure Land teachings brought about the fall of an emperor, and our own country offers similar proof. You should not be in doubt about the matter or consider it strange. The only thing to do now is to abandon evil ways and take up those that are good, to cut off this affliction at the source, to cut it off at the root!

The guest, looking somewhat mollified, said: Though I have not yet probed deeply into the matter, I believe I understand to some degree what you are saying. Nevertheless, both in Kyoto, the capital, and in Kamakura, the headquarters of the shogun, there are numerous eminent Buddhist leaders and key figures in the clergy. And yet none of them has so far appealed to the shogun concerning this affair or submitted a memorial to the throne. You, on the other hand, a person of humble position, think nothing of spewing out offensive accusations. Your

74. This incident is known as the Jōkyū disturbance. The wording of the original has been expanded for clarity.

assertions are open to question and your reasoning lacks authority.

The host said: Though I may be a person of little ability, I have reverently given myself to the study of the Mahayana. A blue fly, if it clings to the tail of a thoroughbred horse, can travel ten thousand miles, and the green ivy that twines around the tall pine can grow to a thousand feet. I was born as the son of the one Buddha, Shakyamuni, and I serve the king of scriptures, the Lotus Sutra. How could I observe the decline of the Buddhist Law and not be filled with emotions of pity and distress?

Moreover, the Nirvana Sutra states: "If even a good priest sees someone slandering the Law and disregards him, failing to reproach him, to oust him or to punish him for his offense, then that priest is betraying Buddhism. But if he takes the slanderer severely to task, drives him off or punishes him, then he is my disciple and one who truly understands my teachings."

Although I may not be a "good priest," I certainly do not want to be accused of "betraying Buddhism." Therefore, in order to avoid such charges, I have cited a few general principles and given a rough explanation of the matter.

Long ago in the Gennin era (1224), petitions to the throne were submitted time and again by the two temples of Enryaku-ji on Mount Hiei and Kōfuku-ji in Nara, and as a result an Imperial command and a letter of instruction from the shogunate were handed down, ordering that the wood blocks used in printing Hōnen's *Senchaku Shū* be confiscated and brought to the Great Lecture Hall of Enryaku-ji temple. There they were burned in order to repay the debt owed to the Buddhas of the past, present and future. In addition, orders were given that the menials who are attached to the Gion Shrine should dig up and destroy Hōnen's grave in Kyoto. Then, Hōnen's disciples Ryūkan, Shōkō, Jōkaku, Sasshō[75] and others were condemned

75. Ryūkan (1148–1227), Shōkō (1162–1238), Jōkaku (1133–1247), Sasshō (dates unknown): Priests of the Jōdo sect. Ryūkan is the founder of the

by the government to exile in distant regions, and were never pardoned.

In view of these facts, how can you say that no one has submitted a complaint to the authorities concerning these matters?

The guest, continuing to speak in a mild manner, replied: One could hardly say that Hōnen is the only one who disparages sutras and speaks ill of other priests, [since you do the same thing yourself]. However, it is true that he takes the 637 Mahayana scriptures with their 2,883 volumes of text, along with all the Buddhas and bodhisattvas and the deities of the heavenly and human worlds, and urges people to "discard, close, ignore and abandon" them. There is no doubt that these four injunctions are his very words; the meaning of the passage is quite clear. But you keep harping on this one little "flaw in the jewel" and severely slandering him for it. I do not know whether he spoke out of delusion or out of true enlightenment. Between you and Hōnen, I cannot tell which is wise and which is foolish, or determine whose assertions are right and whose are wrong.

However, you assert that all the recent disasters are to be traced to the *Senchaku Shū* of Hōnen, speaking quite volubly on that point and elaborating on the meaning of your assertion. Now surely the peace of the world and the stability of the nation are sought by both ruler and subject and desired by all the inhabitants of the country. The nation achieves prosperity through the Buddhist Law, and the validity of the Law is

Chōraku-ji school and also called Kaikū or Muga (his posthumous name). He studied the Tendai doctrine under Kōen at Enryaku-ji temple and lived at Chōraku-ji temple in Kyoto. Shōkō is the founder of the Chinzei school and second patriarch of the Jōdo sect. At first he studied the Tendai doctrine on Mt. Hiei, but he became Hōnen's disciple. Jōkaku first studied the Tendai doctrine, but converted to Hōnen's teaching and advocated the doctrine of one-time recitation which teaches that if one once invokes the name of Amida Buddha he can be reborn in the Pure Land. For this reason, he was excommunicated by Hōnen. Sasshō also studied the Tendai doctrine but later followed Jōkaku's teaching. Still later, he went on to found his own sect.

proven by the people who embrace it. If the nation is destroyed and the people are wiped out, then who will continue to pay reverence to the Buddhas? Who will continue to have faith in the Law? Therefore one must first of all pray for the safety of the nation and then work to establish the Buddhist Law. Now if you know of any means whereby disasters can be prevented and troubles brought to an end, I would like to hear about it.

The host said: There is no doubt that I am the foolish one—I would never dare claim to be wise. However, I would just like to quote a few passages from the scriptures. Concerning the means for insuring order in the nation, there are numerous passages in both Buddhist and non-Buddhist texts, and it would be difficult to cite them all here. Since taking up the study of Buddhism, however, I have frequently given thought to this matter, and it seems to me that prohibiting those who slander the Law and paying respect to monks who follow the Correct Way is the best way to assure stability within the nation and peace in the world at large.

In the Nirvana Sutra we read: "The Buddha said, 'With the exception of one type of person, you may offer alms to all kinds of persons and everyone will praise you.'

"Chunda[76] said, 'What do you mean when you speak of "one type of person"?'

"The Buddha replied, 'I mean the type described in this sutra as violators of the commandments.'

"Chunda spoke again, saying, 'I am afraid I still do not understand. May I ask you to explain further?'

"The Buddha addressed Chunda, saying: 'By violators of the commandments I mean the *icchantika*. In the case of all other types of persons, you may offer alms, everyone will praise you, and you will achieve great rewards.'

---

76. Chunda: A blacksmith in Pava Village who was deeply moved by Shakyamuni's preaching and reverently prepared a meal for him. Soon after leaving Chunda's house, Shakyamuni fell ill and passed away.

"Chunda spoke once more, asking, 'What is the meaning of the term *icchantika* ?'

"The Buddha said, 'Chunda, suppose there should be priests or nuns, lay men or women who speak careless and evil words and slander the True Law, and that they should go on committing these grave acts without ever showing any inclination to reform or any sign of repentance in their hearts. Persons of this kind I would say are following the path of the *icchantika*.

" 'Again there may be those who commit the four grave offenses[77] or are guilty of the five cardinal sins, and who, though aware that they are guilty of serious faults, from the beginning have no trace of fear or contrition in their hearts, or if they do, give no outward sign of it. When it comes to the True Law, they show no inclination to establish it and help to protect it over the ages, but rather speak of it with malice and contempt, their words replete with error. Persons of this kind too I would say are following the path of the *icchantika*. With the exception of this one group of people called *icchantika*, however, you may offer alms to all others and everyone will praise you.' "

Elsewhere in the same sutra, the Buddha spoke in these words: "When I recall the past, I remember that I was the king of a great state in this continent of Jambudvipa. My name was Sen'yo, and I loved and venerated the Mahayana scriptures. My heart was pure and good and had no trace of evil, jealousy or stinginess. Men of devout faith, at that time I cherished the Mahayana teachings in my heart. Once, when I heard the Brahmans slandering these teachings, I had them put to death on the spot. Men of devout faith, as a result of that action, I never thereafter fell into hell."

In another passage it says: "In the past, when the Tathagata

77. Four grave offenses: Those particularly grave among the ten evil offenses. They are killing, stealing, committing adultery and lying.

was the ruler of a nation and practiced the way of the bodhisattva, he put to death a number of Brahmans."

Again it says: "There are three degrees of killings: the lower, middle and upper degrees. The lower degree constitutes the killing of any humble creature, from an ant to any of the various kinds of animals. (Only the killing of a bodhisattva who has deliberately chosen to be born in animal form is excluded.) As a result of a killing of the lower degree, one will fall into the realm of Hell, Hunger or Animality, and will suffer all the pains appropriate to a killing of the lower degree. Why should this be? Because even the animals and other humble creatures possess the roots of goodness, insignificant though those roots may be. That is why a person who kills such a creature must suffer full retribution for his offense.

"Killing any person from an ordinary mortal to an *anaga-min*[78] constitutes what is termed the middle degree. As a consequence of such an act of killing, one will fall into the realm of Hell, Hunger or Animality, and will suffer all the pains appropriate to a killing of the middle degree. The upper degree of killing refers to the killing of a parent, an arhat, a person who has reached the state of *pratyekabuddha* or Realization, or a bodhisattva who has completed his efforts and will never retrogress. For such a crime one will fall into the hell of incessant suffering. Men of devout faith, if someone were to kill an *icchantika*, that killing would not fall into any of the three categories just mentioned. Men of devout faith, the various Brahmans that I have said were put to death—all of them were in fact *icchantika*."

In the *Ninnō* Sutra we read: "The Buddha announced to King Prasenajit, 'Thus I entrust the protection of my teachings to the ruler of the nation rather than to the monks and nuns. Why do I do so? Because the monks and nuns do not possess

---

78. *Anagamin*: (Jap anagon) The third of the four stages which *shōmon* people can attain. Also, one who has attained this stage. The fourth and highest stage is arhat.

the kind of power and authority that the king has.' "

The Nirvana Sutra states: "Now I entrust the True Law, which is unexcelled, to the rulers, the ministers, the high officials, and the four kinds of believers. If anyone should vilify the True Law, then the high officials and four kinds of believers should reprimand him and bring him to order."

It also states: "The Buddha said, 'Kashō,[79] it is because I was a defender of the True Law that I have now been able to attain this diamond-like body[80]. . . . Men of devout faith, defenders of the True Law need not observe the five precepts[81] or practice the rules of proper behavior. Rather they should carry knives and swords, bows and arrows, prongs and lances.' "

Again the Buddha said: "Even though there may be those who observe the five precepts, they do not deserve to be called practitioners of the Mahayana. But even if one does not observe the five precepts, if he defends the True Law, then he may be called a practitioner of the Mahayana. Defenders of the True Law ought to arm themselves with knives and swords, weapons and staves. Even though they carry swords and staves, I would call them men who observe the precepts."

The Buddha likewise said: "Men of devout faith, in past ages in this very city of Kushinagara a Buddha appeared whose name was Kangi Zōyaku Nyorai or the Buddha Joy Increasing. After this Buddha passed away, the True Law that he had taught remained in the world for countless millions of years. Finally, only forty more years were left before the Law was due to come to an end.

"At that time there was a monk named Kakutoku who observed the precepts. There were many monks at this time

79. Kashō: Figure in the Nirvana Sutra who put thirty-six questions to the Buddha and heard the Buddha's teachings. He is different from Mahakashyapa (Jap Kashō), one of the Buddha's ten major disciples.

80. Diamond-like body: A reference to the state of Buddhahood which can neither decline nor be destroyed.

81. Five precepts: A basic code of Buddhism that prohibits killing, theft, adultery, lying and intoxicating drink.

who violated the precepts, and when they heard this monk preaching, they all conceived evil designs in their hearts and, arming themselves with swords and staves, attacked this teacher of the Law.

"At this time the ruler of the kingdom was named Utoku. He received reports of what was happening and, in order to defend the Law, he went at once to the place where the monk was preaching the Law and fought with all his might against the evil monks who did not observe the precepts. As a result, the monk who had been preaching the Law was able to escape grievous injury. But the king received so many wounds from the knives and swords, prongs and lances, that there was not a spot on his body the size of a mustard seed that remained unharmed.

"At this time the monk Kakutoku praised the king, saying, 'Splendid, splendid! You, O king, are now a true defender of the True Law. In ages to come, this body of yours will surely become a boundless vessel of the Law!'

"At that time, the king had already heard the teachings of the Law, and he felt great joy in his heart. Thereupon his life came to an end, and he was reborn in the land of the Buddha Ashuku, where he became the principal disciple of the Buddha. Moreover, all the military leaders, citizens and associates of the king who had fought beside him or had rejoiced in his effort were filled with an unflagging determination to achieve enlightenment, and when they died, all of them were reborn in the land of the Buddha Ashuku.

"Later, the monk Kakutoku also died, and he too was reborn in the land of the Buddha Ashuku, where he became second among the disciples who received the direct teachings of the Buddha. Thus, if the True Law is about to come to an end, this is the way one ought to support and defend it.

"Kashō, the king who lived at that time was I myself, and the monk who preached the Law was the Buddha Kashō.[82]

82. Buddha Kashō: One of the seven ancient Buddhas. Of these seven, the

Kashō, those who defend the True Law enjoy this kind of boundless reward. As a consequence, I have been able to obtain the distinguishing characteristics that I possess today, to adorn myself with them, and to put on the Dharma Body[83] that can never be destroyed."

Then the Buddha declared to the Bodhisattva Kashō: "For this reason, lay believers who wish to defend the Law should arm themselves with swords and staves and protect it in this manner.

"Men of devout faith, in the age of confusion and evil after I have passed away, the nation will fall into neglect and disorder, men will plunder and steal from one another, and the common people will be reduced to starvation. Because of hunger, many men at that time will declare their determination to leave their families and become monks. Men such as these may be called shavepates. When this crowd of shavepates see anyone who is attempting to protect the True Law, they will chase after him and drive him away, or perhaps even kill him or do him injury. That is why I now give permission for monks who observe the precepts to associate with and keep company with laymen who bear swords and staves. For even though they carry swords and staves, I would call them men who observe the precepts. But although they may carry swords and staves, they should never use them to take life."

The Lotus Sutra says: "One who refuses to take faith in this sutra and instead slanders it immediately destroys the seeds for becoming a Buddha in this world. . . . After he dies, he will fall into the hell of incessant suffering."

The meaning of these passages from the sutras is perfectly clear. What need is there for me to add any further explanation? If we accept the words of the Lotus Sutra, then we must understand that slandering the Mahayana scriptures is more serious than committing the five cardinal sins. Therefore

---

Buddha Kashō was the sixth to appear, and Shakyamuni Buddha, the seventh.
83.   Dharma Body: Buddha who is the embodiment of the Law.

one who does so will be confined in the great fortress of the hell of incessant suffering and cannot hope for release for countless aeons. According to the Nirvana Sutra, even though you may give alms to a person who has committed one of the five cardinal sins, you must never give alms to a person who has slandered the Law. He who kills so much as an ant will fall into one of the three evil paths, but he who helps to eradicate slander of the Law will ascend to the state from which there can be no retrogression. Thus the passage tells us that the monk Kakutoku was reborn as the Buddha Kashō, and that King Utoku was reborn as the Buddha Shakyamuni.

The Lotus and the Nirvana sutras represent the very heart of the doctrines that Shakyamuni preached during the five periods of his teaching life. Their warnings must be viewed with the utmost gravity. Who would fail to heed them? And yet those people who forget about the Correct Way and slander the Law put more trust than ever in Hōnen's *Senchaku Shū* and grow blinder than ever in their stupidity.

Thus some of them, remembering how their master looked in life, fashion sculptures and paintings of him, while others, putting faith in his perverse teachings, carve wood blocks with which to print his offensive words. These images and writings they scatter about throughout the area within the seas,[84] carrying them beyond the cities and into the countryside until, wherever honor is paid, it is to the practices of this school, and wherever alms are given, it is to the priests of this sect.

As a result, we see people cutting off the fingers of the images of Shakyamuni and refashioning them to form the gesture appropriate to Amida, or renovating temples formerly ded-icated to Yakushi, the Buddha of the Eastern Region, and fitting them with statues of Amida, the lord of the Western Land. Or we find the ceremony of copying the Lotus Sutra, which has been carried out for over four hundred years on Mount Hiei, being suspended and the copying of the three Pure

84. Area within the seas: Japan. The phrase originally referred to China.

Land sutras substituted in its place, or the annual lectures[85] on the doctrines of the Great Teacher T'ien-t'ai being replaced by lectures on the teachings of Shan-tao. Indeed, the slanderous people and their associates are too numerous to count! Are they not destroyers of the Buddha? Are they not destroyers of the Law? Are they not destroyers of the Priesthood? And all their heretical teachings derive from the *Senchaku Shū*!

Alas, how pitiful, that others should turn their backs on the enlightened prohibitions of the Buddha! How tragic, that they should heed the gross and deluded words of this ignorant monk! If we hope to bring order and tranquillity to the world without further delay, we must put an end to these slanders of the Law that fill the country!

The guest said: If we are to put an end to these people who slander the Law and do away with those who violate the prohibitions of the Buddha, then are we to condemn them to death as described in the passages from the sutras you have just cited? If we do that, then we ourselves will be guilty of inflicting injury and death upon others, and will suffer the consequences, will we not?

In the *Daijuku* Sutra, the Buddha says: "If a person shaves his head and puts on clerical robes, then, whether that person observes the precepts or violates them, both gods and men should give him alms. In doing so, they are giving alms and support to me, for that person is my son. But if men beat and abuse that person, they are beating my son, and if they curse and insult him, they are reviling me."

If we stop to consider, we must realize that, regardless of whether one is good or bad, right or wrong, if he is a priest or monk, then he deserves to have alms and nourishment extended to him. For how could one beat and insult the son and still not cause grief and sorrow to the father? The Brahmans who beat the Buddha's disciple Maudgalyayana to death with their

85.   Annual lectures: Lectures held on the anniversary of T'ien-t'ai's death on November 24 each year.

staves have for a long time been sunk in the hell of incessant
suffering. Because Devadatta murdered the nun Utpalavarna,
he has gone on and on choking in the flames of the Avichi
Hell.[86] Examples from earlier ages make the matter perfectly
clear, and later ages fear this offense most of all. You speak of
punishing those who slander the Law, but to do so would
violate the Buddha's prohibitions. I can hardly believe that such
a course would be right. How can you justify it?

The host said: You have clearly seen the passages from the
sutras that I have cited, and yet you can ask a question like that!
Are they beyond the power of your mind to comprehend? Or
do you fail to understand the reasoning behind them? I
certainly have no intention of censuring the sons of the
Buddha. My only hatred is for the act of slandering the Law.
According to the teachings of the Buddhas who lived prior to
Shakyamuni, slanderous priests would have incurred the death
penalty. But in the sutras preached since the time of Shakyamuni, priests of this type have merely been prevented from
receiving alms. Now if all the four kinds of believers within the
four seas and the ten thousand lands would only cease giving
alms to wicked priests and instead all come over to the side of
the good, then how could any more troubles rise to plague us
or disasters come to confront us?

With this the guest moved off his mat in a gesture of respect,
straightened the collar of his robe, and said: The Buddhist
teachings vary greatly and it is difficult to investigate each
doctrine in full. I have had many doubts and perplexities and
have been unable to distinguish right from wrong.

[Nevertheless, this work by the venerable Hōnen, the *Senchaku Shū*, does in fact exist. And it lumps together all the
various Buddhas, sutras, bodhisattvas and deities and says that
one should "discard, close, ignore and abandon" them. The
meaning of the text is perfectly clear. And as a result of this, the
sages have departed from the nation, the benevolent deities

86.   Avichi Hell: The hell of incessant suffering.

have left their dwelling places, hunger and thirst fill the world and disease and pestilence spread abroad.

Now, by citing passages from a wide variety of scriptures, you have clearly demonstrated the rights and wrongs of the matter. Therefore I have completely forsaken my earlier mistaken convictions, and my ears and eyes have been opened on point after point.

[There can be no doubt that all men, from the ruler down to the common people, rejoice in and desire the stability of the nation and the peace of the world. If we can quickly put an end to the alms that are given to these *icchantika* and insure that continuing support is instead given to the host of true priests and nuns, if we can still these "white waves"[87] that trouble the Ocean of the Buddha and cut down these "green groves" that overgrow the Mountain of the Law, then the world may become as peaceful as it was in the golden ages of Fu Hsi and Shen Nung,[88] and the nation may flourish as it did under the sage rulers Yao and Shun.[89] After that, there will be time to dip into the Waters of the Law and to decide which are shallow doctrines and which are deep, and to pay honor to the pillars and beams that support the House of the Buddha.

The host exclaimed with delight: As the proverb says, the dove has changed into a hawk, the sparrow into a clam![90] How gratifying! You have transformed yourself through your association with me, and like the bramble growing in the hemp field, you have learned to stand up straight! If you will truly

87. White waves: A Chinese term referring to rebels and outlaws. Here, "white waves" indicates Hōnen and other priests of the Pure Land sect as well as the followers of other misleading sects. "The Ocean of the Buddha" signifies Shakyamuni's teachings. The phrases "green groves" and "Mountain of the Law" in the next sentence likewise refer to evil men and Shakyamuni's teachings respectively.

88. Fu Hsi and Shen Nung: Legendary ideal rulers of ancient China. Their ages are said to have been peaceful and ideal ones.

89. Yao and Shun: Also legendary rulers said to have reigned after the time of Fu Hsi and Shen Nung.

90. Expressions that appear in early Chinese literature. They indicate a dramatic change.

give consideration to the troubles I have been describing and put entire faith in these words of mine, then the winds will blow gently, the waves will be calm, and in no time at all we will enjoy bountiful harvests.

But a person's heart may change with the times, and the nature of a thing may alter with its surroundings. Just as the moon on the water will be tossed about by the waves, or the soldiers in the vanguard will be cowed by the swords of the enemy, so, although at this moment you may say you believe in my words, I fear that later you will forget them completely.

[Now if we wish first of all to bring security to the nation and to pray for our present and future lives, then we must hasten to examine and consider the situation and take measures as soon as possible to remedy it.]

[Why do I say this? Because, of the seven types of disasters described in the passage from the *Yakushi* Sutra that I cited earlier, five have already occurred. Only two have yet to appear, the "calamity of invasion from foreign lands" and the "calamity of revolt within one's own domain." And of the three calamities mentioned in the passage from the *Daijuku* Sutra, two have already made their appearance. Only one remains, the "disaster of warfare."

The different types of disaster and calamity enumerated in the *Konkōmyō* Sutra have arisen one after the other. Only that described as "bandits and marauders from other regions invading and plundering the nation" has yet to materialize. This is the only trouble that has not yet come. And of the seven calamities listed in the *Ninnō* Sutra, six are now upon us in full force. Only one has not yet appeared, the calamity that occurs "when enemies rise up on all four sides and invade the nation."]

Moreover, as the *Ninnō* Sutra says, "When a nation becomes disordered, it is the spirits which first show signs of rampancy. Because these spirits become rampant, all the people of the nation become disordered."

Now if we examine the present situation carefully in the

light of this passage, we will see that the various spirits have for some time been rampant, and many of the people have perished. If the first predicted misfortune in the sutra has already occurred, as is obvious, then how can we doubt that the later disasters will follow? If, in punishment for the evil doctrines that are upheld, the troubles that have yet to appear should fall upon us one after the other, then it will be too late to act, will it not?

[Emperors and kings have their foundation in the state and bring peace and order to the age; ministers and commoners hold possession of their fields and gardens and supply the needs of the world. But if bandits come from other regions to invade the nation, or if revolt breaks out within the domain and people's lands are seized and plundered, how can there be anything but terror and confusion? If the nation is destroyed and families are wiped out, then where can one flee for safety? If you care anything about your personal security, you should first of all pray for order and tranquillity throughout the four quarters of the land, should you not?]

[It seems to me that, when people are in this world, they all fear what their lot may be in the life to come. So it is that some of them put their faith in heretical teachings, or pay honor to those who slander the Law. It distresses me that they should be so confused about right and wrong, and at the same time I feel pity that, having embraced Buddhism, they should have chosen the wrong kind. With the power of faith that is in their hearts, why must they vainly give credence to heretical doctrines? If they do not shake off these delusions that they cling to but continue to harbor false ideas, then they will quickly leave the world of the living and fall into the hell of incessant suffering.

Thus the *Daijuku* Sutra says: "Though the ruler of a state may have for countless existences in the past practiced the giving of alms, observed the precepts and abided by the principles of wisdom, if he sees that my Law, the Dharma of

when we pray for Risen Rule we are praying for all of our desires

the Buddha, is in danger of perishing and stands idly by without doing anything to protect it, then all the inestimable store of good causes that he has accumulated through the practices just mentioned will be entirely wiped out. . . . Before long, the ruler will fall gravely ill, and after his life has come to an end, he will be reborn in one of the major hells. . . . And the same fate will befall the ruler's consort, his heir, the high ministers of the state, the lords of cities, the village heads and generals, the magistrates of districts, and the government officials."

The *Ninnō* Sutra states: "If a man destroys the teachings of the Buddha, he will have no filial sons, no harmony with his close relatives, and no aid from the heavenly deities. Disease and evil spirits will come day after day to torment him, disasters will descend on him incessantly, and misfortunes will dog him wherever he goes. And when he dies, he will fall into one of the three realms of Hell, Hunger or Animality. Even if he should be reborn as a human being, he will be destined to become a slave in the army. Retribution will follow as an echo follows a sound or a shadow follows a form. A person writing at night may put out the lamp, but the words he has written will still remain. It is the same with the destiny we create for ourselves in the threefold world."

The second volume of the Lotus Sutra says: "One who refuses to take faith in this sutra and instead slanders it . . . . After he dies, he will fall into the hell of incessant suffering." And in the *Fukyō* chapter in the seventh volume, it says: "For a thousand aeons they dwelt in the hell of incessant suffering and underwent great pain and torment."

In the Nirvana Sutra we read: "If a man separates himself from good friends, refuses to listen to the True Law and instead embraces evil teachings, then as a result he will sink down into the hell of incessant suffering, where he will experience indescribable torment."

When we examine this wide variety of sutras, we find that

they all stress how grave a matter it is to slander the Law. How pitiful, that all men should go out of the gate of the True Law and enter so deep into the prison of these perverse dogmas! How stupid, that they should fall one after another into the snares of these evil doctrines, and remain for so long entangled in this net of slanderous teachings! They lose their way in these mists and miasmas, and sink down amid the raging flames of hell. How they must grieve! How they must suffer!

Therefore you must quickly reform the tenets that you hold in your heart and embrace the one true vehicle, the single good doctrine of the Lotus Sutra. If you do so, then the threefold world will all become the Buddha land, and how could a Buddha land ever decline? The regions in the ten directions will all become treasure realms, and how could a treasure realm ever suffer harm? If you live in a country that knows no decline or diminution, in a land that suffers no harm or disruption, then your body will find peace and security and your mind will be calm and untroubled. You must believe my words, heed what I say!

The guest said: Since it concerns both this life and the lives to come, who could fail to be cautious in a matter such as this? Who could fail to agree with you? Now when I examine the passages you have cited from the sutras and see exactly what the Buddha has said, I realize that slandering is a very grave offense indeed, that violating the Law is in truth a terrible sin. I have put all my faith in one Buddha alone, Amida, and rejected all the other Buddhas. I have honored the three Pure Land sutras and set aside the other sutras. But this was not due to any distorted ideas of my own conception. I was simply obeying the words of the eminent men of the past.[91] And the same is true of all the other persons in the ten directions who follow the Pure Land teachings.

But now I realize that to do so means to exhaust oneself in

91. Eminent men of the past: T'an-luan, Tao-ch'o, Shan-tao, Eshin and Hōnen.

[margin note: "when our ichinen in faith changes—everything changes" "we must lead the people in the right direction, the Gohonzon"]

futile efforts in this life, and to fall into the hell of incessant suffering in the life to come. The texts you have cited are perfectly clear on this point and their arguments are detailed—they leave no room for doubt. With your kind instruction to guide me, I have been able bit by bit to dispel the ignorance from my mind.

Now I hope we may set about as quickly as possible taking measures to deal with these slanders against the Law and to bring peace to the world without delay, thus insuring that I may live in safety in this life and enjoy good fortune in the life to come. But it is not enough that I alone should accept and have faith in your words—we must see to it that others as well are warned of their errors!]

BACKGROUND   On April 28, 1253, Nichiren Daishonin declared the founding of his new Buddhism by chanting Nam-myoho-renge-kyo for the first time, and in August, he went to Kamakura, the seat of the military government, to begin prop-agation. In examining the records, we find that shortly there-after the era-names were changed frequently. The year 1253 was in the Kenchō era. Three years later, in 1256, the era-name was changed to Kōgen, and the next year, to Shōka. Then, two years later, in 1259, it was changed to Shōgen, the follow-ing year to Bunnō, and the year after that to Kōchō. In the space of a mere five years from 1256 until 1261, the era-name was changed no less than five times. An era-name was custom-arily changed for one of two reasons. Foremost was the acces-sion of a new emperor. The other reason was the frequent ap-pearance of disasters or other inauspicious events. The changes in the mid-thirteenth century were for the latter reason.

Although natural disasters occurred often during the final years of the Heian period (794–1185), the year 1256 and every year thereafter for some time saw unusually severe earthquakes, storms, epidemics, droughts, fires and cold spells. For example, on August 6, 1256, a torrential rainstorm in Kamakura caused floods and landslides, taking many lives and devastating the crops. In September an epidemic spread, claiming the lives of the shogun, the regent and other high officials. In the middle of the night on May 18 in the following year there was a strong earthquake, followed by an even greater tremor on August 1. Drought continued from June till July.

Most frightful of all was an earthquake of unprecedented scale which occurred at about eight P.M. on August 23. There were landslides, houses crumbled, yawning fissures opened in the ground, and fires broke out. A large number of people perished. Temblors continued to shake the city throughout the remainder of the year. The year 1259 saw no lessening of natural calamities. A fire in January reduced Jufuku-ji temple and the Hachiman shrine at Tsurugaoka to ashes. A rainstorm which wiped out crops in August led to a shortage of food. Epidemics and famine stalked the city, and corpses littered the streets. The citizenry lost all hope; the government proved powerless to help. In a vain attempt to end their misery, the people turned to priests of the leading sects. This too proved futile.

When Nichiren Daishonin saw the population afflicted with such suffering, he determined to clarify the cause of these misfortunes and the manner of their solution in the light of the Buddhist Law. He journeyed to Jissō-ji temple at Iwamoto in Suruga Province, where he stayed from the beginning of 1258 through the middle of 1260. As a major temple of the Tendai sect in eastern Japan, Jissō-ji housed many important sutras in its library. The Daishonin pored over them all.

As a result, Nichiren Daishonin was able to pinpoint the textual passages which clarified the root cause of the calamities and of the inefficacy of the prayers which had been offered. He decided to remonstrate with the leaders of the government and thereupon wrote the "Risshō Ankoku Ron" (On Securing the Peace of the Land through the Propagation of True Buddhism).

On July 16, 1260, Nichiren Daishonin submitted this document to Hōjō Tokiyori, at that time the retired regent but still the most influential member of the entire Hōjō clan, via Tokiyori's majordomo, Yadoya Mitsunori. In the document he cited the *Ninnō*, *Yakushi*, *Daijuku* and *Konkōmyō* sutras, and affirmed that the fundamental cause of the three calamities and seven disasters was disbelief in the True Law and belief in teachings contradictory to the Buddha's true intent. In other words, mistaken philosophies lead people to act in ways which run counter to the fundamental law or harmony of the universe, thus creating suffering. In particular, the Daishonin regarded Hōnen's otherworldly-oriented teaching of Nembutsu as a major factor responsible for enervating the people and undermining the country. He defined the basis for establishing a peaceful land as belief in the True Law. On the basis of his understanding of the sutras, he warned that if leaders of the government were not awakened to this principle, two great disasters, that is, internal strife and foreign invasion, would occur, plunging the people into great misery. This in essence is the message of the "Risshō Ankoku Ron."

Both internal strife and foreign invasion imply warfare. Nichiren Daishonin's underlying intention was not only to protect his own country from foreign invasion, but to uproot the cruelty and misery of war itself, whether civil or international. In other words, he saw the peace of the land as a primary requisite to individual happiness. This is clear from the concluding portion of the "Risshō Ankoku Ron."

This document is written in scholarly classical Chinese, and to this day it is one of several writings by which Nichiren Daishonin is most often judged. People who are critical of the Daishonin quote it to imply that he was an abrasive fanatic; others find in it the Daishonin's courage to express his convictions in an effort to save the troubled people.

Hōjō Tokiyori made no reply, but there was an unofficial response. The "Risshō Ankoku Ron" incensed the government and religious authorities among whom it was circulated. Instigated by their religious leaders, a group of Nembutsu believers descended on the Daishonin's cottage at Matsubaga-yatsu on the evening of August 27, intending to silence him permanently. The Daishonin escaped, but thereafter he was to enter a period in his life of continual confrontation with danger and oppression.

This document takes the form of a dialogue between a host and a traveler who is stopping at his house. The host, of course, symbolizes Nichiren Daishonin, and the guest represents Hōjō Tokiyori. In the beginning of this document, the host attributes people's sufferings to their belief in erroneous religions. He lays the greatest blame on the proponents of the Nembutsu, or belief in the Buddha Amida. He cites various scriptural references to support his assertions. He then predicts further and more terrifying consequences if the nation continues to pursue false doctrines. "Why do I say this?" he asks. "Because, of the seven types of disasters described in the passage from the *Yakushi* Sutra that I cited earlier, five have already occurred. Only two have yet to appear, the 'calamity of invasion from foreign lands' and the 'calamity of revolt within one's own domain.'" He then exhorts his guest: "Therefore you must quickly reform the tenets that you hold in your heart and embrace the one true vehicle, the single good doctrine of the Lotus Sutra." At the end of the text, the traveler discards his false beliefs, embraces the Daishonin's Buddhism, and pledges to spread it widely.

Let us consider why, in the "Risshō Ankoku Ron," the Daishonin attacks the Jōdo or Pure Land teaching in particular as a fundamental cause of unhappiness. The Pure Land sect in Japan was founded by Hōnen (1133–1212), who advocated the single practice of chanting the name of Amida Buddha in order to attain rebirth in the Pure Land after death. To aid in promulgating this teaching, he wrote the *Senchaku Shū* (The Sole Selection of the Nembutsu Teachings) in 1198 at the age of sixty-six. By the time Nichiren Daishonin appeared, the Pure Land teaching had swept across the country.

There were probably two major reasons for this popularity. One was the evident decadence of the established Buddhist sects. For example, although the Tendai sect held a central position in the religious world, it had incorporated the doctrines of the esoteric Shingon sect into its teachings and deviated from the teaching of the Lotus Sutra upon which it was originally founded. The chief priest of the sect had come to wield political influence, and competition for the position of chief priest intensified. Worse yet, the great temples such as Enryaku-ji, Kōfuku-ji and Tōdai-ji maintained groups of armed monks in order to protect their lands. These temple armies often attempted to settle disputes by force. People grieved over this degradation of the established sects and were spiritually ready for a new religion.

The other reason was a general pessimism deriving from the traditional concept that in the Latter Day of the Law, Buddhism would lose its power for redemption and evil would prevail. This idea became a morose preoccupation. According to scholars of the day, the year 1052 marked the onset of the Latter Day of the Law, and a series of disasters and conflicts seemed to substantiate the hopelessness which this age implied. Because of this succession of misfortunes, people felt their efforts to be futile, and, despairing of happiness in this life, longed to achieve it in the next. Some followers of the Pure Land teaching actually committed suicide out of disgust with life and a desire for rebirth in the Pure Land. Nichiren Daishonin severely attacked the Pure Land teaching for undermining the people's initiative and directing attention away from the reality of this life toward unverifiable promises of bliss after death.

In terms of its view of the relationship between the people's religious beliefs and the realization of a peaceful society, the "Risshō Ankoku Ron" holds an important position in Nichiren Daishonin's writings. It is interesting to note that the document was directed at Hōjō Tokiyori, the most powerful man in the country. Nichiren Daishonin lived at a time of authoritarian government, and the reins of power were held by a single man. By 1260, although Hōjō Tokiyori had formally retired from the position of regent, he still wielded more power than anyone else. The Daishonin probably felt, and with justification, that opening this one man's eyes could help bring about a reformation of the entire society. Today, however, in a society where sovereignty rests with the people, spreading true Buddhism among the people is the most appropriate way to realize the principle of the "Risshō Ankoku Ron."

Another point of significance is this document's assertion that the three calamities and seven disasters stem from the evil nature in human life itself. A reformation of human life can therefore lead to the correction of social and environmental problems. This derives from the Buddhist doctrine of the oneness of life and its environment. Based on this doctrine, the "Risshō Ankoku Ron" explains that a reformation of the individual will bring about a transformation of the environment, and that this individual reformation is made possible through the practice of true Buddhism.

The Izu Exile

I HAVE received the rice-dumplings wrapped in bamboo leaves, saké, dried rice, peppers, paper and other items from the messenger whom you took the trouble of sending. He also conveyed your message that this offering should be kept secret. I understand.

On the twelfth day of the fifth month, having been exiled, I arrived at a beach I had never even heard of before. When I left the boat, still suffering from seasickness, you kindly took me into your care. What destiny brought us together? You might have been a votary of the Lotus Sutra in times past. Now, in the Latter Day of the Law, you were born as a boat-manager named Yasaburō to take pity on me. Being a man, it was perhaps natural for you to act as you did, but your wife might have been less inclined to help me. Nevertheless, she gave me food, brought me water to wash my hands and feet and treated me with great concern. I can only describe this as wondrous.

What caused you to believe in the Lotus Sutra and to serve me during my more than thirty-day stay there? I was hated and resented by the lord and people of the district even more than I was in Kamakura. Those who saw me scowled, while those who merely heard my name were filled with spite. And yet, though I was there in the fifth month when rice was scarce, you secretly fed me. It would almost seem as though my parents had been reborn in Kawana close to Itō in Izu Province.

The fourth volume of the Lotus Sutra states, "[I will send] pureminded men and women to make offerings to the teacher of the Law." The heavenly gods and benevolent deities will assume the form of men and women and present offerings to help one who practices the Lotus Sutra. There is no doubt that you and your wife were born as just such a "pureminded man and woman" and now make offerings to the teacher of the Law, Nichiren.

Since I wrote to you in detail earlier, I will make this letter brief. But I would like to mention one thing in particular. When the lord of this district sent me a request to pray for his recovery from illness, I wondered if I should accept it. But since he showed some degree of faith in me, I decided I would appeal to the Lotus Sutra. If I did, I saw no reason why the Ten Goddesses should not join forces to aid me. I therefore pleaded with the Lotus Sutra, Shakyamuni, Tahō and the other Buddhas throughout the universe, the Sun Goddess, Hachiman and the other deities, both major and minor. I was sure that they would consider my request and respond by curing the lord's illness. Certainly they would never disregard Nichiren's prayer, but would respond as naturally as a person rubs a sore or scratches an itch. And as it turned out, the lord recovered. In gratitude he presented me with a statue of the Buddha which had appeared from the sea along with a catch of fish. He did so because his illness had finally ended, an illness which I am certain was inflicted by the Ten Goddesses. The benefits of his offering will pass on to you and your wife.

We common mortals all have dwelt in the sea of suffering since time without beginning. But now that we have become votaries of the Lotus Sutra, we will without fail become Buddhas who are enlightened to the entity of body and mind which has existed since the beginningless past. We will reveal the unchangeable nature innate within us, as well as the mystic wisdom which enables us to realize the mystic truth. We will enjoy a state of life as indestructible as a diamond. Then how can we be in any way different from the Buddha who appeared from the sea? The Lord Shakyamuni, who declared, "I alone can save them," at a time even more distant than *gohyaku-jintengō*,[1] is none other than each of us. This is the teaching of *ichinen sanzen* expounded in the Lotus Sutra. Our behavior is a personal demonstration of "I am here always, teaching the Law."[2] Thus we are all entities embodying the supreme teaching of the Lotus Sutra and the august life of Shakyamuni Buddha, though ordinary people never realize this. This is the meaning of the passage in the *Juryō* chapter, ". . . the deluded people cannot see me even when I am nearby." The difference between delusion and enlightenment is like the four different views of the grove of sal trees.[3] Let it be known that the Buddha of *ichinen sanzen* is anyone in any of the Ten Worlds who manifests his inherent Buddha nature.

The demon who appeared before Sessen Dōji was Taishaku in disguise. The dove which sought the protection of King Shibi was the god Bishukatsuma.[4] King Fumyō,[5] who was imprisoned in the castle of King Hanzoku, was the Lord

1. The Lord Shakyamuni, . . . at a time even more distant than *gohyaku-jintengō*: Refers not to Gautama Buddha in India, but to the eternal Buddha who has continued to exist since time without beginning. The phrase, "a time even more distant than *gohyaku-jintengō*," indicates that the Daishonin is shifting his reference from the temporal framework of *gohyaku-jintengō* to that of *kuon ganjo*, time without either beginning or end.

2. Lotus Sutra, chap. 16.

3. Four different views of the grove of sal trees: The grove of sal trees was where Shakyamuni expounded his last teaching, the Nirvana Sutra, and died. The four different views represent the four kinds of lands: the land of enlightened and unenlightened beings, the land of transition, the land of actual reward, and the land of eternal light. According to the capacity and life-condition of people, the grove of sal trees is viewed in four different ways, that is, as a grove composed of earth, trees, plants and stone walls; as a place adorned with seven kinds of treasure, including gold and silver; as a place where all Buddhas practice Buddhism; and as the eternal, enlightened land of the Buddha.

4. Bishukatsuma: (Skt Viśvakarman) A god who serves the god Taishaku, who lives on Mt. Sumeru. His story appears in the *Daichido Ron*. When Shakyamuni in a past existence practiced Buddhist austerities as King Shibi,

Shakyamuni himself. The eyes of common mortals cannot see their true identities, but the eyes of the Buddha can. As the sutra states, the sky and the sea both have paths [though we cannot see them] for birds and fish to come and go. A wooden statue of the Buddha is itself a golden one, and a golden statue is a wooden one. Aniruddha's gold was seen first as a hare and then as a corpse.[6] Sand in the palm of Mahanama's[7] hand turned into gold. These things are beyond the grasp of human reason. A common mortal is a Buddha, and a Buddha a common mortal. This is exactly what is meant by *ichinen sanzen* and by the phrase, "[The time is limitless and boundless . . .] since I in fact attained Buddhahood."[8]

Thus it is quite possible that you and your wife have appeared here as reincarnations of the Lord Buddha Shakyamuni in order to help me. Although the distance between Itō and Kawana is short, we are not allowed to communicate openly. I am writing this letter for your future reference. Do

Taishaku assumed the form of a hawk, and Bishukatsuma, that of a dove, as a test of the king's sincerity. In order to save the dove, Shibi gave his life, offering his flesh to the hungry hawk.

5. Fumyō: Name of Shakyamuni when he engaged in the practice of observing precepts in a past existence. King Fumyō and ninety-nine other kings (nine hundred and ninety-nine kings according to another source) were captured by King Hanzoku and were about to be killed. In grief, Fumyō said to King Hanzoku, "When I was taken from my country, I had promised offerings to a certain monk. I am not trying to avoid death, but breaking that promise is hard to bear." King Fumyō received seven days' grace and returned to his country. He gave the monk offerings and transferred the throne to his son. After proclaiming to his people that keeping a promise is the most important precept, he returned to King Hanzoku. Hanzoku was so impressed by Fumyō's sincerity that he released not only Fumyō but the ninety-nine other kings as well. Furthermore, he was converted to Buddhism.

6. Aniruddha's gold was seen first as a rabbit and then as a corpse: Aniruddha was one of the ten major disciples of Shakyamuni and was known as "foremost in divine insight." He was a cousin of Shakyamuni. The Sanskrit, *aniruddha*, means to be unobstructed, or to gratify every wish and be without desire. His story appears in the first volume of T'ien-t'ai's *Hokke Mongu*. Long ago, a pratyekabuddha named Rida engaged in the practice of begging alms, but gained nothing. Seeing this, a poor man offered him barnyard millet. Later, when the poor man went deep into a mountain to find millet for Rida, a rabbit happened to jump on his back and then turned into a corpse. Frightened, he

not discuss these matters with other people, but ponder them yourself. If anyone should learn anything at all about this letter, it will go hard with you. Keep this deep in your heart, and never speak about it. With my deepest regard. Nam-myoho-renge-kyo.

Nichiren

The twenty-seventh day of the sixth month in the first year of Kōchō (1261)

BACKGROUND   This letter was written on June 27, 1261, to Funamori Yasaburō, who lived in Kawana, a small fishing village on the northeastern coast of the Izu Peninsula, about fifty miles west of Kamakura. Nichiren Daishonin was then forty years old and in exile at Izu. Yasaburō was commonly

---

tried to shake it off, but in vain. As soon as he arrived at his house, however, the corpse fell off and turned into gold. Hearing of this, wicked men came to rob him of the gold, but to them it looked like a mere corpse. To the eye of the poor man, however, it was a genuine treasure of gold, and he became wealthy. Ninety-nine aeons later, he was born as Aniruddha.

7.   Mahanama: One of the five *bhikkhus*, or ascetic monks. When Shakyamuni forsook the secular world and entered the religious life, his father, the king, ordered five men to accompany him. They followed and practiced asceticism with Shakyamuni, but left him when he renounced ascetic practices. However, shortly after Shakyamuni attained enlightenment, he preached his first sermon to them at Sarnath, known as the Deer Park, and they became his first disciples. The exact identity of these five ascetics is unknown. According to the *Zōichi Agon* Sutra, however, Mahanama is said to have possessed occult powers. The story of "sand in his palm turning into gold" appears in Ts'ung-i's supplementary note to T'ien-t'ai's three major works on the Lotus Sutra.

8.   Lotus Sutra, chap. 16. Shakyamuni explained his original enlightenment by saying that he had actually attained enlightenment in *gohyaku-jintengō*, revealing his true identity. Nichiren Daishonin revealed the deeper meaning of the phrase, "since I in fact attained Buddhahood." In his orally transmitted teachings, he states that "I" indicates all people of the Ten Worlds in the universe, while "attain" means to open and reveal. Accordingly, "attain Buddhahood" signifies that people of the Ten Worlds can reveal their eternally inherent Buddha nature.

known as Funamori (literally, "boat-manager") since he ran a fishing business. He and his wife protected the Daishonin during his exile, even at the risk of their lives, and were converted to the Daishonin's Buddhism. The Daishonin later sent several letters of thanks to them for their help during the almost two years of his exile in Izu.

In 1260, Nichiren Daishonin had submitted the "Risshō Ankoku Ron" (On Securing the Peace of the Land through the Propagation of True Buddhism) to Hōjō Tokiyori, the former regent. In this treatise, the Daishonin asserted that Japan slandered the True Law and encouraged false doctrines, especially Nembutsu. The letter was a lengthy thesis and attributed the chaos of the age to religious decadence. Not only did his warning go unheeded, but a group of Nembutsu followers attacked his cottage at Matsubagayatsu in an attempt to kill him. The Daishonin narrowly escaped to Shimōsa Province, staying for a time at the home of Toki Jōnin, his follower and an influential lord. But in less than a year, his sense of mission compelled him to return to Kamakura to resume his preaching.

The Nembutsu priests, alarmed at his success in attracting followers, contrived to have charges brought againt him before the Kamakura government. The regent at the time was Hōjō Nagatoki. His father was Shigetoki, a Nembutsu adherent and confirmed enemy of the Daishonin. Without investigation or trial, the regent accepted the charges and, on May 12, 1261, ordered Nichiren Daishonin banished to Itō on the Izu Peninsula. Izu was a stronghold of the Nembutsu sect, and exile there posed great personal danger to the Daishonin.

Government officials who were to carry the Daishonin to Izu by boat apparently did not take him as far as Itō. Instead, they abandoned him on a beach at Kawana where he would be at the mercy of local citizens. Yasaburō, who lived nearby, happened to pass by and took the Daishonin to his own house, where he offered shelter and food. After Nichiren Daishonin had spent about a month at Yasaburō's house, the lord of the

Itō district, Itō Sukemitsu, learned of the Daishonin's presence. Seriously ill, Lord Itō sent a messenger, asking the Daishonin to come to pray for his recovery. Itō recovered and gratefully presented the Daishonin with a statue of the Buddha retrieved from the sea.

When the Daishonin went to Itō to pray for the lord's recovery, both Yasaburō and his wife were concerned about the Daishonin's safety. Yasaburō therefore sent a messenger to him at Itō with various offerings. "The Izu Exile" is the Daishonin's reply brought back by the messenger. In this letter, Nichiren Daishonin expresses his heartfelt thanks for the protection which the couple extended to him and says that they acted as Buddhist gods. He also states that there is no essential difference between a common mortal and a Buddha when people understand the principle of *ichinen sanzen* and embody it in their own lives. Finally, he urges Yasaburō to keep their communication secret for his own protection, since associating with an exile was forbidden by law.

Only six months after the Daishonin's term of exile began, the people of Kamakura were shocked by the news that Hōjō Shigetoki had died of a mysterious disease. In time, apparently at the suggestion of the former regent Hōjō Tokiyori, the government issued a pardon, and Nichiren Daishonin returned to Kamakura in February 1263.

Rationale for Submitting
the Risshō Ankoku Ron

IN the first year of the Shōka era (1257), when the reverse marker of Jupiter was in the sector of the sky with the cyclical sign *hinoto-mi*, on the twenty-third day of the eighth month, at the time when the Hour of the Dog gives way to the Hour of the Boar (9:00 P.M.), there occurred an earthquake of unprecedented magnitude. In the second year of the same era (1258), cyclical sign *tsuchinoe-uma*, on the first day of the eighth month, there was a great wind. In the third year (1259), cyclical sign *tsuchinoto-hitsuji*, a major famine occurred. In the first year of the Shōgen era (1259), cyclical sign *tsuchinoto-hitsuji*, disease was rampant, and throughout the four seasons of the second year (1260), cyclical sign *kanoe-saru*, the sickness continued to rage without abating. By this time, more than half the ordinary citizens of the nation had been laid low by death. The rulers of the country, alarmed at this state of affairs, turned to the scriptures of Buddhism and the non-Buddhist writings for help, ordering that various prayers be offered. These, however, failed to produce the slightest effect. On the contrary, famine and disease raged more fiercely than ever.

I, Nichiren, observing this state of affairs, proceeded to consult the various Buddhist scriptures. There I discovered the reason why these prayers are without effect and on the contrary actually make the situation worse, along with passages of proof to support it. In the end I had no other recourse than to compile a work to present my findings, entitling it "Risshō Ankoku Ron." In the first year of the Bunnō era (1260), cyclical sign *kanoe-saru*, on the sixteenth day of the seventh month, at the Hour of the Dragon (7:00–9:00 A.M.), I handed it to the lay monk Yadoya for presentation to His Lordship, the late lay monk of Saimyō-ji.[1] This I did solely that I might repay the debt of gratitude that I owe to my native land.

The essence of my work, the "Risshō Ankoku Ron," is as follows. Long ago it was said that this country of Japan would be ruled by seven heavenly deities, five earthly deities, and a hundred kings, reigning one after another in succession. During the reign of Emperor Kimmei, the thirtieth of the human sovereigns, Buddhism was for the first time brought to Japan from the kingdom of Paekche.[2] From that time until the reign of Emperor Kammu, a period of some 260 years that saw the reigns of twenty or more sovereigns, all the various Buddhist scriptures were brought to Japan, as well as the six sects[3] of Buddhism. At this time, however, the Tendai and Shingon sects had not yet been introduced.

During the reign of Emperor Kammu, there was a young monk named Saichō, who was a disciple of Priest Gyōhō of Yamashina Temple. (He later came to be known by the title Great Teacher Dengyō.) He made a thorough study of the six sects that had been introduced to Japan earlier, as well as of the Zen sect, but none of these seemed to satisfy him. Some forty years earlier, in the reign of Emperor Shōmu, a Chinese monk named Ganjin had come to Japan and brought with him the commentaries of the Great Teacher T'ien-t'ai. When Saichō read these, he for the first time came to understand in essence the true meaning of Buddhism.

---

1. Lay monk of Saimyō-ji: The retired regent, Hōjō Tokiyori.
2. Paekche: An ancient state on the Korean Peninsula.
3. Six sects: Sanron, Jōjitsu, Hossō, Kusha, Ritsu and Kegon, the six major sects of Buddhism which flourished in the ancient Japanese capital of Nara.

In the fourth year of the Enryaku era (785), Saichō founded a temple on Mount Hiei[4] in order to insure the continuance of peace in heaven and on earth. Emperor Kammu paid honor to the new establishment, designating it as a place of worship where prayers should be offered to the guardian star of the ruler. He ceased to heed the teachings of the six sects and instead gave wholehearted allegiance to the perfect doctrines of the Tendai sect.

In the thirteenth year of the Enryaku era (794), the emperor moved the capital from Nagaoka to the city of Heian.[5] In the twenty-first year of the same era (802), on the nineteenth day of the first month, the emperor summoned fourteen learned scholars of the six sects from the seven great temples of Nara, including such monks as Gonsō and Chōyō,[6] to the temple called Takao-dera, and ordered them to engage Saichō in debate. These enlightened masters of the six sects were not able to hold their own against Saichō even for a single exchange of opinions, but shut their mouths so tightly one might have mistaken them for noses. The "Five Teachings" of the Kegon sect, the "Three Periods" of the Hossō sect, the "Two Store-houses" and "Three Eras" propounded by the Sanron sect[7]— all of these doctrines were demolished by Saichō. The doctrines

4. Temple on Mount Hiei: Enryaku-ji, the head temple of the Tendai sect and site of the ordination center of Mahayana Buddhism. Dengyō petitioned the throne for permission to erect the ordination center, and it was completed by his successor, Gishin.

5. Heian: The ancient name of Kyoto.

6. Gonsō and Chōyō: Gonsō (758–827) was a priest and scholar of the Sanron sect at Daian-ji temple in Nara. Kōbō Daishi, founder of the Japanese Shingon sect, was his disciple. Details concerning Chōyō are unknown.

7. These are systems by which these sects sought to classify the body of Buddhist scriptures. The "Five Teachings" of Kegon divides the sutras into Hinayana, early Mahayana, advanced Mahayana, abrupt teachings and perfect teachings. The "Three Periods" of the Hossō sect divides the sutras into: 1) teachings that all is existence; 2) teachings that all is void; and 3) teachings of the Middle Way. The Sanron's "Two Storehouses" are teachings for *shōmon* and teachings for bodhisattvas, and the "Three Eras" of that sect are: 1) teachings that both the subjective mind and its object exist; 2) teachings that only the mind exists; and 3) teachings that both mind and object are void.

of the six sects not only were refuted, but in fact served to reveal that the other debaters were all guilty of slandering the Law. On the twenty-ninth day of the same month, the emperor handed down an edict criticizing the fourteen monks who had opposed Saichō. The fourteen monks in turn drew up a letter apologizing for their conduct and submitted it to the emperor.

Thereafter, one sovereign after another paid allegiance to Mount Hiei, treating it with even greater deference than a filial son shows toward his father and mother, regarding it with greater awe than the common people manifest before the might of the ruler. At times the rulers issued edicts to it, at other times they were obliged to give their approval to its unjust demands. We may note in particular that Emperor Seiwa[8] was able to ascend the throne as a consequence of the powerful prayers of Priest Eryō of Mount Hiei. The emperor's maternal grandfather, the Kujō Minister of the Right, for this reason submitted a written pledge of his fidelity to Mount Hiei. Minamoto no Yoritomo, the founder of the Kamakura shogunate, it will be recalled, was a descendant of Emperor Seiwa. And yet the government authorities in Kamakura, though they may or may not be following the correct course in their administration, ignore and turn their back on Mount Hiei. Have they no fear of the punishment of Heaven?

Later, in the time of the Retired Emperor Gotoba, during the Kennin era (1201–04), there appeared two men, Hōnen and Dainichi,[9] who in their arrogance believed that their

8.   Emperor Seiwa (850–880): Prince Korehito, fourth son of the Emperor Montoku. According to tradition, Montoku was unable to decide whether he should name Korehito or another of his sons at his successor, and had the two princes hold a *sumō* match to settle the matter. It is said that Korehito won because of the prayers offered on his behalf by the priest Eryō.

9.   Dainichi: A twelfth-century Japanese priest who spread the Zen teachings before Eisai, the founder of the Rinzai school. He was also called Nōnin. Because he was criticized for not having received his teachings from a master, in 1189 he sent his two disciples to China to have his teachings authenticated by

understanding surpassed that of all others. Their bodies were possessed by evil spirits, and they went about deluding the people of both high and low station throughout the country, until everyone had become a Nembutsu believer or else was hastening to join the Zen sect. Those who continued to pay respect to Mount Hiei became surprisingly few and lacking in ardor, and throughout the country, the monks who were authorities on the Lotus Sutra or the Shingon teachings found themselves ignored and rejected.

As a result, the deities Tenshō Daijin, Hachiman, and the gods of the seven shrines of the Sannō, who guard and protect Mount Hiei, as well as the various other benevolent deities who protect the different parts of the nation, were no longer able to taste the flavor of the Dharma. Their power and brilliance waned, and they abandoned the country. Thus the evil demons were able to gain access to the nation and to bring about disasters and calamities. These disasters, as I stated in my "Risshō Ankoku Ron," were omens signifying that our country would in the end be destroyed by a foreign nation.

Later, in the first year of the Bun'ei era (1264), cyclical sign *kinoe-ne*, on the fifth day of the seventh month, a comet appeared in the east, and its light shone over the whole country of Japan. This is an evil portent such as has never been seen before since the beginning of history. None of the authorities on the Buddhist scriptures or the secular writings could understand what had brought about such an ill omen. I became even more grieved and distressed. Now, nine years after I presented my work, the "Risshō Ankoku Ron," to the authorities, in the intercalary first month of this year (1268), this letter has arrived from the great kingdom of the Mongols. The events that have occurred match the predictions made in my work as exactly as do the two halves of a tally.

---

a Zen master named Cho-an of Mt. Yü-wang. Thereafter he named his sect the Nihon Daruma or Japanese Bodhidharma sect.

The Buddha left this prediction, saying: "More than one hundred years after my passing, a ruler known as the Great King Ashoka will appear in the world and will spread my relics far and wide." In the reign of King Chao, the fourth ruler of the Chou dynasty, the Grand Historian Su Yu made this prediction: "One thousand years from now, the teachings [of the Buddha] will be spread throughout this country." Crown Prince Shōtoku predicted: "After my death, when two hundred years or more have passed, the city of Heian will be established in the province of Yamashiro." And the Great Teacher T'ien-t'ai predicted: "Two hundred years or more after my death, a person will be born in an eastern country who will spread my Correct Law." All of these predictions were fulfilled to the letter.

When I, Nichiren, observed the great earthquake of the Shōka era, and the great wind and famine that occurred in the same era, as well as the major outbreak of disease that took place in the first year of the Shōgen era, I made a prediction, saying: "These are omens indicating that this country of ours will be destroyed by a foreign nation." I may seem to be congratulating myself on having made such a prediction, though in fact, of course, if our country should be destroyed, it would most certainly mean the destruction of the Buddhist teachings as well.

The eminent Buddhist monks of our time seem to be of one mind with those who slander the Law. In fact, they do not even understand the true meaning of the teachings of their own sects. It is certain that, if they should receive an Imperial command or instructions from the government authorities to offer prayers in an effort to avert the evils that beset the nation, they would only make the Buddhas and deities angrier than they are already, and then the nation could not help but face ruin.

I, Nichiren, understand the steps that should be taken to

remedy the situation. Other than the sage of Mount Hiei,[10] I am the only person in all of Japan who does. Just as there are not two suns or two moons, so two sages are not to be found standing side by side. If these words of mine are false, then may I be punished by the Ten Goddesses, the ten daughters of the demon mother who protect this Lotus Sutra that I embrace. I say all this solely for the sake of the nation, for the sake of the Law, and for the sake of others, not for my own sake. I will be calling upon you in person, and so I am informing you of this. If you do not heed my advice, you will surely regret it later.

Respectfully,
Nichiren

Bun'ei era, fifth year (1268), cyclical sign *tsuchinoe-tatsu*, fourth month, fifth day

BACKGROUND In January of 1268, an envoy from Khubilai Khan arrived in Kamakura with a message demanding, in veiled terms, that Japan acknowledge fealty to the Mongol Empire. The envoy was sent back empty-handed, and the government began to prepare for war. At this time Nichiren Daishonin wrote the rationale for submitting the "Risshō Ankoku Ron" and sent it to a man named Hōkan-bō. Little is known about this individual; his name is that of a priest, but he would appear to have been active in government circles. In this letter the Daishonin explains the circumstances leading up to his writing of the "Risshō Ankoku Ron," and points out that the arrival of the Mongol emissary has substantiated the prophecy of foreign invasion made in that treatise.

In October, he sent letters to eleven high-ranking political and religious leaders including Hōjō Tokimune and the priests Dōryū of Kenchō-ji temple and Ryōkan of Gokuraku-ji

10. Sage of Mount Hiei: The Great Teacher Dengyō.

temple, pointing out that the predictions in his "Risshō Ankoku Ron" were now being fulfilled and demanding the opportunity to demonstrate the validity of his teachings in public religious debate. However, his appeal fell on deaf ears.

Postscript to the Rissho Ankoku Ron

I COMPILED the above work in the first year of the Bunno
era (1260), when the reverse marker of Jupiter was in the
sector of the sky with the cyclical sign *kanoe-saru*. That is, I
began the work during the Shōka era (1257–58) and completed
it in the first year of the Bunnō era.

In the first year of the Shōka era (1257), cyclical sign *hinoto-mi*, on the twenty-third day of the eighth month, at the time
when the Hour of the Dog gives way to the Hour of the Boar
(9:00 P.M.), there was a severe earthquake. Observing this event,
I began compiling the work. Later, in the first year of the
Bunnō era, on the sixteenth day of the seventh month, I presented
it to His Lordship, the late lay monk of Saimyō-ji,[1] by way of
Yadoya Zemmon.[2] Still later, in the first year of the Bun'ei era
(1264), cyclical sign *kinoe-ne*, on the fifth day of the seventh
month, when a great comet appeared, I became even more
certain of the origin of these disasters. Then, on the eighteenth
day of the intercalary first month of the fifth year of the Bun'ei
era (1268), nine years after the first year of the Bunnō era, when
I submitted the "Rishō Ankoku Ron," a letter came from the
great kingdom of the Mongols that lies to the west, threatening

1. Lay monk of Saimyō-ji: *See* p. 62, footnote 1.
2. Yadoya Zemmon: Yadoya Mitsunori, a lay priest and majordomo to
Hōjō Tokiyori.

69

to attack our country. Again, in the sixth year of the same era (1269), a second letter arrived. Thus the prediction that I made in the "Risshō Ankoku Ron" has already proved to be true. In view of this, we may suppose that the predictions I made will continue to come true in the future as well.

This work of mine has now been substantiated by fact. But this has in no regard happened because of my powers. Rather it has come about as a response to the true words contained in the Lotus Sutra.

Copied on the eighth day of the twelfth month of the sixth year of the Bun'ei era (1269), cyclical sign *tsuchinoto-mi*

BACKGROUND   In 1269, Mongol emissaries again arrived at Dazaifu, the government outpost on the southern island of Kyushu. Nichiren Daishonin is believed to have sent off another round of letters to top officials, which again failed to produce a response. The "Postscript to the 'Risshō Ankoku Ron'" dated December 8, 1269, was appended to a copy of the "Risshō Ankoku Ron," which he himself made, and warns that the prophecies made in that document more than nine years ago were now coming true.

The Opening of the Eyes

Part One

T HERE are three categories of people that all men and women should respect. They are the sovereign, the teacher, and the parent. There are three types of doctrines that are to be studied. They are Confucianism, Brahmanism, and Buddhism.

Confucianism describes the Three Rulers,[1] the Five Emperors,[2] and the Three Kings,[3] which it calls the Heaven-Honored Ones. These men are depicted as the heads and eyes of the government officials and the pillars and beams of the populace. In the age before the Three Rulers, people lived like animals and did not even know who their own fathers were. But from the time of the Five Emperors on, they learned to identify both their father and mother and to treat them according to the dictates of filial piety. Thus Shun, the last of the Five Emperors, served his father with reverence, though the latter was stubborn and hard-headed. Also, the governor of P'ei, after he became the first emperor of the Han dynasty, continued to pay

---

1. Three Rulers: Fu Hsi, Shen Nung and Huang Ti, legendary rulers of ancient China said to have realized model governments.

2. Five Emperors: Shao Hao, Chuan Hsü, Ti Kao, T'ang Yao and Yü Shun. They reigned after the Three Rulers.

3. Three Kings: King (or Emperor) Yü of the Hsia dynasty, King T'ang of the Yin dynasty and King Wen of the Chou dynasty. They reigned after the Five Emperors.

great respect to his father, the Venerable Sire. King Wu[4] of the Chou dynasty made a wooden image of his father, the Earl of the West, and Ting Lan[5] fashioned a statue of his mother. All of these men are models of filial piety.

The high minister Pi Kan,[6] seeing that the Yin dynasty was on the path to ruin, strongly admonished the ruler, though it cost him his head. Hung Yen,[7] finding that his lord, Duke Yi, had been killed, cut open his own stomach and inserted the duke's liver in it before he died. These men may serve as models of loyalty.

Yin Shou was the teacher of Emperor Yao, Wu Ch'eng was the teacher of Emperor Shun, T'ai-kung Wang[8] was the teacher of King Wen, and Lao Tzu was the teacher of Confucius.[9] These teachers are known as the Four Sages. Even the Heaven-Honored Ones bow their heads to them in respect, and all people press their palms together in reverence. Sages such as these have left behind writings that run to over three thousand volumes in such works as the *Three Records*, *Five Canons*, and *Three Histories*.[10] But all these writings in the end

4.   When King Wu decided to revolt against Emperor Chou of the Yin dynasty, he carved a wooden figure of his father, who had cherished the same desire, before setting out on his campaign.

5.   During the Later Han dynasty, Ting Lan, who had lost his mother at the age of fifteen, made a statue of her and served it as if she were still alive.

6.   Emperor Chou was so absorbed in his affection for his consort, Ta Chi, that he totally neglected the government. When Pi Kan remonstrated with him, Emperor Chou flew into a rage and had him killed.

7.   Duke Yi of the state of Wei loved cranes and lived extravagantly, losing the support of the public. While his minister Hung Yen was away on a journey, an enemy attacked Wei and killed Duke Yi. They ate the duke's flesh, except his liver, and then left the land. Returning, Hung Yen saw the disastrous scene and wept. He cut open his stomach and inserted the duke's liver in it to save him from shame and dishonor.

8.   T'ai-kung Wang: General who served King Wen and, after the king's death, served King Wu, Wen's son. He fought valorously in the battle with Emperor Chou of the Yin dynasty and contributed to the prosperity of the Chou dynasty.

9.   This assertion is found in the *Chuang Tzu* and the *Shih Chi* (Records of the Historian).

10.   *Three Records*, *Five Canons*, and *Three Histories*: The *Three Records* are

do not advance beyond the three mysteries. The first of the three mysteries is Being.[11] This is the principle taught by the Duke of Chou and others. The second mystery is Non-Being[12] which was expounded by Lao Tzu. The third is Both Being and Non-Being,[13] which is the mystery set forth by Chuang Tzu. Mystery denotes darkness. Some say that, if we ask what existed before our ancestors were born, we will find that life was born out of the primal force, while others declare that eminence and obscurity, joy and sorrow, right and wrong, gain and loss occur simply as part of the natural order.

These are theories that are cleverly argued, but which fail to take cognizance of either the past or the future. Mystery, as we have seen, means darkness or obscurity, and it is for this reason that it is called mystery. It is a theory that deals with matters only in terms of the present. Speaking in terms of the present, the Confucians declare that one should abide by the principles of benevolence and righteousness[14] and thereby insure safety to oneself and peace and order to the state. If one departs from these principles, they say, then one's family will be doomed and one's house overthrown. But although the wise and worthy men who preach this doctrine are acclaimed as sages, they know nothing more about the past than an ordinary person unable to see his own back, and they understand as little about the future as a blind man who cannot see what lies in front of him.

If, in terms of the present, one brings order to his family,

said to record the deeds of the Three Rulers. The *Five Canons* are the writings of the Five Emperors. The *Three Histories* are the works of the Three Kings.

11. Being: The principle that all phenomena emerge from the interaction of two diametrically opposed forces, the Yang and Yin. The Yang and Yin originate from the primal force.

12. Non-Being: The principle that all existences in the universe spring from Non-Being and ultimately return to Non-Being. In practical terms this view urges detachment from worldly affairs.

13. Both Being and Non-Being: The principle that all things have the two fundamental aspects of Being and Non-Being.

14. Principles of benevolence and righteousness: First two of the five constant virtues taught by Confucius.

carries out the demands of filial piety, and practices the five constant virtues of benevolence, righteousness, propriety, wisdom and good faith, then his associates will respect him and his name will become known throughout the country. If there is a wise ruler on the throne, he will invite such a man to become his minister or his teacher, or may even cede his position to him. Heaven too will come to protect and watch over such a man. Such were the so-called Five Elders[15] who gathered about and assisted King Wen and King Wu of the Chou dynasty, or the twenty-eight generals of Emperor Kuang-wu of the Later Han, who were likened to the twenty-eight constellations of the sky.[16] But since such a man knows nothing about the past or the future, he cannot assist his parents, his sovereign, or his teacher in making provisions for their future lives, and he is therefore guilty of failing to repay the debt he owes them. Such a person is not a true wise man or sage.

Confucius declared that there were no wise men or sages in his country, but that in the land to the west there was one named Buddha who was a sage.[17] This indicates that non-Buddhist teachings should be regarded as the first step toward Buddhist doctrine. Confucians first taught the doctrine of propriety and music[18] so that, when the Buddhist writings were brought to China, the concepts of the precepts, meditation and wisdom[19] could be more readily grasped. They taught the ideals of ruler and minister so that the distinction between superior and subordinate could be made clear, they

15. Their names are unknown.
16. Twenty-eight constellations of the sky: *See* p. 9, footnote 19.
17. This is found in the *Lieh Tzu*, an early Taoist text.
18. In ancient times, the Chinese regarded propriety and music as requisite for enhancing one's sense of morality, to maintain social order and for cultivating one's aesthetic sense.
19. Precepts, meditation and wisdom: The three types of learning, considered to cover all aspects of Buddhist doctrine and practice. The purpose of precepts is to stem injustice and stop evil. Meditation indicates focusing one's mind and achieving tranquillity. Wisdom signifies that which enables one to master his illusions and realize the truth.

taught the ideal of parenthood so that the importance of filial piety could be appreciated, and they explained the ideal of the teacher so that men might be taught to follow.

The Great Teacher Miao-lo writes: "The propagation of Buddhism truly depends on this. The doctrines of propriety and music must first be set forth, after which the principles of truth can be introduced."[20] T'ien-t'ai states: "In the *Konkōmyō* Sutra it is recorded that 'All the good teachings that exist in the world derive from this sutra. To have a profound knowledge of this world is itself Buddhism.' "[21] In the *Maka Shikan* we read: "I, the Buddha, have sent three sages[22] to teach the people of China." In the *Guketsu*, Miao-lo's commentary on the *Maka Shikan*, we read: "The *Shōjōhōgyō* Sutra states that Bodhisattva Gakkō appeared in that land under the name Yen Hui, Bodhisattva Kōjō appeared there as Confucius, and Bodhisattva Kashō appeared as Lao Tzu. Since the sutra is speaking from the point of view of India, it refers to China as 'that land.' "

Secondly, we come to the non-Buddhist teachings of India. In Brahmanism we find the two deities Shiva, who has three eyes and eight arms, and Vishnu. They are hailed as the loving father and compassionate mother of all living beings and are also called Heaven-Honored and sovereign. In addition, there are three men, Kapila, Uluka, and Rishabha,[23] who are known as the three ascetics. These ascetics lived somewhere around eight hundred years before the time of the Buddha. The teachings expounded by the three ascetics are known as the Four Vedas, and number sixty thousand works.

Later, in the time of the Buddha, there were the six non-Buddhist teachers, who studied and transmitted these various

20. *Maka Shikan Bugyōden Guketsu*, vol. 6.
21. *Maka Shikan*, vol. 6.
22. Three sages: Confucius (the founder of Confucianism), Yen Hui (Confucius' disciple) and Lao Tzu (the founder of Taoism).
23. Kapila, Uluka and Rishabha: Kapila was a founder of the Sankhya school, one of the six philosophical schools in ancient India. Uluka was also called Kanada, a founder of the Vaisheshika school, one of the above six schools. Rishabha's teachings are said to have prepared the way for Jainism.

non-Buddhist scriptures and acted as tutors to the kings of the five regions of India.[24] Their teachings split into ninety-five or ninety-six different lines, forming sect after sect. The banners of their pride were lifted up higher than the highest heaven, and their dogmatic rigidity was harder than metal or stone. But in their skill and depth of understanding, they surpassed anything known in Confucianism. They were able to look into the past and perceive two, three, or even seven existences, a period of eighty thousand aeons, and they could likewise know what would happen eighty thousand aeons in the future. As the fundamental principle of their doctrine, some of these sects taught that causes produce effects, others taught that causes do not produce effects, while still others taught that causes both do and do not produce effects. Such were the basic doctrines of these non-Buddhist schools of thought.

The devout followers of the non-Buddhist teachings observe the five precepts[25] and the ten good precepts,[26] practice a lesser form of meditation and, ascending through the worlds of form and formlessness,[27] believe they have attained nirvana when they reach the highest level of the threefold world. But although they make their way upward bit by bit like an inchworm, they fall back from the highest level and descend instead into the three evil paths. Not a single one succeeds in remaining on the level of heaven, though they believe that once a person has attained that level, he will never descend from it. Each approves and practices the doctrines taught by his teacher and stoutly abides by them. Thus some of them bathe three times a day in the Ganges even on cold winter days, while

24.   Five regions of India: That is, the whole of India. The five regions are the eastern, southern, western, northern and central parts of India.

25.   Five precepts: *See* p. 35, footnote 81.

26.   Ten good precepts: Prohibitions against the ten evils of killing, theft, adultery, lying, flattery, defaming, duplicity, greed, anger, and ignorant views.

27.   Worlds of form and formlessness: The two highest worlds of the threefold world. The world of form is a realm in which inhabitants are free from desire and feed on light. The world of formlessness is a realm of spirit which transcends matter.

others pull out the hairs on their head, fling themselves against rocks, expose themselves to fire, burn their bodies, or go about stark naked. Again there are those who believe they can gain good fortune by sacrificing many horses, or who burn grasses and trees, or make obeisance to every tree they encounter.

Erroneous teachings such as these are too numerous to be counted. Their adherents pay as much respect and honor to the teachers who propound them as the various deities pay to the god Taishaku or the court ministers pay to the ruler of the empire. But not a single person who adheres to these ninety-five types of higher or lower teachings ever escapes from the cycle of birth and death. Those who follow teachers of the better sort will, after two or three rebirths, fall into the lowest states of existence, while those who follow evil teachers will fall into the lowest states in their very next rebirth.

And yet the final conclusion of these non-Buddhist teachings constitutes an important means of entry into Buddhism. Some of them state, "A thousand years from now, the Buddha will appear in the world,"[28] while others state, "A hundred years from now, the Buddha will appear in the world."[29] The Nirvana Sutra remarks: "All scriptures or teachings, from whatever source, are ultimately the revelation of Buddhist truth. They are not non-Buddhist teachings." And in the Lotus Sutra it is written, "They [the Buddha's disciples] will display the three poisons and appear to cherish misleading philosophies. This is the means by which my disciples save the people."

Thirdly, we come to Buddhism. One should know that the Enlightened One, the Buddha, is a Great Teacher for all living beings, a Great Eye for them, a Great Pillar, a Great Helmsman, a Great Field of Plenty. The Four Sages and Three Ascetics of the Confucian and Brahmanical scriptures and teachings are referred to as sages, but in fact they are no more than common

28. Source unknown.
29. Source unknown.

mortals who have not yet been able to eradicate the three illusions. They are referred to as wise men, but in fact they are no more than children who cannot understand the principles of cause and effect. With their teachings for a ship, could one ever cross over the great sea of birth and death? With their teachings for a bridge, could one ever escape from the maze of the six lower worlds of existence? But the Buddha, our Great Teacher, has advanced beyond even the higher states of re-birth,[30] let alone the lower cycle of birth and death.[31] He is able to wipe out the very root of fundamental ignorance,[32] let alone the petty delusions that appear in the branches and leaves of thought and desire.

This Buddha, from the time of his enlightenment at the age of thirty until his entry into nirvana when he was eighty, expounded his sacred teachings for a period of fifty years. Each word, each phrase he spoke is the truth; not a sentence, not a verse was uttered in error. The words of the sages and wise men preserved in the scriptures and teachings of Confucianism and Brahmanism, as we have noted, are free of error, and the words match the spirit in which they were spoken. But how much more true is this in the case of the Buddha, who from countless aeons in the past has never spoken in error! In comparison to the non-Buddhist scriptures and teachings, the doctrines that he expounded over a period of fifty years represent the Great Vehicle, the true words of the Great Man. Everything that he preached, from the dawn of his enlightenment until the evening that he entered into nirvana, is none other than the truth.

The doctrines that the Buddha taught over a period of fifty

30. Higher states of rebirth: The births and deaths which men of the two realms (Learning and Realization) as well as bodhisattvas undergo as they advance in their practice. This process transcends the cycle of the six lower worlds (from Hell through Heaven) and eventually leads to enlightenment.

31. Lower cycle of birth and death: The cycle of birth and death in the six lower worlds.

32. Fundamental ignorance: Fundamental darkness of the true nature of one's life, which gives rise to all desires and illusions.

years number eighty thousand.[33] They fall into various categories such as Hinayana works and Mahayana works, provisional and true sutras, exoteric and esoteric teachings,
detailed and rough discourses, truths and fallacies, correct and
incorrect views. But among these, the Lotus Sutra represents
the correct teachings of Shakyamuni Buddha, the true words
of the Buddhas of the ten directions in the past, present and
future. The sutras, numerous as the sands of the Ganges, that
the Buddha preached during the first forty or so years of his
teaching career, belong to the time when, as the Buddha said,
he had "not yet revealed the truth."[34] The eight years during
which he preached the Lotus Sutra he called the time when he
"now must reveal the truth."[35] Thus Tahō Buddha came forth
from the earth to testify that "All that you have expounded is the
truth,"[36] and the Buddhas that are emanations of the original
Buddha gathered together and extended their tongues up to
the Brahma-heaven in testimony.[37] These words are perfectly
clear, perfectly understandable, brighter than the sun on a clear
day or the full moon at midnight. Look up to them and believe
them, and when you turn away, cherish them in your heart!

The Lotus Sutra contains two important teachings.[38] The
Kusha, Jōjitsu, Ritsu, Hossō and Sanron sects have never heard
even so much as the name of these teachings. The Kegon and

33.   Eighty thousand: Not an exact number. This figure is often used in
Buddhist scriptures to indicate "a great many."
34.   A passage from the *Muryōgi* Sutra, chap. 2, which reads, "In these more
than forty years, I have not yet revealed the truth."
35.   A passage from the second chapter of the Lotus Sutra which reads,
"The World-Honored One has long expounded his doctrines and now must
reveal the truth."
36.   A passage from the eleventh chapter of the Lotus Sutra.
37.   This is described in the *Jinriki* (21st) chapter of the Lotus Sutra and
represents the truth of the Buddha's teaching.
38.   Two important teachings: The theory of *ichinen sanzen* found in the
theoretical teaching of the Lotus Sutra, and the actuality of *ichinen sanzen*
revealed in the essential teaching of the Lotus Sutra. The latter may be further
interpreted in two ways: as the reality of Shakyamuni Buddha's enlightened
life, and as the life of the original Buddha or the Law of Nam-myoho-renge-
kyo, which the Daishonin embodied in the Gohonzon.

Shingon sects, on the other hand, have surreptitiously incorporated these doctrines and made them the heart of their
own teachings. The doctrine of *ichinen sanzen*[39] is found in
only one place, hidden in the depths of the *Juryō* chapter of the
essential teaching of the Lotus Sutra. The Bodhisattvas Nagarjuna and Vasubandhu were aware of it but did not bring it
forth into the light. The Great Teacher T'ien-t'ai alone embraced it and kept it ever in mind.

The concept of *ichinen sanzen* begins with an understanding
of the mutual possession of the Ten Worlds or states of
existence. But the Hossō and Sanron sects speak only of eight
worlds[40] and know nothing of the entirety of the Ten Worlds,
much less of the concept of their mutual possession. The Kusha,
Jōjitsu and Ritsu sects derive their teachings from the *Agon*
sutras. They are aware only of the six worlds, the six lower
states of existence, and know nothing of the other four worlds
that represent the higher levels of existence. They declare that
in all the ten directions there is only one Buddha, and do not
preach that there is a Buddha in any of the ten directions. Of
the principle that "All sentient beings possess the Buddha
nature,"[41] they of course say nothing at all. They refuse to
acknowledge that even a single person possesses the Buddha
nature. In spite of this, one will sometimes hear members of the
Ritsu and Jōjitsu sects declaring that there are Buddhas in all
the ten directions or that all beings possess the Buddha nature.
This is because, at some time since the passing away of the
Buddha, the men of these sects have appropriated these doctrines of Mahayana Buddhism and incorporated them into the
teachings of their own sect.

Similarly, in the period before the appearance of Buddhism,
the proponents of Brahmanism were not so bound up in their

39. Doctrine of *ichinen sanzen*: Here refers to the Law of Nam-myoho-
renge-kyo.
40. Eight worlds: Hell, Hunger, Animality, Anger, Humanity (or Tranquillity), Heaven (or Rapture), Bodhisattva and Buddhahood.
41. Nirvana Sutra.

own views. But after the appearance of the Buddha, when they had listened to and observed the Buddhist religion, they became aware of the shortcomings of their own teachings. They then conceived the clever idea of appropriating Buddhist teachings and incorporating them into the doctrines of their own sect, and as a result they fell into even deeper error than before. These are examples of the type of heretical teachings known as *fubukkyō* and *gakubuppōjō*.[42]

The same thing occurred in the case of China. Before Buddhism was brought to China, Confucianism and Taoism were rather naive and childish affairs. But in the Later Han, Buddhism was introduced to China and challenged the native doctrines. In time, as Buddhism became more popular, there were certain Buddhist monks who, because they had broken the precepts, were forced to return to secular life, or who elected to join forces with the native creeds. Through such men, Buddhist doctrines were introduced and surreptitiously incorporated by the Confucian and Taoist sects.

In volume five of the *Maka Shikan* we read: "These days there are many devilish monks who renounce their vows and return to lay life. Fearing that they will be punished for their action, they then go over to the side of the Taoists. Hoping to gain fame and profit, they speak extravagantly of the merits of Lao Tzu and Chuang Tzu, usurping Buddhist concepts and reading them into the Taoist scriptures. They twist what is lofty and force it into a mean context, they destroy what is exalted and drag it down among the base, striving to put the two on an equal level."

Miao-lo, in his *Guketsu*, comments on this passage as follows: "Though they are monks, they destroy the teachings of Buddhism. Some renounce their vows and return to lay life, as

---

42. *Fubukkyō* and *gakubuppōjō*: *Fubukkyō* indicates those who incorporate the Hinayana teachings into their own school and claim that it is their own doctrine. *Gakubuppōjō* indicates those who plagiarize Buddhist ideas and set forth the Mahayana teaching as the doctrine of their own school. They seem to learn Buddhism but later lose the correct view.

Wei Yüan-sung[43] did. Then, as laymen, they work to destroy the teachings of Buddhism. Men of this kind steal and usurp the correct teachings of Buddhism and use them to supplement and bolster the heretical writings. The passage on 'twisting what is lofty . . . ,' means that, adopting the outlook of the Taoists, they try to place Buddhism and Taoism on the same level, to make equals of truth and falsehood, though reason tells us that this could never be. Having once been followers of Buddhist teachings, they steal what is correct and use it to bolster what is erroneous. They twist the lofty doctrines of the twelve divisions[44] and eighty thousand writings of the Buddhist canon and force them into the mean context of Lao Tzu's two chapters and five thousand words, using them to interpret the base and erroneous words of that text. This is what is meant by 'destroying what is exalted and dragging it down among the base.' " These comments should be carefully noted, for they explain the meaning of the foregoing description of events.

The same sort of thing happened within Buddhism itself. Buddhism was introduced to China during the Yung-p'ing era (58–75 A.D.) of the Later Han dynasty, and in time replaced the Confucian and Taoist teachings as the orthodox doctrine of the land. But differences of opinion developed within the orthodox doctrine, resulting in the so-called three sects of the south and seven sects of the north, which sprang up here and there like so many orchids or chrysanthemums. In the time of the Ch'en and Sui dynasties, however, the Great Teacher T'ien-t'ai overcame these various sects and returned Buddhism once more to its primary objective of saving all living beings.

Later, the Hossō and Shingon sects of Buddhism were introduced from India, and the Kegon sect also made its appearance. Among these sects, the Hossō sect set itself up as an

43. Wei Yüan-sung: Buddhist monk in China in the sixth century. Out of a desire for fame and profit, he began to associate with a group of Taoists and finally returned to lay life.

44. Twelve divisions: Classification of all the sutras according to style and content.

arch rival of the T'ien-t'ai sect, because their teachings are contradictory to each other like fire and water. Later, when Hsüan-tsang and Tz'u-en,[45] the founders of the Hossō sect in China, closely examined the works of T'ien-t'ai, they came to realize that the views of their own sect were in error. Although they did not openly repudiate their own sect, it appears that in their hearts they switched their allegiance to the T'ien-t'ai teachings.

From the beginning the Kegon and Shingon sects were both provisional sects based upon provisional sutras. But Shan-wu-wei and Chin-kang-chih, who introduced the esoteric teachings to China, usurped the T'ien-t'ai doctrine of *ichinen sanzen* and made it the core of the teachings of their sect, adding the practice of *mudras* and *mantras*[46] and convincing themselves that their teachings surpassed T'ien-t'ai's. As a result, students of Buddhism, unaware of the real facts, came to believe that the doctrine of *ichinen sanzen* was to be found in the *Dainichi* Sutra that had been brought from India. Similarly, in the time of the Kegon patriarch Ch'eng-kuan, the T'ien-t'ai doctrine of *ichinen sanzen* was surreptitiously incorporated and used to interpret the passage in the *Kegon* Sutra that reads, "The mind is like a skilled painter." People are unaware that this is what happened.

In the case of our own country of Japan, Kegon and the other sects that comprised the six Nara sects were introduced to Japan before the Tendai and Shingon sects. The Kegon, Sanron, Hossō and other Nara sects argued and contended, as inimical to one another as water and fire. When the Great Teacher Dengyō appeared in Japan, he not only exposed the errors of the six Nara sects, but also made it clear that the

45.   Tz'u-en (632–682): A priest of the T'ang dynasty and direct successor to Hsüan-tsang, founder of the Fa-hsiang (Hossō) sect. He engaged in the translation of sutras.

46.   *Mudras* and *mantras: Mudras* are gestures made by joining the fingers together in a variety of ways so as to symbolize religious doctrine and enlightenment. *Mantras* are secret words and mystic syllables which are supposed to embody esoteric powers.

Shingon sect had stolen the principles of the Lotus Sutra as expounded by T'ien-t'ai and made them the heart of the teachings of its own sect. The Great Teacher Dengyō called upon the leaders of the other sects to set aside their arbitrary views and interpretations and to examine matters solely in the light of the scriptures themselves. As a result, in debate he was able to defeat eight eminent monks of the six Nara sects, then twelve monks, then fourteen, then over three hundred, including Kōbō Daishi. Soon there was not a single person in all Japan who did not acknowledge allegiance to the Tendai sect, and the great temples of Nara, the Shingon temple Tō-ji in Kyoto, and other temples throughout all the provinces became subordinate to the head temple of the Tendai sect at Mount Hiei. The Great Teacher Dengyō also made it clear that the founders of the various other sects of Buddhism in China, by acknowledging allegiance to the doctrines of the Great Teacher T'ien-t'ai, had escaped committing the error of slandering the true teachings of Buddhism.

Later, however, conditions in the world declined and men became increasingly shallow in wisdom. They no longer studied or understood the profound doctrines of the Tendai sect, and the other sects became more and more firmly attached to their prejudiced views. Eventually, the six Nara sects and the Shingon sect turned upon and attacked the Tendai sect. The latter, growing ever weaker, in the end found that it was no match for the other sects. To aggravate the situation, absurd new sects such as Zen and Jōdo appeared and began attacking the Tendai sect as well, and more and more of its lay believers transferred their allegiance to these unorthodox teachings. In the end, even those monks who were looked up to as the most eminent leaders of the Tendai sect all admitted defeat and lent their support to the heretical sects. Not only Tendai but Shingon and the six Nara sects as well were forced to yield their lands and estates to the new heretical sects, and the true teachings ceased to be propagated. As a result, the Sun Goddess, the God Hachiman, the Mountain King of Mount Hiei, and the other benevolent deities who guard the nation, no longer able to taste the flavor of the true teachings, departed from the land. Demons came forward to take their place, and it became apparent that the nation was doomed.

Here I would like to state my humble opinion that the teachings expounded by the Buddha Shakyamuni during the first forty or so years of his teaching differ markedly from those expounded in the Lotus Sutra during the last eight years of his life. Contemporary scholars have already expressed the opinion, and it is my conviction as well, that the chief difference lies in the fact that the Lotus Sutra teaches that persons in the two realms of *shōmon* (Learning) and *engaku* (Realization) can attain Buddhahood,[47] and that the Buddha Shakyamuni in reality attained enlightenment at an inconceivably distant time in the past.[48]

When we examine the Lotus Sutra, we see that it predicts that Shariputra will become the Flower Light Tathagata, that Mahakashyapa will become the Light Bright Tathagata, Subhuti will become the Wonderful Form Tathagata, Katyayana will become the Jambunada Golden Light Tathagata, Maudgalyayana will become the Tamalapattra Sandalwood Fragrance Buddha, Purna will become the Law Bright Tathagata, Ananda will become the Mountain Sea Wisdom Unrestricted Power King Buddha, Rahula will become the Stepping on Seven Treasure Flowers Tathagata,[49] the five hundred and seven hundred *shōmon* and *engaku* disciples will become the Universal Brightness Tathagatas, the two thousand *shōmon*

47. This truth is expounded in the theoretical teaching, or the first fourteen chapters, of the Lotus Sutra.

48. This is revealed in the *Juryō* (16th) chapter, in the essential teaching, or the latter fourteen chapters, of the Lotus Sutra.

49. The eight persons mentioned in the text, from Shariputra to Rahula, are counted among the ten major disciples of Shakyamuni Buddha. Shariputra was known as the foremost in wisdom among all the *shōmon* disciples of the Buddha. It was prophesied in the *Hiyu* (third) chapter that he would attain Buddhahood. Mahakashyapa was known as the foremost in ascetic practice

who have more to learn or do not have more to learn will become the Treasure Form Tathagatas, the nuns Mahaprajapati and Yashodhara will become the Tathagatas Gladly Seen by All Sentient Beings and Form Resplendent with Ten Million Lights respectively.[50]

Thus, if we examine the Lotus Sutra, we will realize that these persons are worthy of great honor. But when we search through the scriptures containing the teachings expounded in the periods previous to the Lotus Sutra, we find to our regret that the situation is far different.

The Buddha Shakyamuni, the World-Honored One, is a man of truthful words. Therefore he is designated the Sage and the Great Man. In the non-Buddhist scriptures of India and China there are also persons called worthy men, sages, or heavenly ascetics because they speak words of truth. But because the Buddha surpasses all these, he is known as the Great Man.

When he expounded the Lotus Sutra, the Buddha said that "the Buddhas appear in this world for one great reason."[51] He also said, "In these more than forty years I have not yet revealed the truth,"[52] that "The World-Honored One has long

---

(*dhuta*) to purify the mind and body, Subhuti as the foremost in understanding the doctrine of *kū*, Katyayana as the foremost in debating, and Maudgalyayana as the foremost in occult powers. The *Juki* (sixth) chapter of the Lotus Sutra predicts that these four disciples will attain Buddhahood. Purna, noted as the foremost in eloquence, was given a prediction of Buddhahood in the *Gohyaku-deshi-juki* (eighth) chapter. Ananda heard more of the Buddha's teachings than any other disciples and it was prophesied in the *Ninki* (ninth) chapter that he would attain Buddhahood. Rahula, known as the foremost in inconspicuous observance of the precepts, also received a prophecy of Buddhahood in the same chapter.

50.   The prophecy of Buddhahood for the five hundred and seven hundred *shōmon* and *engaku* disciples appears in the *Gohyaku-deshi-juki* (eighth) chapter, and for the two thousand *shōmon*, in the ninth chapter. Mahaprajapati and Yashodhara were, respectively, Shakyamuni's aunt and wife. The *Kanji* (13th) chapter predicts that both of them will attain Buddhahood.

51.   Lotus Sutra, chap. 2.

52.   *Muryōgi* Sutra, chap. 2. The *Muryōgi* (Infinite Meaning) Sutra is an introduction to the Lotus Sutra, and thus, in a broad sense, is regarded as a part of the Lotus Sutra's teachings.

expounded his doctrines and now must reveal the truth,"[53] and that, "Honestly discarding the provisional teachings, I will expound the Supreme Law."[54] Tahō Buddha added his testimony to the words of the Buddha, and the emanations of the Buddha put forth their tongues as a token of assent. Who, then, could possibly doubt that Shariputra will in the future become the Flower Light Tathagata, that Mahakashyapa will become the Light Bright Tathagata, or that the other predictions made by the Buddha will come true?

Nevertheless, all the sutras preceding the Lotus Sutra also represent the true words of the Buddha. The *Kegon* Sutra states: "The Great Medicine King Tree, which is the wisdom of the Buddha, has only two places where it will not grow and bring benefit to the world. It will not grow if it falls into the vast void which is the deep pit of the *shōmon* and the *engaku*, or if it is drowned in the profoundly heretical and passion-bound waters of those unworthy beings who destroy the roots of goodness within themselves."

This passage may be explained as follows. In the Snow Mountains[55] there is a huge tree that has numberless roots. It is called the Great Medicine King Tree and is the monarch of all the trees that grow in the continent of Jambudvipa.[56] It measures 168,000 *yojana*[57] in height. All the other trees and plants of Jambudvipa depend upon the roots, branches, flowers and fruit of this tree to attain their own flowering and fruition. Therefore this tree is employed as a metaphor for the Buddha nature, and the various other trees and plants stand for all the

53. Lotus Sutra, chap. 2.
54. Ibid.
55. Snow Mountains: The Himalayas.
56. Jambudvipa: (Jap *ichiembudai*) According to ancient Indian cosmology, one of four continents lying, respectively, to the north, south, east and west of Mt. Sumeru, the highest of all mountains. The southern continent is called Jambudvipa because there is a grove of *jambu* trees there.
57. *Yojana*: (Jap *yujun*) A unit of distance in ancient India, said to be the distance which an army could cover in a day. It is commonly thought to have been approximately twenty-four kilometers.

sentient beings of the world. But this great tree will not grow in a fiery pit or in the watery circle. The fiery pit is used as a metaphor for the state of mind of the *shōmon* and the *engaku*, and the watery circle[58] is used as a metaphor for the life-condition of men of incorrigible disbelief. The scripture is saying that these two categories of beings will never attain Buddhahood.

The *Daijuku* Sutra states: "There are two types of persons who are destined to die and not to be reborn, and who in the end will never be able to understand or repay their obligations. One is the *shōmon* and the other is the *engaku*. Suppose that a person falls into a deep pit. That person will be unable to benefit himself or to benefit others. The *shōmon* and the *engaku* are like this. They fall into the pit of nirvana and can benefit neither themselves nor others."

The more than three thousand volumes of the non-Buddhist writings of China on the whole stress two principles, namely, filial piety and loyalty to the sovereign. But loyalty is nothing more than filial piety extended to persons outside the family. Filial piety may be described as lofty. Though heaven is lofty, it is no loftier than the ideal of filial piety. Filial piety may be called deep. Though earth is deep, it is no deeper than filial piety. Sages and worthy men are the product of families where filial piety is taught. It goes without saying, therefore, that persons who study the teachings of Buddhism must also observe the ideal of filial piety and understand and repay their obligations. The disciples of the Buddha must without fail understand the four types of obligation[59] and know how to repay them.

In addition, Shariputra, Mahakashyapa and the other disciples, who belonged to the two realms of *shōmon* and *engaku*,

58. Watery circle: According to ancient Indian belief, one of four circles made, respectively, of gold, water, wind, and *kū*, which supported the earth.
59. Four types of obligation: One's debt of gratitude to one's parents, teacher, sovereign, and the three treasures of Buddhism.

carefully observed the two hundred and fifty precepts[60] and the three thousand rules of conduct,[61] practiced the three types of meditation,[62] carried out the teachings of the *Agon* sutras, and freed themselves from the illusions of thought and desire in the threefold world. They should therefore have been models in the understanding and repaying of obligations.

And yet the Buddha declared that they were men who did not understand obligation. He said this because, when a man leaves his parents and home and becomes a monk, he should always have as his goal the salvation of his father and mother. But these men belonged to the two realms of *shōmon* and *engaku*, and although they thought they had attained nirvana for themselves, they did nothing to benefit others. And even if they had done a certain amount to benefit others, they themselves were bound to a path whereby they could never attain Buddhahood, and could therefore never bring salvation to their parents. Thus, contrary to what one might expect, they became known as men who did not understand their obligations.

In the Vimalakirti Sutra we read: "Vimalakirti[63] once more questioned Monju, saying, 'What are the seeds of Buddhahood?' Monju replied, 'All the delusions and defilements are the seeds of Buddhahood. Even though a person commits

60. Two hundred and fifty precepts: Precepts for the monks of Hinayana Buddhism.

61. Three thousand rules of conduct: Rules for Hinayana monks based on the two hundred and fifty precepts.

62. Three types of meditation: Three types of meditation taught in the *Kusha Ron*. The first indicates a meditation for lay people who have not yet extinguished delusions. The second indicates a meditation for lay people who carry out a definite practice, but their meditation is still not free from delusions and earthly desires. The third meditation enables one to attain wisdom completely free from delusions—meditation for those who enter the priesthood.

63. Vimalakirti: (Jap Yuimakitsu) Rich merchant of the city of Vaishali and a lay believer who embraced Mahayana Buddhism. The Vimalakirti Sutra depicts him as refuting the Hinayana ideal of the *shōmon* disciples.

the five cardinal sins and is condemned to the hell of incessant suffering, he is still capable of aspiring to the lofty status of Buddhahood.'"

The same sutra also says: "Good listeners, let me give you a metaphor. The plains and highlands will never bring forth the stems and blossoms of the lotus or the water lily. But the muddy fields that are low-lying and damp—that is where you will find these flowers growing."

It also says: "One who has already become an arhat and achieved the level of truth that goes with arhatship[64] can never conceive the desire to attain Buddhahood or to realize the Buddha nature in himself. He is like a man who has destroyed the five sensory organs and therefore can never again enjoy the five delights that go with them."

The point of this sutra is that the three poisons of greed, anger and stupidity are the seeds of Buddhahood, and the five cardinal sins of killing one's father, etc., are likewise the seeds of Buddhahood. Even if the high plains should bring forth lotus flowers, the two states of *shōmon* and *engaku* would never lead to Buddhahood. The text is saying that, when the goodness of these two states is compared with the evils of the state of common delusion, it will be found that, though the evils of common delusion can lead to Buddhahood, the virtue of the *shōmon* and the *engaku* never can. The various Hinayana sutras censure evil and praise virtue. But this sutra, the Vimalakirti, condemns the virtue of the *shōmon* and the *engaku* and praises the evil of the common mortal. It would almost appear that it is not a Buddhist scripture at all, but rather the teachings of some heretical school. But the point is that it wants to make absolutely clear that the *shōmon* and the *engaku* can never become Buddhas.

The *Hōdō Darani* Sutra states: "Monju said to Shariputra,

64. Arhatship: The highest state of Hinayana enlightenment in which all delusions are said to be eradicated. Those who have achieved this state are called arhats.

'Can a withered tree put forth new blossoms? Can a mountain stream turn and flow back to its source? Can a shattered rock join itself together again? Can a scorched seed send out sprouts?' Shariputra replied, 'No.' Monju said, 'If these things are impossible, then why do you come with joy in your heart and ask me if Buddhahood has been predicted for you in the future?' "

The passage means that, just as a withered tree puts forth no blossoms, a mountain stream never flows backward, a shattered rock cannot be joined, and a scorched seed cannot sprout, so those in the two states of *shōmon* and *engaku* can never attain Buddhahood. In their case the seeds of Buddhahood have been scorched.

In the *Daibon Hannya* Sutra we read: "All you heavenly beings, if you have not yet conceived a desire for Buddhahood, now is the time to do so. If you should once enter the realm of *shōmon*, you would no longer be capable of conceiving such a desire for Buddhahood. Why is this? Because you would be outside the world of birth and death." This passage indicates that the Buddha is not pleased with the persons in the two realms of *shōmon* and *engaku* because they do not conceive the desire for Buddhahood, but he is pleased with the heavenly beings because they do conceive such a desire.

The *Shuryōgon* Sutra states: "If a person who has committed the five cardinal sins should hear of this powerful meditation[65] and should conceive the desire for the highest enlightenment, then, contrary to what you might believe, he would be capable of attaining Buddhahood. But, World-Honored One, an arhat who has cut off all desires is like a broken vessel. He will never be worthy or capable of receiving this meditation."

The Vimalakirti Sutra says: "Those who give alms to you are cultivating for themselves no field of fortune. Those who give support to you will instead fall into the three evil paths."

65. This powerful meditation: The meditation which is supposed to prevent one from being troubled by desire and delusion.

This passage means that the human and heavenly beings who give support to the sage monks such as Mahakashyapa and Shariputra will invariably fall into the three evil paths. Sage monks such as these, one would suppose, must be the eyes of the human and heavenly worlds and the teachers of all beings, second only to the Buddha himself. It must have been very much against common expectation that the Buddha spoke out time and again against such men before the great assemblies of human and heavenly beings, as we have seen him do. Was he really trying to scold his own disciples to death ? In addition, he employed countless different metaphors in expressing his condemnation of the *shōmon* and the *engaku*, calling them donkey milk as compared to the cow's milk of the bodhisattva, clay vessels as compared to vessels of gold, or the glimmer of a firefly as compared to the light of the sun.

He did not speak of this in one word or two, in one day or two, in one month or two, in one year or two, or in one sutra or two, but over a period of more than forty years, in countless sutras, addressing himself to great assemblies of countless persons, condemning the *shōmon* and the *engaku* without a single extenuating word. Thus everyone learned that his condemnation was true. Heaven learned it and earth learned it, not merely one or two persons but a billion learned and heard of it, as did all the human and heavenly beings, the *shōmon* and the *engaku*, and the great bodhisattvas gathered in assembly from the worlds of the ten directions, the worlds of form and formlessness, the six heavens of the world of desire,[66] the four continents[67] and the five regions of India, and the heavenly beings of the threefold world, the dragon kings, and the ashuras. Then each of these beings returned to his own land, explaining the teachings of the Buddha of the present world

66. Six heavens of the world of desire: The world of desire, first of the threefold world, contains both the first six heavens in the realm of Heaven and the five lower worlds from Hell to Humanity. In these six heavens desires are said to be satisfied.

67. Four continents: *See* footnote 56.

one by one to the inhabitants of his respective land, so that there was not a single being in the countless worlds of the ten directions who did not understand that Mahakashyapa, Shariputra and those like them would never attain Buddhahood and that it was wrong to give them alms and support.

In the Lotus Sutra preached during the last eight years of his life, however, the Buddha suddenly refuted his earlier position and instead taught that persons in the two stages of *shōmon* and *engaku* can in fact attain Buddhahood. Could the human and heavenly beings gathered in the great assembly to listen to him be expected to believe this? Would they not rather reject it, and in addition, begin to entertain doubts about all the sutras preached in the earlier periods? They would wonder if all the teachings put forward in the entire fifty years of the Buddha's preaching were not, in fact, empty and erroneous doctrines.

To be sure, there is a passage in the *Muryōgi* Sutra that says, "In these more than forty years, I have not yet revealed the truth." Nevertheless, one might wonder if the devil had not taken on the Buddha's form and preached this sutra of the last eight years, the Lotus Sutra. In the sutra, however, the Buddha describes quite specifically how his disciples in the *shōmon* and *engaku* realms will attain Buddhahood and reveals the time and the lands in which they will appear, the names they will bear, and the disciples they will teach. Thus it becomes apparent that there is a contradiction in the words of the Buddha. This is what people mean when they say that his own sayings are at variance with themselves. This is why the Brahmanists laugh at the Buddha and call him the great prevaricator.

But just as the human and heavenly beings in the great assembly were feeling downcast in the face of this contradiction, Tahō Buddha, who dwells in the world of Treasure Purity in the east, appeared in a tower decorated with seven kinds of treasures[68] and measuring five hundred *yojana* high

68. Tower decorated with seven kinds of treasures: The Treasure Tower adorned with seven kinds of precious materials, including gold and silver,

and two hundred and fifty *yojana* wide. The human and heavenly beings in the great assembly accused the Buddha of contradicting his own words, and although the Buddha answered in one way or another, he was in considerable embarrassment, being unable to dispel their doubts, when the Treasure Tower emerged out of the ground before him and ascended into the sky. It came forth like the full moon rising from behind the eastern mountains in the dark of night. The Treasure Tower ascended into the sky, clinging neither to the earth nor to the roof of the heavens, but hanging in midair, and from within the tower a pure resounding voice issued, speaking words of testimony. As the Lotus Sutra describes it: "At that time a loud voice issued from the Treasure Tower, speaking in praise, 'Excellent, excellent! Shakyamuni, World-Honored One, for the sake of the multitude you skillfully preach the Lotus Sutra, the great wisdom to save all beings equally, which is the Law taught to the bodhisattvas and the doctrine cherished and guarded by the Buddhas. It is as you say. Shakyamuni, World-Honored One, all that you have expounded is the truth!'"

Elsewhere the Lotus Sutra says: "At that time the World-Honored One manifested his great spiritual powers[69] in the presence of Monju and the other hundreds of thousands of billions of bodhisattvas who had from past times lived in the *saha* world, . . . as well as the human beings and nonhuman beings. He extended his long broad tongue[70] till it reached upward to the Brahma-heaven. Then he emitted light from all his pores[71] until it reached the worlds of the ten directions, and

which is described in the *Hōtō* (11th) chapter of the Lotus Sutra.

69. Great spiritual powers: The ten great mystic powers Shakyamuni Buddha displayed in the *Jinriki* (21st) chapter to show the greatness of the Lotus Sutra and the significance of propagation after his death. After Shakyamuni manifested these ten great mystic powers, he transferred the Mystic Law to the Bodhisattvas of the Earth.

70. This indicates that the Buddha's words are true and valid.

71. This indicates that the Buddha's wisdom universally illuminates the ten directions.

all the other Buddhas seated on the lion king thrones under the jewel trees throughout the universe did the same, extending their long broad tongues and emitting innumerable rays of light."[72]

And in another chapter[73] it says: "All the Buddhas who had gathered from the ten directions of the universe returned to their respective lands, . . . and the Buddha ordered that the Treasure Tower of Tahō Buddha return to its original place."

In the past, when the Buddha preached for the first time after attaining enlightenment,[74] the Buddhas of the ten directions appeared to counsel and encourage him, and various great bodhisattvas were dispatched to him. When he preached the *Hannya* Sutra, he covered the major world system[75] with his long tongue, and a thousand Buddhas appeared in the ten directions. When he preached the *Konkōmyō* Sutra, the four Buddhas[76] appeared in the four directions, and when he preached the *Amida* Sutra, the Buddhas of the six directions[77] covered the major world system with their tongues. And when he preached the *Daijuku* Sutra, the Buddhas and bodhisattvas of the ten directions gathered in the Great Treasure Chamber that stands on the border between the worlds of form and desire.

But when we compare the auspicious signs that accompanied these sutras with those accompanying the Lotus Sutra, we find that they are like a yellow stone compared to gold, a white cloud to a white mountain, ice to a silver mirror, or the color

72. Lotus Sutra, chap. 21.
73. Another chapter: The *Zokurui* (22nd) chapter of the Lotus Sutra.
74. This indicates the preaching of the *Kegon* Sutra.
75. Major world system: In modern terms, a galaxy. Buddhist scriptures describe three kinds of world systems. The smallest, a minor world system, consists of a world with a sun, moon, and planets, and would be similar to today's concept of a solar system. One thousand minor world systems constitute a medium world system, and one thousand medium world systems form a major world system.
76. Four Buddhas: Ashuku Buddha in an eastern land of the universe, Hōsō Buddha in a southern land, Muryōju Buddha in a western land, and Mimyōshō Buddha in a northern land.
77. Six directions: East, west, north, south, up and down.

black to the color blue—a person with clear vision can distinguish one from the other, but the bleary-eyed, the squint-eyed, the one-eyed and the wrong-viewed will be likely to confuse them.

Since the *Kegon* Sutra was the first sutra to be preached, there were no previous words of the Buddha for it to contradict, and so it naturally raised no doubts. In the case of the *Daijuku* Sutra, *Hannya* Sutra, *Konkōmyō* Sutra, and *Amida* Sutra, the Buddha, in order to censure the Hinayana ideal of the *shōmon* and *engaku* realms, described the pure lands of the ten directions, and thereby inspired bodhisattvas and common mortals to aspire to attain them. Thus he caused the *shōmon* and *engaku* to abandon the ideal of Hinayana.

Again, because there are certain differences between the Hinayana sutras and the Mahayana sutras mentioned above, we find that in some cases Buddhas appeared in the ten directions, in others great bodhisattvas were dispatched from the ten directions, or it was made clear that the particular sutra was expounded in the worlds of the ten directions, or that various Buddhas came from the ten directions to meet in assembly. In some cases, it was said that Shakyamuni Buddha covered the major world system with his tongue, while in others it was the various Buddhas who put forth their tongues. All of these statements are intended to combat the view expounded in the Hinayana sutras that in the worlds of the ten directions there is only one Buddha.

But in the case of the Lotus Sutra, it differs so greatly from the previous Mahayana sutras that Shariputra and the other *shōmon* disciples, the great bodhisattvas, and the various human and heavenly beings, when they heard the Buddha preach it, were led to think, "Is this not a devil who has taken on the Buddha's form?"[78] And yet those bleary-eyed men of the Kegon, Hossō, Sanron, Shingon and Nembutsu sects all seem to think that their own particular sutras are exactly the same as

78. Lotus Sutra, chap. 3.

the Lotus Sutra. That is what I call wretched perception indeed!

While the Buddha was still in this world, there were undoubtedly those who set aside the sutras he had taught during the first forty or more years of his career and embraced the Lotus Sutra. But after he passed away, it must have been difficult to find persons who would open and read this sutra and accept its teachings. To begin with, the sutras preached earlier run to countless words, while the Lotus Sutra is limited in length. The earlier sutras are numerous, but the Lotus Sutra is no more than a single work. The earlier sutras were preached over a period of many years, but the Lotus Sutra was preached in a mere eight years.

Moreover, the Buddha, as we have seen, has been called the great liar, and therefore one can hardly be expected to believe his words. If one makes a great effort to believe the unbelievable, he can perhaps bring himself to believe in the earlier sutras but not in the Lotus Sutra. Nowadays, there are many persons who appear to believe in the Lotus Sutra, but in fact they do not really believe in it. It is only when someone assures them that the Lotus Sutra is the same as the *Dainichi* Sutra, or that it is the same as the *Kegon* Sutra or the *Amida* Sutra, that they are pleased and become converts to the faith. If someone tells them that the Lotus Sutra is completely different from all the other sutras, they will not listen to him, or even if they should listen, they would not think that the person was really speaking the truth.

Nichiren has this to say. It is now over seven hundred years since Buddhism was introduced to Japan.[79] During that time, only the Great Teacher Dengyō truly understood the Lotus Sutra, but no one is willing to heed this fact which Nichiren has been teaching. It is just as the Lotus Sutra says: "To seize Mount Sumeru and fling it far off to the measureless Buddha lands—

79. According to one of the oldest extant histories, the *Nihon Shoki* (Chronicles of Japan), Buddhism was introduced to Japan in 552 A.D.

that is not difficult . . . But in the evil times after the Buddha's passing to be able to preach this sutra—that is difficult indeed!"[80]

The teachings I am expounding are in complete accord with the sutra itself. But as the Nirvana Sutra, which was designed to propagate the Lotus Sutra, says: "In the troubled times of the Latter Day of the Law, those who slander the True Law will occupy all the land in the ten directions, while the supporters of the True Law will possess no more land than can be placed on top of a fingernail." What do you think of that? Would you say that the people of Japan who oppose me can be squeezed into the space of a fingernail? Would you say that I, Nichiren, occupy the ten directions? Consider the matter carefully.

In the reign of a wise king, justice will prevail, but when a foolish king reigns, then injustice will have supremacy. One should understand that, in similar fashion, when a sage is in the world, then the true significance of the Lotus Sutra will become apparent.

In my remarks here, I have been contrasting the early sutras with the theoretical teaching of the Lotus Sutra, and it would appear as though the early sutras are in a position to prevail. But if they really win out over the theoretical teaching of the Lotus Sutra, then it means that Shariputra and the others who are in the two realms of *shōmon* and *engaku* will never be able to attain Buddhahood. That would surely be lamentable!

I turn now to the second important teaching of the Lotus Sutra.[81] Shakyamuni Buddha was born in the Kalpa of Continuance, in the ninth small kalpa,[82] when the span of human

---

80. A passage from the *Hōtō* (11th) chapter, a part of the verse section explaining the six difficult and nine easy acts.

81. Second important teaching of the Lotus Sutra: The revelation of the fact that Shakyamuni Buddha attained enlightenment countless aeons ago. This doctrine appears in the *Juryō* (16th) chapter of the essential teaching of the Lotus Sutra. The first important teaching is the doctrine that persons in the two realms of *shōmon* and *engaku* can attain Buddhahood. This doctrine is expounded in the theoretical teaching of the Lotus Sutra.

82. Kalpa of Continuance, in the ninth small kalpa: The second of the four

life was diminishing and measured a hundred years. He was the grandson of King Simhahanu and the son and heir of King Shuddhodana. As a boy he was known as Crown Prince Siddhartha, or the Bodhisattva All Goals Completed. At the age of nineteen he became a monk, and at thirty he achieved Buddhahood. At Buddha Gaya, his place of enlightenment, he first revealed the ceremony[83] of Vairochana Buddha of the Lotus Treasury World and expounded the ten mysteries, the six forms,[84] and the supreme, mystic law of the perfect harmony of the phenomenal world. At that time the Buddhas of the ten directions appeared before him, and all the bodhisattvas gathered about like clouds. In view of the place where Shakyamuni preached, the capacity of the listeners, the presence of the Buddhas, and the fact that it was the first sermon, is there any reason the Buddha could have concealed or held back the supreme law? Therefore the *Kegon* Sutra says: "He displayed his power at will and expounded a sutra of true perfection."

The work, which consists of sixty volumes, is indeed a sutra of true perfection in its every word and phrase. It may be compared to the wish-granting gem which, though it is a

stages of formation, continuance, decline and disintegration which a world is said to go through. Each of these four stages lasts for twenty small kalpas or aeons. A small kalpa is approximately sixteen million years long. According to the *Kusha Ron*, during the kalpa of continuance, the human life span is said to undergo a repeated cycle of decrease and increase. In the first hundred years of the kalpa it numbers eighty thousand years. Each hundred years it decreases by a factor of one year, until it finally measures ten years. Thereafter, it increases by one year every hundred years until it again measures eighty thousand years. In the Kalpa of Continuance, this decrease and increase (consisting of one small kapla) is repeated twenty times. Shakyamuni Buddha appeared in the ninth period of decrease.

83.   This ceremony is depicted in the *Kegon* Sutra.

84.   Ten mysteries and the six forms: Doctrines of the *Kegon* Sutra. The ten mysteries represent the ten characteristics of the interdependency of all things and phenomena. The six forms represent the six aspects of everything: the whole containing the parts, the interdependency of the parts making the whole, the unity of the parts in the whole, the variety of the parts, the variety making the whole, and the identity of the parts.

single gem, is the equal of a countless number of gems. For the single gem can rain down ten thousand treasures which are equal to the treasures brought forth by ten thousand gems. In the same way, one word of the *Kegon* Sutra contains all the meaning encompassed in ten thousand words. The passage that expounds the identity of "mind, Buddha, and all living beings" represents not only the core of Kegon teachings, but of the teachings of the Hossō, Sanron, Shingon and Tendai sects as well.

In such a superb sutra, how could there be any truths that are hidden from the hearer? And yet we find the sutra declaring that persons in the two realms of *shōmon* and *engaku* and those who belong to the category of incorrigible disbelief can never attain Buddhahood. Here is the flaw in the gem. Moreover, in three places the sutra speaks of Shakyamuni Buddha as attaining enlightenment for the first time in India. It thus hides the fact that, as revealed in the *Juryō* chapter of the Lotus Sutra, Shakyamuni Buddha actually attained enlightenment in the remote past. Thus, the *Kegon* Sutra is in fact a chipped gem, a moon veiled in clouds, a sun in eclipse. How incomprehensible!

The *Agon*, *Hōdō*, *Hannya*, and *Dainichi* sutras, since they were expounded by the Buddha, are splendid works, and yet they cannot begin to compare with the *Kegon* Sutra. Therefore one could hardly expect that doctrines concealed even in the *Kegon* Sutra would be revealed in these sutras. Thus we find that the *Zō-Agon* Sutra speaks of Shakyamuni Buddha as having "attained enlightenment for the first time in India," the *Daijuku* Sutra says, "It is sixteen years since the Buddha first attained enlightenment," and the Vimalakirti Sutra states, "For the first time the Buddha sat beneath the tree and through his might conquered the devil." Likewise, the *Dainichi* Sutra describes the Buddha's enlightenment as having taken place "some years ago when I sat in the place of meditation," and the

Ninnō Hannya Sutra refers to it as an event of "twenty-nine years ago."

It is hardly surprising that these sutras should speak in this fashion. But there is something that is an astonishment to both the ear and the eye. This is the fact that the *Muryōgi* Sutra also speaks in the same way. In the *Muryōgi* Sutra, the Buddha denies the *Kegon* Sutra concept of the phenomenal world as created by the mind alone, the *Daijuku* Sutra concept of the ocean-imprint meditation[85] and the *Hannya* Sutra concept of the identity and non-duality of all beings when he declares, "I have not yet revealed the truth." The *Muryōgi* Sutra regards the practices taught in the previous sutras as the "kalpa after kalpa of training" that the bodhisattva must undergo in order to attain Buddhahood. However, the same sutra says, "Previously I went to the place of meditation and sat upright beneath the Bodhi tree, and after six years, I was able to attain the supreme enlightenment," using the same type of language as the *Kegon* Sutra when it talks of Shakyamuni Buddha having "attained enlightenment for the first time in India."

Strange as this may seem, we may suppose that, since the *Muryōgi* Sutra is intended to serve as an introduction to the Lotus Sutra, it deliberately refrains from speaking about doctrines to be revealed in the Lotus Sutra itself. But when we turn to the Lotus Sutra itself, we find that, in the sections[86] where the Buddha discusses the three realms of *shōmon, engaku* and

85. The *Daijuku* Sutra says that during this meditation, the spiritual and physical functions of all beings are reflected within the mind of a bodhisattva, just as all things are reflected in the ocean.

86. In the *Hōben* (second) chapter of the Lotus Sutra, Shakyamuni expounded the Ten Factors to teach that all people have the Buddha nature, thus providing a theoretical basis for the assertion that all people can become Buddhas. Subsequently, in the same chapter, Shakyamuni declares that the goal of Buddhist practice is not the three realms of *shōmon* (Learning), *engaku* (Realization) and Bodhisattva, but the supreme state of Buddhahood. In the following chapters he predicts that the people in the realms of *shōmon* and *engaku* will attain Buddhahood. These are the sections which "discuss the three realms of *shōmon, engaku* and Bodhisattva as provisional goals."

Bodhisattva as provisional goals, he says: "The true entity of all phenomena can only be understood and shared between Buddhas."[87] "The World-Honored One has long expounded his doctrines and now must reveal the truth," he says elsewhere, and, "Honestly discarding the provisional teachings, I will expound the Supreme Law." Moreover, Tahō Buddha testifies to the verity of the eight chapters[88] of the theoretical teaching in which these passages occur, declaring that these are all true. We would suppose, therefore, that in them there would be nothing held back or concealed. Nevertheless, the Buddha hides the fact that he attained enlightenment countless aeons ago, for he says: "When I first sat in the place of meditation and gazed at the tree and walked about it, . . . "[89] This is surely the most astounding fact of all.

In the *Yujutsu* chapter, a multitude of bodhisattvas who had not been seen previously in the more than forty years of the Buddha's preaching career suddenly appear, and the Buddha says, "I taught them, and caused them for the first time to aspire to enlightenment." Bodhisattva Miroku, puzzled by this announcement, says: "World-Honored One, when you were crown prince, you left the palace of the Shakyas and sat in the place of meditation not far from the city of Gaya, where you attained the supreme enlightenment. A mere forty years or so have passed since then. In that short period of time, how could you have accomplished so much great work as a Buddha?"

In order to dispel this doubt and puzzlement, the Buddha then preaches the *Juryō* chapter. Referring first to the version of the events presented in the earlier sutras and the theoretical teaching of the Lotus Sutra, he says: "All the human and heavenly beings and the ashuras at present believe that Shakyamuni Buddha, after leaving the palace of the Shakyas, sat in

87. Lotus Sutra, chap. 2.
88. Eight chapters: Eight chapters from the *Hōben* (second) chapter to the *Ninki* (ninth) chapter.
89. Lotus Sutra, chap. 2.

the place of meditation not far from the city of Gaya and there attained the supreme enlightenment." But then, in order to dispel their doubts, he says: "However, men of devout faith, the time is limitless and boundless—a hundred, thousand, ten thousand, hundred thousand, nayuta aeons—since I in fact attained Buddhahood."

All the provisional sutras such as the *Kegon*, *Hannya* and *Dainichi* not only conceal the fact that people in the two realms of *shōmon* and *engaku* can attain Buddhahood, but they also fail to make clear that the Buddha attained enlightenment countless aeons in the past. These sutras are guilty of two errors. First, because they teach that the ten worlds of existence are separate from one another, they fail to move beyond the provisional doctrines and to reveal the doctrine of *ichinen sanzen* as it is expounded in the theoretical chapters of the Lotus Sutra. Second, because they teach that Shakyamuni Buddha attained enlightenment for the first time in India and do not explain his true identity, they fail to reveal the fact, stressed in the essential teaching, that the Buddha attained enlightenment countless aeons ago. These two great doctrines are the core of the Buddha's lifetime teachings and the very heart and marrow of all the sutras.

The *Hōben* chapter, which belongs to the theoretical teaching, expounds the doctrine of *ichinen sanzen*, making clear that persons in the two realms of *shōmon* and *engaku* can achieve Buddhahood. It thus avoids committing one of the two errors perpetrated in the earlier sutras. But it nevertheless fails to reveal that the Buddha attained enlightenment countless aeons ago. Thus the true doctrine of *ichinen sanzen* remains unclear and the attainment of Buddhahood by persons in the two realms is not properly affirmed. Such teachings are like the moon seen in the water, or rootless plants that drift on the waves.

When we come to the chapters of the Lotus Sutra that put forth the essential teaching, then the belief that Shakyamuni

obtained Buddhahood for the first time in India is demolished,
and the effects of the four teachings[90] are likewise demolished.
When the effects of the four teachings are demolished, the
causes[91] are likewise demolished. Thus the cause and effect of
the ten worlds of existence as expounded in the earlier sutras
and the theoretical teaching of the Lotus Sutra are wiped out,
and the cause and effect of the Ten Worlds in the essential
teaching are revealed. This is the doctrine of original cause and
original effect. It reveals that the nine other worlds are all
present in the beginningless Buddhahood, and that the Buddhahood is inherent in the beginningless nine other worlds.
This is the true mutual possession of the Ten Worlds, the true
hundred worlds and thousand factors, the true *ichinen sanzen*.

When we consider the matter in this light, we can see that
the Vairochana Buddha described in the *Kegon* Sutra, the
Shakyamuni described in the *Agon* sutras,[92] and the provisional
Buddhas described in the *Hōdō* and *Hannya* sutras such as the
Konkōmyō, *Amida* and *Dainichi* sutras are no more than
reflections of the Buddha of the *Juryō* chapter, like reflections of
the moon that float on the surfaces of various large and small
bodies of water. The scholars of the various sects of Buddhism,

90. Effects of the four teachings: T'ien-t'ai classified Shakyamuni's sutras
into four groups, according to content: *zōkyō*, which corresponds to the
Hinayana teachings; *tsūgyō*, or lower provisional Mahayana teachings; *bekkyō*, a
higher level of provisional Mahayana; and *engyō*, or true Mahayana. *Engyō*
translates literally as "perfect teaching." The perfect teaching in the true sense
of the word is the Lotus Sutra, the Buddha's highest teaching. Superficially,
however, the teachings of some sutras are similar to those of the Lotus Sutra.
From a broad perspective, these teachings are also included in *engyō*. The four
teachings in the text are mentioned in this broad context. Accordingly, the four
teachings here indicate all of the pre-Lotus Sutra teachings. "The effects of the
four teachings" indicates the enlightenment one is supposed to attain by
practicing the four teachings. However, the Lotus Sutra denies the attainment
of enlightenment by those teachings.

91. Causes: Practices of the four teachings for the attainment of Buddhahood.

92. In the *Agon* sutras Shakyamuni preaches Hinayana teachings. Therefore, Shakyamuni in the *Agon* sutras is inferior to the Shakyamuni who
preaches the Mahayana teachings.

confused by the doctrines of their own sect and unaware of the teachings of the *Juryō* chapter of the Lotus Sutra, mistake the reflection in the water for the actual moon, some of them entering the water and trying to grasp it in their hands, others to snare it with a rope. As T'ien-t'ai says, "They know nothing of the moon in the sky, but gaze only at the moon in the pond."[93]

Nichiren has this to remark. Though the Lotus Sutra teaches that persons in the two realms of *shōmon* and *engaku* can attain Buddhahood, this view tends to be overshadowed by the opposite view propounded in the sutras that precede the Lotus Sutra. How much more so is this the case with the doctrine that the Buddha attained enlightenment countless aeons ago! For in this case, it is not the Lotus Sutra as a whole that stands in contradiction to the earlier sutras, but the essential teaching of the Lotus Sutra that stands in contradiction both to the earlier sutras and to the chapters of the Lotus Sutra that deal with the theoretical teaching. Moreover, of the chapters of the Lotus Sutra that deal with the essential teaching, all of them with the exception of the *Yujutsu* and *Juryō* chapters take the view that Shakyamuni Buddha attained enlightenment for the first time in India.

The forty volumes of the Nirvana Sutra, preached by the Buddha on his deathbed in the grove of sal trees, as well as the other Mahayana sutras except the Lotus Sutra, have not one single word to say about the fact that the Buddha attained enlightenment countless ages ago. They speak of the *hosshin* or Dharma body of the Buddha as being without beginning and without end, but they do not reveal that the other two bodies, the *hōshin* or wisdom body, and the *ōjin* or manifested body,[94]

---

93.   *Hokke Gengi*, vol. 7.

94.   *Hosshin, hōshin* and *ōjin*: The three bodies, or enlightened properties, of the Buddha (Jap *sanjin*). The *hosshin*, or Dharma body of the Buddha, is the entity of the Buddha's life, the *hōshin*, or wisdom body, indicates the spiritual aspect of the Buddha's life and the *ōjin*, or manifested body, the physical aspect of the Buddha's life, or his merciful action to save all people.

are the same in nature as the Dharma body. How, then, can we expect men to cast aside the vast body of writings represented by the earlier Mahayana sutras, the Nirvana Sutra, and the majority of the chapters in the Lotus Sutra that deal with the theoretical and essential teachings, and put all their faith simply in the two chapters *Yujutsu* and *Juryō* ?

If we examine the origins of the sect called Hossō, we find that, nine hundred years after Shakyamuni passed away in India, there was a great teacher of doctrine called Asanga.[95] At night, he entered the halls of Tushita,[96] where he came before Bodhisattva Miroku and received instruction in the teachings propounded by the Buddha during his lifetime. In the daytime, he worked to propagate the Hossō doctrines in the state of Ayodhya.[97] Among his disciples were various great teachers of doctrine such as his younger brother Vasubandhu, Dharmapala, Nanda and Shilabhadra.[98] The great ruler, King Shiladitya,[99] converted to his teachings, and in time the people of all the five regions of India abandoned their arrogance and declared themselves followers of his faith.

95.   Asanga: Scholar of the Consciousness-Only doctrine. He was born to a Brahman family in Gandhara in northern India. Vasubandhu was his younger brother. After renouncing secular life, he initially studied the Hinayana teachings but was dissatisfied with these doctrines and made efforts to master the Mahayana teachings as well. When Vasubandhu became attached to Hinayana teachings, Asanga converted him to Mahayana Buddhism.

96.   Tushita: Fourth of the six heavens in the world of desire, one division of the threefold world.

97.   Ayodhya: A state in northeast India. Asanga was a native of Gandhara, but lived most of his life in Ayodhya.

98.   Dharmapala, Nanda, Shilabhadra: Dharmapala was one of the ten great scholars of the Vijnaptimatrata (Consciousness-Only) school. He became the head of the Nalanda Monastery. The Hossō sect originates from this Vijnaptimatrata school. Nanda was also one of the ten great scholars of this school. Shilabhadra was Dharmapala's disciple. When Hsüan-tsang visited the Nalanda Monastery, Shilabhadra, then head of the monastery, transmitted the teachings of the Vijnaptimatrata school to him.

99.   Shiladitya: Ruler in India during the former half of the seventh century. He had faith in Buddhism and built many stupas. He is said to have shown special favor to Shilabhadra and Hsüan-tsang.

The Chinese monk Hsüan-tsang journeyed to India, spending seventeen years visiting one hundred and thirty or more states in India. He rejected all the other teachings of Buddhism, but brought back the doctrines of the Hossō sect to China and presented them to the wise sovereign, Emperor T'ai-tsung of the T'ang. Hsüan-tsang numbered among his disciples such men as Shen-fang, Chia-shang, P'u-kuang, and K'uei-chi.[100] He preached his teachings in the great temple in the capital city of Ch'ang-an called Tz'u-en-ssu and spread them through more than three hundred and sixty districts of China.

In the reign of Emperor Kōtoku, the thirty-seventh sovereign of Japan, the monks Dōji and Dōshō[101] went to China and studied these doctrines, and on their return preached them at Yamashina Temple.[102] In this way, the Hossō sect became the leading sect of Buddhism throughout all three lands of India, China and Japan.

According to this sect, in all the teachings of the Buddha, from the *Kegon* Sutra, the earliest of the sutras, to the Lotus and Nirvana sutras that were preached last, it is laid down that those who do not possess the innate nature to become Buddhas and those predestined for the realms of *shōmon* and *engaku*[103] can

100.   K'uei-chi: Also called Tz'u-en from the name of the temple where he lived. *See* footnote 45.
101.   Dōji (675–744) and Dōshō (629–700): Dōji was the third patriarch of the Sanron sect in Japan, He is said to have been well versed in the Hossō as well as the Sanron doctrines. He went to China in 701. Dōshō was the founder of the Hossō sect in Japan. In 653, he went to China and studied the Hossō doctrines under Hsüan-tsang.
102.   Yamashina Temple: The old name of Kōfuku-ji temple, the head temple of the Hossō sect.
103.   Those who do not possess the innate nature . . . the realms of *shōmon* and *engaku*: According to the Hossō sect, by nature people are divided into the following five groups—the group predestined for *shōmon*, the group predestined for *engaku*, the group predestined for bodhisattva, the indeterminate group and the group without the Buddha nature. The first two groups have no prospect for attaining Buddhahood. The third group can eventually attain Buddhahood because they have the seed of Buddhahood within. The fourth or indeterminate group may eventually attain any of the realms of *shōmon*, *engaku*

never become Buddhas. The Buddha, they say, never con-
tradicts himself. Therefore, if he has once declared that these
persons will never be able to attain Buddhahood, then, even
though the sun and moon may fall to the earth and the great
earth itself may turn upside down, that declaration can never be
altered. In the earlier sutras those who do not possess the innate
nature to become Buddhas or those predestined for the realms
of *shōmon* and *engaku* were said to be incapable of attaining
Buddhahood. Therefore, even in the Lotus or Nirvana Sutra it
is never said that they can in fact do so.

"Close your eyes and consider the matter," the members of
the Hossō sect would say. "If it had in fact been plainly stated in
the Lotus and Nirvana sutras that those who do not possess the
innate nature to become Buddhas or those predestined for the
two realms can actually attain Buddhahood, then why would
not the great teachers of doctrine such as Asanga and Vasubandhu or eminent monks such as Hsüan-tsang and Tz'u-en
have taken notice of this fact? Why did they not mention it in
their own writings? Why did they not accept the belief and
transmit it to later ages? Why did not Asanga question
Bodhisattva Miroku about it? People like you, Nichiren, claim
that you are basing your assertions on the text of the Lotus
Sutra, but in fact you are simply accepting the biased views of
men like T'ien-t'ai, Miao-lo, and Dengyō and interpreting the
text of the sutra in the light of their teachings. Therefore you
claim that the Lotus Sutra is as different from the earlier sutras
as fire from water."

Again, there are the Kegon and Shingon sects, which are
incomparably higher in level than the Hossō and Sanron
sects.[104] They claim that the doctrines that persons in the

---

or Bodhisattva. The fifth, the group without the Buddha nature, have no
prospect for attaining Buddhahood. It follows, therefore, that the group
predestined for bodhisattva and some of the indeterminate group can attain
Buddhahood.

104. Hossō and Sanron sects: *See* p. 17, footnote 41. The Sanron sect is
often compared with the Hossō sect. It denies the reality of existence on the

realms of *shōmon* and *engaku* may attain Buddhahood and that
the Buddha achieved enlightenment countless aeons ago are to
be found not only in the Lotus Sutra, but in the *Kegon* and
Dainichi sutras as well.

According to these sects, the Kegon patriarchs Tu-shun,
Chih-yen, Fa-tsang and Ch'eng-kuan, and the Shingon masters
Shan-wu-wei, Chin-kang-chih and Pu-k'ung were far more
eminent than T'ien-t'ai or Dengyō. Moreover, they claim that
Shan-wu-wei's teachings descend in an unbroken line from the
Buddha Mahavairochana. How could men like this, who are
manifestations of the Buddha, possibly be mistaken, they ask.
They point to the passage in the *Kegon* Sutra that reads: "Some
people perceive that an inestimable number of aeons have
passed since the Buddha Shakyamuni attained enlightenment,"
or the passage in the *Dainichi* Sutra that says: "I[105] am the
source and beginning of all things." Why, they ask, would
anyone claim that it is the *Juryō* chapter of the Lotus alone that
expounds the doctrine that the Buddha attained enlightenment
long ago? Persons who do so are like frogs at the bottom of a
well who have never seen the great sea, or ignorant hill folk
who know nothing of the capital. "You people look only at the
Juryō chapter and know nothing of the *Kegon*, *Dainichi* and the
other sutras! Do you suppose that in India and China and Silla
and Paekche[106] people believe, as they do in Japan, that these
two doctrines are limited to the Lotus Sutra alone?"

As we have seen, the Lotus Sutra, which was preached over a
period of eight years, is quite different from the earlier sutras
preached over a period of some forty years. If one had to
choose between the two, one ought by rights to choose the
Lotus Sutra, and yet the earlier sutras in many ways appear to
be superior.

---

basis of the doctrine of *kū*. In contrast, the Hossō sect asserts that all phenomena
are derived from the *alaya*-consciousness.

105.   "I" means Mahavairochana Buddha.

106.   Silla and Paekche: Ancient states in the Korean Peninsula.

While the Buddha was still alive, there would have been good reasons for choosing the Lotus Sutra. But in the ages since his passing, the teachers and scholars have in most cases shown a preference for the earlier sutras. This has made it extremely difficult to believe in the Lotus Sutra. In addition, the Former and the Middle Days of the Law are coming to an end, sages and worthy men grow fewer and fewer, and deluded persons constantly increase in number. People are prone to make mistakes even in shallow, worldly affairs, so how much more likely are they to be mistaken about the profound Buddhist teachings that lead to enlightenment?

Vatsiputriya and the ascetic, Vaipulya,[107] were keen and perceptive, but still they confused the Hinayana and Mahayana sutras. Muku and Matō[108] were very clever by nature, but they could not distinguish properly between the provisional teachings and the true teachings. These men lived during the thousand-year period known as the Former Day of the Law, not far removed in time from the Buddha himself, and in the same country of India, and yet they fell into error, as we have seen. How much more likely, therefore, that the people of China and Japan should do so, since these countries are far removed from India and speak different languages from it?

As many centuries have passed since the Buddha's death, men have grown increasingly dull by nature, their life span diminishes steadily,[109] and the poisons of greed, anger and stupidity continue to multiply. The Buddhist scriptures are all

107. Vatsiputriya and Vaipulya: Vatsiputriya studied the Hinayana teachings but reduced them to the level of non-Buddhist teachings. Vaipulya incorporated the Mahayana teachings into non-Buddhist teachings in order to elevate the latter.

108. Muku and Matō: Sanskrit unknown. Muku is said to have opposed Vasubandhu and died insane. Matō was a scholar of the Sankhya school, one of the six philosophical schools in ancient India. It is said that he was refuted by Tokue, one of the ten great scholars of the Vijnaptimatrata school, and vomited blood until he died.

109. This age is a period of decrease, in which the human life span is said to diminish. This is mentioned in the treatise *Kusha Ron*. *See also* footnote 82.

misunderstood. Who these days has the wisdom to interpret them correctly?

Therefore the Buddha predicted in the Nirvana Sutra: "In the Latter Day of the Law, those who abide by the true teachings will occupy no more land than can be placed on top of a fingernail, while those who slander the true teachings will occupy all the lands in the ten directions."

In the *Hōmetsujin* Sutra[110] we find this passage: "Those who slander the true teachings will be as numerous as the sands of the Ganges, but those who abide by the true teachings will be no more than one or two pebbles." Though five hundred or a thousand years go by, it will be difficult to find even a single person who believes in the true teachings. Those who fall into the evil states of existence because of ordinary crimes will be as insignificant in number as the space of a fingernail, but those who do so because of violations of the Buddhist teachings will occupy all the lands in the ten directions. More monks than laymen, and more nuns than laywomen, will fall into the evil states of existence.

Here Nichiren would like to make a statement. Already over two hundred years have passed since the world entered the Latter Day of the Law. I was born in a remote land far from India, a person of low station and a priest of humble learning. During my past lifetimes through the six lower paths, I have perhaps at times been born as a great ruler in the human or heavenly worlds, and have bent the multitudes to my will as a great wind bends the branches of the small trees. And yet at such times I was not able to become a Buddha.

I studied the Hinayana and Mahayana sutras, beginning as an ordinary practitioner with no understanding at all and gradually moving upward to the position of a great bodhisattva.

110. *Hōmetsujin* Sutra: The translator of the Chinese version is unknown. This sutra describes how the Buddha's teachings disappear after his death. It also explains that in the Latter Day of the Law devils appear in the form of priests and carry out slanderous acts against the Law.

For one aeon, two aeons, countless aeons I devoted myself to the practices of a bodhisattva, until I had almost reached the state where I could never fail to attain Buddhahood. And yet I was dragged down by the powerful and overwhelming influence of evil, and I never attained Buddhahood. I do not know whether I belong to the third group[111] of those who heard the preachings of the sons of Daitsū Buddha and yet failed to attain enlightenment even when one son was reborn in the world as Shakyamuni Buddha, or whether I faltered and fell away from the teachings which I heard long before Daitsū Buddha, at *gohyaku-jintengō*, and thus have been reborn in this form.

While one is practicing the teachings of the Lotus Sutra, he may surmount all kinds of difficulties occasioned by the evil forces of worldly life, or by the persecutions of rulers, heretics, or the followers of the Hinayana sutras. And yet he may encounter someone like Tao-ch'o, Shan-tao, or Hōnen,[112] monks who seemed thoroughly conversant with the teachings of the provisional and the true Mahayana sutras but who were in fact possessed by devils. Such men seem to praise the Lotus Sutra most forcefully, but in fact they belittle the people's ability to understand it, claiming that "its principles are so

111.   Third group: Reference to the story of Daitsū Buddha and his sixteen sons which appears in the seventh chapter of the Lotus Sutra. In the remote past of *sanzen-jintengō*, Daitsū Buddha preached the Lotus Sutra to his sixteen sons. These sons then preached the sutra to the people, some of whom attained enlightenment. These people belong to the first group. The second group comprises those who took faith in the sutra at that time but later discarded their faith, accepting lower teachings of Hinayana Buddhism. However, these people heard the Lotus Sutra again and attained enlightenment when the sixteenth son appeared in India as Shakyamuni Buddha. The third group is those who heard the Lotus Sutra in *sanzen-jintengō* but did not take faith in it and could not attain Buddhahood even when reborn in the lifetime of Shakyamuni Buddha.

112.   Tao-ch'o (562–645), Shan-tao (613–681) and Hōnen (1133–1212): Priests of the Jōdo sect. Tao-ch'o was the second patriarch of the Jōdo sect in China, and Shan-tao was the third patriarch of the sect. Hōnen was the founder of the Jōdo sect in Japan.

profound that few can comprehend them."[113] They mislead others by saying, "Not a single person has ever attained Buddhahood through that sutra"[114] or "Not one person in a thousand can reach enlightenment through its teachings."[115] Thus, over a period of countless lifetimes, men are deceived more often than there are sands in the Ganges, until they abandon their faith in the Lotus Sutra and descend to the teachings of the provisional Mahayana sutras, abandon these and descend to the teachings of the Hinayana sutras, and eventually abandon even these and descend to the teachings and scriptures of the non-Buddhist doctrines. I understand all too well how, in the end, men have come in this way to fall into the evil states of existence.

I, Nichiren, am the only person in all Japan who understands this. But if I utter so much as a word concerning it, then parents, brothers and teachers will surely criticize me and the government authorities will take steps against me. On the other hand, I am fully aware that if I do not speak out, I will be lacking in compassion. I have considered which course to take in the light of the teachings of the Lotus and Nirvana sutras. If I remain silent, I may escape harm in this lifetime, but in my next life I will most certainly fall into the hell of incessant suffering. If I speak out, I am fully aware that I will have to contend with the three obstacles and the four devils. But of these two courses, surely the latter is the one to choose.

If I were to falter in my determination in the face of government persecutions, however, I would not be able to fulfill my course. In that case, perhaps it would be better not to speak out. While thinking this over, I recalled the teachings of the *Hōtō* chapter on the six difficult and nine easy acts. Persons like myself who are of paltry strength might still be able to lift

113.   Tao-ch'o's *Anraku Shū*.
114.   Ibid.
115.   Shan-tao's *Ōjō Raisan*.

Mount Sumeru and toss it about; persons like myself who are lacking in spiritual powers might still shoulder a load of dry grass and yet remain unburned in the fire at the end of the kalpa of decline;[116] and persons like myself who are without wisdom might still read and memorize as many sutras as there are sands in the Ganges. But such acts are not difficult, we are told, when compared to the difficulty of embracing even one phrase or verse of the Lotus Sutra in the Latter Day of the Law. Nevertheless, I vowed to summon up a powerful and unconquerable desire for the salvation of all beings, and never to falter in my efforts.

It is already over twenty years since I began proclaiming my doctrines. Day after day, month after month, year after year I have been subjected to repeated persecutions. Minor persecutions and annoyances are too numerous even to be counted, but the major persecutions number four. Among the four, twice I have been subjected to persecutions by the government itself.[117] The most recent one has come near to costing me my life. In addition, my disciples, my lay followers, and even those who have merely listened to my teachings have been subjected to severe punishment and treated as though they were guilty of treason.

In the *Hosshi* chapter of the Lotus Sutra we read: "Since hatred and jealousy abound even during the lifetime of the Buddha, how much worse will it be in the world after his passing?" The *Hiyu* chapter states: "They will despise, hate, envy and bear grudges against those who read, recite, transcribe and embrace this sutra." And the *Anrakugyō* chapter says: "The people will be full of hostility, and it will be extremely difficult to believe." The *Kanji* chapter states: "There will be

116.   Fire at the end of the kalpa of decline: A world was said to go through a continuous cycle of formation, continuance, decline and disintegration, each of these four phases lasting for one medium kalpa. The end of the kalpa of decline is marked by a great fire which consumes the world.

117.   These persecutions mean the exiles to the Izu Peninsula and Sado Island.

many ignorant people who will curse and speak ill of us," and, "They will address the rulers, high ministers, Brahmans and great patrons of Buddhism . . . slandering and speaking evil of us, saying, 'These are men of perverted views.' " It is also stated in the *Kanji* chapter: "Again and again we will be banished," and, in the *Fukyō* chapter, "They would beat him with sticks and staves, and stone him with rocks and tiles."

The Nirvana Sutra records: "At that time there were a countless number of non-Buddhists who plotted together and went in a group to King Ajatashatru of Magadha and said, 'At present there is a man of incomparable wickedness, a monk called Gautama.[118] All sorts of evil persons, hoping to gain profit and alms, have flocked to him and become his followers. They do not practice goodness, but instead use the power of spells and magic to win over men like Mahakashyapa, Shariputra and Maudgalyayana.' "

T'ien-t'ai says: "It will be 'much worse' in the future because the Lotus Sutra is so hard to teach."[119] Miao-lo says: "Those who have not yet freed themselves from impediments are called 'hostile ones,' and those who take no delight in listening to the doctrine are called 'jealous ones.' "[120] The leaders of the three southern and seven northern sects of Buddhism in China, as well as the countless other scholars of China, all regarded T'ien-t'ai with resentment and animosity. Thus Tokuichi[121] said: "See here, Chih-i,[122] whose disciple are you? With a tongue less than three inches long you slander the teachings that come from the Buddha's long broad tongue!"[123]

Priest Chih-tu[124] writes in his work *Tōshun*: "Someone questioned me, saying, 'While the Buddha was in the world,

118. Gautama: Surname of Shakyamuni Buddha.
119. *Hokke Mongu.*
120. *Hokke Mongu Ki.*
121. Tokuichi: Priest of the Hossō sect in eighth-century Japan. He had a debate with the Great Teacher Dengyō and was defeated.
122. Chih-i: T'ien-t'ai.
123. *Shugo Kokkai Shō.*
124. Chih-tu: A disciple of the Great Teacher Miao-lo.

there were many who were resentful and jealous of him. But now, in the years after his passing, when we preach the Lotus Sutra, why are there so many who try to make trouble for us?' I replied, 'It is said that good medicine tastes bitter. This sutra, which is like good medicine, dispels attachments to the five vehicles and establishes the one supreme teaching. It reproaches common mortals and censures sages, denies Mahayana and refutes Hinayana. It speaks of the heavenly devils as poisonous insects and calls the heretics evil demons. It censures those who cling to Hinayana beliefs, calling them mean and impoverished, and it dismisses bodhisattvas as beginners in learning. For this reason, heavenly devils hate to listen to it, heretics find their ears offended, persons in the *shōmon* and *engaku* realms are dumbfounded, and bodhisattvas flee in terror. That is why all these types of persons try to make trouble for us. The Buddha was not speaking nonsense when he predicted that we would face "much hatred and jealousy."''"

The Great Teacher Dengyō in his *Kenkai Ron* writes: "The superintendents of priests [in the capital of Nara] submitted a memorial to the throne, saying: 'Just as in the Western Hsia land of Central Asia there was an evil Brahman named Devil Eloquence who deceived people, so now in this eastern realm of Japan there is a shave-pated monk who spits out crafty words. Creatures like this will attract to themselves those who are of like mind and will deceive and mislead the world.' I replied to these charges by saying: 'Just as in the Ch'i dynasty of China we heard of the superintendent of priests, Hui-kuang, who arrogantly attacked T'ien-t'ai, so now in our own country we see these six superintendents of priests who oppose me. How true was the Buddha's prediction that after his death his followers would face greater opposition than ever.'"

In the *Hokke Shūku*, the Great Teacher Dengyō also says: "The propagation of the true teaching will begin in the age when the Middle Day of the Law ends and the Latter Day opens, in a land to the east of T'ang and to the west of Katsu,[125] among people stained by the five impurities who live in a time of conflict. The sutra says, 'Since hatred and jealousy abound even during the lifetime of the Buddha, how much worse will it be in the world after his passing?' There is good reason for this statement."

When a little boy is given moxibustion treatment, he will hate his mother for a time; when a seriously ill person is given good medicine, he will complain without fail about its bitterness. And we meet with similar complaints about the Lotus Sutra, even in the lifetime of the Buddha. How much more severe is the opposition after his passing, especially in the Middle and Latter Days of the Law and in a far-off country like Japan? As mountains pile upon mountains and waves follow waves, so do persecutions add to persecutions and criticisms augment criticisms.

During the Middle Day of the Law, one man alone, the Great Teacher T'ien-t'ai, understood and expounded the Lotus Sutra and the other sutras. The other Buddhist leaders of both northern and southern China hated him for it, but the two wise sovereigns, Emperor Wen of the Ch'en dynasty and Emperor Yang of the Sui, gave him an audience to establish the correctness of his views in debate with his opponents. Thus in time he ceased to have any more opponents. At the end of the Middle Day of the Law, one man alone, the Great Teacher Dengyō, knew how to expound the Lotus Sutra and the other sutras in the same manner as the Buddha himself. The seven great temples of Nara rose up like hornets against him, but the two wise sovereigns, Emperor Kammu and Emperor Saga, gave him the opportunity to make clear the correctness of his views, and thereafter there was no further trouble.

It is now over two hundred years since the Latter Day of the

125. Katsu: A Tungusic nation that ruled over the northeastern part of China and northern Korea in the sixth and seventh centuries.

Law began. The Buddha predicted that conditions would be much worse after his passing, and we see the portents of this in the quarrels and wranglings that go on today because unreasonable doctrines are prevalent. And as proof of the fact that we are living in an age of chaos and confusion, the contestants in these doctrinal debates are not called together so that they may settle the matter fairly, but instead I am sent into exile and my very life is imperiled.

When it comes to understanding the Lotus Sutra, I have only a minute fraction of the vast ability that T'ien-t'ai and Dengyō possessed. But in my ability to endure persecution and the wealth of my compassion for others, I believe I would put them to shame. As a votary of the Lotus Sutra, I firmly believe that I will come under the protection of the gods, and yet I do not see the slightest sign of this. On the contrary, I fall under growing accusation for the crimes I am said to commit. In view of this, am I perhaps then not a votary of the Lotus Sutra after all? Or have the numerous benevolent deities of heaven who vowed to protect the votary of the Lotus Sutra perhaps taken leave and departed from this land of Japan? I find myself in much perplexity.

But then I recall the twenty lines of verse in the *Kanji* chapter of the fifth volume of the Lotus Sutra in which the eighty myriads of millions of nayutas of bodhisattvas describe the persecutions they will endure after the Buddha's death for the sake of the Lotus Sutra. If I, Nichiren, had not been born in this land of Japan, then the words of the Buddha predicting such persecutions would have been a great prevarication, and those countless bodhisattvas would have been guilty of the same crime as that of Devadatta, of lying and misleading others.

The *Kanji* chapter says: "There will be many ignorant people who will curse and speak ill of us, and will attack us with swords and staves, with rocks and tiles."[126] Look around

126. In the twenty-line verse of the *Kanji* (13th) chapter, Shakyamuni prophesied that the three powerful enemies would arise to persecute the

you in the world today—are there any monks other than Nichiren who are cursed and vilified because of the Lotus Sutra or who are attacked with swords and staves? If it were not for Nichiren, the prophecy made in this verse of the sutra would have been sheer falsehood.

The same passage says: "There will be monks in that evil age with perverse views and hearts that are fawning and crooked,"[127] and, "They will preach the Dharma to white-robed laymen and will be respected and revered by the world as though they were arhats who possess the six supernatural powers.[128]"[129] If it were not for the teachers of the Nembutsu, Zen and Ritsu sects of our present age, then Shakyamuni Buddha, who uttered these prophecies in the sutra, would have been a teller of great untruths.

The passage likewise says: "Constantly going about among the populace, . . . They will address the rulers, high ministers, Brahmans and great patrons of Buddhism . . . slandering and speaking evil of us." If the monks of today did not slander me to the authorities and condemn me to banishment, then this passage in the sutra would have remained unfulfilled.

"Again and again we will be banished," says the sutra. But if Nichiren had not been banished time and again for the sake of the Lotus Sutra, what would these words "again and again" have meant? Even T'ien-t'ai and Dengyō were not able to fulfill this prediction, that they would be banished "again and again," much less was anyone else. But because I have been born at the beginning of the Latter Day of the Law, the "fearful and evil age" described in the sutra, I alone have been able to live these words.

votaries of the Lotus Sutra in the Latter Day of the Law. This passage represents the first of the three powerful enemies.

127.   This passage indicates the second of the three powerful enemies.

128.   Six supernatural powers: See p. 15, footnote 36.

129.   This passage indicates the third of the three powerful enemies, that is, those who enjoy the respect of the general public and who, in fear of losing fame or profit, induce the authorities to persecute the votary.

As other examples of prophecies that were fulfilled, in the *Fuhōzō* Sutra it is recorded that Shakyamuni Buddha said, "One hundred years after my passing, a ruler known as the Great King Ashoka will appear." In the *Maya* Sutra he said, "Six hundred years after my passing, a man named Bodhisattva Nagarjuna will appear in southern India." And in the *Daihi* Sutra he said, "Sixty years after my passing, a man named Madhyantika[130] will establish his base in the Dragon Palace." All of these prophecies came true. Indeed, if they had not, who would have faith in the Buddhist sutras?

Thus the Buddha decided the time when the votary of the Lotus Sutra should appear, describing it as a "fearful and evil age," "a latter age," "a latter age when the Law will disappear," and "the final five hundred years," as attested by both the two Chinese versions of the Lotus Sutra, *Shō-hokekyō* and *Myōhō-renge-kyō*.[131] At such a time, if the three powerful enemies predicted in the Lotus Sutra did not appear, then who would have faith in the words of the Buddha? If it were not for Nichiren, who could fulfill the Buddha's prophecies concerning the votary of the Lotus Sutra? The three sects of southern China and seven sects of northern China, along with the seven great temples of Nara, are numbered among the enemies of the Lotus Sutra in the time of the Middle Day of the Law. And if that is so, then how could the Zen, Ritsu and Nembutsu priests of the present time hope to escape a similar label?

With this body of mine, I have fulfilled the prophecies of the sutra. The more the government authorities rage against me, the greater is my joy. For instance, there are certain Hinayana bodhisattvas who, having not yet freed themselves from de-

130. Madhyantika: A disciple of Ananda. He is regarded as one of the twenty-four successors of the Buddhist teachings.

131. *Shō-hokekyō* and *Myōhō-renge-kyō*: Two of the three extant Chinese versions of the Lotus Sutra. The three are *Shō-hokekyō* translated by Dharmaraksha, *Myōhō-renge-kyō* by Kumarajiva, and *Tempon-hokekyō* by Jnanagupta and Dharmagupta. Among these versions, Kumarajiva's *Myōhō-renge-kyō* has been read more widely than the other two.

lusion, voluntarily choose to be born in evil circumstances so they may help others. In order to accomplish this, they will create bad karma that they have no desire to create. Thus, if one of them sees that his mother and father have fallen into hell and are suffering greatly, he will deliberately create the appropriate karma in hopes that he too may fall into hell and share their suffering. To suffer for the sake of others is a joy to him. It is the same with me in fulfilling the prophecies. Though at present I must face trials that I can scarcely endure, I rejoice when I think that in the future I will escape being born into an evil state of existence.

And yet the people doubt me, and I too have doubts about myself. Why do the gods not assist me? The various guardian deities of Heaven made their vow before the Buddha. Even if the votary of the Lotus Sutra were an ape rather than a man, if he announced that he was a votary of the Lotus Sutra, then I believe the gods should rush forward to fulfill the vow they made before the Buddha. Does their failure to do so mean that I am in fact not a votary of the Lotus Sutra? This doubt lies at the heart of this piece I am writing. And because it is the most important concern of my entire life, I will raise it again and again here and emphasize it more than ever, before I attempt to answer it.

Prince Chi-cha[132] in his heart had promised to give the Lord of Hsü the precious royal sword that he wore. Therefore, when he later found that the Lord of Hsü had died, he placed the sword on his grave. Wang Shou,[133] having drunk water from

132.   Chi-cha: Son of Shou-meng, king of Wu in China. In 544 B.C. he was ordered to visit other countries as an envoy. At that time, he was given a valuable sword. When he happened to be passing through the country of Hsü, the lord of the state saw Chi-cha's sword and wanted it, though he did not dare say so. Chi-cha understood the lord's desire and in his heart promised to give him the sword after he had fulfilled his mission and returned to Hsü. However, when he came back to Hsü, he found the lord already dead. True to his promise, Chi-cha offered the sword at the lord's grave.

133.   Wang Shou: The details of the story are unknown; it symbolizes Wang Shou's deep gratitude for the natural environment and sense of integrity.

a river, carefully tossed a gold coin into the water as payment. Hung Yen, finding that his lord had been killed, cut open his stomach and inserted his lord's liver in it before he died. These were worthy men, and they knew how to fulfill their obligations. How much more so, then, should this be the case with great sages like Shariputra and Mahakashyapa, who observed every one of the two hundred and fifty precepts and the three thousand rules of conduct, and had cut themselves off from the illusions of thought and desire[134] and separated themselves from the threefold world? They are worthy to be the teachers of Bonten, Taishaku and the other gods of Heaven, and the eyes of the multitude. During the first forty or more years of the Buddha's preaching, these men, because they belonged to the *shōmon* and *engaku* realms, were disliked and pushed aside with admonitions that they could "never attain Buddhahood." But when they had tasted the medicine of immortality in the Lotus Sutra, they were like scorched seeds that sprout, a shattered rock joined together again, or withered trees that put forth blossoms and fruit. Through the Lotus Sutra, it was revealed that they would attain Buddhahood after all, though they had yet to enter the eight phases of a Buddha's existence.[135] Why, then, do they not do something to repay their obligation to the sutra? If they do not do so, they will show themselves to be inferior to the worthy men I have mentioned earlier, and in fact be no more than animals who have no understanding of obligation.

The turtle that Mao Pao[136] saved did not forget to repay the

134.   Illusions of thought and desire: First of the three categories of illusion established by T'ien-t'ai. *See* Three illusions in the Glossary.

135.   Eight phases of a Buddha's existence: 1) descending from Heaven; 2) entering the mother's body; 3) coming out of the mother's body; 4) renouncing secular life; 5) conquering devils; 6) attaining enlightenment; 7) preaching the Law; and 8) entering nirvana.

136.   When Mao Pao was walking along the Yangtze River, he saw a fisherman catch a turtle and prepare to kill it. He bought the turtle and put it back in the water. Later, Mao Pao was defeated by a powerful general called Stone Tiger. When he fled in retreat to the Yangtze River, the turtle which he

obligation of the past. The great fish of the K'un-ming Pond,[137] in order to repay the man who had saved his life, presented a bright pearl in the middle of the night. Even these creatures understood how to fulfill their obligations, so why shouldn't men who are great sages?

Ananda was the second son of King Dronodana,[138] and Rahula was the grandson of King Shuddhodana. Both men were born into very distinguished families but, because they had attained the level of arhat, they were prevented from ever reaching Buddhahood. And yet, during the eight-year assembly at Eagle Peak when the Lotus Sutra was preached, it was revealed that Ananda would become the Mountain Sea Wisdom [Unrestricted Power King] Buddha and that Rahula would become the Buddha Stepping on Seven Treasure Flowers. No matter what great sages these men were or how distinguished their families, if it had not been for the revelation in the Lotus Sutra, who would have paid respect to them?

King Chieh of the Hsia dynasty and King Chou of the Yin dynasty[139] were lords of an army of ten thousand chariots and commanded the allegiance of the entire populace of their kingdoms. But because they governed despotically and brought about the downfall of their dynasties, people speak of Chieh and Chou as the epitome of evil men. Even a beggar or a

---

had saved earlier appeared and carried Mao Pao on its back to the opposite shore.

137.   The K'un-ming Pond was a pond constructed by Emperor Wu of the Former Han dynasty. One day he saw a fish in the pond suffering because of a hook caught in its throat. The emperor felt pity for the fish and removed the hook, putting the fish back into the water. Later, to repay his obligation, the fish offered a bright pearl to the emperor.

138.   Dronodana: Younger brother of King Shuddhodana, the father of Shakyamuni.

139.   Emperor Chieh and Emperor Chou: Evil rulers of antiquity. Because Emperor Chieh, the seventeenth ruler of the Hsia dynasty, perpetrated every possible atrocity, he was overthrown by his enemies and the Hsia dynasty perished. Emperor Chou, the last ruler of the Yin dynasty, was a slave to his consort, Ta Chi, and totally misgoverned the country. He was defeated by King Wu of the Chou dynasty.

leper, if he is likened to Chieh and Chou, will be enraged at the insult. [Thus we see that power and position alone do not necessarily insure that one will be respected.]

If it had not been for the Lotus Sutra, then who would ever have heard of the twelve hundred *shōmon*[140] and the countless other *shōmon* who would attain Buddhahood through the sutra, and who would have listened to their voices? No one would have read the Buddhist sutras compiled by the thousand *shōmon* disciples,[141] nor would there be any paintings or statues of them set up and worshiped. It is entirely due to the power of the Lotus Sutra that these arhats are revered and followed. If these *shōmon* were to separate themselves from the Lotus Sutra, they would be like a fish without water, a monkey without a tree, a baby without the breast, or a people without a ruler. Why, then, do they abandon the votary of the Lotus Sutra?

In the sutras that precede the Lotus Sutra, the *shōmon* are depicted as acquiring the Heavenly Eye and the Wisdom Eye in addition to their physical eyes. In the Lotus Sutra, we are told that they are also provided with the Dharma Eye and the Buddha Eye.[142] Their eyesight can penetrate any of the worlds in the ten directions. How then could they fail to see me, the votary of the Lotus Sutra, right here in the *saha* world? Even if I were an evil man who had said a word or two against them, or even if I cursed and reviled the *shōmon* for a year or two, a kalpa or two, or a countless number of kalpas, and went so far as to threaten to take up swords and staves against them, so long as I maintain my faith in the Lotus Sutra and act as its votary, then they should never abandon me.

A child may curse his parents, but would the parents for that

140.   Twelve hundred *shōmon*: *Shōmon* disciples who received a prophecy of attaining Buddhahood in the eighth chapter of the Lotus Sutra. Each of them was given the title of Universal Brightness Tathagata.

141.   Thousand *shōmon* disciples: The disciples who gathered after the Buddha's death at the first great assembly to compile his teachings.

142.   Heavenly Eye, Wisdom Eye, Dharma Eye and Buddha Eye: Four of the five types of vision. Eye here means perceptive faculty. *See* Five types of vision in the Glossary.

reason cast him aside? The young owls eat their mother, but the mother nevertheless does not abandon them. The *hakei*[143] beast kills its father, but the father does nothing to prevent this. If even animals behave like this, then why should great sages like the *shōmon* abandon the votary of the Lotus Sutra?

The four great *shōmon* disciples[144] of the Buddha, in the passage that deals with their belief and understanding, proclaimed: "Now have we become true *shōmon*,[145] for we take the voice (*shō*) of the Buddha's Way and cause it to be heard (*mon*) among all beings. Now have we become true arhats, for among all the gods, men, demons and Bontens of the various worlds, everywhere in their midst we deserve to receive offerings. The Buddha in his great beneficence makes use of a rare thing[146] to comfort and teach us and bestow benefit upon us. In countless millions of kalpas, who could ever repay him? Though men offer him their hands and feet,[147] bow their heads to the ground in obeisance, and present him with all manner of alms, none of them could repay him. Should they bear him on the crown of their heads or carry him on their two shoulders, through kalpas numerous as the sands of the Ganges exhausting their hearts in reverence; should they offer him delicious foods, numberless jeweled garments and articles of bedding, potions and medicines of every kind; should they use oxhead sandalwood and all kinds of rare gems to erect a stupa shrine, spreading jeweled garments over the ground; should they perform these acts and use these things as offerings through

143.   *Hakei*: Details unknown. The *hakei* is said to be bigger than a tiger.

144.   Four great *shōmon* disciples: Maudgalyayana, Mahakashyapa, Katyayana and Subhuti. The passage appears in the fourth chapter of the Lotus Sutra. In this chapter, they say they have realized that the purpose of Buddhist practice is to attain Buddhahood and not to attain Learning, Realization or Bodhisattva.

145.   *Shōmon* literally means to hear (*mon*) the voice (*shō*) of the Buddha. In this passage, a true *shōmon* is defined as one who engages in altruistic practice, that is, causing the voice (*shō*) of the Buddha to be heard (*mon*).

146.   Rare thing: The supreme teaching or Lotus Sutra.

147.   Offer him their hands and feet: To serve the Buddha and practice his teachings.

kalpas numerous as the sands of the Ganges, still they could never repay him."

In the various sutras preached during the earlier period of the Buddha's life, which have been compared to four inferior flavors,[148] the *shōmon* disciples were depicted on countless occasions as subjected to all kinds of abuse and shamed before the great assembly of human and heavenly beings. Thus we are told that the sound of Mahakashyapa's weeping and wailing echoed through the entire universe,[149] that Subhuti was so dumbfounded that he almost went off and left the alms bowl[150] he had been carrying, that Shariputra spat out the food he was eating,[151] and that Purna was berated for being the kind who would put filth in a precious jar.[152]

When the Buddha was at the Deer Park, he extolled the *Agon* sutras and enjoined men to observe the two hundred and fifty precepts, warmly praising those who did so, and yet before long, as we have seen, he turned about and began

148. Four inferior flavors: The pre-Lotus Sutra teachings. T'ien-t'ai divided Shakyamuni's teachings into five periods—Kegon, Agon, Hōdō, Hannya and Hokke-Nehan. He compared these to the five flavors produced in the processing of milk—the flavors of fresh milk, cream, curdled milk, butter and ghee (a kind of highly clarified butter). The four flavors thus indicates all sutras before the Lotus Sutra.

149. This story appears in the Vimalakirti Sutra. When Mahakashyapa heard Vimalakirti speak about enlightenment, he could not understand it at all and wept over the fact that he did not inherently possess the seed of Buddhahood. The Vimalakirti Sutra relates that the sound of his weeping echoed throughout the universe.

150. This story is also found in the Vimalakirti Sutra. One day Subhuti came to Vimalakirti, asking for alms. Vimalakirti filled Subhuti's bowl but told him that he did not deserve to receive alms and that those who offered alms to him would invariably fall into the three evil paths. At that time Subhuti was so shocked that he almost went off without his alms bowl.

151. This story is in the *Daichido Ron*. When Shakyamuni Buddha reproached Shariputra for eating impure food, Shariputra was so surprised that he spat it out. Impure food is so called because it is not an offering made from the offerer's heart. The implication is that one who receives alms from slanderers is not qualified to attain enlightenment.

152. This story appears in the Vimalakirti Sutra. When Shakyamuni Buddha saw Purna preaching the Hinayana teachings to the people, he told Purna that he should not put impure things into a precious vessel.

condemning such men. He is guilty, we would have to say, of making two different and completely contradictory pronouncements.

Thus, for example, the Buddha cursed his disciple Devadatta, saying, "You are a fool who licks the spit of others!" Devadatta felt as though a poison arrow had been shot into his breast, and he cried out in anger, saying, "Gautama is no Buddha! I am the eldest son of King Dronodana, the elder brother of Ananda and a cousin of Gautama. No matter what kind of evil conduct I might be guilty of, he ought to admonish me in private for it. But to publicly accuse me of faults in front of this great assembly of human and heavenly beings—is this the behavior appropriate to a Great Man or a Buddha? He showed himself to be my enemy in the past when he stole the woman I intended to marry,[153] and he has shown himself my enemy at this gathering today. From this day forward, I vow to look upon him as my greatest enemy for lifetime after lifetime and age after age to come!"

When we stop to consider, we note that, of the *shōmon* disciples, some were originally from Brahman families who followed non-Buddhist doctrines, or were leaders of various non-Buddhist sects who had converted kings to their teachings and were looked up to by their followers. Others were men of aristocratic families or the possessors of great wealth. But they abandoned their exalted positions in life, lowered the banners of their pride, cast off everyday clothing and wrapped their bodies in the humble, dingy-hued robes of a Buddhist monk. They threw away their white fly whisks, their bows and arrows, and took up a solitary alms bowl, becoming like paupers and beggars and following the Buddha. They had no dwellings to protect them from the wind and rain, and very little in the way of food or clothing by which to sustain life.

153. In the period before Shakyamuni renounced the secular life, he married Yashodhara, a beautiful woman whom Devadatta had wished to marry. As a result, Devadatta nurtured a grudge against Shakyamuni.

Moreover, all the people of the five regions of India and the four seas were disciples or supporters of the non-Buddhist religions, so that even the Buddha himself was on nine occasions forced to suffer major hardships.

Thus, for example, Devadatta hurled a great stone at him, King Ajatashatru loosed a wild elephant on him, and King Ajita for a period of ninety days would give him and his followers nothing but horse fodder to eat. At a Brahman city, he was offered stinking rice gruel, and a Brahman woman named Chinchamanavika, tying a bowl to her belly, claimed to be pregnant with his child.

Needless to say, the Buddha's disciples were likewise forced to suffer frequent hardships. Thus, numerous members of the Shakya clan were killed by King Virudhaka, and countless of the Buddha's followers were trampled to death by wild elephants that were set upon them. The nun Utpalavarna was killed by Devadatta,[154] the disciple Kalodayin was buried in horse dung,[155] and the disciple Maudgalyayana was beaten to death by a Brahman named Chikujō. In addition, the six non-Buddhist teachers banded together and slandered the Buddha before King Ajatashatru and King Prasenajit, saying, "Gautama is the most evil man in the whole continent of Jambudvipa. Wherever he may be, his presence heralds the onset of the three calamities and the seven disasters. As the numerous rivers gather together in the great sea and the groves of trees cluster on the great mountains, so do crowds of evil men gather about Gautama. The men called Mahakashyapa, Shariputra, Maudgalyayana and Subhuti are examples. All those who are born in human form should place loyalty to the sovereign and filial piety above all else. But these men have been so misled by

154. Because Utpalavarna reproved Devadatta for being a great enemy of Buddhism, he was so enraged that he beat her to death.
155. Kalodayin was a handsome man of fine presence. One day when he was going about begging, a woman offered him alms. Her husband happened to see this and was enraged. He killed Kalodayin and cast the body in a manure pit and put horse dung over the corpse to hide it.

Gautama that they disregard the teachings of their parents, abandon their families and, defying the commandments of the king, go to live in the mountain forests. They should be expelled from this country. It is because they are allowed to remain that the sun, moon and stars manifest sinister phenomena and many strange happenings occur in the land."

The *shōmon* disciples did not know how they could possibly bear this slander. Then, as if to add to their hardship, [the Buddha himself began to denounce them]. They found it difficult to follow him. Now and then, hearing him condemn them in great assemblies of human and heavenly beings, and not knowing how to behave, they only became more confused.

On top of all this, they had to face the greatest hardship of all, as revealed in the Vimalakirti Sutra, when the Buddha addressed the *shōmon* disciples, saying: "Those who give alms to you are cultivating for themselves no field of fortune. Those who give support to you will instead fall into the three evil paths." According to this passage, these words were spoken in the gardens of Ambapali in the city of Vaishali. There Bonten, Taishaku, the deities of the sun and moon, the Four Heavenly Kings, and the various gods of the threefold world, along with earth gods, dragon gods, and other beings as numerous as the sands of the Ganges, had gathered in a great assembly, when the Buddha said, "The human and heavenly beings who give alms to Subhuti and the other monks will fall into the three evil paths." After the human and heavenly beings had heard this, would they be likely to go on giving alms to the *shōmon* disciples? It would almost appear as though the Buddha were deliberately attempting through his words to inflict death upon those who were in the two realms of *shōmon* and *engaku*. The more sensible persons in the assembly were no doubt repelled by the Buddha's action. Nevertheless, the *shōmon* disciples were able to obtain enough of the alms given to the Buddha to keep themselves alive, meager though the amount was.

When I consider the situation, it occurs to me that, if the

Buddha had passed away after preaching the various sutras delivered in the first forty or more years of his career, and had never lived to preach the Lotus Sutra in the later eight years, then who would ever have offered alms to these *shōmon* disciples? They would by now have fallen into the realm of Hunger.

But after more than forty years of preaching various sutras, it was as though the bright spring sun appeared to melt the frigid ice, or a great wind arose to dispel the dew from countless grasses. With one remark, in one moment, the Buddha wiped away his earlier pronouncements, saying, "I have not yet revealed the truth." Like a great wind scattering the dark clouds or the full moon in the vast heavens, or like the sun shining in the blue sky, he proclaimed, "The World-Honored One has long expounded his doctrines and now must reveal the truth." With the brilliance of the sun or the brightness of the moon, it was revealed in the Lotus Sutra that Shariputra would become the Flower Light Tathagata and Mahakashyapa would become the Light Bright Tathagata. Because of the Lotus Sutra, which is a phoenix among writings, a mirror or a diviner's tortoise shell, after the Buddha's passing, these *shōmon* disciples were looked up to by the human and heavenly supporters of Buddhism as though they were actual Buddhas.

If the water is clear, then the moon will not fail to be reflected there. If the wind blows, then the grass and trees will not fail to bow before it. And if there is a true votary of the Lotus Sutra, then the sages, the *shōmon* disciples, should not fail to go to his side, though they might have to pass through a great fire to do so, or make their way through a great rock. Though Mahakashyapa may be deep in meditation,[156] does he

156.   When Mahakashyapa felt that death was approaching, he went to Mt. Kukkutapada in Magadha, Central India, where he entered into meditation and died. It is said that Mahakashyapa will reappear when Bodhisattva Miroku appears in the world, 5,670 million years after the Buddha's death.

intend to do nothing about the situation? I am completely perplexed. Is this not the period of "the fifth five hundred years"? Is the prediction about "worldwide *kōsen-rufu*"[157] mere nonsense? Is Nichiren not the votary of the Lotus Sutra? Are the *shōmon* disciples protecting those who disparage the Lotus Sutra as a written teaching and who put forth their great lies about what they call a "special transmission"?[158] Are they guarding those who write "Discard! close! ignore! abandon!,"[159] urging men to put an end to the teachings of the Lotus Sutra and to throw away the texts, and who cause the ruin of the temples where they are taught? The *shōmon* disciples and the various deities of Heaven swore before the Buddha to protect the votary of the Lotus Sutra, but now that they see how fierce are the great persecutions of this age of chaos, have they decided to withhold their aid? The sun and the moon are still up in the sky. Mount Sumeru has not collapsed. The sea tides ebb and flow and the four seasons proceed in their normal order. Why then is there no sign of aid for the votary of the Lotus Sutra? My doubts grow deeper than ever.

In the sutras preached before the Lotus Sutra, the Buddha is shown predicting that various great bodhisattvas and heavenly and human beings will attain Buddhahood in the future. But trying to realize such predictions is like trying to grasp the moon in the water, like mistaking the reflection for the actual object—it has the color and shape of the object but not the

---

157. "The fifth five hundred years" and "worldwide *kōsen-rufu*": References to a passage from the *Yakuō* (23rd) chapter of the Lotus Sutra, which reads, "In the fifth five hundred years after my death, accomplish worldwide *kōsen-rufu* and never allow its flow to cease."

158. Special transmission: A tenet of the Zen sect. This sect denies the sutras, maintaining that the Buddha's enlightenment is not transmitted by the Buddhist scriptures but is transferred from mind to mind.

159. Discard! close! ignore! abandon!: A quotation from Hōnen, the founder of the Jōdo sect in Japan, which appears in his treatise *Senchaku Shū*. In this work, he insists that people discard everything but the three basic sutras of his sect.

reality. Likewise, the Buddha would seem to be displaying profound kindness in making such predictions, but in fact it is little kindness at all.

When Shakyamuni had first attained enlightenment and had not yet begun to preach, more than sixty great bodhisattvas, including Dharma Wisdom, Forest of Merits, Diamond Pennant, and Diamond Storehouse, appeared from the various Buddha lands of the ten directions and came before the Buddha. There, at the request of the bodhisattvas Chief Wise, Moon of Deliverance, and others, they preached the doctrines of the ten stages of security, the ten stages of practice, the ten stages of devotion, the ten stages of development,[160] etc. The doctrines that these great bodhisattvas preached were not learned from Shakyamuni Buddha.[161] At that time, Bonten and other deities of the worlds of the ten directions came together and preached the Dharma, but again it was not something they had learned from Shakyamuni.

These great bodhisattvas, deities, dragons, etc. who appeared at the assembly described in the *Kegon* Sutra were beings who had attained the stage of *fushigi* enlightenment[162] in the period before Shakyamuni. Perhaps they were disciples of Shakyamuni Buddha when he was carrying out bodhisattva practices in previous incarnations, or perhaps they were disciples of previous Buddhas of the worlds of the ten directions. In any event, they were not disciples of the Shakyamuni who was born in India and who attained enlightenment at the age of thirty.

It was only when the Buddha set forth the four types of teachings in the *Agon*, *Hōdō* and *Hannya* sutras that he finally

160. These four kinds of ten stages partially comprise the fifty-two stages of bodhisattva practice, together with the first ten stages of faith and the last two stages—*tōgaku* (the stage almost equal to enlightenment) and *myōkaku* (enlightenment).

161. The *Kegon* Sutra explains that these great bodhisattvas devoted themselves to religious practice under Vairochana Buddha.

162. *Fushigi* enlightenment: *Fushigi* literally means mystic. *Fushigi* enlightenment is a kind of Mahayana enlightenment.

acquired disciples. And although there were doctrines preached by the Buddha himself, they were not his own. Why do I say this? Because the *bekkyō* and *engyō*, the two higher types of teachings, as set forth in the *Hōdō* and *Hannya* sutras, do not differ in meaning from the *bekkyō* and *engyō* as set forth in the *Kegon* Sutra. The *bekkyō* and *engyō* teachings given in the *Kegon* Sutra are not the *bekkyō* and *engyō* teachings of Shakyamuni Buddha. They are the *bekkyō* and *engyō* teachings of Hōe (Dharma Wisdom) and the other great bodhisattvas mentioned earlier. These great bodhisattvas may appear to most people to have been disciples of Shakyamuni Buddha, but in fact it would be better to call them his teachers. Shakyamuni listened to these bodhisattvas preaching and, after gaining wisdom and understanding, proceeded to set forth the *bekkyō* and *engyō* teachings of the *Hōdō* and *Hannya* sutras. But these differ in no way from the *bekkyō* and *engyō* teachings of the *Kegon* Sutra.

Therefore we know that these bodhisattvas were the teachers of Shakyamuni. These bodhisattvas are mentioned in the *Kegon* Sutra, where they are called *zenchishiki* or men of "good influence." To call a person a *zenchishiki* means that he is neither one's teacher nor one's disciple. The two types of teachings called *zōkyō* and *tsūgyō* are offshoots of the *bekkyō* and *engyō* teachings. Anyone who understands the *bekkyō* and *engyō* teachings will invariably understand the *zōkyō* and *tsūgyō* teachings as well.

A teacher is someone who teaches his disciples things that they did not previously know. For example, in the ages before the Buddha, the heavenly and human beings and followers of non-Buddhist religions were all disciples of the two deities and the three ascetics.[163] Though their doctrines branched off to form ninety-five different schools, they all remained faithful to the views of the three ascetics. Shakyamuni also studied these doctrines and for a time became a disciple of the non-Buddhist

163.   Two deities and the three ascetics: The two deities are Shiva and Vishnu, and the three ascetics are Kapila, Uluka and Rishabha.

teachers. But after spending twelve years in various difficult and easy practices,[164] he came to understand the principles of suffering, emptiness, impermanence and non-ego.[165] Therefore he ceased to call himself a disciple of the non-Buddhist teachings and instead proclaimed himself the possessor of a wisdom acquired from no teacher at all. Thus in time the heavenly and human beings came to look up to him as a great teacher.

It is clear, therefore, that during the first forty or more years of his preaching career, the so-called period of the four flavors, Shakyamuni Buddha was a disciple of Hōe and the other great bodhisattvas. Similarly, he was the ninth disciple of Bodhisattva Monju.[166] This is also the reason why the Buddha repeatedly declares in the earlier sutras, "I never preached a single word."

When Shakyamuni Buddha was seventy-two, he preached the *Muryōgi* Sutra on Eagle Peak in the kingdom of Magadha. At that time he denied all the sutras he had preached during the previous more than forty years, and all the fragmentary teachings derived from those sutras, saying, "In these more than forty years, I have not yet revealed the truth." At that time, the great bodhisattvas and the various heavenly and human beings hastened to gather around and implore the

164. After he renounced secular life, Shakyamuni engaged in various practices for twelve years until he attained enlightenment. It is said that for the former six years he engaged in ascetic practice and for the latter six years he engaged in the practice of meditation. These two types of practices correspond to "difficult and easy practices."

165. These principles indicate enlightenment as described in Hinayana teachings.

166. This story appears in the first chapter of the Lotus Sutra. In the distant past, Monju appeared as Bodhisattva Myōkō, a disciple of Nichigatsu Tōmyō Buddha. After the Buddha's death, Myōkō continued to embrace the Lotus Sutra which his teacher had expounded. The Buddha had fathered eight sons before his death. These sons of the departed Buddha practiced under Myōkō until they attained Buddhahood. The last of them to attain Buddhahood was called Nentō Buddha, under whom Shakyamuni practiced the sutra for enlightenment in a previous existence.

Buddha to reveal the true doctrine. In fact, in the *Muryōgi* Sutra he mentioned one teaching that appeared to be true,[167] but he did not elaborate on it. It is like the moment when the moon is about to rise. The moon is still hidden behind the eastern hills, and though its glow begins to light the western hills, people cannot yet see the body of the moon itself.

In the *Hōben* chapter of the Lotus Sutra, when the Buddha first briefly explained why the three vehicles should be rejected and the supreme vehicle embraced, he also briefly explained the concept of *ichinen sanzen*, speaking the true thoughts that were in his mind. But because this was the first time he had touched on the subject, it was only dimly apprehended, like the first note of the cuckoo heard by someone drowsy with sleep, or like the moon appearing over the rim of the hill but veiled in thin clouds. Shariputra and the others, startled, called the deities, dragon gods and great bodhisattvas together, begging for instruction. As the sutra says: "The various deities and dragon gods were numberless as the sands of the Ganges; the various bodhisattvas seeking to be Buddhas were great in number, eighty thousand. And from the myriads of millions of lands the wheel-turning kings[168] arrived. With palms pressed together and reverent minds, all wished to hear the teaching of perfect endowment."

The passage indicates that the persons requested to hear a doctrine such as they had not heard in the previous more than forty years, one that differed from the four flavors and the three teachings.[169] With regard to the line "they wish to hear the

167. In the *Muryōgi* Sutra, Shakyamuni Buddha used the term "true entity," but did not reveal what the true entity is.

168. Wheel-turning kings: Kings who rule the four continents surrounding Mt. Sumeru by turning the wheels of the Law. These wheels are of four kinds: gold, silver, copper and iron. The Gold-wheel-turning King rules all four lands; the Silver-wheel-turning King, the eastern, western, and southern lands; the Copper-wheel-turning King, the eastern and southern lands; and the Iron-wheel-turning King, the southern land.

169. Three teachings: *Zōkyō*, *tsūgyō* and *bekkyō*. Those teachings preached prior to the Lotus Sutra.

teaching of perfect endowment," it may be noted that the Nirvana Sutra states: "Sad[170] indicates perfect endowment." The *Daijō Shiron Gengi Ki*[171] states: "*Sad* connotes six. In India the number six implies perfect endowment."[172] In his annotation on the Lotus Sutra, Chia-hsiang[173] writes: "*Sad* means perfect endowment." In the eighth volume of his *Hokke Gengi*, T'ien-t'ai remarks, "*Sad* is a Sanskrit word, which is translated as *myō*." Bodhisattva Nagarjuna, in the heart of his thousand-volume *Daichido Ron*, comments, "*Sad* signifies six." (Nagarjuna was thirteenth in the lineage of the Buddha's successors, the founder of the Shingon, Kegon and other sects, a great sage who had ascended to the forty-first stage of bodhisattva practice and whose true identity was the Tathagata Hōun Jizaiō.)

The title *Myōhō-renge-kyō* is of course Chinese. In India, the Lotus Sutra is called *Saddharmapundarika sutra*. The following is the *mantra* concerning the heart of the Lotus Sutra composed by Shan-wu-wei:

> Nōmaku sammanda bodanan (Hail to the universal Buddha)
> on (the three-bodied Tathagata)
> a a annaku (who opens, shows, enlightens, causes us to enter)
> saruba boda (all the Buddha's)
> kinō (wisdom and)
> sakishubiya (understanding)
> gyagyanō samsoba (so that we understand the empty nature)
> arakishani (and display a departure from defilement)

170. *Sad* corresponds to *sad* of *Saddharmapundarika sutra*, the Sanskrit name of the Lotus Sutra.
171. *Daijō Shiron Gengi Ki*: "Annotation of the Four Mahayana Theses." This treatise, which belongs to the Sanron sect, was written by Hui-chün.
172. It is said that in India six was the base of the ancient numerical system.
173. Chia-hsiang: A priest of the Sanron sect in China.

satsuri daruma (the correct Dharma)
fundarikya (white lotus)
sotaran (sutra)
ja (enters)
un (everywhere)
ban (causing us to dwell)
koku (in joy)
bazara (with steadfast)
arakishaman (protection,)
un (void, without form, without desire)
sohaka (absolutely achieved)

This *mantra*, which expresses the heart of the Lotus Sutra, was found in the iron tower in southern India.[174] In this *mantra*, the words *satsuri daruma* mean "correct Dharma." *Satsu* means *shō* (correct). *Shō* is the same as *myō* (mystic), *myō* is the same as *shō*. *Shōhokke* is the same as *Myōhokke*. And when the two syllables *Namu* are prefixed to the title *Myōho-renge-kyō*, we have the formula *Nam-myōhō-renge-kyō*.[175]

Myō means *gusoku* (perfect endowment). Six refers to the six types of practices leading to perfection.[176] When the persons ask to hear the teaching of perfect endowment, they are asking how they may gain the perfect endowment of the six practices of the bodhisattvas. In the word *gusoku*, the element *gu* (possession) refers to the mutual possession of the Ten Worlds, while the element *soku* (perfect) means that, since there is mutual possession of the Ten Worlds, then any one world contains all the other worlds, indicating that this is "perfect." This Lotus Sutra is a single work consisting of eight volumes, twenty-eight chapters, and 69,384 characters. To each and

---

174. The Shingon sect asserts that Nagarjuna received the *Dainichi* Sutra from Bodhisattva Kongōsatta along with other esoteric teachings preserved in an iron tower in southern India.

175. The exact transliteration is *Namu-myōhō-renge-kyō*, but it is correctly pronounced Nam-myoho-renge-kyo.

176. Six types of practices leading to perfection: The six *paramitas*. See Six paramitas in the Glossary.

every character is attached the word *myō* or "mystic," making it a Buddha endowed with the thirty-two distinguishing features and eighty physical characteristics.[177] Each of the Ten Worlds manifests its own Buddha nature. As Miao-lo writes, "If even the Buddha nature is present in all the Ten Worlds, then all the other worlds will of course be present, too."[178]

According to the *Hōben* chapter, the Buddha replied to the request of his listeners by saying, "I wish to open the door of Buddha wisdom to all beings." The term "all beings" here refers to Shariputra and it also refers to men of incorrigible disbelief. It also refers to the nine worlds, thus fulfilling the words of the Buddha, "All beings are numberless—I vow to save them."[179] As the Buddha says in the *Hōben* chapter, "At the start I pledged to make all people perfectly equal to me, without any distinction between us. By now the original vows that I made have already been fulfilled."

All the great bodhisattvas, heavenly beings and others, when they had heard the doctrine of the Buddha and comprehended it, said: "From past times we have heard the World-Honored One preach on various occasions, but we have never heard anything to match the profoundness and wonder of this superior Dharma !"

The Great Teacher Dengyō comments: " 'From past times we have heard the World-Honored One preach on various occasions' refers to the fact that they had heard him preach the great doctrines of the *Kegon* Sutra and other sutras in the time previous to the preaching of the Lotus Sutra. 'We have never heard anything to match the profoundness and wonder of this

177.   Thirty-two distinguishing features and eighty physical characteristics: Attributes of the Buddha described in the provisional teachings. These unusual qualities awed the people and awoke in them a desire for the Buddha's teachings. They signify the Buddha's wisdom, ability, mercy, etc.

178.   *Maka Shikan Bugyōden Guketsu*, vol. 5.

179.   One of the four universal vows of a Buddha or bodhisattva. The other three are to remove all earthly desires, to study all the Buddhist teachings, and to attain the supreme enlightenment through the practice of Buddhism.

superior Dharma' means that they had never heard the doctrine of the unique, supreme vehicle propounded in the Lotus Sutra."[180]

They understood, that is, that none of the previous Mahayana sutras such as the *Kegon*, *Hōdō*, *Hannya*, *Jimmitsu*, and *Dainichi*, which are numerous as the sands of the Ganges, had ever made clear the great principle of *ichinen sanzen*, which is the core of all the teachings of the Buddha's lifetime, or the bone and marrow of those teachings, the doctrines that those in the two realms of *shōmon* and *engaku* shall achieve Buddhahood and that the Buddha attained enlightenment countless aeons ago.

180.   *Shugo Kokkai Shō.*

Part Two

From this time forward, the great bodhisattvas as well as Bonten, Taishaku, the gods of the sun and moon, and the Four Heavenly Kings, became the disciples of Shakyamuni Buddha. Thus, in the *Hōtō* chapter of the Lotus Sutra, the Buddha treats these great bodhisattvas as his disciples, admonishing and instructing them in these words: "I say to the great assembly: After I have passed away, who can protect and maintain, read and recite this sutra? Now in the presence of the Buddha let him come forward and speak his vow!" This was the solemn way he addressed them. And the great bodhisattvas in turn were, in the words of the sutra, "like the branches of small trees when a great wind blows them." Like the *kusha* grass[1] bending before a great wind or like rivers and streams drawn to the great ocean, so were they drawn to the Buddha.

But it was still a relatively short time since the Buddha had begun to preach the Lotus Sutra on Eagle Peak, and what he said seemed to his listeners dreamlike and unreal. The Treasure Tower had first appeared to confirm the correctness of the theoretical teaching in the first part of the Lotus Sutra, and after that the Treasure Tower prepared the way for the expounding of the essential teaching. The Buddhas of the ten directions gathered in assembly, Shakyamuni Buddha announcing that "all of these are emanations of my being." The Treasure Tower hung in the air, with Shakyamuni and Tahō seated side by side in it, as though both the sun and the moon had appeared side by side in the blue sky. The great assembly of human and heavenly beings were ranged about the sky like stars, and the Buddhas

1. *Kusha* grass: A kind of lily used in religious ceremonies.

who were emanations of Shakyamuni Buddha were on the ground, seated on their lion king thrones[2] under jewel trees.

In the Lotus Treasury World described in the *Kegon* Sutra, the Buddhas in their property-of-wisdom aspect all dwell in their separate lands. Buddhas of other worlds do not come to the present world and call themselves emanations of Shakyamuni, as happened in the case of the Lotus Sutra, nor do Buddhas of this world go to other worlds. Only Hōe and the others of the four bodhisattvas[3] come and go.

As for the Nine Honored Ones of the Eight Petals and the Thirty-seven Honored Ones,[4] described in the *Dainichi* and *Kongōchō* sutras, although they appear to be incarnations of the Buddha Dainichi or Mahavairochana, they are not dignified Buddhas who possess all the three properties of a true Buddha.

The thousand Buddhas[5] described in the *Daibon Hannya* Sutra and the Buddhas of the six directions represented in the *Amida* Sutra never assembled in this world, as did the Buddha's emanations in the Lotus Sutra. The Buddhas who are described in the *Daijuku* Sutra as assembling in this world, on the other hand, were not emanations of Shakyamuni. Similarly, the four Buddhas of the four directions[6] depicted in the *Konkōmyō* Sutra are merely their own incarnations.[7]

Thus, in the various sutras other than the Lotus Sutra,

2. Lion king throne: A Buddha's throne or seat. A Buddha is likened to the lion, king of beasts, because of his fearlessness.

3. Four bodhisattvas: Bodhisattvas Hōe, Kudokurin, Kongōdō and Kongōzō who appear in the *Kegon* Sutra.

4. Nine Honored Ones of the Eight Petals and the Thirty-seven Honored Ones: Symbolism found in the Shingon sutras. Eight petals represent the lotus blossom. On four of the eight petals, four Buddhas seat themselves, while four bodhisattvas sit on the other four. Dainichi Buddha is situated in the center of the lotus. This scene is described in the *Dainichi* Sutra. The *Kongōchō* Sutra depicts thirty-seven Buddhas and bodhisattvas including Dainichi Buddha.

5. According to the *Daibon* Sutra, a thousand Buddhas appeared in the ten directions, but they did not assemble on the occasion when the *Daibon* Sutra was preached.

6. Four Buddhas of the four directions: See p. 95, footnote 76.

7. Incarnations here mean the manifold forms which a Buddha himself assumes. Emanations are the manifestations of one true Buddha.

Shakyamuni does not assemble Buddhas who carry out different austerities and practices and who possess the three properties of a true Buddha, nor does he identify them as emanations of himself. Only in the *Hōtō* chapter of the Lotus Sutra does he do so. This chapter, then, is intended as an introduction to the *Juryō* chapter that follows later. Shakyamuni Buddha, who we believed had attained enlightenment for the first time only some forty or more years previously, calls together Buddhas who had become enlightened as long ago as one or even ten aeons in the past, and declares that they are emanations of himself. This is a far cry indeed from the Buddha's usual preaching on the equality of all Buddhas, and in fact a cause of great astonishment. If Shakyamuni had attained enlightenment for the first time only some forty years earlier, there could hardly have been so many beings in the ten directions who had received his instruction. And even if he was privileged to possess emanations, there would have been no benefit in his showing them to his listeners. T'ien-t'ai, describing what went on in the astonished minds of the assembly, says: "It was evident to them that Shakyamuni Buddha possessed numerous emanations. Therefore they understood that he must have attained enlightenment in the far distant past."[8]

In addition, a multitude of great Bodhisattvas of the Earth appeared, rising up out of the ground. Even Fugen and Monju, the leading disciples of Shakyamuni, could not compare to them. The great bodhisattvas described in the assemblies in the *Kegon*, *Hōdō* and *Hannya* sutras and the *Hōtō* chapter of the Lotus Sutra, or Kongōsatta and the others of the sixteen great bodhisattvas of the *Dainichi* Sutra, when compared with these newly arrived bodhisattvas, seemed like a pack of apes or monkeys, with the new bodhisattvas appearing among them like so many Taishakus. It was as though great ministers of court should mingle with humble mountain folk. Even

8. *Hokke Gengi*, vol. 9.

Miroku, who was to be the next Buddha after Shakyamuni, was perplexed by them, to say nothing of the lesser personages in the assembly.

Among these innumerable great bodhisattvas there were four great sages called Jōgyō, Muhengyō, Jyōgyō and Anryūgyō. In the presence of these four, the other bodhisattvas suspended in the air or seated on Eagle Peak could not bear to gaze on them face to face or try to match the workings of their minds. Even the four bodhisattvas of the *Kegon* Sutra, the four bodhisattvas of the *Dainichi* Sutra,[9] or the sixteen great bodhisattvas of the *Kongōchō* Sutra,[10] when in the presence of these four, were like bleary-eyed men trying to peer at the sun, or like humble fishermen appearing in audience before the emperor. These four were like T'ai-kung Wang and the others of the Four Sages of ancient China,[11] who towered above the multitude. They were like the Four White-haired Recluses of Mount Shang[12] who assisted Emperor Hui of the Han dynasty. Solemn, dignified, they were beings of great and lofty stature. Aside from Shakyamuni Buddha, Tahō Buddha and the emanations of Shakyamuni Buddha from the ten directions, they were worthy of acting as teachers to all beings.

Then Bodhisattva Miroku began to consider the matter in his mind. He said to himself, "Since Shakyamuni Buddha was a crown prince, and during the forty-two years since he gained

9. Four bodhisattvas of the *Dainichi* Sutra: Monju, Fugen, Miroku and Kannon.

10. Sixteen great bodhisattvas of the *Kongōchō* Sutra: The four bodhisattvas who follow each of the Buddhas of the four quarters of the universe.

11. The other three sages are Yin Shou, Wu Ch'eng and Lao Tzu. *See* p. 72, footnote 8.

12. Four White-haired Recluses of Mount Shang: Emperor Kao-tsu (256–195 B.C.), founder of the Han dynasty, tried to disown his son, the future Emperor Hui. Hui's mother, Empress Lü, persuaded four eminent recluses who lived on Mount Shang to become his advisors. They were known as Master Tung-yüan, Scholar Lu-li, Ch'i Li-chi and Master Hsia-huang. On seeing these four recluses, the emperor was so impressed by their dignity that he finally accepted Hui as his successor.

enlightenment at the age of thirty up until this gathering on Eagle Peak, I have known all the bodhisattvas of this world, and all the great bodhisattvas that have come from the worlds of the ten directions to attend this assembly. Moreover, I have visited all the pure and impure lands of the ten directions, sometimes as the Buddha's emissary, at other times on my own initiative, and I have become acquainted with all the great bodhisattvas of those various countries. Now who are these great bodhisattvas who have appeared from the earth, and what kind of Buddha is their teacher? Surely he must be a Buddha who surpasses even Shakyamuni, Tahō and the emanations from the ten directions! From the violence of the rain, you can judge the greatness of the dragon that caused it to fall; from the size of the lotus flower, you can tell the depth of the pond that produced it.[13] Now from what country did these great bodhisattvas come, under what Buddha did they study, and what great Dharma do they practice?"

Thus did Miroku wonder to himself, becoming so puzzled that he was unable to utter a sound. But, perhaps through the Buddha's power, he was at last able to put his doubts into words, saying: "The incalculable thousands of myriads of millions of bodhisattvas in a great multitude such as the past has never seen . . . This great, majestic, vigorously advancing multitude of bodhisattvas . . . who preached the Dharma for their sake, instructing them and leading them to their present state? As whose followers did they first turn to the Way? What Buddha's teachings do they proclaim? . . . World-Honored One, from past times I have never seen their like! I beg you to explain where they come from, the name of the land. Though I am constantly visiting other countries, I have never seen the likes of them! Within all this multitude, I do not recognize a single person. Suddenly they have come out of the ground—I beg you to explain the reason!"[14]

13. This sentence is found in the *Hokke Mongu*.
14. Lotus Sutra, chap. 15.

T'ien-t'ai comments on this: "From the time immediately after his enlightenment when Shakyamuni preached the *Kegon* Sutra up until the present gathering on Eagle Peak, bodhisattvas had continuously come from the ten directions to gather in assembly. Their numbers were unlimited, but Miroku, with the wisdom and power appropriate to the Buddha's successor-to-be, had seen and come to know them all. And yet among the newly arrived multitude, he did not recognize a single person—this in spite of the fact that he had traveled in the ten directions, had served various Buddhas, and was well known among the multitude."[15]

Miao-lo comments: "Wise men can see omens and what they foretell, as snakes know the way of snakes."[16]

The meaning of these passages of scripture and commentary is perfectly clear. In effect, from the time of Shakyamuni's enlightenment up until the assembly on Eagle Peak, in all the lands of the ten directions, no one had ever seen or heard of beings such as these bodhisattvas that came forth from the earth.

The Buddha, replying to Miroku's doubts, said: "Ajita,[17] . . . these persons whom you and the others have never seen before, they are bodhisattvas whom I converted and guided after I had attained supreme enlightenment in this *saha* world. I tamed their hearts and caused them to develop a longing for the Way."[18]

He also said: "When I was in the city of Gaya,[19] seated beneath the Bodhi tree, I attained the highest form of enlightenment and turned the wheel of the unparalleled Law. Thereafter I taught them, and caused them for the first time to aspire to enlightenment. And now all dwell in the stage where

15. *Hokke Mongu*, vol. 9.
16. *Hokke Mongu Ki*, vol. 9.
17. Ajita: An epithet of Miroku, meaning "invincible."
18. Lotus Sutra, chap. 15. The following passage is also found in the same chapter.
19. Gaya: A city in Magadha, sixty miles southwest of Pataliputra.

they will never backslide . . . Ever since the long distant past I have been teaching and guiding the members of this multitude."

But Miroku and the other great bodhisattvas were further perplexed by these words of the Buddha. When the Buddha preached the *Kegon* Sutra, Hōe and countless other great bodhisattvas appeared in the assembly. Miroku and the others wondered who they could be, but the Buddha said, "They are my good friends," and they thought this must be true. Later, when the Buddha preached the *Daijuku* Sutra at the Great Treasure Chamber[20] and the *Daibon Hannya* Sutra at the White Heron Lake,[21] great bodhisattvas appeared in the assembly and Miroku and the others supposed that they too were friends of the Buddha.

But these great bodhisattvas who had newly appeared out of the earth were older and more distinguished-looking than those earlier bodhisattvas. One might conclude that they were the teachers of the Buddha, and yet he had "caused them for the first time to aspire to enlightenment," and, when they were still young, had converted them and made them his disciples. It was this that Miroku and the others found so profoundly perplexing.

Prince Shōtoku[22] of Japan was the son of Emperor Yōmei, the thirty-second sovereign of Japan. When he was six years old, elderly men came to Japan from the states of Paekche and Koguryŏ in Korea and from the land of China. The six-year-old prince thereupon exclaimed, "These are my disciples!" and the old men in turn pressed their palms together in reverence and said, "You are our teacher!" This was a strange happening indeed.

There is a similar story found in a secular work. According

20.   Great Treasure Chamber: Treasure chamber supposed to stand on the border between the worlds of form and desire.
21.   White Heron Lake: Lake which existed in the Bamboo Grove Monastery in Rajagriha, Magadha.
22.   Shōtoku: *See* p. 13, footnote 30.

to this work, a man was walking along a road when he saw by the roadside a young man of about thirty who was beating an old man of about eighty. When he asked the reason, the young man replied, "This old man is my son."

Bodhisattva Miroku, continuing to doubt, said, "World-Honored One, when you were crown prince, you left the palace of the Shakyas and sat in the place of meditation not far from the city of Gaya, where you attained the supreme enlightenment. A mere forty years or so have passed since then. In that short period of time, how could you have accomplished so much great work as a Buddha?"[23]

The various bodhisattvas who had attended the numerous assemblies held in the forty-some years since the Buddha preached the *Kegon* Sutra had raised doubts at each assembly. The Buddha dispelled these doubts for the benefit of the multitude. But this present doubt concerning the bodhisattvas who had appeared out of the earth was the greatest doubt of all. It surpassed even the doubt entertained by Daishōgon and the others of the eighty thousand great men described in the *Muryōgi* Sutra when the Buddha, after declaring in the previous forty-some years of his teaching that enlightenment was something that required countless aeons to attain, now announced that it could be attained in a very short time.

According to the *Kammuryōju* Sutra, King Ajatashatru, led astray by Devadatta, imprisoned his father and was on the point of killing his mother, Lady Vaidehi. Reprimanded by the physician Jivaka and the court minister Chandraprabha, however, he spared his mother's life. At that time she had an interview with the Buddha and began by posing this question: "What sin have I committed in the past that I should have given birth to this evil son? And, World-Honored One, through what cause have you come to be related to a person as evil as your cousin Devadatta?"

Of the two doubts raised here, the second is the more

23. Lotus Sutra, chap. 15.

perplexing, the question of why the Buddha should be related to an evil person like Devadatta. A wheel-turning king, we are told, is never born into the world along with his enemies, nor is the god Taishaku to be found in the company of demons. The Buddha had been a merciful personage for countless aeons. Yet the fact that Shakyamuni was related to Devadatta might make one doubt whether he was indeed a Buddha at all. The Buddha, however, did not answer the question of Lady Vaidehi. Therefore, if one reads only the *Kammuryōju* Sutra and does not examine the *Devadatta* chapter of the Lotus Sutra, he will never know the truth of the matter.[24]

In the Nirvana Sutra, Bodhisattva Kashō posed thirty-six questions to the Buddha, but even these cannot compare to this question concerning the bodhisattvas who appeared from the earth. If the Buddha had failed to dispel the doubts concerning this matter, the sacred teachings of his entire lifetime would have amounted to no more than froth on the water, and the members of the multitude would have remained tangled in the snare of doubt. That was why it was so important for him to preach the *Juryō* chapter.

Later, when the Buddha preached the *Juryō* chapter, he said: "All the human and heavenly beings and the ashuras at present believe that Shakyamuni Buddha, after leaving the palace of the Shakyas, sat in the place of meditation not far from the city of Gaya and there attained the supreme enlightenment." This passage expresses the view held by all the great bodhisattvas from the time when Shakyamuni first attained enlightenment until the preaching of the *Anrakugyō* chapter[25] of the Lotus Sutra. "However, men of devout faith," the Buddha con-

24.   The *Devadatta* chapter reveals the master–disciple relationship between Devadatta and Shakyamuni in their previous existence. In a previous existence Shakyamuni was a king. In order to learn the Mahayana teachings, he served a hermit named Ashi for one thousand years. After relating this story, he identifies the king as himself and Ashi as Devadatta. He is now the teacher of the man who once taught him. The *Devadatta* chapter thus provides the answer to the question posed in the *Kammuryōju* Sutra.

25.   *Anrakugyō* chapter: The fourteenth chapter of the sutra and the last

tinued, "the time is limitless and boundless—a hundred, thousand, ten thousand, hundred thousand, nayuta aeons—since I in fact attained Buddhahood."

Three places in the *Kegon* Sutra the Buddha said: "I have attained enlightenment for the first time in India." In the *Agon* sutras he speaks of having "for the first time attained enlightenment;" in the Vimalakirti Sutra he says, "For the first time the Buddha sat beneath the tree"; in the *Daijuku* Sutra, "It is sixteen years since the Buddha first attained enlightenment"; in the *Dainichi* Sutra, "some years ago when I sat in the place of meditation"; in the *Ninnō* Sutra, "twenty-nine years since my enlightenment"; in the *Muryōgi* Sutra, "previously I went to the place of meditation"; and in the *Hōben* chapter of the Lotus Sutra, "when I first sat in the place of meditation." But now all these passages have been exposed as gross falsehoods by this single pronouncement in the *Juryō* chapter.

When Shakyamuni Buddha revealed that he had gained enlightenment in the far distant past and had since then been constantly in the world, it became apparent that all the other Buddhas were emanations of Shakyamuni. When the Buddha preached the earlier sutras and the theoretical chapters of the Lotus Sutra, the other Buddhas present were pictured as practicing various religious austerities and disciplines side by side with Shakyamuni Buddha. Therefore the people who pay devotion to one or another of these Buddhas as the object of worship customarily look down on Shakyamuni Buddha. But now it becomes apparent that Vairochana Buddha of the *Kegon* Sutra and the various Buddhas of the *Hōdō*, *Hannya* and *Dainichi* sutras are all in fact followers of Shakyamuni Buddha.

When Shakyamuni gained enlightenment at the age of thirty, he seized the *saha* world away from Bonten and the Devil of the Sixth Heaven, who had ruled it previously, and made it his own. In the earlier sutras and the theoretical

---

chapter of the theoretical teaching. In the theoretical teaching, Shakyamuni did not reveal his original attainment of Buddhahood in the distant past.

chapters of the Lotus Sutra, he called the regions of the ten directions "pure lands" and spoke of the present world as an "impure land." But now he has reversed this in the *Juryō* chapter, revealing that this world is the true land and the so-called pure lands of the ten directions are impure lands, mere provisional lands.

Since the Buddha of the *Juryō* chapter is revealed as the eternal Buddha, it follows that the great bodhisattvas such as Monju and Miroku, and the great bodhisattvas from other realms are in fact disciples of Shakyamuni Buddha. If, among all the numerous sutras, this *Juryō* chapter should be lacking, it would be as though there were no sun and moon in the sky, no supreme ruler in the nation, no gems in the mountains and rivers, and no spirit in man.

Nevertheless, Ch'eng-kuan, Chia-hsiang, Tz'u-en, Kōbō and others, learned men of provisional sects such as Kegon and Shingon, in order to praise the various sutras upon which their provisional doctrines are based, go so far as to say, "The Buddha of the *Kegon* Sutra is 'the Buddha in his property-of-wisdom aspect,' while the Buddha of the Lotus Sutra is merely 'the Buddha in his property-of-action aspect.' "[26] Or they say, "The Buddha of the *Juryō* chapter of the Lotus Sutra is in the region of darkness, while the Buddha of the *Dainichi* Sutra occupies the position of enlightenment."[27]

As clouds obscure the moon, so calumnious ministers can obscure the man of true worth. A yellow stone, if people praise it, may be mistaken for a jewel, and ministers who are skilled in flattery may be mistaken for worthy men. In this impure age we live in, scholars and students are confused by the slanderous assertions of the kind of men I have mentioned above, and they do not appreciate the true worth of the jewel of the *Juryō* chapter. Even among the men of the Tendai sect there are those who have become so deluded that they cannot distinguish the

26. *Kegon-kyō Goron*, vol. 1.
27. *Hizō Hōyaku*, written by Kōbō.

gold of the Lotus Sutra from the mere stones that are the earlier sutras.

One should consider the fact that, if the Buddha had not attained enlightenment in the distant past, there could not have been so many people who were converted to his teachings. The moon is not stingy with its shining, but if there is no water to catch its rays, then its reflection will not be seen. The Buddha may be very anxious to convert all people, but if he cannot establish some connection with them, then he cannot go through the eight phases of a Buddha's existence. Thus, for example, the *shōmon* disciples attained the first stage of security and the first stage of development,[28] but because they followed the teachings that preceded the Lotus Sutra and sought only to regulate and save themselves, they had to postpone the attainment of the eight phases of a Buddha's existence to some future lifetime.

If Shakyamuni Buddha had actually attained enlightenment for the first time at the age of thirty, then when he preached the Lotus Sutra, Bonten, Taishaku, the gods of the sun and moon and the Four Heavenly Kings who have ruled the present world from countless ages in the past would have been disciples of Shakyamuni Buddha for no longer than a period of forty-some years. During the eight years when he preached the Lotus Sutra, the beings who assembled to listen to him would have been unable to accept as their master a person who had so recently come to prominence and would have deferred instead to Bonten, Taishaku and the other deities who had from ages past been the lords of this world.

But now that it has become apparent that Shakyamuni Buddha attained enlightenment countless aeons ago, then the Bodhisattvas Nikkō and Gakkō, who attend the Buddha

28.   First stage of security and the first stage of development: The first of the ten stages of security and the first of the ten stages of development, which comprise part of the fifty-two stages of bodhisattva practice. *See also* Fifty-two stages of bodhisattva practice in the Glossary.

Yakushi of the eastern region, the Bodhisattvas Kannon and Seishi, who attend the Buddha Amida of the western region, along with the disciples of all the Buddhas of the worlds of the ten directions and the great bodhisattvas who are disciples of the Buddha Dainichi as they are shown in the *Dainichi* and *Kongōchō* sutras—all of these beings are disciples of Shakyamuni Buddha. Since the various Buddhas themselves are emanations of Shakyamuni Buddha, it goes without saying that their disciples must be disciples of Shakyamuni. And of course the various deities of the sun, moon and stars, who have dwelt in this world from countless ages in the past, must likewise be disciples of Shakyamuni Buddha.

Nevertheless, the sects of Buddhism other than Tendai have gone astray concerning the true object of worship. The Kusha, Jōjitsu and Ritsu sects take as their object of worship the Shakyamuni Buddha who eliminated illusions by practicing thirty-four kinds of spiritual purification.[29] This is comparable to a situation in which the heir apparent of the supreme ruler of a state mistakenly believes himself to be the son of a commoner. The four sects of Kegon, Shingon, Sanron and Hossō are all Mahayana schools of Buddhism. Among them the Hossō and Sanron sects worship a Buddha who is comparable to the Buddha in the superior property-of-action aspect.[30] This is like the heir of the supreme ruler supposing that his father was a member of the samurai class. The Kegon and Shingon sects look down upon Shakyamuni Buddha and declare that Mahavairochana or Dainichi Buddha should be the true object of worship. This is like the heir looking down upon his own father, the supreme ruler, and paying honor to one who is not

29. A Hinayana practice for eradicating the illusions of thought and desire.
30. When Shakyamuni Buddha preached the earlier sutras, he manifested various aspects of Buddhahood according to the superiority or inferiority of the sutras. When he expounded the *zōkyō* teachings and *tsūgyō* (higher than *zōkyō*) teachings, he manifested himself respectively as the Buddha in the inferior property-of-action aspect and the Buddha in the superior property-of-action aspect.

even related to him by blood simply because that person pretends to be the Dharma King. The Jōdo sect considers itself to be most closely related to the Buddha Amida, who is an emanation of Shakyamuni, and rejects Shakyamuni himself. The Zen sect behaves like a person of low birth who makes much of his own achievements and despises his father and mother. Thus the Zen sect rejects both the Buddha and the sutras. All of these sects are misled concerning the true object of worship. They are like the people who lived in the age before the Three Rulers of ancient China and did not know who their own fathers were. In that respect, the people of that time were no different from birds and beasts.

The men of these sects who are ignorant of the teachings of the *Juryō* chapter are similarly like beasts. They do not understand to whom they are obligated. Therefore Miao-lo states: "Among all the teachings of the Buddha's lifetime, there is no place other than the *Juryō* chapter where the true longevity of the Buddha is revealed. A person ought to know how old his father and mother are. If a son does not even know how old his father is, he will also be in doubt as to what lands his father presides over. Though he may be idly praised for his talent and ability, he cannot be counted as a son at all!"[31]

The Great Teacher Miao-lo lived in the T'ien-pao era (742–755) in the latter part of the T'ang dynasty. He is saying that if one makes a deep and thorough examination of the Sanron, Kegon, Hossō and Shingon sects and the sutras upon which they are based, but fails to become acquainted with the Buddha of the *Juryō* chapter, he is no more than a talented animal who does not even know what lands his father presides over. "Though he may be idly praised for his talent and ability" refers to men like Fa-tsang and Ch'eng-kuan of the Kegon sect or Shan-wu-wei of the Shingon sect. These teachers had talent and ability, yet they were like sons who do not even know their own father.

31. *Hokke Gohyakumon Ron.*

The Great Teacher Dengyō was the patriarch of both esoteric and exoteric Buddhism in Japan.[32] In his *Hokke Shūku* he writes: "The sutras that the other sects are based upon give expression to the mother-like nature of the Buddha. But they convey only a sense of love and are lacking in a sense of fatherly sternness. It is only the Tendai sect, based upon the Lotus Sutra, that combines a sense of both love and sternness. The sutra is a father to all the worthy men, sages, those in the stages of learning and beyond learning, and those who have awakened in themselves the mind of the bodhisattva."[33]

The sutras that form the basis of the Shingon and Kegon sects do not even contain the terms "sowing," "maturing" and "harvest," much less the doctrine [of the sowing of the seeds of Buddhahood, the maturing of the seeds, and the eventual attainment of Buddhahood] to which these terms refer. When the sutras of the Kegon and Shingon sects assert that their followers will enter the first stage of development and achieve Buddhahood in the same lifetime, they are putting forth the teachings of the provisional sutras alone, teachings that conceal the role of the past.[34] To expect to attain fruition without having the seed first sowed is like the eunuch Chao Kao[35]

32.   When Dengyō went to China, he chiefly studied T'ien-t'ai's teachings which are based on the Lotus Sutra. In Japan he asserted the supremacy of the Lotus Sutra. However, when he came back to Japan, he also brought esoteric teachings with him. Because he brought them earlier than Kōbō, founder of the esoteric Shingon sect in Japan, he is regarded as the patriarch of both esoteric and exoteric Buddhism in Japan.

33.   A sense of fatherly sternness stands for the seed of Buddhahood, and a sense of motherly love represents the nurturing of the seed to maturity. The earlier sutras do not reveal the seed of Buddhahood. Therefore, they are unable to help people attain Buddhahood. On the other hand, the Lotus Sutra contains the seed of Buddhahood as well as the blessing of maturing.

34.   That is, they do not reveal the Buddha's attainment of enlightenment in the distant past.

35.   Chao Kao (d. 207 B.C.): Minister to Shih-huang-ti (259–210 B.C.), first emperor of the Ch'in dynasty. When Shih-huang-ti died of illness, the eunuch official Chao Kao issued a false edict setting the emperor's youngest son on the throne. He brought about the death of the emperor's eldest son, as well as many generals and high ministers and finally the second emperor. He wielded power

attempting to seize Imperial power in China or the monk Dōkyō[36] trying to become emperor of Japan.

The various sects argue with one another, each claiming that its sutra contains the true seeds of enlightenment. I do not intend to enter the argument. I will let the sutras speak for themselves. Thus the Bodhisattva Vasubandhu, speaking of the seeds of enlightenment implanted by the Lotus Sutra, designates them "the seeds without peer."[37] And these seeds of enlightenment are the doctrine of *ichinen sanzen* as expounded by the Great Teacher T'ien-t'ai.

The seed of enlightenment of the various Buddhas described in the *Kegon* Sutra, the other various Mahayana sutras and the *Dainichi* Sutra, is the one doctrine of *ichinen sanzen*. And the Great Teacher T'ien-t'ai was the only person who was capable of perceiving the truth of this doctrine. Ch'eng-kuan of the Kegon sect usurped the doctrine of *ichinen sanzen* and used it to interpret the passage in the *Kegon* Sutra that reads: "The mind is like a skilled painter."

The *Dainichi* Sutra of the Shingon sect contains no mention of the fact that the *shōmon* and *engaku* can attain Buddhahood, that the Buddha Shakyamuni achieved enlightenment countless aeons ago, or of the doctrine of *ichinen sanzen*. But after Shan-wu-wei came to China, he had occasion to read the *Maka Shikan* by T'ien-t'ai and came to gain wisdom and understanding. He then usurped the doctrine of *ichinen sanzen*, using it to interpret the passages in the *Dainichi* Sutra on "the reality of the mind" or that which reads, "I[38] am the source and beginning of all things," making it the core of the Shingon teachings but

---

and attempted to control the throne. He was finally killed by the third ruler, Shih-huang-ti's grandson.

36. Dōkyō (d. 772 A.D.): Monk who cured Empress Kōken of illness. Taking advantage of her favor, he commanded power and attempted to take the throne, but failed.

37. In his *Hokke Ron*, Vasubandhu asserted the superiority of the Lotus Sutra over all other sutras from ten viewpoints. "The seeds without peer" is the first of them.

38. "I" means Mahavairochana Buddha.

adding to it the practice of *mudras* and *mantras*. And in comparing the relative merits of the Lotus Sutra and the *Dainichi* Sutra, he declared that while the two agree in principle, the latter is superior in practice. The mandalas of the two worlds[39] symbolize the attaining of Buddhahood by the *shōmon* and *engaku* and the mutual possession of the Ten Worlds, but are these doctrines to be found anywhere in the *Dainichi* Sutra? Those who claim so are guilty of the grossest deception!

Therefore the Great Teacher Dengyō writes: "The school of Shingon Buddhism that has recently been brought to Japan deliberately distorts its teachings to suit its purposes,[40] while the Kegon school that was introduced earlier attempts to disguise the fact that it was influenced by the doctrines of T'ien-t'ai."[41]

Suppose someone were to go to some wild region like the island of Ezo (Hokkaido) and recite the famous poem:

> How I think of it—
> dim, dim in the morning mist
> of Akashi Bay,
> that boat moving out of sight
> beyond the islands.[42]

If the person told the ignorant natives of Ezo that he himself had composed the poem, they would probably believe him. The Buddhist scholars of China and Japan are equally gullible.

39. Mandalas of the two worlds: The Womb World mandala of the *Dainichi* Sutra and the Diamond World mandala of the *Kongōchō* Sutra. The terms *womb* and *diamond* here indicate respectively the all-inclusiveness or productivity and the wisdom of Dainichi, or Mahavairochana, Buddha.

40. When Shan-wu-wei came from India to China in the reign of Emperor Hsüan-tsung, the T'ien-t'ai sect had established the supremacy of the Lotus Sutra. Shan-wu-wei induced I-hsing, a priest of the T'ien-t'ai sect, to write a treatise on the *Dainichi* Sutra and to assert the supremacy of the *Dainichi* Sutra over the Lotus with respect to the practice of *mudras* and *mantras*.

41. *Ebyō Shū.*

42. Poem from the ninth volume of the *Kokin Waka Shū* (Collection of Ancient and Modern Poetry).

The Chinese priest Liang-hsü[43] of the T'ien-t'ai sect writes: "The doctrines of the Shingon, Zen, Kegon, Sanron . . . can at best serve as a kind of introduction to the Lotus Sutra."[44] We are told that Shan-wu-wei was subjected to punishment by Emma, the King of Hell, no doubt because of his mistaken view that the *Dainichi* Sutra is superior to the Lotus Sutra. Later he had a change of heart and became an enthusiastic supporter of the Lotus Sutra, which is why he was spared further punishment. As evidence, when he, Pu-k'ung and the others devised mandalas to symbolize the teachings of the Shingon sect, they placed the Lotus Sutra in the center of the two worlds as the supreme ruler, with the Womb World mandala of the *Dainichi* Sutra and the Diamond World mandala of the *Kongōchō* Sutra to the left and right as ministers to the ruler.

When Kōbō of Japan drew up a theoretical statement of the Shingon teachings, he was influenced by the Kegon sect and assigned [the *Kegon* Sutra to the ninth stage of advancement and] the Lotus Sutra to the eighth stage.[45] But when he taught the practices and ceremonies to his disciples Jitte, Shinga, Enchō, Kōjō and the others, he placed the Lotus Sutra in a central position, above the two worlds of the Womb and the Diamond as Shan-wu-wei and Pu-k'ung did.

In a similar case, Chia-hsiang of the Sanron sect, in his ten-volume *Hokke Genron*, assigned the Lotus Sutra to the fourth of the five periods of teachings,[46] claiming that it opened the way of the bodhisattva to the *shōmon* and *engaku*. Later, however, he

43. Liang-hsü: Ninth successor to T'ien-t'ai. In 851, when Chishō, the fifth patriarch of the Tendai sect in Japan, came to China, he studied the teachings of the T'ien-t'ai sect under Liang-hsü.

44. A rephrasing of the *Juketsu Shū*.

45. In his *Jūjūshin Ron*, Kōbō explained ten stages of mind's development. He placed a follower of the Lotus Sutra in the eighth stage, and a follower of the *Kegon* Sutra in the ninth. Ultimately he placed a follower of the Shingon teaching in the highest, tenth stage, because he is one who has obtained the secret teaching.

46. In his *Hokke Genron*, Chia-hsiang asserted that the Lotus Sutra was inferior to the *Hannya* Sutra.

became converted to the teachings of T'ien-t'ai. He ceased giving lectures, dismissed his disciples, and instead served the Great Teacher T'ien-t'ai for a period of seven years, personally carrying T'ien-t'ai on his back when T'ien-t'ai mounted an elevated seat for preaching.

Again, Tz'u-en, the founder of the Hossō sect, in his seven-volume and twelve-volume *Daijō Hōon Girin Jō*,[47] states: "The One Vehicle doctrine set forth in the Lotus Sutra is a mere expedient; the Three Vehicle doctrine represents the truth." He also makes many similarly absurd pronouncements. But in the fourth volume of the *Hokke Genzan Yō Shū*, he is represented as saying that "both doctrines are to be accepted," thus bringing flexible interpretation to the tenets of his own sect. Although he said that both doctrines were acceptable, in his heart he supported the T'ien-t'ai teachings on the Lotus Sutra.

Ch'eng-kuan of the Kegon sect wrote a commentary on the *Kegon* Sutra in which he compared the *Kegon* and Lotus sutras and declared that the Lotus Sutra appears to be a mere expedient doctrine. But elsewhere he wrote: "I believe that the teachings of the T'ien-t'ai sect represent the truth. In doctrine and principle they agree completely with those of my own sect." From this it would appear, would it not, that he regretted his earlier pronouncement.

Kōbō is a similar example. If one has no mirror, he cannot see his own face, and if one has no opponents, he cannot learn of his own errors. The scholars of the Shingon and the other various sects were unaware of their errors. But after they were fortunate enough to encounter the Great Teacher Dengyō, they became conscious of the mistakes of their own particular sects.

The various Buddhas, bodhisattvas, and heavenly and human beings described in the sutras that preceded the Lotus may seem to have gained enlightenment through the particular

47. The original consists of seven volumes and its revision, of twelve volumes.

sutras in which they appear. But in fact they attained enlightenment only through the Lotus Sutra. The first of the general vows taken by Shakyamuni and the other Buddhas to "save the countless sentient beings"[48] finds fulfillment through the Lotus Sutra. That is the meaning of the passage in the *Hōben* chapter of the Lotus Sutra in which Shakyamuni declares: "By now the original vows that I made have already been fulfilled."

In view of these facts, I believe that the devotees and followers of the various provisional sutras such as the *Kegon*, *Kammuryōju* and *Dainichi* sutras will undoubtedly be protected by the Buddhas, bodhisattvas and heavenly beings of the respective sutras that they uphold. But if the votaries of the *Dainichi*, *Kammuryōju* and other sutras should set themselves up as the enemies of the votary of the Lotus Sutra, then the Buddhas, bodhisattvas and heavenly beings will abandon them and will protect the votary of the Lotus Sutra. It is like the case of a filial son whose father opposes the ruler of the kingdom. The son will abandon his father and support the ruler, for to do so is the height of filial piety.

The same thing applies to Buddhism. The Buddhas, bodhisattvas and the Ten Goddesses described in the Lotus Sutra lend their protection to Nichiren, the votary of the Lotus. And in addition, the Buddhas of the six directions and the twenty-five bodhisattvas of the Jōdo sect,[49] the 1,200 venerable ones[50] of the Shingon sect, and the various venerable ones and benevolent guardian deities of the seven sects[51] also protect Nichiren. It is like the case of the Great Teacher Dengyō, who was protected by the guardian deities of the seven sects.

48. Save the countless sentient beings: *See* p. 138, footnote 179.

49. The Buddhas of the six directions are Ashuku Buddha in the east, Nichigatsu Tōmyō Buddha in the south, Amida Buddha in the west, Enken Buddha in the north, Shishi Buddha below and Bonnon Buddha above. The twenty-five bodhisattvas protect all who worship Amida Buddha. They are Bodhisattvas Kannon, Seishi, Yakuō and so on.

50. 1,200 venerable ones: Venerable Buddhas, bodhisattvas and others inscribed on the two Shingon mandalas (*see* footnote 39).

51. Seven sects: The six Nara sects (*see* Glossary) and the Shingon sect.

I, Nichiren, have this to say. The gods of the sun and moon and the other deities were present in the two places and three assemblies[52] when the Lotus Sutra was preached. If a votary of the Lotus Sutra should appear, then, like iron drawn to a magnet or the reflection of the moon appearing in the water, they will instantly come forth to take on his sufferings for him and thereby fulfill the vow that they made in the presence of the Buddha. But they have yet to come and inquire of my well-being. Does this mean that I am not a true votary of the Lotus Sutra ? If that is so, then I must examine the text of the sutra once more in the light of my conduct and see where I am at fault.

Question: What eyes of wisdom allow you to perceive that the Nembutsu, Zen and other sects of our time are the enemies of the Lotus Sutra and evil companions who are ready to mislead all people ?

Answer: I do not state arbitrary opinions, but merely hold up the mirror of the sutras and commentaries so that the slanderers of the Law may see their ugly faces reflected there and perceive their errors. But, blind men that they are, they seem incapable of doing so.

In the *Hōtō* chapter of the Lotus Sutra we read: "At that time Tahō Buddha in the Treasure Tower gave half of his seat to Shakyamuni Buddha . . . At that time, the great multitude saw the two Buddhas seated with legs crossed on the lion throne in the tower of seven treasures . . . Shakyamuni Buddha addressed the four kinds of believers in a loud voice, saying, 'Who among you will propagate the Lotus Sutra throughout the *saha* world ? Now is the time to do so ! Before

52. Two places and three assemblies: The scene where Shakyamuni preached the Lotus Sutra. The two places are atop Eagle Peak and in the air. The three assemblies are: the first assembly at Eagle Peak, the assembly in the air, and the second assembly at Eagle Peak. The first assembly at Eagle Peak continues from the first chapter through the first half of the *Hōtō* (11th) chapter. The assembly in the air lasts from the latter half of the *Hōtō* chapter to the *Zokurui* (22nd) chapter, and the second assembly at Eagle Peak from the *Yakuō* (23rd) chapter to the *Fugen* (28th) chapter.

long, I will enter nirvana. The Buddha hopes there is someone
to whom he can entrust this Lotus Sutra.'"

This is the first pronouncement of the Buddha.

Again the chapter reads: "At this time the World-Honored
One, wishing to repeat the announcement that he had just
made, spoke in verse:

> 'The Sainted Lord, World-Honored One [Tahō Buddha],
> though he passed into nirvana long ago,
> seats himself in the Treasure Tower,
> coming here for the sake of the Law.
> You people, why then do you also
> not strive for the sake of the Law? . . .
> My emanations,
> these numberless Buddhas
> who are like the sands of the Ganges,
> they have come, desiring to hear the Law . . .
> Each has abandoned his precious land
> as well as his host of disciples,
> the heavenly and human beings, dragons and gods,
> and all the offerings they give him—
> to make certain that the Law will long endure,
> they have come to this place . . .
> It is like the branches of small trees
> when a great wind blows them.
> Through this expedient means
> they make certain that the Law will long endure.
> So I say to the great assembly:
> After I have passed away,
> who can protect and maintain,
> read and recite this sutra?
> Now in the presence of the Buddha
> let him come forward and speak his vow!'"

This is the second proclamation of the Buddha. The passage
continues:

" 'Tahō Buddha, myself
and the emanations of myself
who have gathered here—
they know the intention of my words . . .
Men of devout faith,
each of you must consider carefully!
This is a difficult matter—
it is proper that you take a great vow.
The other sutras
number as many as the sands of the Ganges,
but though you expound them all,
that is not worthy to be considered difficult.
To seize Mount Sumeru
and fling it far off
to the measureless Buddha lands—
that too is not difficult . . .
But after the Buddha's passing,
in the time of evil,
to be able to preach this sutra—
that is difficult indeed! . . .
When the fires come at the end of the kalpa,[53]
to load dry grass on one's back
and enter the fire without being burned—
that is not difficult.
But after my passing,
to be able to preserve this sutra
and expound it to even one person—
that is difficult indeed! . . .
Men of devout faith,
after my passing,
who can receive and embrace,
read and recite this sutra?
Now in the presence of the Buddha
let him come forward and speak his vow!' "

53.   Fires come at the end of the kalpa: *See* p. 114, footnote 116.

This is the third admonition from the Buddha. The fourth and fifth admonitions are found in the *Devadatta* chapter and I will deal with them later.

The meaning of these passages from the sutra is right before our eyes, obvious as the sun suspended in the blue sky or a mole on a white face. And yet the blind ones, those with perverse eyes, the one-eyed, those who believe no one but their own teachers, and those who cling to biased views cannot see it!

For those who are determined to surmount all difficulties and have set their hearts on the Truth, I will try to explain and point out the way. But they must understand that the Truth is more rarely met with than the peaches of immortality[54] that grow in the garden of the Queen Mother of the West, or the udumbara flower[55] that blooms only once every three thousand years in the age of a wheel-turning monarch. Moreover, the conflict among the sects over their superiority surpasses the eight years of warfare when Liu Pang and Hsiang Yü[56] battled for the empire of China, the seven years when Minamoto no Yoritomo and Taira no Munemori[57] fought for the islands of Japan, the struggles between Taishaku and the ashuras, or between the dragon kings and the garuda birds at the Icy Lake.[58]

54.   The Queen Mother of the West is a legendary goddess in China. The peaches in her garden are said to bear fruit once in three thousand years.
55.   The udumbara flower is said to bloom once every three thousand years to herald the appearance of a gold-wheel-turning monarch in the world.
56.   Liu Pang and Hsiang Yü took advantage of the confusion following the death of Shih-huang-ti, the first emperor of the Ch'in dynasty, to raise an army and overthrow the dynasty. Thereafter, the two engaged in a protracted struggle for power. This ended in the victory of Liu Pang, who founded the Han dynasty in 206 B.C.
57.   The Minamoto clan, led by Minamoto no Yoritomo (1147–1199), waged a long campaign to wrest political power from the Taira clan. The Tairas were finally defeated at Dannoura, and Taira no Munemori (1147–1185), the last head of his clan, died in the battle. Minamoto no Yoritomo subsequently established the Kamakura shogunate.
58.   Dragon kings and the garuda birds at the Icy Lake: The garuda are gigantic birds in Indian mythology that are said to feed on dragons. The Icy Lake, located at the summit of the Snow Mountains, contains cool, clear water

This Truth that I am speaking of has made its appearance twice in the country of Japan. You should understand that it appeared once with the Great Teacher Dengyō and again with Nichiren. But the sightless ones doubt this, and they do not have the strength to believe. Shakyamuni Buddha, Tahō Buddha and the Buddhas of the ten directions gathered together and judged the relative merits of all the sutras of Japan, China, India, the palace of the Dragon King, the heavens, and all the other worlds of the ten directions, and this is the sutra they chose.

Question: Do sutras such as the *Kegon*, *Hōdō*, *Hannya*, *Jimmitsu*, *Ryōga*, *Dainichi* and Nirvana belong to the "nine easy acts" group or the "six difficult acts" group?

Answer: Tu-shun, Chih-yen, Fa-tsang and Ch'eng-kuan of the Kegon sect, who were all masters of the three divisions of the Tripitaka,[59] stated that both the Lotus Sutra and the *Kegon* Sutra belong to the "six difficult acts" category. Though in name they are two different sutras, they are identical in their teachings and principles. It is similar to the statement, "Though the four views of reality are separate, the truth they point to is identical."[60]

Hsüan-tsang and Tz'u-en of the Hossō sect state that the *Jimmitsu* Sutra and the Lotus Sutra both expound the Consciousness-Only doctrine. They date from the third period of the Buddha's teaching[61] and belong to the "six difficult" category.

which removes all sufferings. This lake is said to be inhabited by a dragon king.

59.   Three divisions of the Tripitaka: Sutras, rules of discipline and treatises on the Buddhist doctrines. Tripitaka literally means "three baskets" but here indicates the three divisions of the Buddhist canon.

60.   *Maka Shikan*, vol. 6. "The truth" here indicates the enlightenment set forth in Hinayana teachings. The quotation indicates that although the way to this enlightenment is divided into four, all of these equally lead to enlightenment.

61.   The Hossō sect divides all of Shakyamuni's teachings into three. The first period contains the doctrine of the Four Truths, which corresponds to the Hinayana teaching. The second period includes the teachings which assert that the essential nature of all things is *kū*. This doctrine is intended to refute

Chia-hsiang of the Sanron sect asserts that the *Hannya* Sutra and the Lotus Sutra are different names for a single entity, two sutras that preach one Truth.

Shan-wu-wei, Chin-kang-chih and Pu-k'ung of the Shingon sect say that the *Dainichi* Sutra and the Lotus Sutra are identical in principle and that both belong to the "six difficult" category. But the Japanese Shingon leader Kōbō says that the *Dainichi* Sutra belongs neither to the "six difficult" nor the "nine easy" category. The *Dainichi* Sutra, according to him, stands apart from all the other sutras preached by Shakyamuni Buddha, since it was preached by Dainichi Buddha, the Buddha in his property-of-Law aspect. Likewise, some persons assert that, since the *Kegon* Sutra was preached by the Buddha in his property-of-wisdom aspect, it stands outside the categories of "six difficult" and "nine easy."

Such, then, are the views put forth by the founders of these four sects. The thousands of followers of these sects likewise subscribe to the same views.

I must observe sadly that, although it would be simple enough to point out the error of the views put forward by these men, if I did so, the people of today would not even look in my direction, much less listen to me. They would go on in their erroneous ways, and in the end would slander me to the rulers of the country and put my life in jeopardy. Nevertheless, our merciful father Shakyamuni Buddha, when he faced his end in the grove of sal trees, stated as his dying instructions that we are to "rely on the Law and not upon persons."[62] "Not relying upon persons" means that, when persons of the first, second, third and fourth ranks[63] preach, even though they are bodhi-

---

attachment to the Hinayana teachings. The *Hannya* Sutra belongs to the second period. The teachings in the third period reveal the Consciousness-Only doctrine and refute extreme attachment to the doctrine of *kū*. The third period includes the *Jimmitsu*, Lotus, *Kegon* and Nirvana sutras. Among them, the *Jimmitsu* Sutra is most highly valued by the Hossō sect.

62. Nirvana Sutra.

63. Persons of the first, second, third and fourth ranks: Reliable Buddhist

sattvas such as Fugen or Monju whose enlightenment almost approaches that of the Buddha, if they do not preach with the sutra in hand, following its teachings faithfully, then they are not to be accepted.

It is also laid down that one should "rely on the sutras that are complete and final and not on those which are not complete and final."[64] We must therefore look carefully among the sutras to determine which are complete and final and which are not, and put our faith in the former. Bodhisattva Nagarjuna in his *Jūjūbibasha Ron* states: "Do not rely on treatises that distort the sutras; rely only on those that are faithful to the sutras." The Great Teacher T'ien-t'ai says: "That which accords with the sutras is to be accepted and heeded. But put no faith in anything that in word or meaning fails to do so."[65] The Great Teacher Dengyō says: "Depend upon the preachings of the Buddha and do not put faith in traditions handed down orally."[66] Enchin or Chishō Daishi says: "In transmitting the teachings, rely on the written words."[67]

To be sure, the leaders of the various sects whose opinions I have quoted above all base themselves on some groups of sutras and treatises in attempting to establish which teachings are the most superior. But these men all cling firmly to the doctrines of their own sect and perpetuate the erroneous views handed down from their predecessors, so that their judgments are characterized by "twisted interpretations and personal feel-

---

teachers who appear after the Buddha's death. They are classified into four ranks according to the levels of their understanding. In his *Hokke Gengi* T'ien-t'ai applied the fifty-two stages of bodhisattva practice to the four ranks. The persons of the first rank correspond to those who have not yet attained the first stage of security. The persons of the second rank are those in the ten stages of security. The persons of the third rank are those in the ten stages of practice and the ten stages of devotion. The persons of the fourth rank are those in the ten stages of development and the stage of *tōgaku* in which one has almost approached the enlightenment of the Buddha.

64. Nirvana Sutra.
65. *Hokke Gengi*, vol. 10.
66. *Hokke Shūku*.
67. *Juketsu Shū*.

ings." Their doctrines are no more than private opinions that have been dressed up and glorified.

The non-Buddhist sects of such men as Vatsiputriya and Vaipulya, which appeared in India after the Buddha's death, are even more wrong in their views and more cunning in their doctrines than their counterparts before the Buddha [because they borrowed ideas from Buddhism.] Similarly, since the introduction of Buddhism to China in the Later Han dynasty, non-Buddhist views and writings have become even more wrong and cunning than the pre-Buddhist writings of Confucianism that deal with the Three Rulers and Five Emperors of antiquity. Also the leaders of the Kegon, Hossō, Shingon and other sects, jealous of the orthodox teachings of the T'ien-t'ai sect, brazenly interpret the words of the true sutra [i.e., the Lotus Sutra] in such a way that they will accord with the provisional teachings.

Those who seek the truth of Buddhism, however, should reject such one-sided views, whether they are of their own sects or of other sects, and should not treat others with contempt.

In the *Hosshi* chapter of the Lotus Sutra, the Buddha says: "Among all the sutras I have preached, now preach, and will preach, this Lotus Sutra is the most difficult to believe and the most difficult to understand."

Miao-lo remarks: "Though other sutras may call themselves the king among sutras, there is none that announces itself as foremost among all the sutras preached in the past, now being preached, or to be preached in the future."[68] He also says: "Faced with this wonderful sutra that surpasses all those of past, present and future, there are those who persist in going astray. They commit the grave fault of slandering the Truth and for many long aeons are condemned to hell."[69]

Startled by these passages in the sutra and its commentaries, I examined all the sutras and the expositions and commentaries

68. *Hokke Mongu Ki*, vol. 7.
69. *Hokke Gengi Shakusen*, vol. 6.

of the various teachers, and found that my doubts and suspicions melted away. But now those foolish Shingon priests rely upon their *mudras* and *mantras* and believe that the Shingon sect is superior to the Lotus Sutra, simply because Jikaku Daishi and their other teachers have assured them that Shingon is superior. Their views are not worthy of discussion.

The *Mitsugon* Sutra says: "The *Jūji*,[70] *Kegon*, *Daiju*, *Jinzū*, *Shrimala* and the other sutras all derive from this sutra. Thus the *Mitsugon* Sutra is the greatest of all the sutras."

The *Daiun* Sutra states: "This sutra is the wheel-turning monarch among all sutras. Why is this? Because in this sutra is set forth the doctrine of the constancy of the Buddha nature as the true nature of all beings."

The *Rokuharamitsu* Sutra says: "All the correct teachings expounded by the countless Buddhas of the past and the eighty-four thousand wonderful laws that I have expounded are in this sutra and may as a whole be divided into five categories: 1. sutra; 2. vinaya; 3. abhidharma; 4. prajnaparamita; 5. dharani.[71] The works in these five collections will instruct and enlighten sentient beings. Among sentient beings there may be those who cannot accept and abide by the sutras, vinaya, abhidharma and prajnaparamita, or there may be sentient beings who commit various evil acts such as the four grave offenses,[72] the eight grave offenses,[73] or the five cardinal

70. *Jūji* Sutra: The *Jūji* chapter of the *Kegon* Sutra is regarded as a single sutra, called the *Jūji* Sutra.

71. Vinaya, abhidharma, prajnaparamita, dharani: Vinaya means the discipline, or monastic rules, one of the three divisions of the canon, or Tripitaka. Abhidharma are commentaries on Buddhist doctrines. Prajnaparamita is the highest of the six *paramitas* or the virtue of wisdom which enables one to attain enlightenment. Dharani are syllables which are supposed to possess esoteric powers.

72. Four grave offenses: Killing, stealing, carnality and lying. These four grave prohibitions are for monks, while the eight serious offenses are prohibitions for nuns.

73. Eight grave offenses: Besides the four grave offenses, (5) obscene contact with a male; (6) any sort of improper association (leading to carnality); (7) concealing the misbehavior (of an equal or inferior); (8) following a monk

sins that lead to the hell of incessant suffering, or slander the Mahayana sutras and disbelieve Buddhism itself. In order to wipe out such crimes, give rapid release to the offenders and allow them to enter into nirvana at once, I preached for their sake this collection of dharanis.

"These five divisions of the Dharma are compared to the flavors of milk, cream, curdled milk, butter and ghee respectively, with ghee as the finest. The division containing the dharanis compares to ghee. Ghee has the finest and most subtle flavor among the five substances enumerated above and is capable of curing various sicknesses and easing the minds and bodies of sentient beings. Similarly, the dharani division stands foremost among the five divisions of the teachings because it can do away with grave offenses."

The *Gejimmitsu* Sutra states: "At that time the Bodhisattva Shōgishō addressed the Buddha, saying, 'World-Honored One, in the first period of your teaching when you were in the Deer Park in Varanasi, for the sake of those who wished merely to embark upon the way of the *shōmon*, you expounded the doctrine of the four noble truths,[74] in this way turning the wheel of the Correct Law. This was a very wonderful thing, a very rare thing. No heavenly or human being in any of the countless worlds had ever been able to expound such a doctrine as this before. And yet the wheel of the Law that you turned at that time left room for improvement, left room for doubt. It was not yet final in meaning and offered ample opportunity for dispute.

"'Then, World-Honored One, in the second period of your teaching, for the sake of those who wished merely to practice the way of the Great Vehicle,[75] you taught that all phenomena

---

whose offense has been exposed.

74.   Four noble truths: Basic teachings of Hinayana Buddhism. The first is that all existence is suffering. The second is that suffering is caused by selfish craving. The third is that selfish craving must be eliminated. The fourth is that selfish craving can be eliminated by following the eightfold path.

75.   Great Vehicle: The way of bodhisattvas.

are without distinctive natures of their own, that there is no birth or death, that all things are basically in a state of quietude, and that the nature of beings as they exist constitutes nirvana. You turned the wheel of the Correct Law, although you did not reveal the whole truth. This was even more wonderful, an even rarer thing. But the wheel of the Law that you turned at that time left room for improvement, left room for doubt. It was not yet final in meaning and offered ample opportunity for dispute.

" 'Now, World-Honored One, in the third period of your teaching, for the sake of those who wish to practice the vehicle that saves all beings, you taught that all phenomena are without distinctive natures, that there is no birth or death, that all things are basically in a state of quietude, and that the nature of beings as they exist constitutes nirvana—and then you have taught that the "nature" you spoke of itself lacks anything that can be called a nature. You have turned the wheel of the Correct Law and expounded these doctrines in their perfect form. This is most wonderful, the rarest thing of all. This wheel of the Law that you have turned leaves no room for improvement, no room for doubt. It is truly complete and final in meaning and offers no opportunity for dispute.' "

The *Daihannya* Sutra says: "By listening to the laws of the secular world and Buddhism, all beings may through expedient means be brought to understand and embrace the profound principles of *prajna* or wisdom. And they will also come to understand and embrace the truth that, through *prajna*, all actions carried out in the present world can be seen to partake of the Dharma nature,[76] and that there is nothing whatsoever that is outside the Dharma nature."

The first volume of the *Dainichi* Sutra states, "Master of Secrets,[77] there is a Great Vehicle practice which arouses the

76.   Dharma nature: The real, unchanging nature innate in the phenomenal world.

77.   Master of Secrets: Kongōsatta. Dainichi Buddha is said to have transferred the law to Kongōsatta.

mind that is unrelated to things and leads one to understand
that all phenomena are without individual natures. Why is
this? Because in past times those who practiced this way were
able to observe the *alaya*-consciousness[78] and that which is
stored in it, and to realize that individual natures are illusory."

The same sutra also says, "Master of Secrets, these men in
this way cast aside the concept of egolessness and came to
realize that the mind exists in a realm of freedom and that the
individual mind has from the beginning never known birth [or
death]."

It also says: "*Kū* or emptiness is by nature removed from the
sense organs and their objects. It has no form nor boundaries,
but is a kind of void that transcends all theory. It represents the
ultimate in the absence of individual nature."

It also says, "The Buddha Dainichi or Mahavairochana
addressed the Master of Secrets, saying, 'Master of Secrets,
what is the meaning of enlightenment? It means to understand
one's own mind as it truly is.'"

The *Kegon* Sutra states, "Among the various beings of all the
different worlds, there are few who seek to practice the vehicle
of the *shōmon*. There are still fewer who seek that of the *engaku*,
and those who seek the Great Vehicle are extremely rare. To
seek the Great Vehicle is relatively easy to do, but to have faith
in the doctrines of this sutra is difficult in the extreme. And how
much more difficult is it to accept this sutra, keep its teachings
correctly in mind, practice them as directed, and understand
their true meaning.

"To take the major world system and hold it on the top of
your head without moving for the space of a kalpa is not such a
difficult thing to do. But to have faith in the doctrines of this
sutra is difficult in the extreme. For the space of a kalpa to offer
musical instruments to all the sentient beings who are as
countless as the dust particles of the major world system will

78. *Alaya*-consciousness: The deepest of the eight consciousnesses. It is
regarded as giving rise to all phenomena, knowledge and experience.

not gain you much merit. But to have faith in the doctrines of this sutra will gain you merit in great quantity. To hold ten Buddha lands in the palm of your hand and remain stationary in the midst of the air for the space of a kalpa is not so difficult to do. But to have faith in the doctrines of this sutra is difficult in the extreme. For the space of a kalpa to offer musical instruments to all the sentient beings who are as countless as the dust particles of those ten Buddha lands will not gain you much merit. But to have faith in the doctrines of this sutra will gain you merit in great quantity. For the space of a kalpa you may honor and give alms to the various Buddhas who are as countless as the dust particles of those Buddha lands. But if you can accept and abide by the doctrines of this chapter, you will gain vastly greater merit."

The Nirvana Sutra says, "Although belief in the various Mahayana sutras will bring inestimable merit, there is no way to describe how much greater is the merit gained by belief in this sutra. It is a hundred times, a thousand times, a billion times greater, greater in a way that is beyond calculation or simile. Men of devout faith, milk comes from the cow, cream is made from milk, curdled milk is made from cream, butter is made from curdled milk, and ghee is made from butter. Ghee is the finest of all. He who eats it will be cured of all illnesses, for all kinds of medicinal properties are contained in it. Men of devout faith, the Buddha is like this. The Buddha brought forth the twelve divisions of the sacred writings. From among these twelve divisions he brought forth the sutras,[79] from among the sutras he brought forth the Mahayana sutras, from the Mahayana sutras he brought forth the *Hannyaharamitsu* sutras, and from the *Hannyaharamitsu* sutras he brought forth the Nirvana Sutra. The Nirvana Sutra is comparable to ghee. Ghee here is a metaphor that stands for the Buddha nature [inherent within all beings]."

79.   Sutras: Here, one of the twelve divisions of the canon, the parts in prose style which discourse on doctrines.

When we compare these sutras that I have just quoted with the Lotus Sutra, the greatest of "past, present and future" with its "six difficult and nine easy acts," it stands out like the bright moon beside the tiny stars, or Mount Sumeru, highest of all mountains, beside the other eight mountains which surround it. And yet Ch'eng-kuan of the Kegon sect, Tz'u-en of the Hossō sect, Chia-hsiang of the Sanron sect, and Kōbō of the Shingon sect, all men who were believed to possess the Buddha eye of wisdom, did not understand the [above phrases of the] Lotus Sutra. How then could the ordinary scholars of the time, who appear to be quite blind, be expected to judge the difference between the Lotus Sutra and the other ones! This difference is as plain as black and white, or Mount Sumeru side by side with a mustard seed, yet these men go astray. It is hardly surprising, therefore, that they are also confused by the doctrines as vast as the sky derived from all the sutras. Unless one can perceive the relative profundity of the various writings, he cannot judge the worth of the doctrines that derive from them.

The teachings of the sutras often differ from volume to volume and must be understood in their proper order. Since it is difficult to judge the worth of these teachings, I will quote further passages and try to help the ignorant to understand.

When it comes to kings, there are great kings and minor kings, and in any matter whatsoever, there are parts and there is the whole. We have talked about the simile of the five flavors of milk, cream, curdled milk, butter and ghee, but we must understand when this simile is being applied to Buddhist teachings as a whole and when it is being applied to one part of those teachings.

The *Rokuharamitsu* Sutra teaches that sentient beings can attain enlightenment, but it says nothing about the enlightenment of insentient beings. And of course it mentions nothing about the doctrine that Shakyamuni Buddha attained enlightenment countless ages in the past.

The *Rokuharamitsu* Sutra claims that the dharanis are comparable to ghee, but they cannot in fact even compare with the Nirvana Sutra, which compares itself with ghee, much less with the theoretical and essential teachings of the Lotus Sutra. And yet Kōbō Daishi of Japan, misled by this sutra, assigned the Lotus Sutra to the fourth category, comparing it to the flavor of butter. If the so-called ghee of the dharanis cannot even match the so-called ghee of the Nirvana Sutra, then how could he possibly make such an obvious mistake? And yet he writes that "the teachers of China in their competition have stolen the ghee!,"[80] calling T'ien-t'ai and others thieves. And in a boastful vein he writes, "What a pity it is that the worthy men of ancient times were not able to taste this ghee!"[81]

I will point out the truth for the sake of my followers. If others do not choose to believe it now, they will eventually come to take faith after suffering from the bad karma they will create for themselves. By tasting a single drop, one can tell the flavor of the great ocean, and by observing a single flower in bloom, one can predict the advent of spring. One does not have to cross the water to far-off China, spend three years traveling to Eagle Peak in India,[82] enter the palace of the Dragon King the way Nagarjuna did, encounter the Bodhisattva Miroku the way Asanga did,[83] or be present at the two places and three assemblies when Shakyamuni preached the Lotus Sutra, in order to judge the relative merits of the Buddha's teachings. It is said that snakes can tell seven days in advance when a flood is going to occur. This is because they are akin to dragons, who make the rain fall. Crows can tell what lucky or unlucky events

80.   *Ben Kemmitsu Nikyō Ron.*
81.   Ibid.
82.   This refers to the Chinese monk Fa-hsien's journey to India. Deploring the lack of Buddhist scriptures in China, he left Ch'ang-an in 399 to seek them. He went overland to India and there learned Sanskrit and studied the sutras, writings on discipline and other Buddhist treatises. In 414 he returned by sea to China with many sutras and Buddha images.
83.   Asanga is said to have ascended to the Tushita Heaven and there inherited the teachings from Bodhisattva Miroku.

are going to take place throughout the course of a year. This is because in a past existence they were diviners. Birds are better at flying than human beings. And I, Nichiren, am better at judging the relative merits of sutras than Ch'eng-kuan of the Kegon sect, Chia-hsiang of the Sanron sect, Tz'u-en of the Hossō sect, and Kōbō of the Shingon sect. That is because I follow in the footsteps of the teachers T'ien-t'ai and Dengyō. But Ch'eng-kuan and the others, because they did not heed the teachings of T'ien-t'ai and Dengyō, could not avoid committing the error of slandering the truth.

I, Nichiren, am the richest man in all of present-day Japan. I have dedicated my life to the Lotus Sutra, and my name will be handed down in ages to come. If one is lord of the great ocean, then all the gods of the various rivers will obey him. If one is king of Mount Sumeru, then the gods of the various other mountains cannot help but serve him. If one can understand the doctrine of the "six difficult and nine easy acts" of the Lotus Sutra, then, without reading the other sutras, he can command the allegiance of all their Buddhas and bodhisattvas.

In addition to the three pronouncements of the Buddha in the *Hōtō* chapter of the Lotus Sutra, the *Devadatta* chapter contains two enlightening admonitions. [The first reveals that Devadatta will attain Buddhahood.] Devadatta was a man of incorrigible disbelief, of the type called *icchantika*, and yet it is predicted that he will in the future become a Buddha called Heavenly King. The forty volumes of the Nirvana Sutra state that all beings, including the *icchantika*, possess the Buddha nature, but the actual proof of that is found in this chapter of the Lotus Sutra. There are countless other persons such as the monk Sunakshatra[84] or King Ajatashatru who have committed the five cardinal sins and slandered the truth, but Devadatta is

---

84. Sunakshatra: A priest who devoted himself to Buddhist austerities and attained a limited form of enlightenment. But he was arrogant and thought he had mastered Buddhism. Later he turned to non-Buddhist teachings and discarded his faith in Buddhism. He opposed the Buddha, and is said to have fallen into hell alive.

cited as one example to represent all the countless others; he is the chief offender, and it is assumed that all lesser offenders will fare as he does. Thus it is revealed that all those who commit the five or the seven cardinal sins[85] or who slander the Truth or are inherently opposed to taking faith will become Buddhas like the Tathagatha Heavenly King. In the Lotus Sutra, poison turns into sweet dew, the finest of all flavors.

[The second admonition concerns the fact that the Dragon King's daughter attained Buddhahood.] When she attained Buddhahood, this does not mean simply that one person did so. It reveals the fact that all women will attain Buddhahood. In the various Hinayana sutras that were preached before the Lotus Sutra, it is denied that women can ever attain Buddhahood. In the Mahayana sutras other than the Lotus Sutra, it would appear that women can attain Buddhahood. But they may do so only after they have changed into some other form. It is not the kind of immediate attainment of Buddhahood that is encompassed in the doctrine of *ichinen sanzen*. Thus it is an attainment of Buddhahood in name but not in reality. The Dragon King's daughter is, as the phrase has it, "one example that stands for all the rest."[86] When the Dragon King's daughter attained Buddhahood, it opened up the possibility of attaining Buddhahood for all women of later ages.

Confucianism preaches filial piety and care for one's parents, but it is limited to this present life. It provides no way for one to assist one's parents in their future lives, and the Confucian sages and worthies are therefore sages and worthies in name only and not in reality. Brahmanism, though it recognizes the existence of past, present and future lives, similarly offers no means to assist one's parents to a better life in the future. Buddhism alone can do so, and thus it is the true way of sages

85.   Seven cardinal sins: The five cardinal sins (*see* entry in the Glossary) and two others: (6) killing a monk of high virtue and (7) killing a teacher.
86.   *Hokke Mongu Ki*, vol. 7.

and worthies. But in the Hinayana and Mahayana sutras preached before the Lotus Sutra, and in the sects based on these sutras, to gain salvation even for oneself is impossible. One can hardly hope to do anything for one's parents either. The possibility exists in theory but not in fact. Only with the preaching of the Lotus Sutra, in which the Dragon King's daughter attained Buddhahood, did it become evident that the attainment of Buddhahood was a possibility for all the mothers of the world. And when it was revealed that even an evil man such as Devadatta could attain Buddhahood, it became evident that Buddhahood was a possibility for all the fathers of the world. The Confucians have their *Classic of Filial Piety*, but the Lotus Sutra is the *Classic of Filial Piety* of Buddhism. This ends my discussion of the two admonitions contained in the *Devadatta* chapter.

Awed by the five proclamations of the Buddha made in the *Hōtō* and *Devadatta* chapters, the countless bodhisattvas promised the Buddha that they would propagate the Lotus Sutra, as described in the *Kanji* chapter. I shall hold up this passage of the sutra like a bright mirror so that all may see how the present-day leaders of the Zen, Ritsu and Nembutsu sects and their lay followers are guilty of slandering the Law.

On the twelfth day of the ninth month of last year, between the hours of the Rat and the Ox (11:00 P.M. to 3:00 A.M.), this person named Nichiren was beheaded.[87] It is his soul that has come to this island of Sado and, in the second month of the following year, snowbound, is writing this to send to his close followers. The description of the evil age in the *Kanji* chapter seems terrifying, but because I have dedicated myself to the True Law, I, Nichiren, have nothing to be terrified about. Those observing me will be awestruck. This treatise is the bright mirror of Shakyamuni, Tahō, and all the other Buddhas of the ten directions in which contemporary Japan is reflected.

87.   This refers to the Tatsunokuchi Persecution which occurred in 1271.

At the same time, it may be regarded as a keepsake from me.

In the *Kanji* chapter of the Lotus Sutra, the bodhisattvas, addressing the Buddha, say: "We beg you not to worry. After the Buddha has passed away, in an age of fear and evil we will preach far and wide. There will be many ignorant people who will curse and speak ill of us, and will attack us with swords and staves, but we will endure all these things. There will be monks in that evil age with perverse views and hearts that are fawning and crooked who will say they have attained what they have not attained, being proud and boastful in heart. Or there will be forest-dwelling monks wearing clothing of patched rags and living in retirement who will claim they are practicing the true Way, despising and looking down on the rest of mankind. Greedy for profit and nourishment, they will preach the Dharma to white-robed laymen and will be respected and revered by the world as though they were arhats who possess the six supernatural powers. These men with evil in their hearts, constantly thinking of worldly affairs, will borrow the name of forest-dwelling monks and take delight in proclaiming our faults . . . Constantly they will go about among the populace, seeking in this way to slander us. They will address the rulers, high ministers, Brahmans and great patrons of Buddhism as well as the other monks, slandering and speaking evil of us, saying, 'These are men of perverted views who preach the doctrines of heretical sects!' . . . In a muddied kalpa, in an evil age there will be many different things to fear. Demons will take possession of others and through them curse, revile and heap shame on us . . . The evil monks of that muddied age, failing to understand the Buddha's expedient means, how he preaches the Dharma in accord with what is appropriate, will confront us with foul language and angry frowns; again and again we will be banished."

Miao-lo, in the eighth volume of his *Hokke Mongu Ki*, comments as follows: "In this passage, three types of arrogance are cited. First there is a section that exposes persons of mistaken views. This represents the arrogance and presumption of the ordinary populace. Next there is a section that exposes the arrogance and presumption of certain members of the Buddhist clergy. Third is a section that exposes the arrogance and presumption of those who pretend to be sages. Of these three types of arrogance, the first can be endured. The second is more formidable than the first, and the third is the most formidable of all. This is because the second is harder to recognize for what it really is, and the third is even harder to recognize."

Priest Chih-tu writes in the *Tōshun*: "First, in the section dealing with the 'ignorant people,' there is a verse telling how the votaries of the Lotus Sutra must endure evils inflicted by the body, mouth and mind of their opponents. This refers to evil men among the ordinary populace. Next, in the section on the 'monks in that evil age,' there is a verse that deals with arrogant members of the Buddhist clergy. Third, in the section on the 'forest-dwelling monks,' there are three verses dealing with members of the clergy who pretend to be sages and use their position to act as leaders of all the other evil persons." And the same text goes on to say: "The section that begins 'Constantly they will go about among the populace' describes how these men will appeal to the government authorities, slandering the Law and defaming its supporters."

In the ninth volume of the Nirvana Sutra we read: "Men of devout faith, there are persons called *icchantika*, persons of incorrigible disbelief. They pretend to be arhats, living in deserted places and speaking slanderously of the Mahayana sutras. When ordinary people see them, they suppose that they are all true arhats and speak of them as great bodhisattvas." It also says: "At that time, this sutra will be preached throughout the continent of Jambudvipa. In that age there will be evil monks who will do violence to this sutra and destroy its unity, losing 'the color, scent and flavor' of the True Law that it contains. These evil men will read and recite this sutra, but they will ignore and put aside the profound and vital principles that the Buddha has expounded in it and replace them with ornate rhetoric and meaningless talk. They will tear off the first part of the sutra and stick it on at the end, tear off the end and put it at the beginning, put the end and the beginning in the middle and the middle at the beginning or the end. You must understand that these evil monks are the companions of the devil."

The six-volume *Hatsunaion* Sutra[88] states: "There are also *icchantika* who resemble arhats but who commit evil deeds. There are also arhats who resemble *icchantika* but display merciful hearts. The *icchantika* who look like arhats spend their time slandering the Mahayana sutras to the populace. The arhats who look like *icchantika*, on the other hand, are critical of the *shōmon* and go about preaching Mahayana doctrines. They address the populace, saying, 'You and I are all bodhisattvas. Why? Because each and every one of us possesses the Buddha nature.' But the populace will probably call such men *icchantika*."

In the Nirvana Sutra, the Buddha speaks as follows: "After I have passed away and after the Former Day of the Law has ended and the Middle Day of the Law has begun, there will be monks who will give the appearance of abiding by the rules of monastic discipline. But they will scarcely ever read or recite the sutras, and instead will crave all kinds of food and drink to nourish their bodies. Though they wear the robes of a monk, they will go about searching for alms like so many huntsmen, spying sharply and stalking softly. They will be like a cat on the prowl for mice. And constantly they will reiterate these words: 'I have attained the state of arhat!' Outwardly they will seem to be wise and good, but within they will harbor greed and jealousy. [And when they are asked to preach the Dharma,] they will conceal it, like Brahmans who have taken a vow of

88. Six-volume *Hatsunaion* Sutra: One of the Chinese versions of the Nirvana Sutra, translated by Fa-hsien.

silence. They are not true monks—they merely have the appearance of monks. Consumed by their erroneous views, they slander the True Law."

In the light of the sun and moon that are the Lotus and Nirvana sutras, or in the bright mirrors that are the writings of Miao-lo and Chih-tu, we can discern without a trace of doubt the ugly faces of the people of Zen, Ritsu and Nembutsu in present-day Japan. The *Kanji* chapter of the Lotus Sutra says: "After the Buddha has passed away, in an age of fear and evil," and the *Anrakugyō* chapter says: "In the evil age hereafter," "in the latter age," and "in the latter age when the Law is on the point of disappearing." The *Fumbetsu Kudoku* chapter says: "In the evil-filled Latter Day of the Law"; the *Yakuō* chapter says, "In the fifth five hundred years," etc. The *Kanzetsu* chapter of the Dharmaraksha translation of the Lotus Sutra says, "In the latter age" and "in the latter age to come." The same type of language is found in the translation of the Lotus Sutra made by Jnanagupta and Dharmagupta. T'ien-t'ai states: "In the Middle Day of the Law, the three sects of southern China and the seven sects of northern China are the enemies of the Lotus Sutra."[89] And Dengyō states: "At the end of the Middle Day of the Law, the scholars of the six Nara sects are the enemies of the Lotus Sutra."[90]

In the time of T'ien-t'ai and Dengyō, the three types of enemies mentioned above had not yet appeared. But we must recall that when Shakyamuni Buddha and Tahō Buddha sat side by side in the Treasure Tower like the sun and the moon and the Buddhas who were emanations of Shakyamuni had come from the ten directions and were ranged beneath the trees like so many stars, then it was said that, after the thousand years of the Former Day of the Law and the thousand years of the

89. Source unknown, possibly a rephrasing of the *Hokke Gengi*, vol. 10.
90. Source unknown, possibly a rephrasing of the *Hokke Shūku* or the *Kenkai Ron*.

Middle Day of the Law, at the beginning of the Latter Day of the Law, there would be three types of enemies of the Lotus Sutra. How could this pronouncement made by the eighty myriads of millions of nayutas of bodhisattvas have been an empty or a false prediction?

It is now some twenty-two hundred years since the Buddha passed away. Even if it were possible to point straight at the earth and miss it, if the flowers were to cease blooming in spring, still I am certain that these three powerful enemies are bound to appear in the land of Japan. If so, then who is to be numbered among the three enemies? And who is to be accounted a votary of the Lotus Sutra? It is a troubling question. Are we—I and my disciples—to be numbered among the three enemies? Or are we to be numbered among the votaries of the Lotus Sutra? It is a troubling question.

In the twenty-fourth year of the reign of King Chao, the fourth ruler of the Chou dynasty in ancient China (trad. date 1028 B.C.), on the night of the eighth day of the fourth month, a five-colored light spread across the sky from north to south until all was as bright as noon. The earth shook in six different ways, and though no rain fell, the rivers and streams, wells and ponds overflowed with water. All the trees and grasses bloomed and bore fruit. It was a wondrous happening indeed. King Chao was greatly alarmed, but the Grand Historian Su Yu performed divinations and announced, "A sage has been born in the western region." "What will become of our country?" asked King Chao, to which Su Yu replied, "It will suffer no harm. One thousand years from now, the words of this sage will be brought to this country and will bring benefit to all living beings." Su Yu was a scholar of non-Buddhist texts who had not in the slightest degree freed himself from illusions, and yet he was able to know what would happen a thousand years in the future. And just as he predicted, 1,015 years after the Buddha's passing, in the reign of Emperor Ming, the second ruler of the Later Han dynasty, in the tenth year of the Yung-p'ing era (A.D. 67), the doctrines of Buddhism were introduced to China.[91]

On quite a different level is the prediction I have described above that was made by the various bodhisattvas in the presence of Shakyamuni Buddha, Tahō Buddha, and the Buddhas from the ten directions that were emanations of Shakyamuni Buddha. In view of this prediction, how could the three types of enemies of the Lotus Sutra help but be present in Japan today?

In the *Fuhōzō* Sutra, the Buddha is recorded as saying: "After my passing, during the one thousand years of the Former Day of the Law, there will be twenty-four persons in succession[92] who will spread abroad the True Law as I have taught it." Mahakashyapa and Ananda were contemporaries of the Buddha and so we will pass them over. But a hundred years later there was the monk Parshva,[93] six hundred years later the Bodhisattva Ashvaghosha, and seven hundred years later the Bodhisattva Nagarjuna, along with others, all appearing just as the prophecy had said they would.

If so, how could the prophecy in the *Kanji* chapter of the Lotus Sutra be in vain? If this prophecy is at variance with the truth, then the whole Lotus Sutra is at variance with the truth.

91.   The introduction of Buddhism to China in the tenth year of the Yung-p'ing era is described in the *History of the Later Han*.

92.   Twenty-four persons in succession: The successors of Shakyamuni Buddha who appeared in the Former Day and propagated the Buddha's teachings. They are listed in the *Fuhōzō* Sutra or *Fuhōzō Innenden* (The History of the Buddha's Successors), which says that in the days of Aryasinha, the twenty-fourth successor, Buddhism in India was destroyed by King Mirakutsu and the succession ceased. *See* Twenty-four successors in the Glossary.

93.   Parshva: The tenth of the Buddha's twenty-four successors. According to the *Record of the Western Regions*, he was born in northern India and renounced secular life at the age of eight. In obedience to King Kanishka's orders, he summoned four hundred and ninety-nine monks and compiled the Buddhist sutras in Kashmir. This is known as the fourth assembly to compile the Buddha's teachings.

Then the prediction that Shariputra will in the future become the Flower Light Buddha and that Mahakashyapa will become the Light Bright Buddha are all mere lies. In that case, the teachings put forward in the sutras that preceded the Lotus Sutra must be correct, and Shariputra and the other *shōmon* are destined never to achieve Buddhahood. If it is true that one should give alms to a dog or a jackal before one gives them to a *shōmon* such as Ananda, then where do we stand?

In the passage from the *Kanji* chapter of the Lotus Sutra that I quoted earlier, the text mentioned three groups of people, saying first that "There will be many ignorant people," referring second to "monks in that evil age," and third to "monks in their clothing of patched rags." The first category of ignorant people are the important lay believers who support monks in the second and third categories. Accordingly, the Great Teacher Miao-lo, commenting on the persons in the first group, says they represent the arrogance and presumption of "the ordinary populace." And the Priest Chih-tu describes how they will "appeal to the government authorities" in their slanders of the Law and its supporters.

Concerning the second group of enemies of the Lotus Sutra, the sutra says: "There will be monks in that evil age with perverse views and hearts that are fawning and crooked who will say they have attained what they have not attained, being proud and boastful in heart."

Similarly, the Nirvana Sutra says: "In that age there will be evil monks . . . These evil men will read and recite this sutra, but they will ignore and put aside the profound and vital principles that the Buddha has expounded in it."

The *Maka Shikan* says: "If one lacks faith in the Lotus Sutra, he will object that it pertains to the lofty realm of the sages, something far beyond the capacity of his own wisdom to comprehend. If one lacks wisdom, he will become puffed up with arrogance and will claim to be the equal of the Buddha."

We see an example of this in the statement by the Priest Tao-ch'o: "The second reason for rejecting the Lotus Sutra is that its principles are so profound that few can comprehend them."[94] In a similar vein, Hōnen says: "Religious practices other than the Nembutsu do not accord with people's capacities. They are not appropriate for the times."[95]

To combat such views, Miao-lo states in the tenth volume of his *Hokke Mongu Ki*: "Probably the reason people are mistaken in their understanding of this matter is that they fail to realize how great is the benefit gained even by a beginner in the practice of the Lotus Sutra. They assume that benefit is reserved for those who are far advanced in practice and disparage the efforts of beginners. Therefore I will now demonstrate that even a little practice will gain profound benefit, and thereby show how great is the power of the Lotus Sutra."

Similarly, the Great Teacher Dengyō declares: "The Former and Middle Days are almost over, and the Latter Day is near at hand. Now indeed is the time when the One Vehicle expounded in the Lotus Sutra will prove how perfectly it fits the capacities of all people. How do we know this is true? Because the *Anrakugyō* chapter of the Lotus Sutra states that, 'In the latter age when the Law is on the point of disappearing,' [the Lotus Sutra will be expounded far and wide]."[96] And Eshin[97] says: "Throughout all Japan, all people share the same capacity to attain Buddhahood through the perfect teachings [of the Lotus Sutra]."[98]

Now which opinion should we believe, that of Tao-ch'o and Hōnen or that of Dengyō and Eshin? The former has not a scrap of evidence in the sutras to support it. The latter is based firmly upon the Lotus Sutra.

94. *Anraku Shū*.
95. *Senchaku Shū*.
96. *Shugo Kokkai Shō*.
97. Eshin (942–1017): A priest of the Tendai sect. He wrote the *Ōjō Yōshū* and in this work emphasized the need to chant the name of Amida Buddha. He influenced Hōnen. Later he recanted and wrote the *Ichijō Yōketsu*, in which he asserted the supremacy of the Lotus Sutra.
98. *Ichijō Yōketsu*.

Moreover, the Great Teacher Dengyō of Mount Hiei is honored by priests throughout Japan as the master of ordination into the priesthood. How could any priests turn their hearts toward a person like Hōnen, who is possessed by the Devil of the Sixth Heaven, and reject the Great Teacher Dengyō, who established the very ordination ceremonies that these priests themselves underwent? If Hōnen was a truly wise man, why did he not, in his *Senchaku Shū*,[99] mention the passages of explanation by Dengyō and Eshin such as I have quoted above, and resolve the contradiction? He did not do so, because he is the kind of person who hides the teachings of others. When the Lotus Sutra speaks of the second type of enemy, "monks of that evil age," it is referring to men like Hōnen who disregard the precepts and hold perverse views.

The Nirvana Sutra says: "We call ourselves men of perverse views." Miao-lo explains this by saying: "The Buddha is referring to the three types of teachings[100] that preceded the Lotus Sutra and saying that they all may be called perverse views."[101] And the *Maka Shikan* states: "The Nirvana Sutra says, 'Until the time of the Lotus Sutra, we call ourselves men of perverse views.' Perverseness is bad, is it not?"

In the *Guketsu*, Miao-lo states: "Perverseness is bad. Therefore we must understand that only the perfect teachings [which reveal the Truth] are good. But there are two meanings involved here. That which accords with the truth is to be accounted good and that which goes against the truth is to be accounted bad. This is the meaning from the relative standpoint. At the same time, attachment is bad and transcending it is good. From both the relative and absolute points of view, we should abandon all that is bad. To be attached to the perfect teachings [of the three teachings that precede the Lotus Sutra] is

99. *Senchaku Shū*: *See* p. 17, footnote 38.
100. Three types of teachings: *Zōkyō*, *tsūgyō* and *bekkyō*, which indicate the provisional teachings. *See* p. 104, footnote 90.
101. A rephrasing of the *Hokke Gengi Shakusen*, vol. 17.

bad, and to be attached to the lower teachings is of course even worse."

The goods and evils of the non-Buddhist creeds, when compared with the Hinayana sutras, all represent a bad way. Similarly, the good ways expounded in the Hinayana sutras, and in the sutras of the four inferior flavors and the three types of teachings, when compared with the Lotus Sutra, are all perverse and bad. The Lotus Sutra alone represents the true good. The perfection of the sutras preached before the Lotus Sutra is a relative perfection. Compared to absolute perfection, it must still be counted as bad. To hold fast to the three types of teachings expounded before the Lotus Sutra is still to follow a bad way. Even one who practices the highest principles taught in the sutras of that period is still following a bad way. How much more so, then, is someone who would take a work of insignificant doctrine such as the *Kammuryōju* Sutra, which cannot compare even with the *Kegon* and *Hannya* sutras, and substitute it for the Lotus Sutra? Though such a person borrows ideas from the Lotus, he urges people to "discard, close, ignore and abandon" the Lotus and devote themselves to the Nembutsu. That is what Hōnen and his disciples and lay supporters do, and they deserve to be called slanderers of the True Law, do they not?

The *Hōtō* chapter of the Lotus Sutra says of the assembly of Shakyamuni Buddha, Tahō Buddha and the various Buddhas of the ten directions, "To make certain that the Law will endure forever, they have come to this place." And yet Hōnen and the other practitioners of the Nembutsu in Japan declare that "In the Latter Day of the Law, the Lotus Sutra will disappear before the Nembutsu." Are such persons not the enemies of Shakyamuni, Tahō and the other Buddhas?

Concerning the third group of enemies of the Lotus Sutra, the sutra says: "Or there will be forest-dwelling monks wearing clothing of patched rags and living in retirement . . . and they will preach the Dharma to white-robed laymen and will be respected and revered by the world as though they were arhats who possess the six supernatural powers." And the six-volume *Hatsunaion* Sutra states: "There are also *icchantika* who resemble arhats but who commit evil deeds. There are also arhats who resemble *icchantika* but display merciful hearts. The *icchantika* who look like arhats spend their time slandering the Mahayana sutras to the populace. The arhats who look like *icchantika*, on the other hand, are critical of the *shōmon* and go about preaching Mahayana doctrines. They address the populace, saying, 'You and I are all bodhisattvas. Why? Because each and every one of us possesses the Buddha nature.' But the populace will probably call such men *icchantika*."

The Nirvana Sutra says: "After I have passed away . . . [After the Former Day of the Law has ended and] the Middle Day of the Law has begun, there will be monks who will give the appearance of abiding by the rules of monastic discipline. But they will scarcely ever read or recite the sutras, and instead will crave all kinds of food and drink to nourish their bodies. Though they wear the robes of a monk, they will go about searching for alms like so many huntsmen, spying sharply and stalking softly. They will be like a cat on the prowl for mice. And constantly they will reiterate these words: 'I have attained the state of arhat!' Outwardly they will seem to be wise and good, but within they will harbor greed and jealousy. [And when they are asked to preach the Dharma,] they will conceal it, like Brahmans who have taken a vow of silence. They are not true monks—they merely have the appearance of monks. Consumed by their erroneous views, they slander the True Law."

Miao-lo writes concerning persons of this type: "The third [group] is the most formidable of all. This is because the second is harder to recognize for what it really is, and the third is even harder to recognize." And the *Tōshun* states: "Third, in the section on the 'forest-dwelling monks,' there are three verses dealing with members of the clergy who pretend to be sages and use their positions to act as leaders of all the other evil persons."

As for these "members of the clergy who pretend to be sages and use their positions to act as leaders of all the other evil persons"—where in Japan at the present time should we look for them? On Mount Hiei? In Onjō-ji temple? In Tō-ji temple[102] in Kyoto? In the temples of Nara? In the Zen temple Kennin-ji[103] in Kyoto, or the Zen temples Jufuku-ji and Kenchō-ji[104] in Kamakura? We must examine this carefully. Do the words refer to the monks of Enryaku-ji on Mount Hiei who wear helmets on their heads and are dressed in armor? Do they refer to the monks of Onjō-ji who have consecrated their bodies to the Dharma and yet wear suits of mail and carry weapons? But these men do not resemble the forest-dwelling monks "wearing clothing of patched rags and living in retirement" that are described in the sutra, nor do they seem to be the type who are "respected and revered by the world as though they were arhats who possess the six supernatural powers." They are not like the men of the third group who, as Miao-lo said, "are even harder to recognize." It would appear, therefore, that the words refer to men such as Shō-ichi[105] of Kyoto and Ryōkan of Kamakura. Even if they are so denounced, it does not do to hate others. If one has eyes, one should examine the sutra texts and compare one's behavior with them.

The first volume of the *Maka Shikan* states: "There has never been anything to compare to the brightness and serenity of *shikan* style meditation." In the first volume of the *Guketsu*, Miao-lo writes: "From the time when Emperor Ming of the

102. Hiei, Onjō-ji temple and Tō-ji temple: *See* p. 14, footnotes 31, 32.
103. Kennin-ji: A head temple of the Rinzai school of Zen.
104. Jufuku-ji and Kenchō-ji: Temples of the Kenchō-ji branch of the Rinzai school. Kenchō-ji is the head temple of that branch.
105. Shōichi: The founder of Tōfuku-ji temple of the Rinzai school. He studied Zen in China and, after returning to Japan, propagated its teachings in the Imperial court.

Han dynasty dreamt of the Buddha[106] down to the Ch'en dynasty, when the Great Teacher T'ien-t'ai lived, there were many who participated in the Zen sect and received the robe and bowl[107] that were handed down." The *Fuchū*[108] explains this by saying: "The handing down of the robe and bowl refers to the succession of Zen patriarchs from Bodhidharma on down."

In volume five of the *Maka Shikan*, T'ien-t'ai says: "There is a type called Zen men, but their leaders and disciples are blind [to the truth] and lame [in practice], and both leaders and disciples will fall into hell." In the seventh volume, we read: "[I have set forth ten ways to understand and propagate the Dharma.] But the ninth way has nothing in common with the ordinary priests of the world who concentrate on the written word, nor does it have anything in common with the Zen masters who concentrate on practice. Some Zen masters give all their attention to meditation, which is one of the ten ways in my system. But their meditation is shallow and false, totally lacking in the rest of the ten ways. This is no empty assertion. Worthy men of later ages who have eyes to see will understand the truth of what I say."

In the seventh volume of the *Guketsu*, Miao-lo comments on this as follows: " 'Priests who concentrate on the written word' refers to men who gain no inner sight or understanding through meditation but concern themselves only with the externals of the Dharma. 'Zen masters [who] give all their attention to meditation' refers to men who do not learn how to attain the true realm and wisdom of meditation but fix their

106. This event refers to the introduction of Buddhism to China. Emperor Ming was the second emperor of the Later Han dynasty.
107. Robe and bowl: A monk's most important possessions. They symbolize that he has received the precepts. To "receive the robe and bowl" means to inherit the teachings of Zen.
108. *Fuchū*: Ts'ung-i's annotation of T'ien-t'ai's three major works (the *Maka Shikan*, the *Hokke Gengi* and the *Hokke Mongu*).

minds on the mere techniques of breath control. They are incapable of cutting off the basic delusions. 'Some Zen masters give all their attention to meditation, which is one of the ten ways,' means that, for the sake of discussion, T'ien-t'ai gives them a certain degree of recognition, but in the end he withdraws it, concluding that their meditation never leads to true understanding. The Zen men in the world today value only empty meditation and have no familiarity with doctrinal teachings. They put together the eight wrong views[109] and the eight worldly desires[110] and talk about the Buddha as being sixteen feet in height.[111] They lump together the five components[112] and the three poisons and call them the eight wrong views. They equate the six sense organs with the six supernatural powers and the four elements[113] with the four noble truths. To interpret the sutras in such an arbitrary manner is to be guilty of the greatest falsehood. Such nonsense is not even worth discussing."

The seventh volume of the *Maka Shikan* states: "In the past, the Zen master [Bodhidharma] of Yeh and Lo became renowned throughout the length and breadth of China. When he arrived, people gathered around him from all directions like clouds, and when he left for another place, they formed a great

109.   Eight wrong views: The opposite of the Eightfold Path. The eight wrong views are: 1) wrong view; 2) wrong thinking; 3) wrong speech; 4) wrong action; 5) wrong way of life; 6) wrong endeavor; 7) wrong memory; and 8) wrong meditation. These are regarded as the causes of human suffering.

110.   Eight worldly desires: Another term for the eight winds: prosperity, decline, disgrace, honor, praise, censure, suffering and pleasure. People are inclined to be carried away by these eight winds.

111.   The height of the Buddha in his property-of-action aspect (*ōjin*) is considered to be sixteen feet. This height is also a standard for statues of the Buddha.

112.   Five components: First of the three realms of existence—form, perception, conception, volition and consciousness.

113.   Four elements: Earth, water, fire and wind. The ancient Indians believed that all matter is composed of these four elements. They stand, respectively, for the qualities of solidity, moisture, heat and motion.

crowd along the roads. But what profit did they derive from all this bustle and excitement? All of them regretted what they had done when they were on their deathbed."[114]

In the seventh volume of the *Guketsu*, Miao-lo comments: "The text speaks of the 'Zen master of Yeh and Lo.' Yeh is in Hsiang-chou and was the capital of the Ch'i and Wei dynasties. [Bodhidharma,] the founder of Zen, caused Buddhism to flourish there and converted the people of the region. The Great Teacher T'ien-t'ai, out of deference to the people of his time, refrains from naming [Bodhidharma] specifically. Lo refers to the city of Lo-yang."

The six-volume *Hatsunaion* Sutra says: "The extreme is impossible to see. That is, the extremely evil deeds done by the *icchantika* are all but impossible to perceive." Or, as Miao-lo has said, "The third [group] is the most formidable of all. This is because . . . the third is even harder to recognize."

Those without eyes, those with only one eye, and those with distorted vision cannot see these three types of enemies of the Lotus Sutra who have appeared at the beginning of the Latter Day of the Law. But those who have attained a portion of the Buddha eye can see who they are. "They will address the rulers, high ministers, Brahmans and great patrons of Buddhism," says the *Kanji* chapter. And Priest Chih-tu comments in his *Tōshun*: "These men will appeal to the government authorities, slandering the Law and defaming its supporters."

In the past, when the Middle Day of the Law was coming to an end, Gomyō,[115] Shūen[116] and other monks presented

---

114.   This sentence may also be interpreted as, "When Bodhidharma was on his deathbed, they all regretted what they had done."

115.   Gomyō (750–834): A priest of the Hossō sect. He first entered Konkōmyō-ji temple and studied Buddhism under Priest Dōkō. Thereafter, he studied the Consciousness-Only doctrine. In 819 in his petition to the throne, Gomyō condemned Dengyō for seeking permission from the emperor to construct a Mahayana ordination center. He competed with Dengyō in praying for rain, but was unsuccessful.

116.   Shūen (771–835): A priest of the Hossō sect. He was famed as the

petitions to the throne in which they slandered the Great
Teacher Dengyō. Now, at the beginning of the Latter Day of
the Law, Ryōkan, Nen'a[117] and others drew up false documents and presented them to the shogunate. Are they not to be
counted among the third group of enemies of the Lotus Sutra?

Nowadays the followers of the Nembutsu address the
"rulers, high ministers, Brahmans and great patrons of Buddhism" who support the Tendai sect, saying, "The doctrines of
the Lotus Sutra are so profound that we can barely comprehend them. The Dharma it teaches is extremely deep; our
capabilities are extremely shallow." Just as the *Maka Shikan*
says, "They object that it pertains to the lofty realm of the
sages, something far beyond the capacity of their own wisdom
to comprehend."

Again, the men of the Zen sect say: "The Lotus Sutra is a
finger pointing at the moon, but the Zen sect is the moon itself.
Once one has the moon, of what use is the finger? Zen is the
mind of the Buddha. The Lotus Sutra is the word of the
Buddha. After the Buddha had finished preaching the Lotus
Sutra and all the other sutras, he took a single flower and gave it
to Mahakashyapa alone, whereby the disciple understood its
meaning.[118] As a symbol of this tacit communication, he also
presented Mahakashyapa with his own robe, which has been

---

most learned priest in Kōfuku-ji temple. In 802, he debated with Dengyō and
was defeated. Together with Gomyō, he submitted a petition to the throne
opposing Dengyō's plan to construct a Mahayana ordination center on Mt.
Hiei.

117.   Nen'a (1199–1287): The founder of the Chinzei school of the Jōdo
sect. Also called Ryōchū, he is regarded as the third patriarch of the Jōdo sect,
after Hōnen and Benchō.

118.   This Zen story is related in the *Daibontennō-mombutsu-ketsugi* Sutra.
When the Buddha silently held up a flower before the assembly on Eagle Peak,
no one could comprehend the meaning of this gesture. Mahakashyapa alone
understood and smiled faintly. Thereby the Buddha transferred his enlightenment to Mahakashyapa, an enlightenment independent of any sutra. The Zen
sect regards this incident as the origin of its sect. However, the above-
mentioned sutra is said to be an apocryphal work. The Zen sect also asserts that
the enlightenment was handed down from Mahakashyapa to Ananda, from

handed down from one to another by the twenty-eight patriarchs of Indian Zen and so on to the sixth patriarch of Chinese Zen." For many years now, the whole country has been intoxicated and deceived by this kind of absurd nonsense.

Again, the eminent monks of the Tendai and Shingon sects, though nominally representatives of their respective sects, are in fact quite ignorant of their teachings. In the depths of their greed and out of fear of the courtiers and warriors, they lend their support to the assertions of the Nembutsu and Zen followers and sing their praises. Long ago, Tahō Buddha and the various Buddhas who were emanations of Shakyamuni Buddha acknowledged their allegiance to the Lotus Sutra, saying, "We will make certain that the Law will long endure." But now the eminent leaders of the Tendai sect obsequiously testify that "the doctrines of the Lotus Sutra are so profound that one can barely comprehend them." As a result, the Lotus Sutra exists in Japan today in name only—there is not a single person who actually practices it and attains enlightenment. Who can be called a votary of the Lotus Sutra? We see monks who burn down temples and pagodas and are exiled in numbers too great to count. And we see numerous eminent monks who fawn on the courtiers and warriors and are hated for it by the people. Can men such as these be called the votaries of the Lotus Sutra?

Because the predictions of the Buddha are not false, the country is already full of the three types of enemies of the Lotus Sutra. And yet, as though to belie the golden words of the Buddha, there seems to be no votary of the Lotus Sutra as was predicted would appear. How can this be?

But let us consider. Who is it who is cursed and spoken ill of by the populace? Who is the monk who is attacked with

---

Ananda to Shanakavasa, and so on to Bodhidharma, the twenty-eighth patriarch of Indian Zen. Bodhidharma became the founder of Zen in China and transferred his enlightenment to Hui-k'o, the second patriarch of Chinese Zen. The sixth patriarch of Chinese Zen in the quotation refers to Hui-neng.

swords and staves? Who is the monk who, because of the Lotus Sutra, is accused in petitions submitted to the courtiers and warriors? Who is the monk who is "again and again banished," as the Lotus Sutra predicted? Who else in Japan besides Nichiren could fit this description?

But I, Nichiren, am not a votary of the Lotus Sutra, because, contrary to the prediction, Heaven has cast me aside. Who, then, in this present age will be the votary of the Lotus Sutra and fulfill the prophecy of the Buddha?

The Buddha and Devadatta are like a form and its shadow— in lifetime after lifetime, they are never separated. Prince Shōtoku and his archenemy Mononobe no Moriya[119] appeared at the same time, like the blossom and the seed pod of the lotus. If there exists a votary of the Lotus Sutra, then the three types of enemies are bound to exist as well. The three types of enemies have already appeared. Who, then, is the votary of the Lotus Sutra? Let us seek him out and make him our teacher. As the Lotus Sutra says, to find such a person is as rare as for a one-eyed turtle[120] to chance upon a piece of driftwood with a hole just the right size to hold him.

Question: It would surely appear that the three types of enemies are present today, but there is no votary of the Lotus Sutra. If I were to say that you are the votary of the Lotus Sutra, then the following serious discrepancies would become apparent. The *Anrakugyō* chapter of the Lotus Sutra says: "The young sons of the heavenly deities will wait on and serve him. Swords and staves will not touch him, and poison will have no power to harm him." And the same passage continues: "If men curse and speak evil of him, their mouths will be closed and

119.   When Buddhism was introduced to Japan, Mononobe no Moriya, one of the highest ministers, opposed it, while Prince Shōtoku and Soga no Umako, who was also one of the highest ministers, accepted it. In addition, Mononobe no Moriya battled with Soga no Umako over the issue of the succession to the Imperial throne and was defeated.

120.   Lotus Sutra, chap. 27. The story of the one-eyed turtle emphasizes the difficulty of encountering Buddhism. *See also* One-eyed turtle in the Glossary.

stopped up." The *Yakusōyu* chapter says: "They [who have heard the Law] will enjoy peace and security in this life and good circumstances in the next." The *Dharani* chapter says that those who do harm to a votary of the Lotus Sutra will "have their heads split into seven pieces like the branches of the *arijaka* tree." Also, the *Kambotsu* chapter states: "[He who honors the Lotus Sutra] will receive his reward of good fortune in the present age." And it adds: "If anyone shall see a person who embraces this sutra and try to expose the faults or evils of that person, he will in the present age be afflicted with white leprosy, whether what he speaks is the truth or not." [How do you explain these discrepancies?]

Answer: These doubts of yours are most opportune. I will take the occasion to clear up the points that puzzle you. The *Fukyō* chapter of the Lotus Sutra says: "[Bodhisattva Fukyō] was spoken evil of and cursed." And again: "They would beat him with sticks and staves, and stone him with rocks and tiles." The Nirvana Sutra says: "They will be killed or harmed." The *Hosshi* chapter of the Lotus Sutra states: "Hatred and jealousy abound even during the lifetime of the Buddha."

The Buddha encountered acts of hostility, known as the nine great persecutions, such as being wounded in the foot by Devadatta, and yet he was a votary of the Lotus Sutra, was he not? And Bodhisattva Fukyō, who, as we have seen above, was cursed and beaten—was he not a votary of the One Vehicle of the Lotus Sutra? Maudgalyayana was beaten to death by a Brahman called Chikujō [literally meaning a bamboo staff] sometime after the Lotus Sutra predicted that he would attain Buddhahood in a future life. Bodhisattva Kanadeva was the fourteenth patriarch in the lineage of Buddhism in India, and Aryasinha was the twenty-fifth patriarch, and both men were murdered. Were these men not votaries of the Lotus Sutra? The Chinese monk Chu Tao-sheng[121] was banished to Mount

---

121.   Chu Tao-sheng (d. 434): Chinese monk who insisted that even a man of disbelief has the potential to attain Buddhahood, for which he was banished

Su, and the monk Fa-tao was branded on the face and exiled south of the Yangtze River. Were these men not upholders of the One Vehicle of the Lotus Sutra? Among scholars of secular learning, both Po Chü-i[122] and Sugawara no Michizane,[123] who was posthumously revered as the god Tenjin of Kitano, were exiled to distant places, and yet were they not worthy men?

If we consider the meaning of these examples, we must note the following points. Those who did not commit the error of slandering the Lotus Sutra in their previous existences will become votaries of the Lotus Sutra in their present lives. If such persons should be subjected to persecution under a false charge of having committed worldly offenses, then those who persecute them ought to suffer some kind of immediate retribution. It should be like the case of the ashuras who shoot arrows at Taishaku or the garuda birds that try to eat the dragon kings of the Icy Lake, but who both invariably suffer injury themselves instead. And yet the Great Teacher T'ien-t'ai says: "The ills and pains I suffer at present are all due to causes in the past, and the meritorious deeds that I do in my present life will be rewarded in the future."[124] Likewise, the *Shinjikan* Sutra states: "If you want to understand the causes that existed in the past, look at the results as they are manifested in the present. And if you want to understand what results will be

---

from the community of believers. Later, when the Nirvana Sutra was translated into Chinese, his assertion was verified.

122. Po Chü-i (772–846): A poet and official of the T'ang dynasty in China. He lost favor after remonstrating with the government and was exiled to a distant place in south China.

123. Sugawara no Michizane (845–903): A Japanese statesman and scholar of the Heian period (794–1185). He was highly regarded by Emperor Daigo and became one of the highest ministers. But because of groundless accusations made by Fujiwara no Tokihira, another high minister, he was demoted to a far inferior position in Kyushu, the distant southern area. He was versed in history and excelled in poetry and literature. After his death, he was worshiped as a god, and a shrine was consecrated to this new deity at Kitano in Kyoto. Tenjin means "heavenly god."

124. *Hokke Gengi*, vol. 6.

manifested in the future, look at the causes that exist in the present." The *Fukyō* chapter of the Lotus Sutra says: "After expiating his sins."[125] This indicates that Bodhisattva Fukyō was attacked with tiles and stones because he had in the past committed the offense of slandering the Lotus Sutra.

Second, we should note that, if a person is inevitably destined to fall into hell in his next existence, then even though he commits a grave offense in this life, he will suffer no immediate punishment. The *icchantika*, men of incorrigible disbelief, are examples of this.

The Nirvana Sutra states: "Bodhisattva Kashō said to the Buddha, 'World-Honored One, as you have described, the rays of the Buddha's great nirvana enter the pores of all beings.'" It also states: "Bodhisattva Kashō said to the Buddha, 'World-Honored One, how can those who have not yet set their hearts on enlightenment create the causes that will lead to enlightenment?'" The sutra answered the question this way. "The Buddha said to Kashō, 'There may be persons who listen to the Nirvana Sutra and yet claim that they have no need to set their hearts on enlightenment, and instead slander the True Law. Such persons will immediately dream at night of devils and their hearts will be filled with terror. The devils will say to them, "How foolish you are, my friend! If you do not set your heart on enlightenment now, your life span will be cut short!" These persons quake with fear, and as soon as they wake from the dream, they set their hearts on enlightenment. And you should know that such persons will become great bodhisatt-vas.'" In other words, although a person might slander the True Law, if he is not an unspeakably evil person, he will be warned at once in a dream and will have a change of heart.

The *icchantika*, on the other hand, are likened to "dead trees or stony mountains" that can never bring forth growth. They

---

125.   This passage means that Bodhisattva Fukyō expiated his past offense of slandering the Law by being subjected to persecutions on account of the Law, and that he thereby changed his karma and attained Buddhahood.

are "scorched seeds which, although they encounter the sweet rain," will not grow. They are "bright pearls hidden in mud" which can never shine. They are like "persons with a wound on their hands who nevertheless handle poison." Just as "torrents of rain cannot remain suspended in the sky," so will they fall into hell. All these various similes illustrate the fact that *icchantika* of the most evil type will invariably fall into the hell of incessant suffering at the time of their successive rebirths. Therefore they do not suffer any immediate punishment in this life. They are like the evil rulers of ancient China, Emperor Chieh of the Hsia dynasty and Emperor Chou of the Yin dynasty. During their reigns, Heaven did not display any unusual manifestations as a warning. That was because their offenses were so grave that their dynasties were already destined to perish.

Third, it would appear that the guardian deities have deserted this country, and that is probably one reason why offenders do not suffer any immediate punishment. In an age that slanders the Law, guardian deities will take their leave and the various heavenly gods will cease to lend their protection. That is why the votaries of the True Law do not receive any sign of divine favor, but on the contrary encounter severe difficulties. The *Konkōmyō* Sutra says: "Those who perform good deeds day by day languish and dwindle in number." We are living in an evil country and an evil age. I have discussed all this in detail in my work entitled "Risshō Ankoku Ron."

This I will state. Let the gods forsake me. Let all persecutions assail me. Still I will give my life for the sake of the Law. Shariputra practiced the way of the bodhisattva for sixty aeons, but he fell from that high position because he could not endure the beratings of the Brahman who begged for his eye.[126] Of those who received the seeds of Buddhahood in the time of

126.   This story is found in the *Daichido Ron*. In the Latter Day of the Law of Sentara Buddha, Shariputra practiced the bodhisattva way. One day, a Brahman begged for Shariputra's eye, and Shariputra gave it to him. But the

gohyaku-jintengō or in the days of Daitsū Buddha (*sanzen-jintengō*), many in later times abandoned the seeds, fell from their high condition and remained in hell because they followed evil companions.

Whether tempted by good or threatened by evil, if one casts aside the Lotus Sutra, he destines himself for hell. Here I will make a great vow. Though I might be offered the rulership of Japan if I will only abandon the Lotus Sutra, accept the teachings of the *Kammuryōju* Sutra and look forward to rebirth in the Western Pure Land, though I might be told that my father and mother will have their heads cut off if I do not recite the Nembutsu—whatever obstacles I might encounter, so long as men of wisdom do not prove my teachings to be false, I will never accept the practices of the other sects! All other troubles are no more to me than dust before the wind.

I will be the Pillar of Japan. I will be the Eyes of Japan. I will be the Great Ship of Japan. This is my vow, and I will never forsake it!

Question: How can you be certain that the exiles and sentences of death imposed on you are the result of karma created in the past?

Answer: A bronze mirror will reflect color and form. The First Emperor of the Ch'in dynasty had a lie-detecting mirror that would reveal offenses committed in this present life. And the mirror of the Buddha's Law makes clear the causal actions committed in the past. The *Hatsunaion* Sutra states: "Men of devout faith, because you committed countless offenses and accumulated much evil karma in the past, you must expect to suffer retribution for everything you have done. You may be reviled, cursed with an ugly appearance, be poorly clad and poorly fed, seek wealth in vain, be born to an impoverished or heretical family, or be persecuted by your sovereign. It is due to

---

Brahman was revolted by the smell of the eye and dropped it, trampling it into the dirt. Seeing this, Shariputra withdrew from the bodhisattva practice and fell into the hell of incessant suffering for countless aeons.

the blessings obtained by protecting the Law that one can diminish in this lifetime his suffering and retribution."

This sutra passage conforms exactly with my own experience. By now all the doubts that I have raised earlier should be dispelled, and thousands of difficulties are nothing to me. But let me show you phrase by phrase how the text applies to me. "You may be reviled," or, as the Lotus Sutra says, "They will despise, hate, envy and bear grudges" against you—and in exactly that manner I have been treated with contempt and arrogance for over twenty years. "You will be cursed with an ugly appearance," "You will be poorly clad"—these too apply to me. "You will be poorly fed"—that applies to me. "You will seek wealth in vain"—that applies to me. "You will be born to an impoverished family"—that applies to me. "You will be persecuted by your sovereign"—that applies to me. The Lotus Sutra says, "Again and again we will be banished," and the passage from the *Hatsunaion* Sutra speaks of having to suffer various kinds of retribution. Can there be any doubt that the passage applies to me?

The passage also says: "It is due to the blessings obtained by protecting the Law that one can diminish in this lifetime his suffering and retribution." The fifth volume of the *Maka Shikan* has this to say on the subject: "The feeble merits produced by a mind only half intent on goodness cannot alter the cycle of birth and death. But if one practices meditation and attains profound insight (*shikan*), so as to control the five components of his life and thus ward off illness and restrain earthly desires, then one can transcend the cycle of birth and death." It also says, "As practice progresses and understanding grows, the three obstacles and four devils emerge, vying with one another to interfere."

From the beginningless past I have been born countless times as an evil ruler who deprived the votaries of the Lotus Sutra of their robes and rations, their fields and crops, much as the people of Japan in the present day go about destroying the temples dedicated to the Lotus Sutra. In addition, I cut off the heads of numberless votaries of the Lotus Sutra. Some of these grave offenses I have already paid for, but there must be some that are not paid for yet. Even if I seem to have paid for them all, there are still ill effects that remain. When the time comes for me to transcend the sufferings of birth and death and attain Buddhahood, it will be only after I have completely freed myself from these grave offenses. My merits are insignificant, but these offenses are grave.

If I practiced the teachings of the provisional sutras rather than those of the Lotus Sutra, then these retributions for my past grave offenses would not appear. When iron is heated, if it is not strenuously forged, the impurities in it will not become apparent. Only when it is subjected to the tempering process again and again will the flaws appear. When one is pressing hemp seeds, if he does not press very hard, he will not get much oil from them. Likewise, when I vigorously berate those throughout the country who slander the Law, I meet with great difficulties. It must be that my actions in defending the Law in this present life are calling forth retributions for the grave offenses of my past. If iron does not come into contact with fire, it remains black, but if it contacts fire, it turns red. If you place a log across a swift stream, waves will pile up like hills. If you disturb a sleeping lion, it will roar loudly.

The Nirvana Sutra says: "It is like the case of a poor woman. She has no house to live in and no one to aid or protect her, and in addition she is beset by illness, hunger and thirst, until she decides to take to the road and beg for a living. While staying at the house of another, she gives birth to a baby, but the master of the house drives her away. Though the baby has just been born, she takes it up in her arms and sets out, hoping to journey to another land. But along the way, she encounters fierce wind and rain, and she is troubled by cold and bitten by mosquitoes, hornets and poisonous insects. Coming at length to the Ganges River, she clasps her child in her arms and begins to cross it. Although the current is very swift, she will not let go of her child, and in the end both mother and child are drowned. But through the merit that the woman gained by her loving tenderness, she is reborn after her death in the Brahma-heaven.

"Monju, if there are men of devout faith who wish to defend the True Law, they should emulate this poor woman crossing the Ganges who sacrificed her life because of her love for her child. Men of devout faith, the bodhisattvas who guard the Law should behave in this way. Do not hesitate to give up your life! Then, although you do not seek enlightenment, enlighten-ment will come of itself, just as the poor woman, though she did not seek to be reborn in the Brahma-heaven, was neverthe-less reborn there."

The Great Teacher Chang-an interprets this story from the Nirvana Sutra in terms of the three obstacles of illusion, karma and retribution. Let us see how he does this. The fact that the woman is called "poor" indicates that the person does not have the treasure of the Law. The fact that she is identified as a woman indicates that the person has a measure of tenderness. The "house of another" signifies a realm of defilement. The child she bears is the heart that has faith in the Lotus Sutra, one of the three factors leading to enlightenment.[127] Being driven out of the house signifies that the person is exiled. The fact that the baby has just been born means that very little time has passed since the person began to have faith in the Lotus Sutra. The fierce wind the woman encounters is the Imperial decree sentencing the person to exile. The mosquitoes and other insects are the "many ignorant people who curse and speak ill" of the votary of the Lotus Sutra. The fact that both mother and child are drowned indicates that, though in the end the person had his head cut off, he never renounced his faith in the Lotus

---

127.   Three factors leading to enlightenment: The innate Buddha nature, the wisdom to realize it and the external cause to manifest it. Here the Daishonin equates faith with wisdom.

Sutra. Being reborn in the Brahma-heaven means being reborn in the realm of Buddhahood.

The power of karmic reward extends to all of the Ten Worlds, even to the realm of Buddhahood. Even though one might go around killing people in Japan, China and other countries, if he does not commit any of the five cardinal sins or does not slander the Law, he will not fall into the hell of incessant suffering. Yet he will be reborn and confined in the other kinds of hell over a period of countless years. Even if one observes a great many rules of discipline and performs a great many good acts, if he performs them with a mind only half intent on goodness, he cannot be reborn in heaven, in the world of form where beings are free from desires. To be born a king in the Brahma-heaven, one must add compassion to the karmic reward that leads to rebirth in the threefold world. The poor woman in the sutra passage was reborn in the Brahma-heaven because of her concern for her child. Her case is different from the ordinary rules of Buddhist practice. Chang-an offers two interpretations of it, but in the end it is nothing other than the loving kindness with which the woman cares for her child that makes the difference. Her concern concentrates on one thing, rather like a concentrated meditation of Buddhism. She thinks of nothing but her child, which is similar to the Buddha's profound mercy. That must be why, although she created no other causes to bring it about, she was reborn in the Brahma-heaven.

The path to Buddhahood is not to be found in the Kegon doctrine that the mind is the only reality,[128] in the eightfold negation[129] of the Sanron sect, in the Consciousness-Only

128.   The Kegon sect asserts that all beings and phenomena arise from the mind and that they do not exist apart from the mind.

129.   Eightfold negation: Eight negative expressions in Nagarjuna's *Chū Ron*: "neither birth nor death, neither cessation nor permanence, neither identity nor difference, neither coming nor going." The doctrine of the eight negations indicates that the Middle Way lies beyond attachment to either existence or nonexistence. In other words, it indicates that the true nature of all phenomena is *kū* and that all phenomena arise from dependent causation.

doctrine of the Hossō sect, or in the Shingon type of meditation on the five elements of the universe.[130] Only the Tendai doctrine of *ichinen sanzen* is the path to Buddhahood. Even in the case of this doctrine of *ichinen sanzen*, we do not possess the kind of wisdom and understanding to comprehend it fully. Nevertheless, among all the sutras preached by the Buddha during his lifetime, the Lotus Sutra alone contains this jewel which is the doctrine of *ichinen sanzen*. The doctrines of the other sutras are merely yellow stones that appear to be jewels. They are like sand, from which you can extract no oil no matter how hard you squeeze it, or a barren woman who can never bear a child. Even a wise man cannot become a Buddha through the other sutras, but with the Lotus Sutra, even fools can plant the seeds that lead to Buddhahood. As the sutra passage I have quoted earlier puts it, "Although you do not seek enlightenment, enlightenment will come of itself."

Although I and my disciples may encounter various difficulties, if we do not harbor doubts in our hearts, we will as a matter of course attain Buddhahood. Do not have doubts simply because Heaven does not lend you protection. Do not be discouraged because you do not enjoy an easy and secure existence in this life. This is what I have taught my disciples morning and evening, and yet they begin to harbor doubts and abandon their faith.

Foolish men are likely to forget the promises they have made when the crucial moment comes. [In the face of persecutions,] some of them feel pity for their wives and children and grieve at the thought of parting from them in this life. In countless births throughout many long aeons they have had wives and children but parted from them in every existence. They have

130.   Shingon type of meditation on the five elements of the universe: An esoteric form of meditation intended to make one understand that the five elements of earth, water, fire, wind and *kū* (latency) correspond to five parts of the body, namely, crown, face, breast, abdomen and knees. The eventual aim is to realize that the body itself is united with the five Buddhas who are embodiments of the five aspects of Dainichi Buddha's wisdom.

done so unwillingly and not because of their desire to pursue the way of the Buddha. Since they must part with them in any case, they should remain faithful to their belief in the Lotus Sutra and make their way to Eagle Peak, so that they may lead their wives and children there as well.

Question: You insist that the followers of the Nembutsu and Zen sects will fall into the hell of incessant suffering. This shows that you have a contentious heart. You yourself are in danger of falling into the realm of the ashuras. Moreover, it is said in the *Anrakugyō* chapter of the Lotus Sutra: "It is undesirable that one should speak of the faults of others or of the other sutras; nor should one regard other priests with contempt." It is because you are going against this passage in the sutra that you have been abandoned by Heaven, is it not?

Answer: The *Maka Shikan* says: "There are two ways to spread the Buddha's teachings. The first is called *shōju* and the second is called *shakubuku*. When the *Anrakugyō* chapter says that one should not speak of the good or bad points of others, it is referring to the *shōju* method. But when the Nirvana Sutra says, 'Carry swords and staves and cut off their heads!' it is referring to the *shakubuku* method. They differ in approach in that one is lenient and the other severe, but they both bring benefit."

In the *Guketsu*, Miao-lo comments on this passage as follows: "With regard to the two ways of spreading the Buddha's teachings, the Nirvana Sutra says, 'Carry swords and staves,' and in the third volume it says that defenders of the True Law need not observe the five precepts or practice the rules of proper behavior. . . . And later on, it tells of how King Sen'yo put to death those who slandered the Law.[131] It also states: 'The new physician, [knowing that the medicine the people had

---

131.   King Sen'yo: A previous incarnation of Shakyamuni Buddha. According to the Nirvana Sutra, vol. 12, King Sen'yo was the ruler of a great kingdom in Jambudvipa (India) and believed in the Mahayana sutras. When Brahmans slandered the Mahayana sutras, he had them put to death. The sutra says that because of this, he was thereafter never in danger of falling into hell.

been using was poison,] forbade them to use it, saying, "If anyone takes any more of this medicine, he will have his head cut off !" [132] These passages all demonstrate how the method of *shakubuku* should be applied to persons who go against the Law. All the sutras and treatises deal with one or the other of these two methods."

In the *Hokke Mongu*, T'ien-t'ai states: "Question: The Nirvana Sutra clearly states that one should support and follow the ruler, bearing bows and arrows and helping to overthrow evil persons. And yet the *Anrakugyō* chapter of the Lotus Sutra says that one should stay away from persons in power and should behave with humility and loving kindness. There seems to be a major contradiction between the sternness of one approach and the gentleness of the other. Why should they differ so ?

"Answer: The Nirvana Sutra speaks mostly about the *shakubuku* approach. But it also mentions dwelling in the state where one looks on all beings as one's own children. Could it say so if it did not have the *shōju* approach ? The Lotus Sutra is concerned mainly with the elucidation of the *shōju* approach. But in the *Dharani* chapter there is also the curse on anyone who offends the Law which says he will have his head split into seven parts. Could it say so if it did not have the *shakubuku* approach ? One should examine both methods and use whichever one accords with the time."

Chang-an, in his commentary on the Nirvana Sutra, writes: "When priests or laymen are defending the Law, the most important thing is for them to adopt the proper basic mental attitude. They should disregard external details, stick to the principles, and in this way spread the teachings of the Nirvana Sutra. Therefore it says that defenders of the True Law need not abide by petty regulations. And that is why it says they

132. According to the Nirvana Sutra, the medicine which the old physician prescribed did harm to the people. To save their lives, the new physician persuaded the king to use stringent measures to prohibit the use of the medicine.

need not practice the rules of proper behavior. In past times the age was peaceful and the Law spread throughout the country. At that time it was proper to observe the five precepts and not to carry staves. But now the age is perilous and the Law is overshadowed. Therefore it is proper to carry staves and to disregard the five precepts. If both past and present were perilous times, then it would be proper to carry staves in both of them. And if both past and present were peaceful times, then it would be proper to observe the five precepts in both of them. You should distinguish between the *shōju* and the *shakubuku* methods and never adhere solely to one or the other."

I suppose the learned priests of the time think it is only natural that one should have doubts about this. Therefore, no matter how I explain and try to persuade my own disciples, they still cannot seem to overcome their doubts, but behave like *icchantika* who do not possess the innate nature to become Buddhas. Therefore I have quoted these passages of explanation from T'ien-t'ai, Miao-lo and others in order to silence their ungrounded criticisms.

These two methods of spreading the Law, *shōju* and *shakubuku*, are like water and fire. Fire hates water, water detests fire. The practitioner of *shōju* laughs with scorn at *shakubuku*. The practitioner of *shakubuku* despairs at the thought of *shōju*. When the country is full of ignorant or evil persons, then *shōju* is the primary method to be applied, as described in the *Anrakugyō* chapter. But at a time when there are many persons of perverse views who slander the Law, then *shakubuku* should come first, as described in the *Fukyō* chapter. It is like using cold water to cool yourself in the hot weather, or longing for a fire when the weather turns cold. Grass and trees are kinsmen of the sun—they suffer in the cold moonlight. Bodies of water are followers of the moon—they lose their true nature when the hot weather comes.

In the Latter Day of the Law, however, both *shōju* and *shakubuku* are to be used. This is because there are two kinds of countries, the country that is passively evil, and the kind that actively seeks to destroy the Law. We must consider carefully to which category Japan at the present time belongs.

Question: If one applies the *shakubuku* method at a time when the *shōju* method would be appropriate, or *shōju* at a time when *shakubuku* would be appropriate, is there any merit to be gained?

Answer: The Nirvana Sutra says: "Bodhisattva Kashō addressed the Buddha, saying, 'The essential body of the Law[133] that you possess is as indestructible as a diamond. But I do not yet understand the means by which you acquired it. Would you tell me?'

"The Buddha replied, 'Kashō, it is because I was a defender of the True Law that I am now able to attain this diamond-like body that abides forever and is never destroyed.[134]

"'Men of devout faith, defenders of the True Law need not observe the five precepts or practice the rules of proper behavior. Rather they should carry knives and swords, bows and arrows.

"'There are priests who preach the Dharma in various ways, but still they are not able to utter "the lion's roar" and refute evil persons who deny the Dharma. Priests of this kind can bring no merit either to themselves or to the populace. You should realize that they are in fact shirkers and idlers. Though they are careful in observing the precepts and maintain spotless conduct, you should realize that they are incapable of attaining Buddhahood.

"'Then at times there are others who fail to observe the precepts and, as soon as they finish listening to the priest, are enraged to the point where they are about to attack him.

133. Essential body of the Law: Dharma body. One of the three properties of the Buddha. *See* Three properties in the Glossary.

134. In the sutra, the Buddha's reply begins with the sentence: "Kashō, it is because I defended the True Law that I was able to attain this diamond-like body." Since this sentence is the same as the following sentence in meaning, the first sentence has been omitted.

Someone who preaches the Dharma in this way, though he may in the end lose his life, is still worthy of being called a person who observes the precepts and brings merit to both himself and others.' "

Chang-an in the passage quoted earlier says: "You should distinguish between the *shōju* and the *shakubuku* methods and never adhere solely to one or the other." And T'ien-t'ai, as we have seen, declared that one should use whichever method "accords with the time." If you do not, you will be like someone who plants seeds at the end of autumn. Though you may carefully tend the field, you are not likely to harvest any rice or grain.

During the Kennin era (1201–1204), two men came to prominence, Hōnen and Dainichi,[135] who spread the teachings of the Nembutsu and Zen sects respectively. Hōnen denied the worth of the Lotus Sutra now that the world has entered the Latter Day of the Law, saying, "Not a single person has ever attained Buddhahood through that sutra," and "Not one person in a thousand can reach enlightenment through its teachings." Dainichi for his part claimed that the true teachings of Buddhism had been transmitted apart from the sutras.[136] These two doctrines have now spread throughout the entire country. The learned priests of the Tendai and Shingon sects fawn on the Nembutsu and Zen followers or fear them the way a dog wags its tail before its master or a mouse fears a cat. These men enter the service of the ruler and the military leaders, where they preach in such a way as to bring about the destruction of the Buddhist Law and the ruin of the country. These Tendai and Shingon leaders in their present existence will fall into the realm of Hunger, and after death will find themselves in the hell of incessant suffering. Even if they retire to the mountain forests and meditate intensively on *ichinen*

135.   Dainichi: *See* p. 64, footnote 9.
136.   The Zen sect asserts that the essence of Buddhism is transferred not through the sutras but from mind to mind.

sanzen, or retire to a quiet spot and devote themselves to the three mysteries of body, mouth and mind,[137] if they do not understand the times or the people's capacity and perceive which of the two methods, *shōju* or *shakubuku*, is appropriate, then they can never free themselves from the sufferings of birth and death.

Question: When you berate the followers of the Nembutsu and Zen sects and arouse their enmity, what merit does that bring?

Answer: The Nirvana Sutra says, "If even a good priest sees someone slandering the Law and disregards him, failing to reproach him, to oust him or to punish him for his offense, then that priest is betraying Buddhism. But if he takes the slanderer severely to task, drives him off or punishes him, then he is my disciple and one who truly understands my teachings."

Chang-an comments on this as follows: "He who injures or brings confusion to the Buddhist Law is an enemy of the Law. If one befriends another person but lacks the mercy to correct him, he is in fact his enemy. But he who is willing to reprimand and correct the offender is one who truly understands and defends the Law, a true disciple of the Buddha. He makes it possible for the offender to rid himself of evil, and thus he acts

137.   Three mysteries of body, mouth and mind: The body, mouth and mind of Dainichi Buddha. The esoteric teaching maintains that the body, mouth and mind of the Buddha are unimaginably profound and beyond common mortal understanding. Therefore they are called "mysteries." Since the body, mouth and mind of the Buddha are omnipresent, all beings are the mystic body of the Buddha, all sounds the mystic mouth (i.e., voice) of the Buddha, and all thoughts the mystic mind of the Buddha. In addition, the esoteric teaching asserts that the body, mouth and mind of common mortals are not essentially different from those of the Buddha, though their Buddha nature is clouded by illusion. In this sense, the body, mouth and mind of a common mortal in their essential nature are also called the three mysteries. From the viewpoint of practice, the esoteric teaching defines the body to be the making of *mudras* with the hands, the mouth to be the recitation of *mantras* (mystic words), and the mind to be meditation on the object of worship. By these three practices, the body, mouth and mind of the common mortal are said to be associated with those of the Buddha. Through this union, one can attain Buddhahood in his present form.

like a parent to the offender. Those who are willing to reproach offenders are disciples of the Buddha. But those who will not oust offenders are enemies of the Buddhist Law."

If we examine the *Hōtō* chapter of the Lotus Sutra, we find Shakyamuni Buddha, Tahō Buddha, and the various Buddhas from the ten directions [who are emanations of Shakyamuni Buddha] gathering together. And why? As the sutra itself says, "To make certain that the Law will long endure, they have come to this place." One may surmise from this that Shakyamuni, Tahō and the other Buddhas intend to insure the future propagation of the Lotus Sutra so that it can be made available to every single living being in times to come. Their concern and compassion are even greater than that of a father and mother who see their only child inflicted with great suffering. Hōnen, however, shows not the least concern about their compassion, but would tightly shut the gates to the Lotus Sutra so that in the future no one would have access to it. Like a person who tricks a demented child into throwing away his treasure, he tries to induce people to discard the Lotus Sutra, a cruel-hearted thing to do indeed!

If someone is about to kill your father and mother, shouldn't you try to warn them? If an evil son who is insane with drink is threatening to kill his father and mother, shouldn't you try to stop him? If some evil person is about to set fire to the temples and pagodas, shouldn't you try to stop him? If your only child is gravely ill, shouldn't you try to cure him with moxibustion treatment? To fail to do so is to act like those people who do not try to put a stop to the Zen and Nembutsu followers in Japan. As Chang-an says, "If one befriends another person but lacks the mercy to correct him, he is in fact his enemy."

I, Nichiren, am sovereign, teacher, father and mother to all the people of Japan. But the men of the Tendai sect [who do not refute the heretical sects] are all great enemies of the people. As Chang-an has noted, "He who makes it possible for an offender to rid himself of evil is acting like a parent to him."

He who has not set his heart upon the Way can never free himself from the sufferings of birth and death. Shakyamuni was cursed by all the followers of non-Buddhist teachings and labeled as a man of great evil. The Great Teacher T'ien-t'ai was regarded with intense enmity by the three Buddhist sects of southern China and the seven sects of northern China, and later in Japan the Hossō monk Tokuichi criticized him for "using his three-inch tongue to try to destroy the five-foot body"[138] of the Buddha. The Great Teacher Dengyō was disparaged by the monks of Nara, who said, "That Saichō has never been to the capital of T'ang China!"[139] But all of these abuses were incurred because of the Lotus Sutra, and they are therefore no shame to the men who suffered them. To be praised by fools—that is the greatest shame. Now that I have been exiled by the authorities, the priests of the Tendai and Shingon sects are no doubt delighted. They are strange and cruel-hearted men.

Shakyamuni appeared in the *saha* world, Kumarajiva journeyed to the Ch'in dynasty in China,[140] and Dengyō likewise went to China, [all so that the Lotus Sutra might be preached and propagated]. Bodhisattvas Kanadeva and Aryasinha sacrificed their bodies. Bodhisattva Yakuō burned his arms as an offering,[141] and Prince Shōtoku stripped off the skin on his arms to write the titles of sutras in blood. Shakyamuni, when he was a bodhisattva, sold his flesh to make offerings, and another time, when he was a bodhisattva named Gyōbō, he

138. *Chūben Gikyō Sen.*
139. These words appear in a petition presented to the emperor by Gomyō, a priest of the Hossō sect, and other eminent priests. The words are also cited in Dengyō's *Kenkai Ron* which he wrote in refutation. Saichō is another name for Dengyō.
140. Kumarajiva accepted an invitation from Yao Hsing, king of the Later Ch'in dynasty, and came to the capital Ch'ang-an as the "teacher of the nation." There he translated 743 Buddhist scriptures from Sanskrit into Chinese.
141. This story appears in the *Yakuō* (23rd) chapter of the Lotus Sutra. In a past life, Yakuō burned his arms as an offering to the Lotus Sutra.

used his bone as a pen to write down the Dharma.[142]

T'ien-t'ai has said that the practice should "accord with the time." The propagation of the Buddhist Law does indeed follow the times. For what I have done, I have been condemned to exile, but it is a small suffering to undergo in this present life and not one worth crying over. In future lives I will enjoy immense happiness, a thought that gives me great satisfaction.

BACKGROUND This treatise is one of Nichiren Daishonin's most important writings, for he revealed himself here to be the Buddha of the Latter Day of the Law who possesses the three virtues of sovereign, teacher and parent. In February 1272, still under the harsh penalty of exile on Sado Island, the Daishonin completed this work and addressed it to Shijō Kingo, one of his trusted disciples. "The True Object of Worship," written one year later, clarifies the object of worship, which allows all people to attain enlightenment, from the viewpoint of the Law. "The Opening of the Eyes" treats the same subject in terms of the Person; that is, it shows Nichiren Daishonin to be the original Buddha who would establish the true object of worship for the happiness of all mankind. The object of worship is the embodiment of the Daishonin's life and the supreme law of the universe, Nam-myoho-renge-kyo.

The Tatsunokuchi Persecution of 1271 and the subsequent exile to Sado Island were the greatest of all persecutions befalling Nichiren Daishonin. His life on the forbidding island was full of hardship; his hut was open to the wind and snow, and he lacked food, clothing and writing materials. In addition

142. According to Nagarjuna's *Daichido Ron*, a devil disguised as a Brahman appeared to Gyōbō Bonji and said, "I will reveal to you the Buddha's teaching if you are prepared to inscribe it by using your skin as paper, your bone as a pen and your blood as ink." When Gyōbō demonstrated his seeking mind by complying, the devil disappeared and a real Buddha appeared to teach him the Law.

to his physical suffering he was troubled by the news that many of his followers in Kamakura had abandoned their faith. Moreover, jealous Nembutsu priests posed a continual threat to his life. The shadow of death always haunted him. Under these circumstances, Nichiren Daishonin wrote this treatise to encourage his disciples as though it were his last will and testament.

Nichiren Daishonin expressed his conviction as the Buddha of the Latter Day of the Law in the Gosho, "On the Buddha's Behavior": "After everyone had gone, I began to put into shape a work in two volumes, called 'Kaimoku Shō' (The Opening of the Eyes), which I had been working on since the eleventh month of the previous year. I wanted to record the wonder I had experienced, in case I should be beheaded. The essential message in this work, which I entrusted to Shijō Kingo's messenger, is that the destiny of Japan depends solely upon me. A house without pillars collapses and a man without a soul is dead. I am the soul of the people of Japan."

Nichikan Shonin, the twenty-sixth high priest of Nichiren Shoshu, explains in his exegesis of this work that the title "The Opening of the Eyes" means to open eyes that are blind. He writes, "Because the eyes of all people in Japan are clouded by their adherence to provisional teachings, they cannot recognize the three virtues of the original Buddha. Therefore it is as though they were blind." He goes on to explain that this treatise was written to open the eyes of all mankind to the original Buddha who possesses all of the three virtues: the virtue of sovereign, or the power to protect the people; the virtue of teacher, or the wisdom to lead them to enlightenment; and the virtue of parent, or the compassion to save them from unhappiness. A passage from this treatise reads, "On the twelfth day of the ninth month of last year, between the hours of the Rat and the Ox (11:00 P.M. to 3:00 A.M.), this person named Nichiren was beheaded. It is his soul that has come to this island of Sado . . . " It was through the Tatsunokuchi

Persecution that Nichiren Daishonin completed his transient mission as Bodhisattva Jōgyō, the leader of the Bodhisattvas of the Earth, and revealed his true identity as the original Buddha of *kuon ganjo*. "This person named Nichiren was beheaded" means the death of a common mortal named Nichiren, and "it is his soul that has come to this island of Sado" indicates that from then on the Daishonin was to reveal in full his enlightenment as the Buddha of the Latter Day of the Law.

In this treatise, Nichiren Daishonin begins by saying, "There are three categories of people that all men and women should respect. They are the sovereign, the teacher, and the parent." He then proceeds to examine to what extent these three virtues are possessed by teachings of increasing profundity, beginning with Confucianism, and progressing upward through Taoism, Brahmanism, Hinayana Buddhism, provisional Mahayana teachings, the theoretical teaching of the Lotus Sutra, and the essential teaching of the Lotus Sutra. The three virtues are a theme running throughout the entire Gosho; they are a standard for evaluating the relative depth of various teachings. Ultimately, the Daishonin will declare that he himself is the sovereign, teacher and parent for all people in the Latter Day of the Law, indicating that he is the Buddha of that age.

The Daishonin sets up a comparison between the provisional and true teachings of Buddhism. Every teaching of the Buddha reveals some truth, but all the provisional teachings were meant only to lead to the essential teaching of the Lotus Sutra. The Daishonin reveals the core of the essential teaching, saying, "The doctrine of *ichinen sanzen* is found in only one place, hidden in the depths of the *Juryō* chapter of the essential teaching of the Lotus Sutra." He attributes the cause of the miseries and disasters ravaging Japan to the confusion in Buddhism and the failure to recognize the supremacy of the Lotus Sutra.

He then cites two reasons why the sutra is supreme. One is that the theoretical teaching (former half of the Lotus Sutra) reveals that people in the state of *shōmon* (Learning) and *engaku*

(Realization) can attain enlightenment, a possibility utterly denied in the previous forty-two years of the Buddha's preaching. The predictions in the theoretical teaching that Shariputra and others of the two vehicles will attain Buddhahood substantiate the mutual possession of the Ten Worlds and the statement that Buddhahood is open to all.

The other reason is that, in the essential teaching (the latter half of the Lotus Sutra), Shakyamuni Buddha denied that he had first attained enlightenment in India, and instead revealed his original enlightenment in the unfathomably remote past—a time called *gohyaku-jintengō*. The Daishonin points out the difficulty which later scholars had in believing the Buddha's new revelation in the Lotus Sutra. The Buddha himself predicted this, saying that among all sutras, the Lotus Sutra is "the most difficult to believe and the most difficult to understand." People tended to believe the mass of sutras preached during the first forty-odd years rather than the one solitary sutra which contradicted all the others. The Daishonin, however, takes the position that only the revelation of the truth of Buddhism can save the nation from the miseries which have been brought about by false interpretations of the Buddha's teachings. This conviction, he says, has moved him to propagate the Lotus Sutra in spite of the persecution which he knew his action would incur. He alone has experienced the reality of the sutra's words: "Since hatred and jealousy abound even during the lifetime of the Buddha, how much worse will it be in the world after his passing?"

Next the Daishonin raises a major question. If he is in fact the votary of the sutra, he ought to be protected by the heavenly gods, but in actuality he has suffered incomparably greater persecutions than any faced by T'ien-t'ai, Dengyō or others. If he is truly the votary of the Lotus Sutra, then why do the gods not protect him as they vowed in the sutra that they would? This apparent failure was a major cause of doubt among his disciples at the time of the Sado exile. He writes, "This doubt lies at the heart of this piece I am writing. And because it is the most important concern of my entire life, I will raise it again and again here and emphasize it more than ever, before I attempt to answer it."

The second part of the Gosho introduces the scene of the ceremony of the Lotus Sutra where, in the *Yujutsu* (15th) chapter, Shakyamuni Buddha summons forth countless bodhisattvas from beneath the earth. The assembly is awed by their noble appearance. Who are these bodhisattvas, they wish to know. Shakyamuni replies that they are his disciples. This statement provokes grave doubt and consternation. Shakyamuni has been a Buddha for only slightly more than forty years. How could he possibly have trained innumerable bodhisattvas in so short a span of time? Shakyamuni's answer is to expound the *Juryō* (16th) chapter, in which he reveals that he had actually attained enlightenment in the unfathomably remote past. It therefore becomes apparent that all the other Buddhas of other sutras are his emanations and all bodhisattvas are his disciples. Moreover, the three virtues of Shakyamuni Buddha of the *Juryō* chapter are the highest of those of any Buddha or sage discussed so far. Nichiren Daishonin makes it clear that the Buddha of the *Juryō* chapter is the teacher of all Buddhas and sutras. In this chapter the Buddha revealed his supreme teaching. All the other sutras are shown to be a means whereby the people are led to the highest teaching of all—the Lotus Sutra, the core of which is the *Juryō* chapter.

At this point in the Gosho an implicit analogy begins to emerge. The doubt held by Shakyamuni's disciples about how he could possibly have taught the Bodhisattvas of the Earth leads to the revelation of his true identity as the Buddha who attained enlightenment countless aeons ago. Similarly, the doubt held by the Daishonin's disciples about why he was seemingly not protected and did not lead a peaceful life leads to an understanding of his true identity as the Buddha of the Latter Day.

Having so far expounded the superiority of the Lotus Sutra, the Daishonin introduces the principle of sowing, maturing and harvest. When Shakyamuni revealed his Buddhahood in the remote past, he pointed directly toward the original cause of his own enlightenment. The Daishonin, by referring to the seed of Shakyamuni Buddha's enlightenment, points toward the supreme law whereby all Buddhas attain enlightenment— Nam-myoho-renge-kyo. This law is what lies in the depths, not on the surface, of the *Juryō* chapter. Nam-myoho-renge-kyo is the seed of enlightenment. Nichiren Daishonin is the Buddha of True Cause—because he directly taught the original or true cause for attaining Buddhahood. And his Buddhism is called the Buddhism of sowing because it implants the seed of enlightenment in the lives of those who practice it. In this light, he possesses the virtues of sovereign, teacher and parent for all mankind. The Daishonin declares that the bodhisattvas and heavenly gods should be protecting him and helping him to spread the Mystic Law which is the essence of the Lotus Sutra, as they vowed to Shakyamuni that they would do.

Each sutra has its own claim to excellence, a fact which led to much confusion in later times. Giving examples, the Daishonin shows that each sutra contains statements to the effect that it is superior to all teachings which preceded it. But only the Lotus Sutra declares that it is supreme among all the sutras "I have preached, now preach, and will preach." Having reconfirmed the supremacy of the Lotus Sutra, the Daishonin shows how his life is bound irrevocably to the teachings of that sutra. The three powerful enemies predicted in the *Kanji* (13th) chapter of the Lotus Sutra serve to identify him as the votary of the Lotus Sutra in the Latter Day of the Law. Had he not encountered opposition and hostility as the sutra prophesied, the words of Shakyamuni would have been false. However, the people could not acknowledge the Daishonin as the sutra's votary because he did not seem to be protected by the heavenly gods; rather, he suffered an attempted execution and two exiles. Here the Daishonin gives three reasons, apart from the need to fulfill the sutra's prophecies, why the gods do not protect him. First, if one has committed slander of the Lotus Sutra in previous existences, he will not be protected from persecution. However, by meeting difficulty in the course of Buddhist practice, such slanders can be eradicated. The Daishonin here shows this through his own example. Secondly, when the slander of people is so heavy as to doom them to the state of hell, they do not necessarily receive immediate retribution, even when they persecute the votary of the Lotus Sutra. Thirdly, because the gods forsake a country which is filled with slanderers, those who persecute the votary do not incur immediate punishment. After detailing these reasons, the Daishonin vows to stake his life on the cause of saving all people. He writes, "Let the gods forsake me. Let all persecutions assail me. Still I will give my life for the sake of the Law. . . . I will be the Pillar of Japan. I will be the Eyes of Japan. I will be the Great Ship of Japan. This is my vow, and I will never forsake it!" This is his oath as the Buddha of the Latter Day. As such, his deepest concern was not whether or not he was protected by the Buddhist gods, but rather, to carry out his mission.

Then the Daishonin teaches us that we will definitely attain Buddhahood as long as we do not permit ourselves to be overcome by doubts, even when difficulties befall us. In the final section, he also explains that the means used for Buddhist propagation depend on the country and the capacity of the people. There are two ways to propagate the Lotus Sutra: *shōju*, or gentle arguments, and *shakubuku*, or strict refutation. The Daishonin says that Japan of his day, as a nation of slanderers, requires *shakubuku*. Then he concludes that to remove suffering and give joy to the people is the Buddha's teaching. The Daishonin is alone in refuting and rooting out the cause of human miseries. He is the Buddha who possesses the three virtues—the virtues of sovereign, teacher and parent. No matter what others may say about him, he is not shamed. On the contrary, to be praised by the ignorant would be the greatest shame of all. After all, for Nichiren Daishonin the exile to Sado was only a "small suffering" in this life. Rather, he feels "immense joy" even in exile because of the overall results he was confident would come in the future.

The recipient of this treatise, Shijō Kingo, was a leader of the followers in Kamakura and a samurai who served Ema Mitsutoki of the Hōjō clan. Besides his accomplishment in the martial arts, he was reputed to be a skilled physician. He was converted to the Daishonin's Buddhism around 1256. Kingo helped the Daishonin in various ways to propagate his teachings and resolutely protected his fellow believers. He received thirty-seven (extant) letters from the Daishonin.

A passage from "The Three Kinds of Treasure" describes the bond between them: "Over and over I recall the moment, unforgettable even now, when I was about to be beheaded and you accompanied me, holding the reins of my horse and weeping tears of grief. Nor could I ever forget it in any lifetime to come. If you should fall into hell for some grave offense, no matter how Shakyamuni might urge me to become a Buddha, I would refuse; I would rather go to hell with you." At Tatsunokuchi Shijō Kingo had accompanied the Daishonin, resolved to die with him. Also, he journeyed to Sado Island to visit the Daishonin in exile. Communication with an exile was prohibited, so only a few of the most devout disciples attempted even to send a letter or offering. A personal visit was therefore an extreme risk, especially for Shijō Kingo, who was in the employ of the ruling Hōjō clan. Shijō Kingo also sent his messenger to the Daishonin with writing materials and other necessities. On Sado, the Daishonin completed the "The Opening of the Eyes," and delivered it to Shijō Kingo through his messenger.

Why did the Daishonin entrust this treatise to Shijō Kingo in particular? There are at least four possible reasons. First, the faith demonstrated by Shijō Kingo's willingness to give his life for the Lotus Sutra at Tatsunokuchi might well have qualified him in the Daishonin's mind. Secondly, perhaps Shijō Kingo, who had personally witnessed what occurred at Tatsunokuchi, could best understand the full implication of this document. Thirdly, Shijō Kingo was a central figure among the lay believers in Kamakura. Though he alone may have been able to grasp the profound meaning of "The Opening of the Eyes," the Daishonin may have intended to give guidance and encouragement to all the followers in Kamakura through Kingo. Fourth, the Daishonin may have intended, through Shijō Kingo's example, to stress the importance of the role and mission of the believers who assisted him, as stated in "Propagation by the Wise": "Even if there should be a person of wisdom who embraces Buddhism, how could he propagate it without believers who support him ?"

The Causal Law of Life

I HOPE you will read this letter over and over again together with Tōshirō's wife. The sun dispels darkness, no matter how deep. A woman's heart may be likened to darkness, and the Lotus Sutra to the sun. A baby may not always recognize its mother, but a mother never forgets her own baby. Shakyamuni Buddha may be likened to the mother and a woman to the baby. If two people long for one another, then they will never be parted. But though one person yearns for the other, if the other does not feel the same way, then they will be united at times but separated at others. The Buddha may be likened to the one who always longs for the other, and a woman to the one who does not. But if we truly yearn for Shakyamuni Buddha, how could he ever fail to reveal himself to us?

You may call a rock a jewel, but that does not make it one. You may call a jewel a rock, but it remains a jewel. In our age, the doctrines of the Nembutsu and other sects that are based upon the Buddha's provisional teachings are all like rocks. People may say that the Nembutsu is equal to the Lotus Sutra, but that does not in fact make it so. And people may slander the Lotus Sutra, but that does not affect it any more than calling a jewel a rock affects the jewel.

In the past there was an evil ruler in China named Emperor

Hui-tsung.[1] Led astray by Taoist priests, he destroyed Buddhist statues and sutras and forced all the priests and nuns to return to secular life until not one remained in the religious calling. Among the priests was one named the Learned Doctor Fa-tao who refused to be cowed by the Imperial command. As a result, he was branded on the face and exiled to the region south of the Yangtze River. I was born in an age when the rulers put their faith in the Zen sect, which is fully as heretical as the Taoist priests, and I too, like Fa-tao, have met with great difficulties.

You two women were born as commoners and now live in Kamakura, [the seat of the military government,] yet you believe in the Lotus Sutra without concern for the prying eyes of others or the danger it may pose for your lives. This is nothing short of extraordinary. I can only imagine your faith to be like the magic jewel that, when placed in muddy water, miraculously cleanses it. You are like someone who, when taught something new by a wise man, believes his every word and thus grasps the truth. Is this because Shakyamuni Buddha and the Bodhisattvas Fugen, Yakuō and Shukuōke[2] are dwelling in your hearts? The Lotus Sutra declares that people throughout the world are able to believe in the sutra because of the aid extended by Bodhisattva Fugen.[3]

A woman is like a wisteria, a man like a pine. The wisteria cannot stand for a moment if it is separated from the pine tree that supports it. And yet, in this turbulent age, when you do not even have servants you can rely on, you have sent your

1. Hui-tsung (1082–1135): Eighth ruler of the Sung dynasty in China. He ascended the throne in 1100 but took little interest in ruling, devoting his energies instead to calligraphy and painting. His religious policy was to encourage China's native Taoism and destroy Buddhism. In 1127, his dynasty (Northern Sung) was overthrown by the Jürched (Chin) state.

2. Shukuōke: Bodhisattva who appears in the *Yakuō* (23rd) chapter of the Lotus Sutra to play the role of questioning the Buddha. In this chapter, Shakyamuni Buddha orders Bodhisattva Shukuōke to protect the Lotus Sutra with his occult power.

3. Lotus Sutra, chap. 28.

husband here to Sado Island. This shows that your faith is more solid than the earth, and the earthly gods must certainly realize this. Your faith is loftier than the sky, and the heavenly gods Bonten and Taishaku must also be aware of it. The Buddha taught that people from the very moment of their birth are attended by two messengers called Dōshō and Dōmyō[4] who follow them as closely as their own shadows, never leaving them for an instant. These two take turns reporting to heaven the person's good and evil acts, both major and minor, without overlooking the slightest detail. Therefore, heaven must already know about your great faith. How encouraging!

Nichiren

The fourth month

BACKGROUND   When Shijō Kingo visited Sado Island in April 1272 to see Nichiren Daishonin, the Daishonin entrusted him with this letter for his wife, Nichigennyo. Nichigennyo was a name the Daishonin had given her; it is a combination of *nichi* (sun), *gen* (eyes) and *nyo* (woman). He also named her two daughters, Tsukimaro and Kyō'ō. When Kyō'ō took ill, he encouraged her parents with the famous passage, "Kyō'ō Gozen's misfortunes will change into fortune. Muster your faith and pray to this Gohonzon. Then what is there that cannot be achieved?" Shijō Kingo and his wife received frequent guidance and encouragement from the Daishonin, and devoted themselves wholeheartedly to the practice of his Buddhism throughout their lives.

This writing, "The Causal Law of Life," praises Nichigennyo's faith. At the beginning of the letter, the

4. Dōshō and Dōmyō: Two heavenly messengers said to dwell on one's shoulders from the time of one's birth and to observe his every act. They symbolize the workings of the law of cause and effect in life.

Daishonin urges her to read it with Tōshirō's wife. Little is known about Tōshirō; it is believed that he was one of Kingo's colleagues in the Kamakura military government and that his wife was close to Nichigennyo because of their common faith. Tōshirō's wife was also related to the family of Nanjō Tokimitsu, the lord of Ueno District. In a letter dated August 1275 and addressed to Nanjō Tokimitsu's mother, the Daishonin made a similar remark, encouraging her to read it again and again with Tōshirō's wife. In this way he stressed the unity of believers.

Nichiren Daishonin says, "A woman is like a wisteria, a man like a pine. The wisteria cannot stand for a moment if it is separated from the pine tree that supports it." In a feudalistic society, life was difficult for women since their social status was generally inferior to that of men. Nevertheless, at a time when she had no one else to rely on, Nichigennyo sent her husband to Sado all the way from Kamakura on a journey that was not only difficult but dangerous. For this the Daishonin praised her, saying that her faith was firmer than the earth and loftier than the sky.

Dōshō and Dōmyō are said to be messengers of heaven who accompany a person from the moment of his or her birth and report that person's behavior without omitting the slightest detail. These two beings represent the law of cause and effect, which is central to each person's life. One's every action, whether good or evil, is engraved in the depths of one's life and eventually causes either a good or evil effect. Buddhism asserts that the actions of one's past lives exert an effect on his present life, while his present actions shape the future. Life is eternal, and the law of causality penetrates one's life throughout past, present and future existences.

Earthly Desires Are Enlightenment

I DEEPLY appreciate your recent visit here and your constant concern over the numerous persecutions which have befallen me. I have met these great persecutions as the votary of the Lotus Sutra and do not regret them in the slightest. No life could be more fortunate than mine, no matter how many times one might repeat the cycle of birth and death. Were it not for these troubles, I might have remained in the three or four evil paths. But now, to my great joy, I am sure to sever the cycle of sufferings and attain Buddhahood.

T'ien-t'ai and Dengyō suffered persecutions arising out of hate and jealousy merely because they propagated *ichinen sanzen* of the theoretical teaching. In Japan, this teaching was propagated and handed down successively by Dengyō, Gishin,[1] Enchō,[2] Jikaku and others. Among the many disciples who followed the Great Teacher Jie,[3] the eighteenth chief

1. Gishin (781–833): *See* p. 22, footnote 56.
2. Enchō (771–836): Second chief priest of Enryaku-ji temple. He ultimately corrupted the Tendai doctrines by incorporating into them the esoteric teachings of Shingon.
3. Jie (912–985): Eighteenth chief priest of Enryaku-ji temple, a position he assumed at the age of fifty-five. As chief priest he fostered many capable disciples and contributed greatly to the restoration of the Tendai doctrines and the development of the temple.

priest of the Tendai sect, the leading ones were Danna,[4] Eshin,[5] Sōga[6] and Zen'yu.[7] At that time the sect's teachings were divided in two: Abbot Danna transmitted the doctrinal teachings while Priest Eshin devoted himself to the meditative practices. Doctrine is comparable to the moon and practice, to the sun. Doctrinal studies are shallow, while meditative practices are deep. The teachings expounded by Danna were therefore broad but shallow, while Eshin's teachings were deep but limited.

The teaching which I, Nichiren, am now propagating may seem limited, but it is actually most profound. This is because it goes even deeper than the teachings expounded by T'ien-t'ai and Dengyō. It reveals the three important matters[8] contained in the *Juryō* chapter of the essential teaching. To practice only the seven characters of Nam-myoho-renge-kyo may appear limited, yet since this Law is the master of all Buddhas of the past, present and future, the teacher of all bodhisattvas in the universe, and the guide that enables all human beings to attain Buddhahood, its practice is incomparably profound.

The sutra states, "The wisdom of all Buddhas is infinitely profound and immeasurable."[9] "All Buddhas" means every Buddha throughout the universe and in every age of the past,

4. Danna (953–1007): Another name for Kaku'un, the founder of the Danna school of the Tendai sect. His name derives from the fact that he lived in Danna-in sub-temple on Mt. Hiei. Among Jie's disciples, Danna and Eshin were regarded as the two most distinguished Tendai scholars.

5. Eshin (942–1017): Another name for Genshin, the founder of the Eshin school of the Tendai sect. The name Eshin comes from Eshin-in sub-temple on Mt. Hiei.

6. Sōga (917–1003): One of the disciples of Jie. He led a very humble life in his Buddhist practice, heedless of fame or personal interest. It is said that he presented such a shabby, wretched appearance that people mocked him as a madman. In his later years, however, he is said to have gained wide respect and fostered many disciples.

7. Zen'yu: One of the four main disciples of Jie. Details about him are unknown.

8. Three important matters: The Three Great Secret Laws: the true object of worship, the invocation of Nam-myoho-renge-kyo, and the high sanctuary.

9. Lotus Sutra, chap. 2.

present and future, including both Dainichi Buddha of the Shingon sect and Amida Buddha of the Jōdo sect. It represents every single Buddha and bodhisattva of any sutra or sect whatsoever, from the infinite past to the infinite future, even Shakyamuni Buddha himself.

Next, what is meant by the "wisdom" of all Buddhas? It is the true entity manifested in all phenomena, which Shakyamuni revealed in terms of the Ten Factors to lead all people to enlightenment. What then is this entity? It is nothing other than Nam-myoho-renge-kyo. T'ien-t'ai states, "The profound principle of 'true entity' is the original law of Myoho-renge-kyo."[10] The true entity manifested in all phenomena indicates the two Buddhas Shakyamuni and Tahō [seated together in the Treasure Tower]. Tahō represents all phenomena and Shakyamuni, the true entity. The two Buddhas also indicate the two principles of object (*kyō*) and subject (*chi*), or reality and wisdom. Tahō Buddha signifies the object and Shakyamuni, the subject. Although these are two, they are fused into one in the Buddha's enlightenment.

These teachings are of prime importance. They mean that earthly desires are enlightenment and that the sufferings of life and death are nirvana. When one chants Nam-myoho-renge-kyo even during the sexual union of man and woman, then earthly desires are enlightenment and the sufferings of life and death are nirvana. Sufferings are nirvana only when one realizes that the entity of human life throughout its cycle of birth and death is neither born nor destroyed. The *Fugen* Sutra states, "Even without extinguishing their earthly desires or denying the five desires,[11] they can purify all of their senses and eradicate all of their misdeeds." It is stated in the *Maka Shikan* that "the ignorance and dust of desires are enlightenment and

10. Source unknown.
11. Five desires: Desires arising from the contact of the five sensory organs (the eyes, ears, nose, tongue and skin) with the five sensory objects (form, sound, smell, taste and texture).

the sufferings of birth and death are nirvana." The *Juryō* chapter of the Lotus Sutra says, "This is my constant thought: how can I cause all living beings to gain entry to the highest Way and quickly attain Buddhahood?" And the *Hōben* chapter states, "All phenomena are manifestations of the Law and are essentially eternal." The entity of all phenomena is none other than Nam-myoho-renge-kyo.

It was this most august and precious Lotus Sutra which in the past I trampled underfoot, scowled upon in disgust and refused to believe in. In one way or another, I maliciously ridiculed people who studied the Lotus Sutra and who taught it to at least one other person, thereby passing on the Law for the future. In addition, I did everything I could to hinder them from embracing the sutra by asserting that they could practice it in the next life but it would not benefit them in this life.[12] Slanderous acts such as these have now brought on the many severe persecutions that I have suffered in my lifetime. Because I once disparaged the highest of all sutras, I am now looked down upon and my words go unheeded. The *Hiyu* chapter states that [because one slandered the Lotus Sutra in the past] other people will have no sympathy for him even though he sincerely tries to be friendly with them.

As a votary of the Lotus Sutra, you suffered severe persecutions, yet still you came to my assistance. In the *Hosshi* chapter, the Buddha states, "I will send priests, nuns and lay men and women [to make offerings to the teacher of the Lotus Sutra and hear his preaching of the Law]." If you are not one of these laymen, then to whom else could the passage possibly refer? You have not only heard the Law, but have taken faith in it and since then have followed it without turning aside. How

12. According to the Pure Land sect, the Lotus Sutra is too profound to be understood by common mortals in the evil Latter Day of the Law, and it is therefore a waste of time to embrace it in this lifetime. Rather, they assert, one should chant the Nembutsu and obtain rebirth in the Pure Land, where he can then practice the Lotus Sutra more easily.

wondrous! How extraordinary! Then how can there be any doubt that I, Nichiren, am the teacher of the Lotus Sutra? I have fulfilled the words of the Buddha: "He is the envoy of the Buddha, sent to carry out the Buddha's work."[13] I have propagated the five characters of the daimoku which were entrusted to Bodhisattva Jōgyō when the two Buddhas sat together within the Treasure Tower. Does this not indicate that I am an envoy of Bodhisattva Jōgyō? Moreover, following me as a votary of the Lotus Sutra, you also tell others of this Law. What else could this be but the transmission of the Mystic Law?

Carry through with your faith in the Lotus Sutra. You cannot strike fire from flint if you stop halfway. Bring forth the great power of faith and establish your reputation among all the people of Kamakura and the rest of Japan as "Shijō Kingo of the Hokke sect."[14] Even a bad reputation will spread far and wide. A good reputation will spread even farther, particularly if it is a reputation for devotion to the Lotus Sutra.

Explain all this to your wife, and work together like the sun and the moon, a pair of eyes, or the two wings of a bird. With the sun and the moon, how can you fall into the paths of darkness? With a pair of eyes, how can you fail to behold the faces of Shakyamuni, Tahō and all the other Buddhas of the universe? With a pair of wings, you will surely be able to fly in an instant to the Buddha land of eternal happiness. I will write in more detail on another occasion.

With my deep respect,
Nichiren

The second day of the fifth month

13. Lotus Sutra, chap. 10.
14. Hokke sect: The orthodox stream of Buddhism. It originally indicated T'ien-t'ai's teachings which are based on the Lotus Sutra. Here it refers to the Daishonin's teachings.

BACKGROUND   Toward the end of March 1272, Shijō Kingo sent his messenger to Nichiren Daishonin who was living in exile on Sado Island. The messenger returned to Kamakura with a treatise entitled "The Opening of the Eyes," which the Daishonin had addressed to all of his disciples and entrusted to Shijō Kingo. In this writing, Nichiren Daishonin clearly reveals that he is the Buddha who possesses the three virtues of sovereign, teacher and parent. It states in part, "When it comes to understanding the Lotus Sutra, I have only a minute fraction of the vast ability that T'ien-t'ai and Dengyō possessed. But in my ability to endure persecution and the wealth of my compassion for others, I believe I would put them to shame." Another part reads, "I, Nichiren, am sovereign, teacher, father and mother to all the people of Japan." The Daishonin here defines the true object of worship in terms of the Person, i.e., in terms of the Buddha who eternally guides, protects and nurtures all people in their striving for Buddhahood.

In April 1272, Shijō Kingo journeyed from Kamakura to visit the Daishonin on Sado. It required great courage for Kingo to leave Kamakura. He was then in service to Lord Ema Mitsutoki of the ruling Hōjō clan, the same family who had exiled the Daishonin in the first place. Moreover, the journey itself to Sado and back across the Sea of Japan took almost a month and entailed a long series of hardships.

Nichiren Daishonin had been transferred on April 3 from his hut at Tsukahara to an ordinary residence at Ichinosawa. The number of people on Sado professing faith in his Buddhism had increased, and at the house in which he lived, the landlord's wife became a believer and the landlord himself developed a favorable attitude.

Soon after Shijō Kingo returned to Kamakura, Nichiren Daishonin wrote him this letter, entitled "Earthly Desires Are Enlightenment," on May 2, 1272. It was very likely written out of his gratitude for Kingo's visit. Before the near-execution at

Tatsunokuchi in September 1271, the Daishonin had assumed the role of Bodhisattva Jōgyō, the votary whose appearance had been predicted in the Lotus Sutra. He spent all his time teaching the essence of the sutra and propagating the faith. After Tatsunokuchi, he revealed his true identity as the Buddha from time without beginning who is one with the supreme law of Nam-myoho-renge-kyo. In this Gosho, Nichiren Daishonin teaches his followers the significance of the daimoku from the standpoint of the original Buddha who opens the way to Buddhahood for all mankind. He first states that it is his great joy to meet persecutions as the votary of the Lotus Sutra, because it is the sure way to attaining Buddhahood. "The teaching which I, Nichiren, am now propagating may seem limited, but it is actually most profound. This is because it goes even deeper than the teachings expounded by T'ien-t'ai and Dengyō." He reveals that the ultimate law attained by all the Buddhas throughout time and space is none other than Nam-myoho-renge-kyo of the Three Great Secret Laws.

Also, the Daishonin shows the power of the Law by referring to such profound Buddhist doctrines as the fusion of object (*kyō*) and subject (*chi*) and "earthly desires are enlightenment." This Gosho states, "Although these [*kyō* and *chi*] are two, they are fused into one in the Buddha's enlightenment." It refers to the fusion of the person and the object to which he is enlightened. "Object" or reality means the Gohonzon, the objective embodiment of Buddhahood, while "subject" or wisdom indicates people who develop their innate Buddha wisdom by fusing their lives with the Gohonzon. In a practical sense, the doctrine of "earthly desires are enlightenment" indicates that the mundane cravings of the individual, when tempered by faith in the True Law, become the fuel for enlightenment.

Letter to Gijō-bō

I HAVE carefully reviewed your question about Buddhism. The blessing of the Lotus Sutra can only be understood and shared by Buddhas. It is the kind of enlightenment that even the wisdom of Shakyamuni Buddha's emanations throughout the universe can barely fathom, if at all. This is why, as you well know, the Great Teacher T'ien-t'ai defined the word *myō* [of Myoho-renge-kyo] as that which is mysterious.[1] The Lotus Sutra proclaims a great diversity of practices, but only T'ien-t'ai, Miao-lo and Dengyō were able to understand the heart of them. Among these men, the Great Teacher Dengyō was the reincarnation of T'ien-t'ai [and therefore well versed in the T'ien-t'ai doctrine]. Nevertheless, he sent envoys to China on many occasions in an effort to resolve the common doubts of others concerning the sutra. The essence of the sutra is the mutual possession of the Ten Worlds, one hundred worlds and one thousand factors, and *ichinen sanzen*. This is a doctrine of great importance which was revealed in [T'ien-t'ai's] *Maka Shikan*.

The teaching of the *Juryō* chapter bears special significance for me, Nichiren. The great scholars of Buddhism such as T'ien-t'ai and Dengyō understood it in a general way but did not reveal it in words, and the same was true of Nagarjuna and

1. Introduction to the *Hokke Gengi*.

235

Vasubandhu. The *jigage*, the verse section of the chapter, states, "Single-mindedly yearning to see the Buddha, they do not begrudge their lives." I, Nichiren, have called forth Buddhahood from within my life by living this sentence. This means that I actualized the Three Great Secret Laws, the embodiment of *ichinen sanzen* in the *Juryō* chapter. But let us keep this to ourselves!

Dengyō, the Great Teacher of Mount Hiei, journeyed to China to receive instruction in the profound meaning of this sentence from the sutra. "Single" of "single-mindedly" means the one pure way,[2] and "mind" indicates all phenomena and existences. The Great Teacher T'ien-t'ai explained the Chinese character for "mind" by saying that it consists of four brush strokes representing the moon and three stars and implies that the mind of the common mortal is ultimately pure.[3] My interpretation of the passage is that "single" stands for *myō*, "mind" for *hō*, "yearning" for *ren*, "see" for *ge*, and "Buddha" for *kyō*. In propagating these five characters of Myoho-renge-kyo, one should be willing to give up his life.

"Single-mindedly yearning to see the Buddha" also means to see the Buddha in one's own mind, to concentrate one's mind on seeing the Buddha, and that to see one's own mind is to see the Buddha. I have attained Buddhahood, the eternally inherent three enlightened properties of life,[4] by living this sentence. In teaching this I am sure I surpass T'ien-t'ai and Dengyō, Nagarjuna and Mahakashyapa. Forge ahead in your faith. The Buddha states that one should become the master of

2. One pure way: The true entity permeating all phenomena.
3. Source unknown.
4. Three enlightened properties of life: Here means that Nichiren Daishonin is the original Buddha eternally endowed with the three properties—the truth of a Buddha's life (*hosshin*), the wisdom to perceive that truth (*hōshin*) and the merciful actions of a Buddha to save the people (*ōjin*). "The three enlightened properties" of the original Buddha are defined as *musa* (literally "not created"), a Buddhist term meaning "natural" or "eternally inherent."

his mind rather than let his mind master him.[5] This is why I have emphatically urged you to be willing to give up your body and your life for the sake of the Lotus Sutra. Nam-myoho-renge-kyo, Nam-myoho-renge-kyo.

Nichiren

The twenty-eighth day of the fifth month in the tenth year of Bun'ei (1273)

BACKGROUND   Although this letter is short, it contains some very important principles. It was written on May 28, 1273, to Gijō-bō, who had been the Daishonin's senior at Seichō-ji temple. Only about a month before, Nichiren Daishonin had written "The True Object of Worship," in which he had revealed the object of worship in terms of the Law and the correct practice for enlightenment in the Latter Day. The "Letter to Gijō-bō" restates the profound contents of "The True Object of Worship," though much more concisely.

In Buddhism the mind, besides the conventional implications of heart, psyche and spirit, indicates one's life itself. Buddhism teaches us the law of life, and it shows us how we can develop our inherent Buddhahood. In "The True Object of Worship," Nichiren Daishonin elaborated on "observing the mind." He expounded the object of worship as the key to understanding one's mind.

Buddhist practice is prerequisite for us to "see our minds," that is, to manifest our innate Buddha nature. First, Nichiren Daishonin explains the correct way of practice, and then he states that he appeared in this world in order to establish true Buddhism, the essence of the Buddha's teachings, for all mankind.

5. Nirvana Sutra, chap. 11.

The Daishonin says that, of all the chapters of the Lotus Sutra, the *Juryō* (16th) chapter is especially important to him. He quotes a passage, ". . . single-mindedly yearning to see the Buddha, they do not begrudge their lives . . . ," and notes: "I, Nichiren, have called forth Buddhahood from within my life by living this sentence. This means that I actualized the Three Great Secret Laws, the embodiment of *ichinen sanzen* in the *Juryō* chapter." He concludes that the ultimate meaning of this passage is Nam-myoho-renge-kyo of the Three Great Secret Laws, to which he was enlightened but which remained only in his heart.

This is the first mention in his writings of the Three Great Secret Laws: the invocation (Nam-myoho-renge-kyo), the object of worship (the Dai-Gohonzon, for whose inscription he was preparing), and the place of worship (the sanctuary of the true object, whose construction he would entrust to his disciples). He elaborated on these three in "Repaying Debts of Gratitude" written in 1276.

Hell and Buddhahood

I HAVE received your many gifts. Nothing would please me more than to know that you have communicated with the late Lord Ueno, but I know that that is impossible. Perhaps only in a dream or a vision can you see him. Never fear, though; your late husband must certainly be in the pure land of Eagle Peak, listening and watching over this *saha* world day and night. You, his wife, and your children have only mortal senses, so you cannot see or hear him, but be assured that you will eventually be reunited on Eagle Peak.

Counting all your previous lives, you must have shared the bonds of matrimony with as many men as there are grains of sand in the ocean. However, the man to whom you were wed in this life is your true husband. He is the only one who brought you to practice the teachings of the Lotus Sutra. You should revere him as a Buddha. Indeed, he was a Buddha while alive, and in death, he is a Buddha still. His Buddhahood transcends both life and death. This is the meaning of the profound doctrine of *sokushin jōbutsu*, or attaining enlightenment as a common mortal. The fourth volume of the Lotus Sutra states: "One who sincerely embraces this sutra is thereby embracing Buddhahood."

Neither the pure land nor hell exists outside ourselves; both lie within our own hearts. Awakened to this truth, one is called a Buddha; deluded about it, he is a common mortal. The Lotus Sutra awakens us to this reality, and one who embraces the Lotus Sutra will find that hell is itself the enlightened land.

Even though one may practice the provisional teachings for uncountable aeons, he will only fall into hell if he turns against the Lotus Sutra. These are not my own words; they were proclaimed by Shakyamuni Buddha and confirmed by Tahō Buddha and all of Shakyamuni's emanations throughout the universe. To practice the provisional teachings is to be like a man scorched by fire who enters deeper and deeper into the flames, or like a drowning man sinking to the bottom of the deep waters. Not to embrace the Lotus Sutra is like jumping into fire or water. Those who are deluded by such evil companions as Hōnen, Kōbō and other slanderers of the Lotus Sutra and believe in the *Amida* or *Dainichi* Sutra are falling farther and farther into the fire or sinking deeper and deeper toward the bottom of the water. How can they possibly escape from agony? They will doubtless undergo the terrible heat of the hells of *tōkatsu*, *kokujō* and *mugen*,[1] and the unbearable cold of the hells of *guren* and *daiguren*.[2] The second volume of the Lotus Sutra reads, "After he dies, he will fall into the hell of incessant suffering. [After one aeon he will be reborn only to

1. *Tōkatsu, kokujō* and *mugen*: Metaphorical descriptions of the life-conditions experienced by those in the state of Hell. Descriptions of hell vary according to the different sutras and related treatises. These three are included among the so-called eight hot hells. *Tōkatsu* is the first of these eight hells, where people are said to fight each other viciously with iron claws, or are tortured by guards armed with iron staves and razor-sharp sabers. *Kokujō* is the second of the eight hells, in which people are either sawn in half or slashed by redhot axes according to whether they are longer or wider than a red-hot iron measuring rope. Suffering in *kokujō* is said to be ten times worse than in *tōkatsu*. Those who have committed the five cardinal sins are said to undergo indescribable torture in the last and severest hell, *mugen* (the hell of incessant suffering).

2. Hells of *guren* and *daiguren*: Literally, "blood-red lotus" and "great blood-red lotus," two of the eight cold hells. In "Letter to Niike," Nichiren Daishonin writes: "The hell of the blood-red lotus is so called because the intense cold of this hell makes one double over until his back splits open and the bloody flesh emerges like a crimson lotus flower. And there are hells even more horrible."

fall back into hell, and] he will go through this cycle for countless aeons."

Your late husband has escaped such agonies, for he was a follower of Nichiren, the votary of the Lotus Sutra. A passage from the sutra reads: "Even if they fall into a great fire, they will not be burned. . . . If they are swept away by a great flood, by chanting its name they can straightaway reach shallow water."[3] Another passage reads, "The good fortune of the believer cannot be burned by fire or washed away by water."[4] How reassuring!

You may think of hell, the iron rods of the guards of hell or the rending cries of Abōrasetsu[5] as existing way off in some faraway place, but they are not like that. This teaching is of prime importance, and yet I will impart it to you just as Bodhisattva Monju revealed to the Dragon King's daughter the secret teaching of *sokushin jōbutsu*, that one can attain Buddhahood as a common mortal. Now that you are about to receive that teaching, strive even more earnestly in your faith. One who practices still more earnestly whenever he hears the teachings of the Lotus Sutra is a true seeker of the Way. When T'ien-t'ai stated, "From the indigo, an even deeper blue,"[6] he meant that something dyed with indigo becomes even bluer than the indigo plant itself. For us the Lotus Sutra is the indigo plant, and the growing intensity of our practice is "an even deeper blue."

The word *jigoku* or "hell" can be interpreted to mean digging a hole in the ground. A hole is always dug for one who dies; this is what is called "hell." The flames that reduce his body to ashes are the fires of incessant suffering. His wife, children and relatives hurrying the dead man to his grave are

3. Lotus Sutra, chap. 25.
4. Ibid., chap. 23.
5. Abōrasetsu: (Skt Avorakṣas) Jailers in hell, who have the head of an ox and the hands of human beings. They are said to cut down evildoers with razor-sharp swords.
6. *Maka Shikan*, vol. 1.

the guards of hell, called Abōrasetsu. The plaintive cries of his family are the voices of the guards of hell. The meter-long walking stick of the dead man is the iron rod of torture in hell. The horses and oxen that carry the deceased are the horse-headed and ox-headed demons, and the grave itself is the hell of incessant suffering. The eighty-four thousand earthly desires are eighty-four thousand cauldrons for torturing the dead. The dead man leaving his home is departing on a journey to the mountain of death, while the river beside which his loving children stand in grief is the river of three crossings. It is useless to look for hell anywhere else.

Those who embrace the Lotus Sutra, however, can change all this. For them, hell changes into the enlightened land, the burning fires of agony change into the torch of wisdom of the Buddha in his property-of-wisdom aspect; the dead person becomes a Buddha in his property-of-Law aspect; and the fiery inferno becomes the abode where the Buddha in his property-of-action aspect[7] manifests his great mercy. Moreover, the walking stick is transformed into that of the true entity of the Mystic Law, the river of three crossings becomes the ocean of "sufferings are nirvana," and the mountain of death becomes the towering peak of "earthly desires are enlightenment." Please think of your husband in these terms. To realize all this is to attain enlightenment as a common mortal, and to awaken to it is to open the inner eye of the Buddha wisdom. Devadatta changed the hell of incessant suffering into the enlightened paradise, and the Dragon King's daughter also was able to attain enlightenment without changing her dragon form. The Lotus Sutra can bring enlightenment even to those who at first oppose it. Such great benefits are contained in the single character *myō*.

Bodhisattva Nagarjuna wrote, "[The Lotus Sutra is] like a

7. Property-of-wisdom aspect, property-of-Law aspect and property-of-action aspect: The three enlightened properties with which Buddha is endowed. *See* Three properties of life in the Glossary.

great physician who changes poison into medicine."[8] Miao-lo stated, "How can one find the eternal, enlightened land anywhere outside Buddh Gaya? This *saha* world does not exist outside the Buddha land."[9] He also said, "The true entity is invariably revealed in all phenomena, and all phenomena invariably possess the Ten Factors. The Ten Factors invariably function within the Ten Worlds, and the Ten Worlds invariably entail both life and its environment."[10] The Lotus Sutra reads, "The true entity of all phenomena can only be understood and shared between Buddhas. This reality consists of the appearance, nature . . . and their consistency from beginning to end." A passage from the *Juryō* chapter states, "The time is limitless and boundless . . . since I in fact attained Buddhahood." Here, "I" means all people in the Ten Worlds. All people of the Ten Worlds inherently have in them the Buddha nature; so they dwell in the pure land. A passage from the *Hōben* chapter reads, "All phenomena are manifestations of the Law and are essentially eternal." Birth and death are the constant manifestations of eternal life continuing on through past, present and future. This is nothing to regret or be surprised at. Even all the eight phases of a Buddha's existence[11] are subject to the law of birth and death. The votaries of the Lotus Sutra are enlightened to all this, thereby attaining Buddhahood as common mortals. Since your deceased husband was a votary of this sutra, he doubtless attained enlightenment. You need not grieve so much over his passing. But to grieve is natural, as you are a common mortal. Even saints are sometimes saddened. Although Shakyamuni Buddha's greatest disciples realized the truth of life, they were human also and could not help lamenting his death.

By all means offer devoted prayers for your husband. The

8. *Daichido Ron.*
9. *Hokke Mongu Ki*, vol. 26.
10. *Kongōbei Ron.*
11. Eight phases of a Buddha's existence: *See* p. 122, footnote 135.

words of a wise priest, "Base your heart on the Ninth Consciousness[12] and your practice on the six consciousnesses,[13]"[14] are indeed well said. This letter contains one of Nichiren's most profound teachings. Keep it deep within your heart.

Respectfully,
Nichiren

The eleventh day of the seventh month

BACKGROUND   An ancient Chinese maxim states: "If a sage admonishes his sovereign three times and still is not heeded, he should depart the country." In April of 1274, after winning his release from exile on Sado Island, Nichiren Daishonin remonstrated with the Kamakura government for the third time. He passionately declared to the government leaders that the primary cause for the people's sufferings lay in their belief in misleading religions. As with the first two remonstrations—when he presented the "Risshō Ankoku Ron" in 1260, and at the time of his arrest before the Tatsunokuchi Persecution in 1271—his words were ignored. Nichiren Daishonin decided that he had done all that he could in Kamakura, where priests, officials and many of the people refused to heed his warning. Convinced that the government would not soon recognize its errors, he left Kamakura on May 12, 1274, and settled about thirty kilometers west of Mount Fuji at a small dwelling at the base of Mount Minobu.

His life at Minobu was far from easy. He lived in an out-of-

12.   Ninth Consciousness: The fundamental purifying force that is the essence of our lives—the law of Nam-myoho-renge-kyo itself.
13.   Six consciousnesses: The first six of nine consciousnesses, a classification of the spiritual functions of perception. The first five consciousnesses are the perceptions of the five senses: sight, hearing, smell, taste and touch. The sixth consciousness enables one to integrate the perceptions of the five senses and form judgments about them. See also Nine consciousnesses in the Glossary.
14.   Source unknown.

the-way place, covered with snow in winter and tall weeds in summer. Often he ran short of food and clothing. His chief occupation in retirement was to prepare for the future by inscribing the Dai-Gohonzon and training disciples who could carry on his teachings.

On July 11, 1274, Nichiren Daishonin wrote this letter and addressed it to the mother of Nanjō Tokimitsu. Tokimitsu was the lord of Ueno District, Suruga Province. Also called Lord Ueno, he is famous in the annals of Nichiren Shoshu as the donor of the land for the Head Temple, Taiseki-ji. Tokimitsu's mother staunchly upheld her faith and single-handedly raised her nine children, following the death of her husband in 1265. Nichiren Daishonin wrote this letter in gratitude for offerings she had made for the repose of her late husband.

In this letter, Nichiren Daishonin states that when one embraces the Lotus Sutra, he will be able to realize the pure land inherent within himself, that is, the supreme state of Buddhahood. He encourages Lady Ueno by saying that her late husband must certainly have attained Buddhahood as a votary of the Lotus Sutra. He also explains the profound principle of *sokushin jōbutsu*, or attaining enlightenment as you are.

Curing Karmic Disease

I SEE from your letter that you have been stricken with a painful affliction. Knowing you are in agony grieves me, but, on the other hand, it is cause for delight. The Vimalakirti Sutra states, "Once the wealthy Vimalakirti[1] of his own volition became ill. At that time the Buddha told Bodhisattva Monju to go and visit him and inquire after his illness." The Nirvana Sutra says, "At that time the Tathagata . . . assumed the appearance of one who is ill in body, and lay on his right side like a sick man." The Lotus Sutra states, "[The Tathagata is at ease,] with few ailments and few troubles."[2] The eighth volume of the *Maka Shikan* explains, "Vimalakirti utilized his sickbed in Vaishali[3] to expound his teachings . . . The Tathagata used his death to teach the eternity of life and clarified the power of Buddhism through sickness." Another passage from the *Maka Shikan* says, "There are six causes of illness: 1)

1.   Vimalakirti: *See* p. 89, footnote 63.
2.   Lotus Sutra, chap. 15. This is the answer to a question addressed to Shakyamuni Buddha by the Bodhisattvas of the Earth: "Is the World-Honored One in comfort, with few ailments and few troubles?"
3.   Vaishali: One of the sixteen major countries in ancient India. The Licchavi tribe, to which Vimalakirti belonged, lived here. Vaishali was also one of the Vajji Allied Nations. Shakyamuni Buddha often visited Vaishali to preach Buddhism. After the Buddha's passing, the second assembly for compiling the Buddha's teachings was held there.

disharmony of the four elements;[4] 2) immoderate eating or drinking; 3) poor posture; 4) an attack by demons from without; 5) the work of devils from within, and 6) the effects of karma."

The Nirvana Sutra reads, "There are three types of people whose illness is extremely difficult to cure. They are : 1) those who slander Mahayana Buddhism, 2) those who commit the five cardinal sins, and 3) those of incorrigible disbelief (*icchantika*). People in these categories suffer the worst known maladies."

Another passage from the Nirvana Sutra states, "One who creates evil karma in this life will surely suffer the torments of hell in the next. However, by serving the three treasures, one can avoid falling into hell in the next life, but will instead suffer afflictions of the head, eye or back in this one." The *Maka Shikan* states, "Even if one has committed heavy slanders . . . their retribution can be lessened in this life. Thus, illness occurs when evil karma is about to be dissipated." In his *Daichido Ron*, Bodhisattva Nagarjuna writes, "Question: If that is so, then none of the sutras from the *Kegon* to the *Hannya* is a secret teaching, but the Lotus Sutra is secret. . . . The Lotus Sutra is like a great physician who changes poison into medicine." T'ien-t'ai explained the quotation further, saying, "This sutra enables the people of the two vehicles to attain enlightenment in the same way that a skilled physician can change poison into medicine." Therefore, the *Daichido Ron* reads, "No other sutras are secret, but the Lotus Sutra is secret." The *Maka Shikan* says, "Since the Lotus Sutra can cure [illness], it is also called *myō* or mystic." Miao-lo said, "Because it can cure that which is thought to be incurable, it is called *myō* or mystic."[5]

The Nirvana Sutra relates the following story: "King Ajata-shatru of Rajagriha was wicked by nature . . . He killed his father, but later, in a fit of remorse, he developed a high fever

4. Four elements: *See* p. 191, footnote 113.
5. *Guketsu*, vol. 6.

and boils broke out over his entire body. They were foul and evil-smelling, repelling all who came near. His mother, Vaidehi, tried to help by applying various medicines, but this only made the boils worse; there appeared to be no hope of recovery. The king explained to his mother that the boils had a spiritual cause and did not arise from a disharmony of the four elements, and that therefore ordinary physicians could not cure them. Then the World-Honored One, the compassionate and merciful teacher, entered into a special 'moon-loving' meditation[6] for the king's sake. When he had reached the deepest stage of his meditation, a brilliant ray of light shone forth from the Buddha and fell upon the body of the king. In that instant the boils were healed."

The seventh volume of the Lotus Sutra, the sutra of universal wisdom, says, "This sutra is beneficial medicine for the illnesses of all mankind. If one is ill and can hear of this sutra, his illness will vanish immediately, and he will find perpetual youth and eternal life."

In light of the above quotations, it would seem that your illness cannot have originated anywhere outside the six causes of disease. I will set aside the first five causes for the moment. Illnesses of the sixth, which result from karma, are the most difficult to cure. They vary in severity and one cannot make any fixed pronouncements, but we know that the gravest illnesses result from slandering the Lotus Sutra. Even Shen Nung, Huang Ti,[7] Hua T'o[8] and Pien Ch'üeh[9] threw up their

6. Moon-loving meditation: Here the boundless compassion of the Buddha is compared to the moonlight which releases one from uneasiness and brings him peace of mind.

7. Shen Nung and Huang Ti: Two of the Three Rulers, legendary ideal rulers of ancient China who were skilled in medical matters.

8. Hua T'o: A physician of the Later Han, said to have been especially skilled in surgical operations. When acupuncture and medicine proved ineffectual, he performed surgery under anesthesia. He invented a system of physical exercise which he himself practiced. As a result, he is said to have been still vigorous even at the age of one hundred.

9. Pien Ch'üeh: A physician of the Spring and Autumn period (722–481 B.C.) in China. In his boyhood he learned medical arts and is said to have been

hands, and Jisui, Rusui,[10] Jivaka[11] and Vimalakirti likewise kept silent. Such illnesses can only be cured by the beneficial medicine of Shakyamuni Buddha's Lotus Sutra, as that sutra itself explains.

The Nirvana Sutra, referring to the Lotus Sutra, states, "Even slander of the True Law will be eradicated if one repents and professes faith in the True Law. . . . He should devote himself to the True Law, because no other teaching can save or protect him." The Great Teacher Miao-lo says, "Shakyamuni himself in the Nirvana Sutra says that the Lotus Sutra is the highest of his teachings."[12] He further says, "One who falls to the ground rises by pushing himself up from the ground. In the same way, one with an evil heart who is destined for hell can, by slandering the True Law, be saved by it."[13]

Bodhisattva Vasubandhu was originally a scholar of Hinayana Buddhism. In an effort to prevent Mahayana Buddhism from spreading throughout India, he wrote five hundred treatises on Hinayana Buddhism. He awoke to the error of his views, however, when he talked with Bodhisattva Asanga.[14] Vasubandhu told Asanga that he wanted to cut out his tongue in order to eradicate the error of his former preaching. Asanga restrained him, saying, "Instead, use your tongue to praise

skilled in treating almost all kinds of diseases.

10. Jisui and Rusui: A father and son, both excellent physicians, who are described in the *Konkōmyō* Sutra. According to that sutra, they lived countless aeons ago. At one time, an epidemic broke out and spread through their country. Jisui was too old to perform medical treatment, but Rusui mastered his medical art and, in his father's place, saved the people from the epidemic.

11. Jivaka: An Indian physician in Shakyamuni's time. Immediately after birth he is said to have seized hold of the acupuncture needle and medicine bag. He had devout faith in Buddhism and also served as a minister to King Ajatashatru.

12. *Hokke Mongu Ki.*

13. Ibid.

14. Asanga: Elder brother of Vasubandhu. According to tradition, Vasubandhu heard that his elder brother was ill and went to visit him. Asanga explained that he had become ill with grief thinking of the suffering his younger brother would incur from slandering Mahayana, and persuaded him to renounce his faith in Hinayana. *See also* p. 106, footnote 95.

Mahayana Buddhism." Then Vasubandhu immediately wrote five hundred treatises on Mahayana Buddhism in order to refute Hinayana Buddhism. He also vowed that he would never preach another word of Hinayana Buddhism for the rest of his life. In this way he eradicated his slander and was later reborn in the heaven where Bodhisattva Miroku lives.[15]

Bodhisattva Ashvaghosha, a native of eastern India, was thirteenth among Shakyamuni's successors.[16] At one time Ashvaghosha had been a leader of Brahmanism. However, when he debated with the Buddhist monk Punyayasha[17] over the validity of their respective teachings, he quickly realized the superiority of Buddhism. Ashvaghosha was prepared to behead himself in order to pay for his past offense, saying, "I have been my own worst enemy, leading myself to hell." But Punya-yasha admonished him, saying, "Do not behead yourself! Instead, use your mind and your mouth to praise Mahayana Buddhism." Ashvaghosha soon thereafter wrote the *Daijō Kishin Ron* (Awakening of Faith in the Mahayana), in which he refuted all Brahman teachings as well as Hinayana Buddhism. This marked the beginning of the spread of Mahayana Buddhism in India.

The Great Teacher Chi-tsang[18] of Chia-hsiang temple was among the most outstanding scholar-priests in China. He was the founder of the Sanron sect, and lived in Hui in Wu. Believing that none could equal him in knowledge, he was very haughty. He challenged the Great Teacher T'ien-t'ai to discuss the meaning of the phrase in the Lotus Sutra which

15. Heaven where Bodhisattva Miroku lives: Tushita Heaven, the fourth of the six heavens in the world of desire. Miroku is described in a sutra as having been reborn in this heaven after his death.

16. Shakyamuni's successors: *See* Twenty-four successors in the Glossary.

17. Punyayasha: One of the Buddha's twenty-four successors. A native of Pataliputra in Magadha, he was entrusted with the teachings by Parshva and transferred them to Ashvaghosha.

18. Chi-tsang (549–623): Also called Chia-hsiang, after the name of the temple where he lived. He laid the foundation for the San-lun (Sanron) sect in sixth-century China but later became a follower of T'ien-t'ai.

states: "Of all the innumerable sutras I have taught, now teach, or will teach in the future, the Lotus Sutra is the most difficult to believe and the most difficult to understand." In the debate, Chi-tsang was soundly defeated, and thereupon renounced his misguided beliefs. In order to expiate his heavy slander of the True Law and those who practiced it, he gathered more than one hundred eminent scholars and begged T'ien-t'ai to lecture to them. Chi-tsang used his body as a bridge for the Great Teacher T'ien-t'ai to walk on and supported T'ien-t'ai's feet with his head.[19] Moreover, he served T'ien-t'ai for seven years, cutting firewood and drawing water for him. He ceased giving lectures of his own, dispersed his followers and, in order to purge himself of his great conceit, refrained from reciting the Lotus Sutra.[20] After T'ien-t'ai's death, Chi-tsang had an audience with the emperor of the Sui dynasty to pay his respects. As he was leaving, he clutched His Majesty's knees and tearfully bade him farewell. Sometime later, Chi-tsang looked into an old mirror and, seeing his reflection, condemned himself for his past errors. All these many acts of penitence were done to eradicate his evil karma.

The Lotus Sutra, the supreme vehicle, is the golden teaching of the three sages.[21] Likened to an unsurpassed gem, it ranks highest among all the teachings of the past, present and future. There are passages in the Lotus Sutra which say, "This sutra is superior to all other sutras," and "The Lotus Sutra is the foremost of all teachings." The Great Teacher Dengyō said that

19.   This means that when T'ien-t'ai mounted an elevated seat for preaching, Chi-tsang carried T'ien-t'ai on his back and lifted him up.
20.   That is, Chi-tsang felt he was not qualified to recite the Lotus Sutra. A passage from the Gosho "Requital for the Buddha's Favor" reads, ". . . he [Chi-tsang] said, 'If I were to go on standing before my disciples and lecturing on the Lotus Sutra, they might suppose that I have the ability to understand the sutra correctly, when in fact I do not.' Chi-tsang was both older and more eminent than T'ien-t'ai, and yet, in the presence of others, he deliberately put his teacher T'ien-t'ai on his back and carried him across the river."
21.   Three sages: Shakyamuni Buddha, Tahō Buddha and all the other Buddhas of the ten directions.

[of all the sects in Japan,] the Hokke (Lotus) sect is the very one "founded by Shakyamuni Buddha himself."[22]

I have made a thorough study of the *Dainichi, Kongōchō, Soshitsuji* and other sutras upon which the Shingon sect is based, but have found nothing written in them to justify the claim that these sutras are superior to the Lotus Sutra. This claim appears to be no more than the prejudiced view held by Shan-wu-wei, Chin-kang-chih, Pu-k'ung, Kōbō, Jikaku, Chishō and others. Now, more than ever, I realize that it is the real intent of the Buddhas Shakyamuni and Dainichi to place the Lotus Sutra above all other sutras. When Kōbō Daishi, founder of the Shingon sect in Japan, Jikaku Daishi and Chishō Daishi went to China during the T'ang dynasty, they inherited from Hui-kuo[23] and Fa-ch'üan[24] the distorted doctrines originally held by Shan-wu-wei, Chin-kang-chih and Pu-k'ung. Returning to Japan, they propagated the Lotus Sutra and the Shingon teachings in such a way as to make it seem that the dim light of fireflies—the two Shingon mandalas[25]—outshone the full moon of the Lotus Sutra, the supreme vehicle which surpasses all other sutras of the past, present and future. Not only that, they slandered the Lotus Sutra, saying that it was a work of "childish theory" and that the Buddha of the Lotus Sutra was still in the region of darkness. However, these comments were like a dagger turned against those who made them. It is not the Lotus Sutra but the *Dainichi* Sutra that is filled with childish theory, and it was Dainichi himself who

22. *Hokke Shūku.*
23. Hui-kuo (746–805): The seventh master in the lineage of esoteric (Shingon) Buddhism. He studied esoteric teachings under Pu-k'ung. When Kōbō came to China from Japan, Hui-kuo transferred the doctrines of the Womb World mandala of the *Dainichi* and the Diamond World mandala of the *Kongōchō* Sutra to him.
24. Fa-ch'üan: A Chinese priest of the esoteric teachings. He transferred the doctrines of the esoteric teachings to Jikaku and Chishō when they journeyed to China in 838 and in 853, respectively. He wrote many treatises on the esoteric teachings.
25. Two Shingon mandalas: *See* p. 156, footnote 39.

was in the region of darkness. The roots of the Shingon sect were its founders, and they were warped, to begin with. So how could its branches, their disciples and followers, be otherwise? Contamination at the source of a river will pollute its entire length. Because of this, the tree of Japan has had a long, dark night and is now about to be blighted by an alien frost.

Although you were not in the mainstream of Shingon, you were still a retainer of a patron of that sect. You lived for many years in a house whose family was dedicated to an erroneous sect, and month after month your mind was infected by the teachers of error. Though huge mountains may crumble and the great seas dry up, this offense of yours will not easily pass away. However, because of the influence of past karma and the mercy that the Buddha bestows on you in this lifetime, you have met me and have determined to reform your ways. Therefore you will be spared worse suffering, though at the moment your offense has brought on these boils from which you suffer.

King Ajatashatru suffered from severe boils because he committed the five cardinal sins and slandered the Lotus Sutra. But his boils disappeared instantly when the light produced by the Buddha's "moon-loving" meditation illuminated his body. And, though it had been predicted that the king had only twenty-one days left to live, his life span was extended forty years. In deep appreciation, he rendered full support to one thousand arhats so that they could record the golden teachings of the Buddha,[26] thus enabling the spread of Buddhism in the ages of the Former, Middle and Latter Days of the Law.

Your boils have resulted from only one offense—slandering the Lotus Sutra. The healing power of the Mystic Law you

26. Reference to the first council, which began the task of compiling the Buddha's teachings. In the year when Shakyamuni died, this council was convened, with the support of King Ajatashatru, in Pippala Cave at Rajagriha in Magadha.

now embrace is superior to that of the Buddha's "moon-loving" meditation. There is no reason why your boils cannot be healed and your life extended. If these words of mine do not prove to be true, you should shout, "The Buddha, the eye of the entire world, is a great liar, and the Lotus Sutra of the supreme vehicle is filled with falsehood! The World-Honored One should give me proof if he cares about his good name! All the saints and sages should come to protect me if they do not want to be untrue to their vows!"

A letter cannot convey all that one would like to say, and words cannot fully express what is in the heart. The rest will have to wait until the next time we meet.

Respectfully,
Nichiren

The third day of the eleventh month

BACKGROUND   This letter is a reply to Ōta Jōmyō's report that he was suffering from illness. It was written on November 3, 1275, at Mount Minobu, when Nichiren Daishonin was fifty-four years old. In the preceding year he had left Kamakura for the recesses of Mount Minobu. There, after retiring to an out-of-the-way place, he devoted himself to laying an eternal foundation for his Buddhism as a universal religion.

Ōta Jōmyō was a devout believer living in the province of Shimōsa in central Japan. He was an official of the government and his colleague, Toki Jōnin, is thought to have introduced him to faith in the Daishonin's Buddhism. Both men worked together in that area to protect the Daishonin and propagate his teachings. Around 1278, Ōta was tonsured, though he remained a layman. He assumed the religious name of Myōnichi (Mystic Sun), given him by the Daishonin. He is also called Ōta Nyūdō, *nyūdō* meaning one who is tonsured like a monk but lives outside a temple, usually in his own home. Ōta Jōmyō received many writings, including "On the Three Great Secret Laws," from the Daishonin, a fact which attests to the serious-ness with which he regarded his religion. He died on April 26, 1283, the year after the Daishonin passed away, at the age of sixty-two.

In this letter, Nichiren Daishonin clarifies the fundamental cause of Ōta's illness. He explains that since Ōta Jōmyō had renounced his former faith in the Shingon doctrine and pro-fessed faith in true Buddhism, the evil effect of his past mistaken faith had appeared as sickness so that he could eradicate it once and for all. In other words, his past karma had become manifest so that he could erase it. The Daishonin then assures him of the essential cure for his disease—faith in the Lotus Sutra, that is, the law of Nam-myoho-renge-kyo. Nichiren Daishonin ex-plains that his Buddhism is the supreme medicine for suffering people throughout the world.

A Sage Perceives the Three Existences of Life

A SAGE is one who fully understands the three existences of life—past, present and future. The Three Rulers and the Five Emperors[1] referred to in Confucianism, as well as the Three Sages[2] of ancient China, comprehended only the present; they knew neither the past nor the future. Brahmans, however, were able to see eighty thousand aeons into the past and the future, thus in a small way resembling sages. People of the two vehicles, as mentioned in the Hinayana teachings, were aware of the law of cause and effect working throughout the past, present and future. Hence they were superior to the Brahmans.

The Hinayana bodhisattvas could see three *asōgi*[3] aeons into the past, whereas the bodhisattvas of the lowest Mahayana teachings (*tsūgyō*) spent as many aeons practicing Buddhism as there are dust particles in a world, and the bodhisattvas of the intermediate Mahayana teachings (*bekkyō*) spent myriad kotis of aeons to attain each of the fifty-two stages leading to enlightenment.

1. Three Rulers and the Five Emperors: *See* p. 71, footnotes 1, 2.
2. Three Sages: *See* p. 75, footnote 22.
3. *Asōgi*: *Asamkhya* in Sanskrit, indicating an immeasurable number in ancient India. According to one method of calculation, one *asōgi* is equal to 10^{51} and one aeon is said to be 16 million minus 2,000 years. Altogether three *asōgi* aeons indicates an inconceivable span of time.

In the theoretical teaching of the Lotus Sutra, Shakyamuni Buddha described the period of *sanzen-jintengō*, a time incomparably more distant than any that had been mentioned before. In the essential teaching of the sutra, Shakyamuni revealed the unimaginably remote past called *gohyaku-jintengō*, as well as matters pertaining to uncountable aeons in the future.

From the above it is clear that a thorough understanding of both the past and the future is intrinsic to the nature of a sage. Shakyamuni Buddha accurately predicted the near future, saying that he would enter nirvana in three months' time. Can there then be any doubt about his prediction for the distant future, that *kōsen-rufu* will be achieved in the last of the five-hundred-year periods after his passing? With such perception one can see the distant future by looking at what is close at hand. One can infer what will be from what exists in the present. This is the "consistency from beginning to end"[4] [mentioned in the Lotus Sutra].

Who should be acknowledged as the votary of the Lotus Sutra in the last five-hundred-year period? I did not trust my own wisdom, but because the rebellions and invasion that I had predicted have occurred, I can now trust it. These incidents happened solely to prove me correct.

My disciples should know that I, Nichiren, am the votary of the Lotus Sutra. Since I follow the same practice as Bodhisattva Fukyō, those who despise and slander me will have their heads broken into seven pieces,[5] whereas those who believe in me

4. Consistency from beginning to end: A phrase found in the second chapter of the Lotus Sutra indicating the last of the Ten Factors of Life: the appearance, nature, entity, power, influence, internal cause, relation, latent effect, manifest effect, and the consistency of all these nine factors of life. The Daishonin means here that because there is consistency among the nine factors, from the "appearance," one with the Buddha wisdom can discern the ultimate outcome.

5. Have their heads broken into seven pieces: Reference to a verse in the *Dharani* (26th) chapter of the Lotus Sutra which reads: "Whoever resists our spell/And troubles a preacher of the Dharma,/May his head be split in seven pieces/Like the branches of an *arjaka* tree." It is also said that if one touches an *arjaka* flower its petals open and fall in seven pieces.

will amass good fortune as high as Mount Sumeru.

Question: Why is it that those who slander you have not yet had their heads broken into seven pieces?

Answer: Since ancient times, of all those who slandered saints and sages other than the Buddha, only one or two have suffered punishment by having their heads broken. The crime of abusing Nichiren is not by any means limited to only one or two persons. The entire Japanese nation has been punished simultaneously. What else do you think caused the great earthquake of the Shōka era and the huge comet[6] of the Bun'ei era? I am the foremost sage in the entire world.

Nevertheless, all people, from the ruler on down to the common people, have despised and slandered me, attacked me with sword and staff,[7] and even exiled me.[8] That is why Bonten, Taishaku, the gods of the sun and the moon, and the Four Heavenly Kings incited a neighboring country to punish our land. This was clearly prophesied in the *Daijuku* and *Ninnō* sutras, the Nirvana Sutra and the Lotus Sutra. No matter what prayers may be offered, if the people fail to heed me, this country will suffer calamities such as those that occurred on Iki and Tsushima.

My disciples, you should believe what I say and watch what happens. These things do not occur because I myself am

6. The great quake which flattened the Kamakura area in 1257 prompted the Daishonin to remonstrate with the government in his treatise, "Risshō Ankoku Ron." The huge comet, which appeared in 1264, terrified the people because comets were considered very ominous in those days. Nichiren Daishonin also regarded these extraordinary natural phenomena as portents of the rise of true Buddhism.

7. Attacked me with sword and staff: Reference to the Komatsubara and Tatsunokuchi persecutions. On November 11, 1264, a band of Nembutsu followers, led by a local lord named Tōjō Kagenobu, ambushed Nichiren Daishonin and his disciples at Komatsubara, killing two of them and injuring others. The Daishonin himself suffered a sword cut on his forehead and had his left hand broken. On September 12, 1271, the government made an unsuccessful attempt to execute the Daishonin at Tatsunokuchi beach near Kamakura.

8. Even exiled me: Nichiren Daishonin was exiled to the Izu Peninsula from May 12, 1261 through February 22, 1263, and again to Sado Island from October 10, 1271 through March 13, 1274.

respectworthy, but because the power of the Lotus Sutra is supreme. If I declare myself before the people, they will think that I am boastful, but if I humble myself before them, they will despise the sutra. The taller the pine tree, the longer the wisteria vine hanging from it. The deeper the source, the longer the stream. How fortunate, how joyful! In this impure land, I alone enjoy true happiness.

BACKGROUND   In this Gosho, Nichiren Daishonin defines a sage as one who fully understands the past, present and future. Perception into the three existences of life is a distinctive characteristic of the Buddha; the term "sage," as used in this writing, thus indicates "Buddha." A Buddha's prophecy is not based on intuition, occult power or clairvoyance, but on the strict law of causality which governs life throughout eternity. It is because of his understanding of causality that a Buddha can look at the present and know both the past and future.

Nichiren Daishonin first remonstrated with the government in 1260 by submitting the "Risshō Ankoku Ron "(On Securing the Peace of the Land through the Propagation of True Buddhism). In this treatise he issued a warning to the ruler that the country would be plagued by rebellion at home and foreign invasion unless it ceased its support of erroneous religions. In 1272 a rebellion took place, throwing the nation into confusion. The Hōjō clan was rocked by internal intrigue. Hōjō Tokisuke, an elder half brother of the regent Hōjō Tokimune, conspired to seize power, but his plot was discovered. Two of his accomplices were put to death on February 11, and three days later, Hōjo Tokisuke was beheaded. The rebellion had been stopped before it had a chance to get started, but even the prospect of rebellion caused dire fears throughout the country. Then in October 1274, Mongol forces swept across the islands of Tsushima and Iki located between the western part of Japan and the Korean Peninsula, and attacked

Kyushu, the southernmost part of Japan. In 1281, they attacked Kyushu for the second time. This foreign invasion contributed heavily to the social disruption.

Nichiren Daishonin wrote this short but significant letter in 1275. He had already remonstrated with the shogunate government three times, but to no avail. In 1274 he had been pardoned from exile on Sado Island and returned to Kamakura. Just as he predicted, however, the country itself was plagued internally by rebellion and externally by the formidable Mongol hordes.

Toki Jōnin (Toki Gorō Tanetsugu), the recipient of this letter, was an official serving the Kamakura shogunate on the military tribunal and one of the Daishonin's staunch followers. He lived in Shimōsa, to the northeast of Kamakura. He became a priest but lived at home. Such priests were called *nyūdō*. Toki took the priest's name, Jōnin, and was later given another name, Nichijō, by the Daishonin. He received dozens of writings, many of which involve significant revelations, including "The True Object of Worship." Accurate data is scarce and posthumous biographies are contradictory, though it would appear from the few accurate sources now available that he was born in 1216 and died in 1299. He is believed to have converted to the Daishonin's teachings around 1253.

Defining a sage as one who knows past, present and future, Nichiren Daishonin compares the stature of wise men and Buddhas appearing in both non-Buddhist books and Buddhist sutras and arrives at the conclusion that the Buddha revealed in the essential teaching of the Lotus Sutra is the foremost sage. In the Latter Day of the Law, Nichiren Daishonin declared himself to be the foremost sage in the entire world on the basis of his own accurate prediction. Gauging himself against the standards in the sutras, he drew this conclusion. He concluded that enmity toward him caused the protective gods to enjoin a neighboring country to attack Japan and that the workings of these gods should be attributed to the supreme power of the Mystic Law.

Letter to the Priests of Seichō-ji

L ET us congratulate each other on the coming of the New Year. Since you paid me no visit last year, I am worried whether something unfortunate may have occurred. If you have a chance to call on me, would you borrow for me the *Jūjūshin Ron*,[1] *Hizō Hōyaku*,[2] *Nikyō Ron*[3] and other commentaries of the Shingon sect from the priest Ise-kō? I need them in order to refute the Shingon priests who have for some time been clamoring against me. Bring with you also volumes one and two of the *Maka Shikan*. I would also appreciate the *Tōshun*[4] and the *Fushō Ki*[5] if they are available. Borrow the

---

1. *Jūjūshin Ron*: "Treatise on the Ten Stages of Mind," written around 830 by Kōbō, founder of the Japanese Shingon sect. In this work, he defined ten stages of the mind's development. He placed a follower of the Lotus Sutra in the eighth stage, and a follower of the *Kegon* Sutra in the upper ninth. Ultimately he placed a follower of the Shingon teaching in the upper tenth stage, because such a person has obtained the secret teaching. This treatise consists of ten volumes and asserts the supremacy of the *Dainichi* Sutra, the basic sutra of the Shingon sect.
2. *Hizō Hōyaku*: A three-volume summary of the *Jūjūshin Ron*.
3. *Nikyō Ron*: "A Comparison of Exoteric and Esoteric Buddhism," Kōbō's writing. The full title is *Ben Kemmitsu Nikyō Ron*, also called the *Kemmitsu Nikyō Ron*. In this work, Kōbō compares esoteric teachings with exoteric teachings and asserts the supremacy of the former over the latter. This work also explains each of the ten stages of mind.
4. *Tōshun*: A commentary on T'ien-t'ai's *Hokke Mongu* (Words and Phrases of the Lotus Sutra) written by Chih-tu of the T'ang dynasty.
5. *Fushō Ki*: Miao-lo's commentary on the *Hokke Mongu*.

Shūyō Shū[6] which is owned by Kanchi-bō, the disciple of Enchi-bō. Moreover, I have heard people say that he is in possession of other relevant writings. Please borrow them as well, and tell him that I will return them as soon as possible. This year the question of which Buddhist teachings are right and which are wrong will definitely be resolved.

Tell Jōken-bō, Gijō-bō[7] and other priests on my behalf: "Nichiren has often been on the verge of being killed. Twice he was exiled and once almost beheaded. This is not because of any worldly wrongs on his part. [As a youth,] he received supreme wisdom from the living Bodhisattva Kokūzō. He had been praying to the bodhisattva to become the wisest person in Japan. The bodhisattva must have taken pity on him, for he presented him with a great jewel as brilliant as the morning star, which Nichiren tucked away in his right sleeve. Thereafter, on perusing the entire body of sutras, he was able to discern in essence the relative worth of the eight sects[8] as well as of all the scriptures."

The Shingon sect is especially blameworthy, because it violates the Lotus Sutra. However, it is no easy matter to refute Shingon, so in preparation I first attacked the errors of the Zen and Nembutsu sects. I have good reason for my accusation. I will reserve discussion of the rights or wrongs of Buddhist sects in India and China for some other time, but for Japan, all the people have discarded the righteous teaching of the Lotus Sutra and are therefore without exception destined to fall into the evil states of existence. This is because, at each and every

6. *Shūyō Shū*: Generally, a collection of the fundamental teachings of a Buddhist sect. Here it means a collection of the Tendai doctrines.

7. Jōken-bō and Gijō-bō: Nichiren Daishonin's senior priests at Seichō-ji temple. On April 28, 1253, at Seichō-ji temple, the Daishonin denounced the established sects and declared the founding of his Buddhism, thus incurring the wrath of Tōjō Kagenobu, the local lord of that district. Jōken-bō and Gijō-bō protected the Daishonin, helping him escape arrest by Tōjō's warriors and leave the temple safely.

8. Eight sects: *See* p. 25, footnote 66.

temple, the Shingon sect invariably exists side by side with the Hokke sect[9] just as a shadow follows the body. Thus, to the correct practice of the Lotus Sutra is added the Shingon practice of the eighteen paths,[10] and to its performance of penitence is joined that based on the *Amida* Sutra. And in conferring titles upon scholars of the Tendai sect, the Shingon procedure predominates, while that of the Lotus Sutra is relegated to a secondary position.

In reality, the sutras of Shingon belong to the provisional teachings and are inferior even to the *Kegon* or the *Hannya* sutras. Yet Jikaku and Kōbō were confused on this point and held that the Shingon sutras are equal or even superior to the Lotus Sutra. The ceremony for "opening the eyes"[11] of a newly-made image of the Buddha is therefore conducted with the *mudra* of the Buddha-eye Goddess and the *mantra*[12] of Dainichi Buddha. As a result, all the wooden and painted images of the Buddha in Japan have been rendered soulless and sightless, and in consequence, have been possessed by the Devil of the Sixth Heaven, bringing ruin upon their own worshipers. This is why the Imperial court [in Kyoto] is about to perish. Now the evil teaching of Shingon has made its appearance in Kamakura and threatens to destroy all of Japan.

The Zen and Jōdo sects also hold extremely perverted views. I knew that if I declared this, it would certainly cost me my life. Yet I was determined to requite the favor of Bodhisattva Kokūzō. With this in mind, on the twenty-eighth day of the fourth month in the fifth year of Kenchō (1253), I pointed out

9. Hokke sect: Here, the Tendai sect. *See also* p. 231, footnote 14.

10. Shingon practice of the eighteen paths: Reference to Shingon mandala worship. The Womb World mandala and the Diamond World mandala each include nine central objects of worship. The Shingon followers join their fingers in eighteen ways and meditate on these eighteen objects of worship.

11. Ceremony for opening the eyes: Ceremony for imbuing a newly-made Buddha image with a spiritual property, thus making it an object of worship.

12. *Mudra* and *mantra*: *See* p. 83, footnote 46.

the errors of the various sects for the first time to a small audience including Jōen-bō[13] on the southern side of the image hall in Dōzen-bō's[14] quarters in Seichō-ji temple, located in Tōjō Village in Awa Province. For more than twenty years since then, I have persisted in my declaration without retreating a step. For this reason, I was at times driven from my dwelling and at other times exiled. In former days Bodhisattva Fukyō was beaten with staves; now Nichiren must face the sword.

All the people in Japan, both wise and foolish, from the sovereign down to the common people, say that the priest Nichiren is no match for the scholars, teachers, great masters and sages of old. I waited for the right time to dispel their distrust of me. The time finally came when great earthquakes occurred in the Shōka era (1257), followed by the appearance of a huge comet in the Bun'ei era (1264). Observing these, I made this prediction: "Our country will suffer two terrible disasters, internal strife and foreign invasion. The former will take place in Kamakura, in the form of internecine strife[15] among the descendants of Hōjō Yoshitoki. The latter may come from any direction, but that from the west[16] would be the most violent. This latter will occur solely because of the fact that all the Buddhist sects in Japan are heretical, and Bonten and Taishaku will therefore command other countries to attack us. So long as the country refuses to heed me, it will certainly be defeated, no matter whether it has a hundred, a thousand or even ten thousand generals as brave as Masakado,[17] Sumi-

13.   Jōen-bō: A priest at Renge-ji temple at Hanabusa in Tōjō Village. Renge-ji temple is thought to have been a branch temple of Seichō-ji.
14.   Dōzen-bō (d. 1276): Chief priest of Seichō-ji temple, under whom the Daishonin first studied Buddhism. The Daishonin never forgot his first teacher, and, after the latter's death, wrote "Repaying Debts of Gratitude" as an expression of his gratitude.
15.   Internecine strife: In February 1272, Hōjō Tokisuke, an elder half brother of the regent Hōjō Tokimune, attempted a rebellion but failed.
16.   That from the west: Both in 1274 and in 1281, Mongol forces attacked the southwestern part of Japan.
17.   Masakado (d. 940): A distinguished warrior of the Taira clan who wielded power in eastern Japan.

tomo,[18] Sadatō,[19] Toshihito[20] or Tamura.[21] If these words of mine prove false, then the people are free to believe in the distorted views of the Shingon, Nembutsu and other sects." This is the prediction that I made known far and wide.

I especially warn the priests on Mount Kiyosumi. If they treat me with less respect than they show their own parents or the three treasures, they will become wretched beggars in this life and will fall into the hell of incessant suffering in the next. I will explain why. The villainous Tōjō Saemon Kagenobu[22] once hunted the deer and other animals kept by Seichō-ji and tried to force the priests in the various lodging temples to become Nembutsu believers. At that time I pitted myself against Tōjō and supported the lord of the manor. I composed a fervent oath which read, "If the two temples at Kiyosumi and Futama should come into Tōjō's possession, I will discard the Lotus Sutra!" Then I tied it to the hand of the object of worship,[23] to which I prayed continuously. Within a year, both temples were freed from Tōjō's grasp. Certainly Bodhisattva Kokūzō will never forget this, so how can those priests who make light of me avoid being forsaken by the heavens? Hearing me say this, the more foolish of you may think that I am invoking a curse upon you. That is not so, however. I am warning you simply because it would be a pity if you should fall into the hell of incessant suffering after your death.

Let me say a few words about the nun in the family of the

18. Sumitomo (d. 941): Fujiwara no Sumitomo. A military commander of the Fujiwara clan who subdued a band of pirates in 936.

19. Sadatō (1019–1062): Abe no Sadatō, head of a powerful family in eastern Japan.

20. Toshihito: Fujiwara no Toshihito. A distinguished warrior of the Fujiwara family in the Heian period (794–1185). Little is known about him.

21. Tamura (758–811): Sakanoue no Tamuramaro, a military leader who obtained the Imperial commission of Sei-i Tai Shōgun (Generalissimo for Subjugation of the Barbarians) and established the authority of the Imperial court in the northeastern area of Japan around the early ninth century.

22. Tōjō Saemon Kagenobu: The local lord of Tōjō District in Awa Province, who was an ardent believer in Nembutsu.

23. The object of worship: A statue of Shakyamuni Buddha.

lord of the manor.[24] Being a woman, and a foolish one at that, she must have been turned against me by threats from others. I pity her, for, having forgotten her debt of gratitude, she will fall into one of the evil states of existence in her next life. Despite that, however, she extended great favor to my parents, so I am praying that I may somehow be able to save her from that fate.

The Lotus Sutra is nothing other than a scripture that reveals that Shakyamuni Buddha attained enlightenment at a time even more distant than *gohyaku-jintengō*. It also predicts that Shariputra and the other disciples will become Buddhas in the future. Those who do not believe the sutra will fall into the hell of incessant suffering. Not only did Shakyamuni himself declare all this, but Tahō Buddha also testified to its truth and the Buddhas from the ten directions extended their tongues by way of verification. Furthermore, the Lotus Sutra states that the votary of this sutra will receive the protection of the innumerable Bodhisattvas of the Earth, Bodhisattvas Monju and Kannon, Bonten, Taishaku, the gods of the sun and the moon, the Four Heavenly Kings and the Ten Goddesses. Therefore, there is no other way to attain Buddhahood than by practicing the Lotus Sutra, for it is the only scripture which reveals all things past and future.

I have never seen the province of Tsukushi,[25] nor do I know anything about the Mongol Empire. Yet, because my prediction concerning the Mongols derived from my understanding of all the sutras, it has already come true. Hence, when I say that you will all fall into the hell of incessant suffering because

24. The nun in the family of the lord of the manor: "The lord of the manor" refers to Hōjō Tomotoki, younger brother of Hōjō Yasutoki, the third regent of the Kamakura government. The nun, his wife, was called Nagoe no Ama or Ōama. After the Tatsunokuchi Persecution, she chose to forsake her faith in the Daishonin's Buddhism.

25. Tsukushi: The ancient name for Kyushu, the southern part of Japan, where Mongol forces attacked after sweeping across the islands of Iki and Tsushima.

of your ingratitude, how can my words prove false? You may be safe for the time being, but wait and see what happens later. All of Japan will be reduced to the same miserable state in which the islands of Iki and Tsushima now find themselves. When vast numbers of Mongol hordes close in on the province of Awa, those of you priests who cling to heretical teachings will cringe in terror and finally fall into the hell of incessant suffering, saying, "Now I know that the priest Nichiren was right." What a pity! What a shame!

Nichiren

The eleventh day of the first month

This letter is to be read aloud by the priests Sado[26] and Suke Ajari before the statue of Bodhisattva Kokūzō for all the priests of Seichō-ji to hear.

BACKGROUND   As the title suggests, "Letter to the Priests of Seichō-ji" was addressed to the priests of Seichō-ji temple on Mount Kiyosumi in Kominato, Awa Province. It was written on January 11, 1276, while Nichiren Daishonin was living on Mount Minobu. When the Daishonin was twelve, his parents had sent him to study under Dōzen-bō, the chief priest of nearby Seichō-ji temple. It was here that the Daishonin embarked on a lifelong journey to find and proclaim the unique truth of Buddhism.

Seichō-ji temple itself was the kind of anomaly typical of Buddhist centers of the day. The temple had been founded by a Buddhist priest named Fushigi in 771, who had chopped down

26. Sado (1253–1314): Another name for Nikō. He was one of the six closest disciples of Nichiren Daishonin known as the six senior priests. Details concerning Suke Ajari are unknown.

an oak tree, carved it into an image of Bodhisattva Kokūzō and placed it in a shrine he constructed. Thus the object of worship at Seichō-ji was originally the Bodhisattva Kokūzō. The shrine sank into oblivion, however, until the third high priest of Mount Hiei's Enryaku-ji temple, Jikaku, visited there in the next century. After that, it developed into a prestigious institution in that region.

Seichō-ji became a center for study of the Lotus Sutra, since it belonged to the Tendai sect. But later it fell under the influence of first the Shingon sect with its mystic rituals, and later, the Jōdo sect with its reliance on Amida Buddha. Some time after taking the vows of a priest in 1237, the Daishonin set out to visit the great centers of learning in Japan to further his study of Buddhism and obtain the knowledge he needed to confirm his own enlightenment in the light of the sutras. In 1253, twenty years after he had entered Seichō-ji for the first time, he finally declared the founding of his new Buddhism.

This letter refers to events which took place shortly before his tonsuring ceremony. It states, "[As a youth,] he [Nichiren] received supreme wisdom from the living Bodhisattva Kokūzō. He had been praying to the bodhisattva to become the wisest person in Japan." Thereby he obtained "a great jewel" which enabled him to understand all Buddhist scriptures correctly. Bodhisattva Kokūzō was said to possess the wisdom of universal life, so in this metaphorical way, the Daishonin explains that he awoke to the essence of life. Convinced though he was of his own enlightenment, he needed documentary verification to confirm and deepen his understanding of the truth of Buddhism. For this reason, he left Seichō-ji for Kamakura, the seat of the military government, and then Kyoto and Nara, which were the centers of Buddhism in Japan.

Subsequently, this letter refers to the particularly destructive influence of the Shingon sect which performed esoteric rituals and claimed the supremacy of its teachings over the Lotus Sutra. The Daishonin points out that, although he was per-

secuted for his criticism of Shingon and other sects, his
prediction of internal strife and foreign invasion came true.
Finally, the letter affirms the supremacy of the Lotus Sutra and
warns the priests of Seichō-ji to pay heed to the Daishonin's
advice.

The Three Kinds of Treasure

I HAVE received the various articles from your messenger, including a white winter robe and a string of coins, as well as the goods mentioned in Lord Toki's[1] letter. The persimmons, pears, and fresh and dried seaweed are particularly welcome.

I am most grieved over your lord's illness. Although he has not professed faith in the Lotus Sutra, you are a member of his clan, and it is thanks to his consideration that you are able to make offerings to the sutra. Therefore all of your gifts are in effect prayers for your lord's recovery. Think of a small tree under a large one, or grass by a great river. Though they do not receive rain or water directly, they nonetheless thrive, partaking of dew from the large tree or drawing moisture from the river. The same holds true with the relationship between you and your lord. To give another example, King Ajatashatru was an enemy of the Buddha. But because Jivaka,[2] a minister in the king's court, believed in the Buddha and continually made offerings to him, the blessings accruing from his actions are said to have returned to Ajatashatru.

Buddhism teaches that when the Buddha nature manifests itself from within, it will obtain protection from without. This

1. Lord Toki: *See* p. 261.
2. Jivaka: *See* p. 250, footnote 11.

is one of its fundamental principles. The Lotus Sutra says, "I deeply respect you." The Nirvana Sutra states, "All living things possess the Buddha nature." Ashvaghosha's *Daijō Kishin Ron*[3] says, "When the Buddha nature continuously manifests itself, it will quickly extinguish illusions and reveal the property-of-Law aspect of life."[4] Bodhisattva Maitreya's *Yuga Ron*[5] contains a similar statement. An inconspicuous deed will produce a conspicuous benefit.

The Devil of the Sixth Heaven probably knew the aforementioned principle, and he therefore possessed your colleagues, causing them to invent that preposterous lie[6] in order to prevent you from making offerings to the Lotus Sutra. However, since your faith is profound, the Ten Goddesses must have come to your aid and thus caused your lord's illness. He does not regard you as his enemy, but since he once acted against you in giving credit to the false accusations of your colleagues, he has become seriously ill and the malady persists.

Ryūzō-bō,[7] whom these people count on as their pillar of strength, has already been toppled, and those who spoke falsely of you have contracted the same disease as your lord. Ryōkan is

3. *Daijō Kishin Ron*: "Awakening of Faith in the Mahayana," a treatise which preaches the fundamental doctrines of Mahayana Buddhism and attempts to awaken people to true faith. It has been widely read by Mahayana sects and there are many commentaries on it.

4. Property-of-Law aspect of life: One of the three properties of the Buddha's life. *See* Three properties in the Glossary.

5. Maitreya's *Yuga Ron*: "Treatise on the Yogachara Practice," translated from Sanskrit into Chinese by Hsüan-tsang during the T'ang dynasty. It is said to have been dictated to Asanga by Maitreya—not Shakyamuni's contemporary and close disciple but a Buddhist scholar of third- or fourth-century India.

6. That preposterous lie: The report made by Shijō Kingo's colleagues to Lord Ema that he forcibly tried to disrupt the Kuwagayatsu debate in order to embarrass Ryūzō-bō.

7. Ryūzō-bō: A priest of the Tendai sect. He originally lived at Enryaku-ji temple on Mt. Hiei, the head temple of the Tendai sect, but was banished from Mt. Hiei for allegedly eating human flesh. Later, he appeared in Kamakura and continued preaching from a cottage at Kuwagayatsu. Although he came to enjoy considerable popularity, he was defeated in debate by the Daishonin's disciple, Sammi-bō, in June 1277.

even more slanderous than they. He will probably encounter some bad accident, or stir up major trouble and find himself in serious distress. Surely he will not escape unharmed.

As things stand now, I have a feeling you are in danger. Your enemies are sure to make an attempt on your life. In backgammon, if two stones of the same color are placed side by side, they cannot be hit by an opposing stone. A cart, as long as it has two wheels, does not lurch all over the road. Likewise, if two men go together, an enemy will hesitate to attack. Therefore, no matter what faults you may find with your younger brothers, do not let them leave you alone even for a moment.

Your face bears definite signs of a hot temper. But you should know that the gods will not protect a short-tempered person, no matter how important they may think he is. If you should be killed, even though you might attain Buddhahood after your death, your enemies would be delighted, but we would feel only grief. This would indeed be regrettable. While your foes busy themselves plotting against you, your lord places greater confidence in you than before. Therefore, although they appear to have quieted down, inwardly they are no doubt seething with hate. So you should at all times behave unobtrusively in their presence. Pay greater respect to the other retainers of the clan than you have in the past. For the time being, when members of the Hōjō clan are visiting your lord, refrain from calling on him, even if he should summon you.

If the worst should happen and your lord should die, your enemies would become masterless and would have nowhere to turn, though they do not seem to consider that fact. Unreasoning as they are, when they see you report to work more and more frequently, their hearts are bound to be fired with jealousy and their breath come in pants.

If the young nobles of the Hōjō clan or the wives of those in power should inquire about your lord's illness, no matter who the person may be, get down on your knees, place your hands properly, and reply thus: "His malady is entirely beyond my poor skill to cure. But no matter how often I decline, he insists that I treat him. Since I am in his service, I cannot help but do as he says." Leave your hair untended, and refrain from wearing well-starched court dress, bright robes or other colorful clothing. Be patient and continue in this way for the time being.

Perhaps you are well aware of it, but let me cite the Buddha's prediction about what the Latter Day of the Law will be like. In essence he states, "It will be a chaotic age in which even a sage will find it difficult to live. He will be like a stone in a great fire, which for a while seems to endure the heat but finally chars and crumbles to ashes. Worthy men will advocate the five great principles of humanity,[8] but they themselves will find it hard to practice them." Thus the saying goes, "Do not remain in the seat of honor too long."

Many people have plotted to undo you, but you have avoided their intrigues and emerged victorious. Should you lose your composure now and fall into their trap, you will be, as people say, like a boatman who rows his boat with all his might only to have it capsize just before he reaches the shore, or like a person who is served no tea at the end of his meal.

While you are in your lord's mansion, if you stay in the room assigned to you, nothing will happen to you. But on your way to work at dawn or returning from it at dusk, your enemies are bound to be lying in wait for you. Also, be very careful in and around your house in case someone should be hiding beside the double doors, inside the family sanctuary, under the floor or in the space above the ceiling. This time your foes will use even more cunning in their plots than before. In the end, no one will be more dependable in an emergency than the night watchmen of Egara[9] in Kamakura. However dis-

8. Five great principles of humanity: Also called the five constant virtues: benevolence, righteousness, propriety, wisdom and good faith. They were set forth by Confucianism as the principles by which one should always abide.

9. Night watchmen of Egara: Shijō Kingo's four younger brothers. Their lands were confiscated on account of their belief in the Daishonin's teachings, forcing them to take the lowly position of night watchmen.

agreeable it may be to you, you should associate with them amicably.

Minamoto no Yoshitsune[10] found it utterly impossible to defeat the Heike until he won Shigeyoshi[11] over to his side and in that way vanquished the rival clan. Shogun Minamoto no Yoritomo[12] sought to take revenge on Osada[13] for his father's death, but he would not behead the murderer until after he had conquered the Heike. It is even more vital for you to master your emotions and ally yourself with your four brothers. They had risked their lives to acquire their mansions, and these were confiscated by their lord because of their faith in the Lotus Sutra and because of their belief in Nichiren. Be considerate of those who believe in Nichiren and the Lotus Sutra, no matter what they may have done in the past. Moreover, if they frequent your house, your enemies will be afraid to attack you at night. It is not as if they were trying to avenge their fathers'

10. Minamoto no Yoshitsune (1159–1189): A younger half brother of Minamoto no Yoritomo, founder of the Kamakura government. In 1180, when Yoritomo raised an army against the rival Taira or Heike clan, Yoshitsune joined forces with him and later defeated the Taira army. After the battle, Yoshitsune incurred Yoritomo's displeasure and escaped to the northern part of Japan, but was finally killed by a powerful family in that district.

11. Shigeyoshi: Taguchi Shigeyoshi, the head of a powerful family in Awa, a province in the southern part of Japan. Though a member of the Taira clan, he informed Yoshitsune of the internal conditions of the Taira army as well as the weak points of their position. This helped bring about the downfall of the Taira clan.

12. Minamoto no Yoritomo (1147–1199): The founder of the Kamakura shogunate. He defeated the rival Taira clan at the final battle of Dannoura in 1185, and established a military government in Kamakura. However, he made no attempt to dismantle the government machinery already in existence in Kyoto and deliberately sought recognition for his actions from the emperor and the court. In 1192 he succeeded in obtaining the prestigious military title of shogun.

13. Osada: Osada Tadamune, a samurai in Owari Province in central Japan. In 1159 Minamoto no Yoshitomo, the father of Yoritomo, battled with the Taira army and was defeated. Fleeing, he hid at the house of Osada Tadamune. On the Tairas' order, Osada led Yoshitomo into the bath and there killed him. Later, when Yoritomo raised an army, Tadamune and his son, Kagemune, sided with Yoritomo, but were killed at Yoritomo's command after the fall of the Tairas.

deaths; certainly they do not want their plot to come out into the open. To one such as you who must avoid being seen, these four are the most dependable warriors. Always maintain friendly relations with them. But since you are hot-tempered by nature, you might not take my advice. In that case, it will be beyond the power of my prayers to save you.

Ryūzō-bō and your elder brother plotted evil against you. Therefore, Heaven so contrived that the situation would develop exactly as you wished. Then how can you now dare to go against the wish of Heaven? Even if you had accumulated a thousand or ten thousand treasures, of what use would they be if your lord should forsake you? He already looks to you as if you were his own parent, following you as water follows the shape of its container, longing for you as a calf longs for its mother, relying on you as an elderly person relies on his staff. Is his regard for you not due to the aid of the Lotus Sutra? How envious your fellow retainers must be! You must hurry and bring your four brothers over to your side and report to me how the matter goes. Then I will fervently pray to the gods for your protection. I have already informed them of how deeply you grieve over the death of your father and mother. Shakyamuni Buddha will surely extend them his especial consideration.

Over and over I recall the moment,[14] unforgettable even now, when I was about to be beheaded and you accompanied me, holding the reins of my horse and weeping tears of grief. Nor could I ever forget it in any lifetime to come. If you should fall into hell for some grave offense, no matter how Shakyamuni might urge me to become a Buddha, I would refuse; I would rather go to hell with you. For if you and I should fall into hell together, we would find Shakyamuni Buddha and the Lotus Sutra there. It would be like the moon illuminating the darkness, like cold water pouring into hot, like fire melting ice,

14. The moment: A reference to the Tatsunokuchi Persecution.

or like the sun dispelling the darkness. But if you depart from my advice even slightly, then do not blame me for what may happen.

The plague which is raging at present will, as you predict, strike those in the higher ranks of society at the turn of the year. This is perhaps the design of the Ten Goddesses. For the time being stay calm and observe how things develop. And do not go around lamenting to others how hard it is for you to live in this world. To do so is an act utterly unbecoming to a worthy man. If one behaves in this way, then after he dies, his wife, overcome with sorrow at losing her husband, will tell other people about the shameful things he did, though she has no real intention of doing so. And that will in no way be her fault but solely the result of his own reprehensible behavior.

It is rare to be born a human being. The number of those endowed with human life is as small as the amount of earth one can place on a fingernail. Life as a human being is hard to sustain—as hard as it is for the dew to remain on the grass. But it is better to live a single day with honor than to live to one hundred and twenty and die in disgrace. Live so that all the people of Kamakura will say in your praise that Shijō Kingo is diligent in the service of his lord, in the service of Buddhism, and in his concern for other people. More valuable than treasures in a storehouse are the treasures of the body, and the treasures of the heart are the most valuable of all. From the time you read this letter on, strive to accumulate the treasures of the heart!

I would like to relate an incident that is customarily kept secret. In the history of Japan, there have been two emperors who were assassinated. One of them was the thirty-third emperor Sushun. He was the son of Emperor Kimmei and an uncle of Prince Shōtoku.[15] One day he summoned Prince Shōtoku and said, "We hear that you are a man of unsurpassed wisdom. Examine Our physiognomy and tell Us what you see

15. Shōtoku: See p. 13, footnote 30.

there!" The prince declined three times, but the emperor insisted that he obey the Imperial command. Finally, no longer able to refuse, the prince reverently examined Sushun's physiognomy and then reported, "Your Majesty's countenance indicates that you will be assassinated by someone."

The emperor's complexion changed color. "What evidence do you have to support such a contention?" he asked. The prince replied, "I see red veins running over your eyes. This is a sign that you will incur the enmity of others." Thereupon the emperor asked, "How can We escape this fate?" The prince said, "It is difficult to evade. But there are soldiers known as the five great principles of humanity. As long as you keep these warriors on your side, you will be safe from danger. In the Buddhist scriptures these soldiers are referred to as 'forbearance,' one of the six *paramitas*."

For some time after that, Emperor Sushun faithfully observed the practice of forbearance. But, being irascible by nature, he violated the precept one day when one of his subjects presented him with a young wild boar. He withdrew the metal rod that was attached to his sword scabbard and stabbed the boar in the eyes with it, saying, "One of these days this is what We will do to that fellow We hate!" Prince Shōtoku, who happened to be present, exclaimed, "Ah, what a fearful thing to do! Your Majesty will surely arouse the enmity of others. These very words you have spoken will be the sword that wounds you." The prince then ordered articles of value to be brought out and divided among those who had heard the emperor's remark, [hoping to buy their silence]. One of them, however, told the high minister Soga no Umako[16] about the

16. Soga no Umako (d. 626): The chief minister, who succeeded to this position in 570 upon the death of his father, Soga no Iname. In 587, he defeated the Mononobe family, the strongest opponents of Buddhism. In the following year the prince chosen by Umako ascended the throne to become Emperor Sushun. Under the protection of the Soga clan, Buddhism soon began to flourish, and by the end of the sixth century it was well established in the Yamato area. Unfortunately, Soga no Umako's political record did not match

episode. Umako, believing that he was the one the emperor hated, won over Atai Goma, son of Azumanoaya no Atai Iwai, and had him kill the emperor.

Thus even a ruler on a throne must take care not to give unreserved expression to his thoughts. Confucius held to the proverb, "Nine thoughts to one word," which means that he reconsidered nine times before he spoke. Tan, the Duke of Chou,[17] was so earnest in receiving callers that he would bind up his hair three times in the course of washing it, or spit out his food three times in the course of a meal, in order not to keep them waiting. Think carefully about what I mean by this so you will have no cause to reproach me later. Such thoughtfulness is surely a part of Buddhism.

The key to all of Shakyamuni's teachings is the Lotus Sutra, and the key to the practice of the Lotus Sutra is expounded in the *Fukyō* chapter. What does Bodhisattva Fukyō's profound respect for people signify? The real meaning of the Lord Shakyamuni Buddha's appearance in this world lay in his behavior as a human being. How profound! The wise may be called human, but the thoughtless are no more than animals.

Nichiren

The eleventh day of the ninth month in the third year of Kenji (1277)

BACKGROUND   This letter is dated September 11, 1277, and was addressed to Shijō Kingo in Kamakura. It is called "The Three Kinds of Treasure" because the Daishonin refers to

his pious efforts to promote Buddhism, for he proceeded to consolidate his power by acts of outrageous treachery. He had Emperor Sushun assassinated, and placed on the throne his own niece, Empress Suiko.

17. Tan, the Duke of Chou: Younger brother of Emperor Wu. After Wu's death, Ch'eng, Emperor Wu's son, was still a child, so Tan administered the affairs of state for him as regent.

the treasures in a storehouse, the treasures of the body and the treasures of the heart, and declares the treasures of the heart to be the most valuable. It is also sometimes called "The Story of Emperor Sushun," because in this letter the Daishonin relates the story of an emperor by that name who brought ruin upon himself because of his hot temper.

Around 1274, Shijō Kingo began trying to convert his lord to the Daishonin's Buddhism. Lord Ema did not take kindly to these efforts, and, prompted by false accusations from Kingo's colleagues, reduced the believer's landholdings. The situation worsened in June of that year when Kingo attended a debate between Sammi-bō Nichigyō, a disciple of the Daishonin, and Ryūzō-bō, a follower of the Tendai sect. Kingo's colleagues again slandered him to Lord Ema, claiming he had attempted to disrupt the debate and embarrass Ryūzō-bō.

The Daishonin wrote Shijō Kingo several letters and even drafted a petition to Lord Ema on Kingo's behalf. In these letters, the Daishonin offered much practical advice as well as guidance in faith. He told Kingo that he should carry out his service to his lord with the same dedication that he showed toward Buddhist practice. Later that year, Lord Ema fell ill, and Shijō Kingo used his medical skills to cure him. In 1278, the grateful lord restored and later actually increased Kingo's estate. Shijō Kingo had remained steadfast in his faith through-out the ordeal.

At the beginning of this letter, Nichiren Daishonin tells Shijō Kingo that he should remember his debt of gratitude to his lord, and stresses the Buddhist teaching that fundamental changes within oneself inevitably result in changes in the environment. He also advises Kingo to make an effort to control his temper and not to be swayed by his emotions.

Next, the Daishonin encourages Shijō Kingo warmly by saying, "If you and I should fall into hell together, we would find Shakyamuni Buddha and the Lotus Sutra there." When the Daishonin was about to be executed at Tatsunokuchi, Shijō

Kingo vowed to die by his side. Now Kingo was undergoing a severe ordeal and the Daishonin was exerting all his powers to protect him. This spirit to stand by one another is fundamental to Buddhism. The Daishonin then says that since Kingo was fortunate enough to be born human and encounter the True Law, he should accumulate "the treasures of the heart" and win the respect of others. Finally, by citing the story of Emperor Sushun and other examples of sages such as Confucius, the Daishonin teaches Kingo that he, as a practitioner of true Buddhism, should conduct his daily life admirably and be considerate of others.

The Three Obstacles
and Four Devils

THE two men you sent have arrived here, bringing your various offerings. I also received a message from the Priest Nisshō[1] regarding your faith.

In this letter I want to advise you about what is most important for you. In the Former and Middle Days of the Law, the world did not fall into decline because saints and sages appeared frequently and the gods protected the people. In the Latter Day of the Law, however, people have become so greedy that strife rages incessantly between sovereign and subject, parent and child, elder and younger brother, and all the more so among people who are unrelated. When such conflict occurs, the gods abandon the country and then the three calamities and seven disasters begin, until one, two, three, four, five, six or seven suns appear in the sky.[2] Plants wither and die, large and small rivers dry up, the earth smolders like charcoal and the sea becomes like boiling oil. Eventually flames fill the atmosphere, arising from the hell of incessant suffering and reaching the Brahma-heaven. Such is the devastation that will

1. Nisshō (1221–1323): One of Nichiren Daishonin's six senior priest-disciples. He devoted himself to propagation mainly in Kamakura, but after the Daishonin's death, he was influenced by his former ties with the Tendai sect and turned against the Daishonin's teachings and Nikkō Shonin.
2. One, two, three, four, five, six or seven suns appear in the sky: *See* p. 10, footnote 24.

occur when the world reaches its final dissolution.

Everyone, whether wise or foolish, considers it natural for children to obey their parents, for subjects to be loyal to their sovereign, and for disciples to follow their master. Recently, however, it appears that the people of our day, drunk with the wine of greed, anger and stupidity,[3] make it a rule to betray their sovereign, despise their parents and scoff at their teachers. You should read again and again the previous letter[4] in which I explained that one should of course obey his parents as well as his sovereign and teacher, but should they commit evil, admonishing them is in fact being loyal to them.

Recently your elder brother, Uemon no Sakan, was again disowned by your father. I told your wife when she came to visit me here that he was certain to be disowned again, and since your faith was quite unstable, she should be prepared for the worst. This time I am sure that you will give up your faith. If you do, I have not the slightest intention of reproaching you for it. Likewise, neither should you blame me, Nichiren, when you have fallen into hell. It is in no way my responsibility. It is an undeniable fact that fire can at once reduce even a thousand-year-old field of pampas grass to ashes, and that the merit one has formed over a hundred years can be destroyed with a single careless word.

Your father now seems to have become the enemy of the Lotus Sutra, yet your brother will now become one of its votaries.[5] You, who think only of immediate affairs, will obey your father, and deluded people will therefore praise you for your filial devotion. Munemori[6] obeyed his father's tyrannous

3.   Greed, anger and stupidity: Generally known as the three poisons—the fundamental evils inherent in life which give rise to human suffering.

4.   Previous letter: The "Letter to the Brothers" dated April 16, 1275.

5.   The elder brother Munenaka was of course already a votary of the Lotus Sutra in that he had been practicing the sutra according to the Daishonin's teaching. This statement implies that because Munenaka will willingly accept disinheritance and the accompanying social sanctions rather than renounce his faith, he is in effect giving his life for the Lotus Sutra.

6.   Munemori (1147–1185) and Shigemori (1138–1179): Brothers and

commands and was finally beheaded at Shinohara. Shigemori disobeyed his father and preceded him in death. Who was truly the better son? If you obey your father who is an enemy of the Lotus Sutra and abandon your brother who is a votary of the supreme teaching, are you then being filial? In the final analysis, what you should do is resolve to pursue the way of Buddhism single-mindedly just as your brother is doing. Your father is like King Myōshōgon[7] and you brothers are like the princes Jōzō and Jōgen. The age is different but the principle of the Lotus Sutra remains the same. Recently Hōjō Yoshimasa,[8] the lord of Musashi Province, abandoned his vast territory and his many subjects in order to retire from all worldly affairs. If you ingratiate yourself with your father for the sake of a small private estate, neglect your faith and fall into the evil states of existence, you should not blame me, Nichiren. Yet despite this warning, I feel that this time you will discard your belief.

I state this out of pity because you have been faithful until now, but you may fall into the evil states of existence in spite of your past faith. If, by one chance out of a hundred or a thousand, you should decide to follow my advice, then confront your father and say: "Since you are my father, I should by rights obey you, but since you have become an enemy of the Lotus Sutra, I would be unfilial if I were to do so in this matter. Therefore, I have resolved to break with you and follow my

warriors belonging to the Taira clan, which took control of the Japanese court in the mid-twelfth century and held supreme power until defeated by the Minamoto clan in 1185. The head of the ruling clan, Taira no Kiyomori, installed himself in the highest government position and abused his authority. His first son, Shigemori, virtuous and gentle, remonstrated with his father when he tried to confine the retired emperor Goshirakawa, while the second son, Munemori, obeyed his father and kept the emperor in prison after Shigemori died of illness. This emperor's imprisonment triggered the attack on the Tairas by the Minamoto clan. Munemori was beheaded in 1185.

7. Myōshōgon: Father of Jōzō and Jōgen who appears in the *Myōshōgonnō* (27th) chapter of the Lotus Sutra. *See* Jōzō and Jōgen in the Glossary.

8. Hōjō Yoshimasa (1243–1281): A top official of the Kamakura government who held important posts such as advisor to the regent and provincial governor. He resigned from his position to enter the priesthood in 1277.

brother. If you should disown him, be aware that you are disowning me too." You should not have the slightest fear in your heart. It is lack of courage that prevents one from attaining Buddhahood, although he may have professed faith in the Lotus Sutra many times since the remotest past.

There is definitely something extraordinary in the ebb and flow of the tide, the rising and setting of the moon, and the way in which summer, autumn, winter and spring give way to each other. Something uncommon also occurs when an ordinary person attains Buddhahood. At such a time, the three obstacles and four devils will invariably appear, and the wise will rejoice while the foolish will retreat. I have long been waiting to tell you this, either through my own messenger or by some other means. So I greatly appreciate your sending these messengers to me. I am sure that if you were about to abandon your faith, you would not have sent them. Thinking it may still not be too late, I am writing this letter.

To attain Buddhahood is difficult indeed, more difficult than the feat of placing a needle atop the Mount Sumeru of this world and then casting a thread from atop the Mount Sumeru of another world directly through the eye of this needle. And the feat is even more difficult if it must be done in the face of a contrary wind. The Lotus Sutra states, "During countless millions and millions of aeons of inconceivable duration, rare are the times when this Lotus Sutra has been heard. During countless millions and millions of aeons of inconceivable duration, rare are the times when the Buddhas, the World-Honored Ones, preach this sutra. Therefore, the practitioners after the Buddha's death, on hearing such a sutra as this, should not have any doubts." This passage is extremely unusual even among the twenty-eight chapters of the Lotus Sutra. From the *Jo* to the *Hosshi* chapters, humans, heavenly beings, the four kinds of believers and the eight kinds of lowly beings below the stage of *tōgaku*[9] were many in number, but there was only one

9. *Tōgaku*: Fifty-first stage of bodhisattva practice. T'ien-t'ai classified the

Buddha, Shakyamuni. Thus, these chapters are more important [than the pre-Lotus Sutra teachings] but less important [than those chapters of the Lotus Sutra which describe the ceremony in the air]. The twelve chapters from *Hōtō* to *Zokurui* are the most important of all. This is because in the presence of Shakyamuni Buddha there appeared a tower decorated with many treasures.[10] It was as if the sun had risen in front of the moon. All the Buddhas in the universe were seated under the trees, and it seemed as though the light of a fire shone over all the grass and trees in the universe. It was in this setting that the above passage was expounded.

The Nirvana Sutra states, "People have been suffering since uncountable aeons ago. The bones each individual leaves behind in an aeon pile up as high as Mount Vipula in Rajagriha, and the milk he sucks is equal to the water of the four oceans.[11] The blood one sheds surpasses the quantity of water in the four oceans, and so do the tears he sheds in grief over the death of parents, brothers and sisters, wives, children and relatives. And though one used all the plants and trees growing in the earth to make four-inch tallies to count them, one could not count all the parents one has had in the past existences of life." These are the words the Buddha uttered lying in the grove of sal trees on the final day of his earthly life. You should pay the strictest attention to them. They mean that the number of parents who gave birth to you since innumerable aeons ago could not be counted even with tallies made by cutting all the plants and trees growing on all the worlds of the universe into four-inch pieces.

---

bodhisattva practice into fifty-two stages, the last being *myōkaku*, or full enlightenment. *Tōgaku* is thus the highest state of a bodhisattva.

10. Tower decorated with many treasures: The Treasure Tower of Tahō Buddha which appeared in the *Hōtō* (11th) chapter of the Lotus Sutra. The tower, representing the Buddha nature, appeared in order to signify that Shakyamuni was beginning to expound the essential teaching. *See also* Treasure Tower in the Glossary.

11. Four oceans: In Buddhism, the oceans surrounding Mt. Sumeru on all four sides.

Thus you have had a countless number of parents in your past existences, yet during that time you have never encountered the Lotus Sutra. From this we see that it is easy to have parents, but very difficult to encounter the Lotus Sutra. Now if you disobey the words of a parent, one who is easy to come by, and follow a friend of the Lotus Sutra, one who can rarely be encountered, you will not only be able to attain Buddhahood, but will also be able to lead to enlightenment the parent whom you disobeyed. For example, Prince Siddhartha[12] was the eldest son of King Shuddhodana. His father wanted him to succeed to the throne and rule the nation, and actually ceded the throne to him, but the prince went against his father's wishes and escaped from the castle at night. The king was angry at him for being unfilial, but after Siddhartha had attained Buddhahood, he set about first of all to save his parents, King Shuddhodana and Lady Maya.

No parent would ever urge his son to renounce the world in order to attain enlightenment. But however that may be, in your case, the priests and followers of the Ritsu and Nembutsu sects have egged on your father to join with them so that they may make both you and your brother abandon your faith. I am told that Ryōka-bō[13] is persuading others to chant one million Nembutsu in an attempt to cause discord among people and destroy the seeds of the Lotus Sutra. Hōjō Shigetoki, who built Gokuraku-ji temple for Ryōkan, seemed to be an admirable person. But deluded by the Nembutsu believers, he treated me with enmity, and as a result, he and his entire clan have been all but ruined. Only Hōjō Naritoki, lord of Echigo Province, has survived. You may think that those who believe in Ryōka-bō

12. Siddhartha: The given name of Shakyamuni Buddha before his renunciation of the world.

13. Ryōka-bō (1217–1303): Gokuraku-ji Ryōkan, a priest of the Ritsu sect. Ryōka of Ryōka-bō is a phonetic change of Ryōkan and means "two fires." In March of 1275, a fire broke out in Gokuraku-ji temple where Ryōkan was then living, and the flames spread to the palace of the shogunate. The temple and part of the palace were burnt to the ground. Sarcastically, therefore, Nichiren Daishonin called Ryōkan "Ryōka"-bō (priest double-fire).

are prospering, but you should see what has become of the Nagoe clan,[14] who paid for the building of Zenkō-ji temple, Chōraku-ji temple and a temple to house a huge image of the Buddha! Again, Hōjō Tokimune[15] is the ruler of Japan, but by his conduct he has called down on himself an enemy almost as great as the entire world.

Even if you abandon your brother and take his place in your father's favor, you will never prosper in ten million years. There is no knowing what will become of you even in the near future—you may face ruin in this very lifetime. Therefore, you should resolve to give all your thought to your next existence. Having written all this, it occurs to me that this letter may be futile and I tire of going on. But it may serve as a reminder to you in the future.

With my deep respect,
Nichiren

The twentieth day of the eleventh month

BACKGROUND   This letter was written to Hyōe no Sakan Munenaga, the younger of the Ikegami brothers, on November 20, 1277, three years after Nichiren Daishonin returned from exile on Sado Island. The two Ikegami brothers, Uemon

14.   Nagoe clan: The clan of Hōjō Tomotoki (1193–1245), younger brother of Hōjō Yasutoki, the third regent of the Kamakura government. His clan was called the Nagoe clan after their place of residence. He and his clan, who were earnest believers of the Nembutsu sect, died tragic deaths.

15.   Hōjō Tokimune (1251–1284): The eighth regent of the Kamakura government. In the thirteenth century a new and ruthless race of conquerors, the Mongols, appeared upon the scene in Asia. In 1268, when the Mongol Empire sent the first of a succession of envoys to Japan to demand that it acknowledge fealty to the Mongols, Nichiren Daishonin wrote Tokimune a letter, saying that the government should discontinue its patronage of heretical sects and take faith in true Buddhism, but his warning was not heeded. In 1274 and 1281, the Mongol forces attacked the southern parts of Japan, sending waves of terror throughout the country. The Japanese suffered terrible losses, although a great part of the enemy fleet was destroyed by storms.

no Sakan Munenaka and Hyōe no Sakan Munenaga, were converted to the Daishonin's Buddhism at about the same time as Shijō Kingo. The elder, Munenaka, was the first to accept the faith, probably in 1256, and his younger brother, Munenaga, followed soon after. Both were officials in the Kamakura shogunate and their father, Yasumitsu, held an important post in the government construction office.

Yasumitsu was a devout follower of Ryōkan, the chief priest of the Ritsu sect who was highly active in political affairs. Therefore Munenaka and Munenaga met with stubborn opposition from their father in their Buddhist practice. In April of 1275, Yasumitsu disowned his elder son, who was stronger and more confident in his faith. On hearing the news, the Daishonin wrote the "Letter to the Brothers" to encourage the two by stating that Munenaka's disinheritance was an obstacle of the sort that invariably arises when one earnestly pursues enlightenment, and that, by overcoming this obstacle, they could both change their destiny and gain happiness.

No matter how offensive his sons' religion might have seemed to Yasumitsu, there must have been some other provocation to cause him to take so extreme a measure. The Daishonin suspected Ryōkan's hand in this affair. Ryōkan had long since abandoned any direct attacks on Nichiren Daishonin, but he could easily apply pressure on his own followers. Evidence shows that he persuaded the father, Yasumitsu, to take action against his sons. By disowning Munenaka, Yasumitsu in effect was provoking a rift between the two sons, tempting the weaker Munenaga to trade his beliefs for the right to inherit his father's estate. Yasumitsu failed in this attempt and forgave Munenaka. However, he disowned Munenaka again in 1277, which seems to have greatly shaken the younger Munenaga's confidence. In this letter, "The Three Obstacles and Four Devils," Nichiren Daishonin taught Munenaga the true meaning of filial piety—which is, to convert one's parents to faith in true Buddhism—and encouraged him to persist in his faith throughout his life, citing the example of Jōzō and Jōgen. Thereafter, supported by the Daishonin's guidance and encouragement, Munenaga upheld his faith together with his brother, and in 1278, after a total of twenty-two years' practice, their united efforts finally led their father to accept faith in Nichiren Daishonin's Buddhism.

Two Kinds of Faith

I HAVE duly received your offerings of taro, skewer-dried persimmons, baked rice, chestnuts, bamboo shoots and bamboo containers of vinegar.

There was once a king named Ashoka the Great in India. He reigned over a quarter of the world and, attended by the dragon kings,[1] controlled the rain at his will. He even used demons to do his bidding. At first he was a merciless ruler, but later he was converted to Buddhism. He made offerings to sixty thousand priests each day and erected eighty-four thousand stone stupas. In inquiring into the previous lifetime of this great sovereign, we find that in the days of Shakyamuni Buddha there were two little boys called Tokushō Dōji and Mushō Dōji,[2] who once offered the Buddha a mudpie. Because of this act of sincerity, the elder boy Tokushō was reborn as King Ashoka within one hundred years.

1.   Dragon kings: One of the eight kinds of lowly beings who protect Buddhism. From ancient times, dragon kings and demons were believed to possess supernatural power and produce miraculous phenomena, beyond human wisdom to comprehend. "Attended by the dragon kings, [he] controlled the rain at his will" and "He even used demons to do his bidding" show that King Ashoka was endowed with great good fortune and power.

2.   Tokushō Dōji and Mushō Dōji: According to the *Zō-agon* (Skt Saṃyuktāgama) Sutra, Shakyamuni was once going about begging on the outskirts of the city of Rajagriha when he came upon two little boys playing in the mud. The boys, observing the so-called "thirty-two distinguishing features

The Buddha is of course respectworthy, but when compared with the Lotus Sutra, he is like a firefly beside the sun or the moon. The Lotus Sutra is as superior to Shakyamuni Buddha as heaven is higher than the earth. To present offerings to the Buddha produces such great benefits as to be born a king, yet even greater benefit is obtained by making offerings to the Lotus Sutra. If such a marvelous reward was brought about by the mere offering of a mudpie, how much more will come about as a result of all your various gifts! The Buddha was far from being short of food, but now we are in a land where hunger prevails. Therefore I am certain that the Buddhas Shakyamuni and Tahō and the Ten Goddesses will never fail to protect you.

Today there are people who have faith in the Lotus Sutra. The belief of some is like a fire while that of others is like water. When the former listen to the teachings, their passion flares up like fire, but when by themselves, they are inclined to discard their faith. To have faith like water means to believe continuously without ever regressing. Since you pay frequent visits to me regardless of the difficulties, your belief is comparable to flowing water. It is worthy of great respect!

Is it true that there is illness in your family? If so, it cannot be the work of demons. The Ten Goddesses must be testing the strength of your faith. None of the demons who appeared in the Lotus Sutra would ever dare trouble a votary of the sutra and have their heads broken as punishment.[3] Persist in your

---

of a great man" that the Buddha is said to have possessed, decided that they should make an offering to him and proceeded to shape mudpies. Tokushō Dōji placed them in Shakyamuni's begging bowl while the younger boy Mushō then pressed his palms together in a gesture of reverence. Shakyamuni received the gift of mudpies with a smile. The disciple Ananda, who was accompanying him, asked him why he smiled, whereupon he replied, "I have a reason for smiling, Ananda, and you shall know it. One hundred years after my death, this boy will become a wheel-turning king at Pataliputra who will rule over all regions. His name will be Ashoka, and he will rule through the True Law." It is said that Tokushō Dōji was reborn as King Ashoka and Mushō Dōji, as either his wife or his brother.

3.   Have their heads broken as punishment: *See* p. 258, footnote 5.

faith with the firm conviction that both Shakyamuni Buddha and the Lotus Sutra are free from any falsehood.

With my deep respect,
Nichiren

The twenty-fifth day of the second month

BACKGROUND   In October 1274, the Mongol forces swept across the islands of Tsushima and Iki and attacked Kyushu, the southern part of Japan. The Japanese were terrified that the Mongols would invade Japan again at the next opportunity. During this period of unrest, Nichiren Daishonin's disciples exerted themselves in propagation, especially near Mount Fuji. The *shakubuku* movement was progressing rapidly there under the direction of Nikkō Shonin, who was later to become the second high priest. Many new believers, both priests and laymen, resided in a nearby area known as Atsuhara. Angered by the success of Nikkō Shonin's efforts, the priests of a local Tendai temple began harassing the converts. Eventually, on the pretext of a quarrel over land rights, they sent a band of warriors to attack a number of unarmed farmers of the convert group. Twenty of the farmers were arrested and sent to Kamakura for trial by the government authorities. They were tortured and ordered to quit their faith, but they fearlessly resisted. Three were eventually beheaded.

This incident is known as the Atsuhara Persecution. It is significant that, while earlier persecutions had been aimed chiefly at the Daishonin, this one was directed against his followers. Because the farmers refused to yield, the Daishonin was convinced that his disciples had now grown strong enough in their faith to risk their lives if necessary to uphold the Mystic Law. This motivated him to inscribe the Dai-Gohonzon—the true object of worship for all mankind for eternity—on October 12, 1279.

This letter was written on February 25, 1278, to Nanjō Tokimitsu, the lord of Ueno District, Suruga Province. Tokimitsu had been exceptionally faithful since childhood in the face of all difficulties and had the courage necessary to protect the Daishonin's Buddhism. During the Atsuhara Persecution, he played a crucial role in protecting the suffering believers. His own home was their main refuge. As a lord, he exerted some influence and used it to guard the Daishonin's lay followers and priests. His actions did not meet with approval by the Kamakura government, and unreasonably heavy taxes were levied on his estate. Eventually he could no longer afford to keep a horse—a hardship for a samurai—or to buy clothes for his wife and children.

Moreover, Nanjō Tokimitsu, like the majority of people of Japan, was hard pressed for even basic necessities because the country had been troubled by widespread famine. In spite of his own financial difficulties, however, he continued sending provisions to the Daishonin at Minobu. This letter is a reply in which Nichiren Daishonin expresses his gratitude for Lord Nanjō's offerings and praises him for his deep sincerity.

Persecution by Sword and Staff

THE greatest of all the persecutions which I have suffered were those at Komatsubara in Tōjō,[1] and at Tatsuno-kuchi[2] where I was nearly beheaded. None of the others were direct attempts on my life. I have been reviled, denounced, exiled, falsely accused, and struck across the face, but these were all comparatively minor incidents. I, Nichiren, am the only person in Japan to be abused in both body and mind for practicing the Lotus Sutra. If anyone else has been slandered as I have, it was not because of the Lotus Sutra. One incident I especially can never forget is how Shōfu-bō[3] seized the fifth volume of the Lotus Sutra[4] and struck me across the face with it. His attack on me stemmed from the three poisons of greed, anger and stupidity.

1. Tōjō: Place in Nichiren Daishonin's native province of Awa. On November 11, 1264, the Daishonin was ambushed by Lord Tōjō Kagenobu and his men. In the melee he received a swordcut on his forehead and had his hand broken.
2. Tatsunokuchi: Site of an attempt made by the deputy police chief Hei no Saemon to execute Nichiren Daishonin on September 12, 1271.
3. Shōfu-bō: Originally a follower of Nichiren Daishonin who later abandoned his faith. Although details are unknown, it is thought that around the time of the Izu exile, he started doubting the Daishonin and finally turned against him. When Hei no Saemon and his men went to arrest the Daishonin on September 12, 1271, he accompanied them as Saemon's chief retainer.
4. Fifth volume of the Lotus Sutra: In those days, documents were written on a long roll of paper wrapped around a wooden staff, so they would have had

Once in India there was a jealous woman[5] who hated her husband so much that she smashed everything in the house. Her excessive rage completely altered her appearance; her eyes blazed like the sun and moon, and her mouth seemed to belch fire. She looked exactly like a blue or red demon.[6] She seized the fifth volume of the Lotus Sutra which her husband had been reciting for some years and trampled it savagely with both feet. Later she died and fell into hell, all of her except her feet. Though hell's guardians[7] tried to force them down by beating them with iron staves, her feet remained outside of hell as a result of the relationship, albeit a reverse one, which they had formed with the Lotus Sutra by trampling on it. Shōfu-bō struck me in the face with the fifth volume of the Lotus Sutra because he hated me. Thus he too has formed a reverse relationship[8] with this sutra.

One incident occurred in India, the other in Japan; one was perpetrated by a woman, and the other by a man; in one, a pair of feet committed the violence, and in the other, a pair of

---

considerable force if wielded as a weapon. The twenty-eight chapters of the Lotus Sutra traditionally comprised eight volumes, with two more volumes for the opening and closing sutras. The fifth volume includes four chapters from the twelfth through the fifteenth chapters. A passage from the *Kanji* (13th) chapter states that the votaries of the Lotus Sutra will be attacked by sword and staff.

5. Jealous woman: Story recounted in the *Hokke Denki* of the Chinese priest Seng-hsiang, a collection of the biographies of distinguished priests, along with their commentaries.

6. Blue or red demon: Blue demons (Skt Apasmaraka) were ordinary demons said to disturb human beings. They were often depicted in statues and images. Red demons (Vetala) were said to be hell's guardians with ox- or horse-heads.

7. Hell's guardians: Demon subjects of Emma, the king of Hell, who torment those who have fallen into hell with their iron staves.

8. Reverse relationship: Opposite of positive relationship. A connection with the Lotus Sutra formed by opposing it. Although one who slanders Buddhism must suffer retribution for his slander, he nevertheless forms an eternal bond with Buddhism and can thus ultimately attain Buddhahood. This principle shows the great power of the Lotus Sutra which eventually saves everyone who forms a relationship with it, whether positive or negative.

hands; one happened because of jealousy, and the other because of the Lotus Sutra. However, the same fifth volume of the sutra was involved in both instances. The woman's feet did not enter hell, so why should Shōfu-bō's hands? The woman, however, hated only her husband and not the Lotus Sutra itself, whereas Shōfu-bō hated both the Lotus Sutra and me, Nichiren. Therefore his entire body will enter hell. As the sutra states, "After he dies, he will fall into the hell of incessant suffering."[9] There is no mention of his hands being spared. How pitiful! Eventually, however, he will meet me again and be able to attain Buddhahood, just as the four kinds of arrogant people were ultimately saved by Bodhisattva Fukyō.[10]

The fifth volume contains the heart of the Lotus Sutra, for it reveals that the Dragon King's daughter attained Buddhahood without changing her dragon form. Devadatta represents the spiritual aspect of enlightenment, and the Dragon King's daughter, the physical aspect. The principle of attaining Buddhahood in one's present form can be found nowhere else in Shakyamuni's teaching. The Great Teacher Dengyō enumerated ten outstanding principles in which the Lotus Sutra surpasses all others. One of them is attaining Buddhahood as a common mortal. This is the most important doctrine of the Tendai sect, and a section of the *Hokke Mongu* is entitled, "The Supreme Principle of Attaining Buddhahood as a Common Mortal." It is also a point of controversy between the Shingon and Tendai sects. The Dragon King's daughter attained enlightenment through the power of the Lotus Sutra. Bodhisatt-

9. Lotus Sutra, chap. 3.
10. This story is found in the *Fukyō* (20th) chapter of the Lotus Sutra. The four kinds of arrogant people are priests and nuns, lay men and women who slandered and persecuted Bodhisattva Fukyō when he revered them for their inherent Buddha nature. What he practiced at that time was the Lotus Sutra, and because of their slander of that sutra the people fell into the hell of incessant suffering. Eventually, however, due to the reverse relationship they had formed with the Lotus Sutra, they met Bodhisattva Fukyō again and were able to attain enlightenment.

va Monju stated, "I always proclaim and teach only the Lotus Sutra."[11] The words "only" and "always" are the key to this quotation. However, the *Bodaishin Ron*[12] reads, "[The principle of attaining Buddhahood in one's present form] is found only in the teachings of Shingon." Which "only" is correct? The *Bodaishin Ron* must be mistaken. The *Muryōgi* Sutra states, ". . . in these more than forty years, I have not yet revealed the truth." The Lotus Sutra reads, "The World-Honored One has long expounded his doctrines and now must reveal the truth." Tahō Buddha affirmed that only the Lotus Sutra enables one to attain Buddhahood as a common mortal when he said, "All that you (Shakyamuni Buddha) have expounded is the truth."[13] No matter how repeatedly the believers in provisional doctrines may insist that one can attain enlightenment through the pre-Lotus Sutra teachings, it is as easy to refute their assertions as it is to smash a thousand pieces of earthenware with a single hammer. T'ien-t'ai states, "The practice of the Lotus Sutra is *shakubuku*, the refutation of the provisional doctrines."[14] The Lotus Sutra indeed is the most profound and secret teaching.

Ever since Jikaku, scholars of the Tendai sect have interpreted the passages of the *Hokke Gengi*, *Hokke Mongu* and *Maka Shikan* in one way or another, and have given plausible explanations. Their views, however, are as useless to us now as last year's calendar or yesterday's meal. Even if someone should insist that, in the first five hundred years of the Latter Day of the Law, there exists a way to enlightenment apart from the daimoku of the Lotus Sutra, you should not pursue it, even if it

11. Lotus Sutra, chap. 12.
12. *Bodaishin Ron*: Treatise attributed to Nagarjuna and translated by Pu-k'ung in China. It teaches the importance of a seeking mind for enlightenment. Kōbō, the founder of the Japanese Shingon sect, quoted it frequently to assert the superiority of the esoteric teachings over the Lotus Sutra. Nagarjuna's authorship appears doubtful.
13. Lotus Sutra, chap. 11.
14. *Hokke Gengi*, vol. 9.

is based on the Buddha's teachings, and even less so if it is merely some scholar's opinion. The *Devadatta* chapter of the Lotus Sutra teaches that Devadatta was Shakyamuni Buddha's master in some past existence. He who was once the master is now the disciple, and he who is now the disciple was formerly the master. On pondering this chapter, I, Nichiren, realized that it reveals the profound meaning of the Lotus Sutra through the principle of the oneness of past and present and the inseparability of the one who teaches and the one who learns. Therefore, the merciful Shakyamuni Buddha became the master of the wicked Devadatta, and the wise Monju became the master of the ignorant daughter of the Dragon King. Certainly I, Nichiren, can in no way be inferior to Monju or to Shakyamuni Buddha. The men of Japan are like Devadatta and the women are like the Dragon King's daughter. Whether by following it or opposing it, they shall attain enlightenment through the Lotus Sutra. This is the message of the *Devadatta* chapter.

Next we come to the *Kanji* chapter. Only I, Nichiren, have read with my entire being the twenty-line verse[15] from this chapter, which a vast multitude of bodhisattvas proclaimed in a single voice. Since the Buddha's death, who else in the three countries of India, China and Japan has ever read this verse as I have? No one even claims to have done so, nor do I believe that anyone has. The *Kanji* chapter states, "[There will be many ignorant people who will]. . . . attack us with swords and staves." Perhaps others have been beaten with staves, but I have never heard of any who were injured by the sword.

We know that Bodhisattva Fukyō was attacked with staves, in accordance with the words of the sutra, "They would beat him with sticks and staves, and stone him with rocks and tiles,"

15.   Twenty-line verse: The verse section of the thirteenth or *Kanji* chapter that states that the votaries of the Lotus Sutra will be attacked by swords and staves.

but he was not persecuted by the sword. T'ien-t'ai, Miao-lo, Dengyō and others also escaped persecution by sword and staff, in accordance with the words, "Swords and staves will not touch him."[16] I, Nichiren, however, have been attacked by both. As I mentioned before, I was attacked by the sword at Komatsubara in Tōjō and later at Tatsunokuchi. No one else has been thus assaulted for the sake of the Lotus Sutra even once, but I, Nichiren, have been so assaulted twice. As for being attacked with staves, I have already been struck in the face by Shōfu-bō with the scroll of the fifth volume of the Lotus Sutra. Strangely enough, it is precisely that volume which carries the prediction that the votaries of the Lotus Sutra will be attacked with staves. Shōfu-bō hit me before dozens of people, and, though I knew it was for the sake of the Lotus Sutra, being human, I felt miserable and ashamed. Had I had the strength, I would have wrested the weapon from his hand and trampled it to pieces, except that it was in fact the scroll of the fifth volume of the Lotus Sutra.

This brings to mind a story.[17] A father, anxious about his son's future, thrashed the boy with a bow made of boxwood because he refused to study. At the time, the son resented his father's action and hated the boxwood bow. However, he applied himself to his studies, disciplined his mind and eventually achieved a great self-awakening which also benefited others. In retrospect, he saw that he owed his achievements to his father's thrashings. It is said that in gratitude he erected a stupa made of boxwood to honor his father's memory.

It is the same with me, Nichiren. When I attain Buddhahood, how will I be able to forget my obligation to Shōfu-

16. Lotus Sutra, chap. 14. This refers to one of the benefits which bodhisattvas gain as a result of the peaceful ways of practice set forth in the *Anrakugyō* chapter.
17. This story appears in the *Sangoku Denki* (Biographies of the Three Countries). The son later became Enshō, a chief priest of Enryaku-ji, the head temple of the Tendai sect.

bō? Much less can I forget the thanks I owe to the fifth volume of the Lotus Sutra with which he struck me. When I think of this, I cannot restrain my tears of gratitude.

The *Yujutsu* chapter also explains something about me, because it states that Bodhisattva Jōgyō and others will appear in the Latter Day of the Law to propagate the five characters of Nam-myoho-renge-kyo.[18] I, Nichiren, have appeared earlier than anyone else. How reassuring to think that I will surely be praised by bodhisattvas equal in number to the sands of sixty thousand Ganges Rivers![19] Be that as it may, commit yourself to the Lotus Sutra and have faith in its teachings. You must not only believe in them yourself but also encourage others to do the same, so that you may save your deceased parents and ancestors.

From the time that I was born until today, I, Nichiren, have never known a moment's ease; I have thought only of propagating the daimoku of the Lotus Sutra. I do not know how long I or anyone else may live, but without fail, I will be with you at the time of your death and guide you from this life to the next. All the Buddhas of the past, present and future attain enlightenment between the hours of the Ox and the Tiger.[20] In all three countries of India, China and Japan, the place of Buddhist practice is located to the northeast, in the direction of

18. Nam-myoho-renge-kyo actually consists of seven Chinese characters. Sometimes the first two are omitted when referring to the name of the Law (as distinguished from the invocation).

19. Sands of sixty thousand Ganges Rivers: A typical Indian expression which appears in many Buddhist sutras, meaning "innumerable."

20. Time and direction in ancient Japan were designated by twelve different animals. The Hour of the Rat corresponded to the time from 11:00 P.M. to 1:00 A.M.; the Hour of the Ox, from 1:00 to 3:00 A.M.; and the Hour of the Tiger, from 3:00 to 5:00 A.M. Buddhism traditionally regards these hours as a crucial interval in which life moves from the negative (*yin*) to the positive (*yang*), from sleep to waking, or from death to life. Shakyamuni Buddha, under the Bodhi tree, attained enlightenment during these hours, and Nichiren Daishonin, at the Tatsunokuchi Persecution, revealed his true identity as the original Buddha during the same hours.

the demon gate.[21] These are secret teachings of Buddhism, which are reverently transferred from master to disciple. I will explain in more detail later.

With my deep respect.

As you crave food when hungry, seek water when thirsty, long to see a lover, beg for medicine when ill, or as a beautiful woman desires powder and rouge, so should you put your faith in the Lotus Sutra. If you do not, you will regret it later.

Nichiren

The twentieth day of the fourth month in the second year of Kōan (1279)

BACKGROUND   This Gosho was written on April 20, 1279, when Nichiren Daishonin was fifty-eight years old. In the five years since he had come to live in the recesses of Mount Minobu, the first Mongol invasion had occurred and the second was now clearly imminent. The Daishonin was becoming widely respected for the truth of his prophecies. Owing to Nikkō Shonin's sincere efforts, the propagation of his Buddhism advanced rapidly, notably in the Atsuhara area near Mount Fuji.

The year 1279 was especially significant because on October 12 Nichiren Daishonin inscribed the Dai-Gohonzon, fulfilling the purpose of his advent. Around the same time, farmers of Atsuhara who were believers had experienced harsh persecution by the authorities, culminating in the execution of the three brothers Jinshirō, Yagorō and Yarokurō. The recipient of this letter, Nanjō Tokimitsu, lord of the Ueno area, had been

21.   In correlating hours with spatial direction, the hours of the Ox-Tiger correspond to the northeast, believed to be the location of both Buddhism and demons.

practicing sincerely under the guidance of Nikkō Shonin and, at the time of the Atsuhara Persecution, risked his own safety to protect the farmers. Tokimitsu received some thirty personal letters from the Daishonin.

At the beginning of this Gosho, Nichiren Daishonin reveals the profound meaning of the persecution "by sword and staff." The fact of his being struck with the fifth volume of the Lotus Sutra is no mere coincidence but signifies that he is the votary of that sutra.

The fifth volume of the Lotus Sutra contains the twelfth through the fifteenth chapters. In the body of this Gosho, Nichiren Daishonin explains the significance of these chapters in terms of his own enlightenment. First the Daishonin cites the *Devadatta* (12th) chapter, which predicts that Devadatta will attain enlightenment because he had formed a relationship with Buddhism, albeit a negative or "reverse" one, and in which the Dragon King's daughter attained Buddhahood without changing her dragon form.

The *Kanji* (13th) chapter, particularly the twenty-line verse section, describes the persecutions that votaries of the Lotus Sutra will undergo in an evil latter age. The Daishonin states that only he has "read" this chapter, i.e., lived out its predictions, thus identifying himself as the votary of the Lotus Sutra in the Latter Day of the Law. The *Yujutsu* (15th) chapter relates how numerous bodhisattvas emerged from the earth. Their leader was Bodhisattva Jōgyō, and it was to him that Shakyamuni specifically entrusted the mission of propagation in the Latter Day. By citing this chapter, Nichiren Daishonin identifies himself with Bodhisattva Jōgyō, and indirectly, as the original Buddha.

The statements, "All Buddhas . . . attain enlightenment between the hours of the Ox and the Tiger," and ". . . the place of Buddhist practice is located to the northeast," point to the Daishonin's revelation of his true identity at Tatsunokuchi. The fact that Nichiren Daishonin is the original Buddha is not, from our standpoint, a secret teaching; he calls it a secret teaching because it could not be generally understood by, nor did he widely reveal it to, the people of his time. In the concluding paragraph, Nichiren Daishonin urges Lord Nanjō to have faith in the Gohonzon and turn to the Gohonzon under all circumstances in order to lead a life without regrets.

The Proof of the Lotus Sutra

Nichiren, the votary of the Lotus Sutra

A PERSON who, during the evil age of the Latter Day of the Law, believes in the teachings of the Lotus Sutra just as they are set forth in the sutra—how does the mirror of the Lotus Sutra portray him? Shakyamuni Buddha has left us words from his golden mouth revealing that such a person has already served tens of billions of Buddhas in his past existences.[1] But common mortals in the Latter Day might well doubt the words spoken by one Buddha only. With this thought in mind, Tahō Buddha expressly came all the way from his world of Treasure Purity, many lands to the east. Facing Shakyamuni Buddha, he gave his words of testimony, saying, "All that you have expounded is the truth." If this is so, then there can be no room for doubt about the matter. Nevertheless, the Buddha may have felt that common mortals in the Latter Day of the Law would still be skeptical. Hence he summoned all the Buddhas throughout the ten directions to come and join him in the magnificent act of extending their long broad tongues,[2]

---

1. This is mentioned in the *Hosshi* (10th) chapter of the Lotus Sutra.
2. Long broad tongues: One of the thirty-two distinguishing features of a Buddha. The Buddha's tongue was said to be soft, thin and long enough to touch his forehead. In ancient India, people used to extend their tongues in order to show the truth of their words. The farther a tongue was extended, the greater the verification of the words uttered. It was commonly accepted among Brahmans that those who had a long and broad tongue were free from

which had told nothing but the truth for countless aeons, until they projected into the sky as high as Mount Sumeru.

Since this is the case, when a common mortal in the Latter Day believes in even one or two words of the Lotus Sutra, he is embracing the teaching to which all the Buddhas in the ten directions have given credence. I wonder what good karma I created in the past to have been born as such a person, and I am filled with joy. Shakyamuni's words which I have mentioned above indicate that the blessings that come from having served tens of billions of Buddhas are so great that, even though one may have believed in teachings other than the Lotus Sutra and as a result of this slander been born poor and lowly, he is still able to believe in this sutra during this lifetime. Miao-lo states, "One who falls to the ground rises by pushing himself up from the ground, . . ."[3] Those who slander the Lotus Sutra will fall to the ground of the three evil paths, Humanity or Heaven, yet through the help of the Lotus Sutra they will in the end attain Buddhahood.

Now since you, Ueno Shichirō Jirō, are a common mortal in the Latter Day of the Law and were born into a warrior family, you should by rights be called an evil man, and yet your heart is that of a good man. I say this for a reason. Everyone, from the ruler on down to the common people, refuses to take faith in my teachings. They inflict harm on the few who do embrace them, heavily taxing or confiscating their estates and fields or even in some cases putting them to death. So it is a difficult thing to believe in my teachings, and yet both your mother and your deceased father dared to accept them. Now you have succeeded your father as his heir and, without any persuasion from others, you too have wholeheartedly embraced these

---

falsehood. There are various "tongue-verified" sutras, but the *Jinriki* (21st) chapter of the Lotus Sutra mentions a tongue long enough to reach the heavens, implying the absolute truth of the sutra's teaching.

3.   *Hokke Mongu Ki*. The sentence following this quotation is a restatement of the quotation and is omitted to avoid repetition in the translation.

teachings. Many people, both high and low in rank, have reprimanded or threatened you, but you have refused to give up your faith. Now that you appear certain to attain Buddhahood, the Devil of the Sixth Heaven and other demons are trying to use this illness to intimidate you. But remember that life in this world is limited. Never allow yourself to be intimidated!

And as for you demons—will you cause this disciple of mine to suffer and swallow a sword point first, or embrace a raging fire, or become the archenemy of all the Buddhas throughout the universe and in the three existences of life? How terrible this will be for you! Now, will you cure this man's illness immediately and hereafter give him your protection instead, in this way escaping from the grievous sufferings that are the lot of demons? Or do you prefer to have your heads broken into seven pieces[4] and after your death to fall into the hell of incessant suffering? Bear what I say in mind and do not forget; if you ignore my words, you will regret it later.

The twenty-eighth day of the second month in the fifth year of Kōan (1282)

BACKGROUND This letter was sent through Nikkō Shonin to Nanjō Tokimitsu (Nanjō Shichirō Jirō) on February 28, 1282, when Nichiren Daishonin's death was drawing near. On October 13 of the same year, his great and turbulent life came to an end. This is one of several letters that the Daishonin sent to his beloved disciples in his last year. He had said in a letter to Tokimitsu's mother toward the end of the preceding year: "Due to my decline in health I have refrained from replying to those who sent me letters." As revealed in this letter, however, his profound compassion and consideration for

4. *See* p. 258, footnote 5.

his disciples did not waver in the least. Despite his poor health, the Daishonin took up his writing brush to encourage Tokimitsu so that the latter could overcome his illness. This shows how dedicated Tokimitsu was to the cause of Buddhism and how highly the Daishonin valued him.

Nanjō Tokimitsu was born in 1259 and, young as he was, had already shouldered his deceased father's responsibilities long before the time he received this letter. He was lord of an area called Ueno which covered a vast slope of Mount Fuji including the present compound of Taiseki-ji, the head temple of Nichiren Shoshu. A follower of the Daishonin since child-hood, Tokimitsu was one of the leading lay believers in the Fuji area. Especially during the Atsuhara Persecution, at consider-able risk to himself, he exerted his influence to protect believers in the Fuji area. For these actions, the Daishonin honored him with the title "Sage of Ueno" although he was just twenty-one. He and his wife Myōren consistently made offerings to the Daishonin, even while struggling to raise several children and enduring a burden of heavy taxes imposed on them by authorities who disapproved of their religious convictions.

In this letter, Nichiren Daishonin encouraged the twenty-four-year-old Tokimitsu to overcome his illness. Tokimitsu in fact recovered and lived a long life, and even after the Daishonin's death he served Nikkō Shonin and donated to him the land upon which Taiseki-ji temple now stands. He died in 1332.

The letter is traditionally called "The Proof of the Lotus Sutra," for it mentions that all Buddhas gave credence to the truth of the Lotus Sutra. However, it is also called "On Life and Death" since Tokimitsu was then battling a serious illness. In the letter Nichiren Daishonin assured Tokimitsu he would attain enlightenment because he continued to uphold the Lotus Sutra (Gohonzon) in the face of oppression from the govern-ment. All the Buddhas in the universe agree that the believers of the sutra are sure to attain Buddhahood. He stated that because Tokimitsu appeared certain to attain enlightenment, devils and demons would desperately try to impede him. The Daishonin himself strongly enjoined them to stop harassing his beloved disciple.

Appendix A
Japanese Titles of Gosho
in This Volume

Note: Numbers following Japanese titles refer to the page number in the *Gosho Zenshū*.

Appendix B
Sanskrit Personal Names

Sanskrit Names	Japanese Names
Ajatashatru (Ajātaśatru)	Ajase (阿闍世)
Ajita	Agita (阿耆多)
Ananda (Ānanda)	Anan (阿難)
Aryasinha (Āryasiṃha)	Shishi-sonja (師子尊者)
Asanga (Asaṅga)	Mujaku (無著)
Ashoka (Aśoka)	Asoka (阿育)
Ashvaghosha (Aśvaghoṣa)	Memyō (馬鳴)
Bimbisara (Bimbisāra)	Bimbashara (頻婆舍羅)
Bodhidharma	Daruma (達磨)
Chandraprabha (Chandraprabhā)	Gakkō (月光)
Chinchamanavika (Ciñcamāṇavikā)	Senshanyo (旃遮女)
Chunda (Cunda)	Junda (純陀)
Devadatta	Daibadatta (提婆達多) or Chōdatsu (調達)
Dharmagupta	Darumakikuta (達摩掬多)
Dharmapala (Dharmapāla)	Gohō (護法)
Dharmaraksha (Dharmarakṣa)	Hōgo (法護)
Dronodana (Droṇodana)	Kokubonnō (斛飯王)

Haklena
Jivaka (Jīvaka)
Jnanagupta (Jñānagupta)
Kalodayin (Kālodāyin)
Kanadeva (Kāṇadeva)
Kapila
Kashyapa (Kāśyapa)
Katyayana (Kātyāyana)
Kokalika (Kokālika)
Kumarajiva (Kumārajīva)
Kumarayana (Kumārāyaṇa)
Madhyantika
  (Madhyāntika)
Mahakashyapa
  (Mahākāśyapa)
Mahaprajapati
  (Mahāprajāpati)
Maudgalyayana
  (Maudgalyāyana)
Nagarjuna (Nāgārjuna)
Nanda
Parshva (Pārśva)
Prasenajit
Purna (Pūrṇa)
Pushyamitra (Puṣyamitra)

Rahula (Rāhula)
Rishabha (Ṛṣabha)
Shakyamuni (Śākyamuni)
Shariputra (Śāriputra)

Shilabhadra (Śīlabhadra)
Shiladitya (Śīlāditya)
Simhahanu (Siṃhahanu)
Subhuti (Subhūti)

Kakuroku (鶴勒)
Giba (耆婆)
Janakutta (闍那崛多)
Karudai (迦留陀夷)
Kanadaiba (迦那提婆)
Kabira (迦毘羅)
Kashō Dōji (迦葉童子)
Kasennen (迦旃延)
Kugyari (瞿伽利)
Kumarajū (鳩摩羅什)
Kumaraen (鳩摩羅炎)
Madenchi (末田地)

Kashō (迦葉)

Makahajahadai
  (摩訶波闍波提)
Mokuren (目連)

Ryūju (竜樹)
Nanda (難陀)
Kyōbiku (脇比丘)
Hashinoku-ō (波斯匿王)
Furuna (富楼那)
Hosshamittara-ō
  (弗沙弥多羅王)
Ragora (羅睺羅)
Rokushaba (勒沙婆)
Shakuson (釈尊)
Sharihotsu (舎利弗) or
  Shinshi (身子)
Kaigen (戒賢)
Kainichi-ō (戒日王)
Shishikyō-ō (師子頬王)
Shubodai (須菩提)

Sudaya (Sudāya)   Shuda (須陀)
Sunakshatra (Sunakṣatra)   Zenshō (善星) or Shizen
                               (四禅)
Uluka (Ulūka)   Kuru (拘留) or Urusōgya
                               (漚楼僧佉)
Utpalavarna (Utpalavarṇā)   Renge (蓮華) or Keshiki
                               (華色)
Vaidehi (Vaidehī)   Idaike (韋提希)
Vaipulya   Hōkō (方広)
Vasubandhu   Tenjin (天親) or Seshin (世親)
Vimalakirti (Vimalakīrti)   Yuimakitsu (維摩詰)
Virudhaka (Virūḍhaka)   Haruri-ō (波瑠璃王)
Yashodhara (Yaśodharā)   Yashutaranyo (耶輸多羅女)

Appendix C
Chinese Personal Names

Note: Chinese names are romanized according to the traditional Wade-Giles system. The new pinyin romanization appears in parenthesis.

Chinese Names	Japanese Names
Chang-an (Zhang-an)	Shōan (章安)
Chao (Zhao), King	Shō-ō (昭王)
Chao Kao (Zhao Gao)	Chō Kō (趙高)
Ch'eng-kuan (Cheng-guan)	Chōkan (澄観)
Chia-hsiang (Jia-xiang) or Chi-tsang (Ji-zang)	Kajō (嘉祥) or Kichizō (吉蔵)
Chia-shang (Jia-shang)	Kashō (嘉尚)
Chi-cha (Ji-zha)	Kisatsu (季札)
Chieh (Jie), King	Ketsu-ō (桀王)
Chih-tu (Zhi-du)	Chido (智度)
Chih-yen (Zhi-yan)	Chigon (智儼)
Ching-shuang (Jing-shuang)	Kyōsō (鏡霜)
Chin-kang-chih (Jin-gang-zhi)	Kongōchi (金剛智)
Chou (Zhou), King	Chū-ō (紂王)
Chuang Tzu (Zhuang Zi)	Sōshi (荘子)

Chu Tao-sheng (Zhu Dao-sheng)	Jiku Dōshō (竺道生)
Confucius	Kōshi (孔子)
Fa-ch'üan (Fa-quan)	Hassen (法全)
Fa-tao (Fa-dao)	Hōdō (法道)
Fa-tsang (Fa-zang)	Hōzō (法蔵)
Fu Hsi (Fu Xi) and Shen Nung (Shen Nong)	Fuku Gi (伏羲) and Shin Nō (神農)
Hsiang Yü (Xiang Yu)	Kō U (頂羽)
Hsüan-tsang (Xuan-zang) or Hsüan-chuang (Xuan-zhuang)	Genjō (玄奘)
Hsüan-tsung (Xuan-zong), Emperor	Gensō-tei (玄宗帝)
Huang Ti (Huang Di)	Kō Tei (黄帝)
Hua T'o (Hua Tuo)	Ka Da (華陀)
Hui-kuang (Hui-guang)	Ekō (慧光)
Hui-kuo (Hui-guo)	Keika (恵果)
Hui-tsung (Hui-zong), Emperor	Kisō-tei (徽宗帝)
Hung Yen (Hong Yan)	Kō In (公胤) or Kō En (弘演)
Juan Chi (Ruan Ji)	Gen Seki (阮籍)
Kuang-wu (Guang-wu), Emperor	Kōbu-tei (光武帝)
K'uei-chi (Kui-ji) or Tz'u-en (Ci-en)	Kiki (窺基) or Jion (慈恩)
Lao Tzu (Lao Zi)	Rōshi (老子)
Liang-hsü (Liang-xu)	Ryōsho (良諝)
Liu Pang (Liu Bang)	Ryū Hō (劉邦) or Hai Kō (沛公)
Mao Pao (Mao Bao)	Mō Hō (毛宝)
Miao-lo (Miao-luo)	Myōraku (妙楽) or Keikei (荊渓)
Ming (Ming), Emperor	Mei-tei (明帝)
Pien Ch'üeh (Bian Que)	Hen Jaku (扁鵲)

Pi Kan (Bi Gan)   Hi Kan (比干)

P'ing (Ping), King   Hei-ō (平王)

Po Chü-i (Bo Ju-yi)   Haku Kyoi (白居易) or
                                        Haku Rakuten (白楽天)

P'u-kuang (Pu-guang)   Fukō (普光)

Pu-k'ung (Bu-kong)   Fukū (不空)

Shan-tao (Shan-dao)   Zendō (善導)

Shan-wu-wei (Shan-wu-wei)   Zemmui (善無畏)

Shen-fang (Shen-fang)   Shimbō (神肪)

Ssu-ma (Si-ma)   Shiba (司馬)

Su Yu (Su You)   So Yū (蘇由)

T'ai-kung Wang (Tai-gong   Taikō Bō (太公望)
    Wang)

T'ai-tsung (Tai-zong),   Taisō-tei (太宗帝)
    Emperor

Tan (Dan), the Duke of Chou   Shūkō Tan (周公旦)
    (Zhou)

T'an-luan (Tan-luan)   Donran (曇鸞)

Tao-ch'o (Dao-cho)   Dōshaku (道綽)

T'ien-t'ai (Tian-tai)   Tendai (天台)

Ting Lan (Ding Lan)   Tei Ran (丁蘭)

Tu-shun (Du-shun)   Tojun (杜順)

Wang Shou (Wang Shou)   Ō Ju (王寿)

Wei Yuan-sung (Wei Yuan-   Ei Gensū (衛元嵩)
    song)

Wen (Wen), King   Bunnō (文王)

Wu (Wu), King   Bu-ō (武王)

Wu Ch'eng (Wu Cheng)   Mu Sei (務成)

Wu-tsung (Wu-zong),   Busō-tei (武宗帝)
    Emperor

Yao (Yao) and Shun (Shun)   Gyō (堯) and Shun (舜)

Yen Hui (Yan Hui)   Gan Kai (顔回) or Gan En
                                        (顔淵)

Yi (Yi), Duke   I Kō (懿公)

Yin Shou (Yin Shou)   In Ju (尹寿)

Appendix D
Titles of Buddhist Writings

1. *Agon* sutras: The *Agama* sutras
2. *Amida* Sutra: A Chinese version of the smaller *Sukhava-tivyuha* Sutra. Cf. the *Muryōju* Sutra, the larger *Sukhavativyuha* Sutra
3. *Bodaishin Ron*: Treatise on the Mind Aspiring to Enlightenment
4. *Daichido Ron*: The *Mahaprajnaparamitopadesha*
Treatise on the *Mahaprajnaparamita* Sutra
5. *Daihi* Sutra: The *Mahakarunapundarika* Sutra
The Sutra of Great Compassion
6. *Daijō Hōon Girin Jō*: On the Forest of Meanings in the Mahayana Garden of the Law
7. *Daijō Kishin Ron*: Awakening of Faith in the Mahayana
8. *Daijō Shiron Gengi Ki*: Annotations on Four Mahayana Treatises
9. *Daiju* Sutra: The *Mahavriksha* Sutra
The Sutra of the Great Trees
10. *Daijuku* Sutra: The *Mahasanghata* Sutra
The Sutra of the Great Assembly
11. *Dainichi* Sutra: The *Mahavairochana* Sutra
12. *Daiun* Sutra: The *Mahamegha* Sutra
The Sutra of the Great Cloud
13. *Fuhōzō* Sutra: The Sutra of the Transmission of the Law

14. *Fushō Ki*: Supplement to the Annotations on the Words and Phrases of the Lotus Sutra
15. *Gonjikinyo* Sutra: The Sutra of the Silver-colored Woman
16. *Guketsu*: Abbr. of *Maka Shikan Bugyōden Guketsu* Annotations on the Great Concentration and Insight
17. *Hannya* Sutra: The *Prajnaparamita* Sutra
    The Sutra of Perfect Wisdom
18. *Hatsunaion* Sutra: The *Parinirvana* Sutra
    The Sutra of the Final Nirvana
19. *Hizō Hōyaku*: The Jewel Key to the Store of Mysteries (Summary of the Treatise on the Ten Stages of Mind)
20. *Hōdō Dharani* Sutra: The *Mahavaipulyadharani* Sutra
    The Sutra of the Great Dharani
21. *Hōdō* sutras: The *Vaipulya* sutras
22. *Hōjōjū* Sutra: The Sutra of the Eternity of the Law
23. *Hokke Gengi*: Profound Meaning of the Lotus Sutra
24. *Hokke Genron*: Treatise on the Profundity of the Lotus Sutra
25. *Hokke Genzan*: In Praise of the Profundity of the Lotus Sutra
26. *Hokke Mongu*: Words and Phrases of the Lotus Sutra
27. *Hokke Mongu Ki*: Annotations on the Words and Phrases of the Lotus Sutra
28. *Hokke Shūku*: On the Supremacy of the Lotus Sutra
29. *Hōmetsujin* Sutra: The Sutra of the Decline of the Law
30. *Jimmitsu* Sutra: Also *Gejimmitsu* Sutra
    The *Sandhinirmochana* Sutra
    The Sutra of Profound Understanding
31. *Jinzū* Sutra: The Sutra of Supernatural Powers
32. *Jōmyō* Sutra: Also *Yuima* Sutra
    The Vimalakirti Sutra
33. *Jūji* Sutra: The Sutra of the Ten Stages

34. *Jūjūbibasha Ron*: The *Dashabhumivibhashashastra*
   A Commentary on the Ten Stages
35. *Jūjūshin Ron*: Treatise on the Ten Stages of Mind
36. *Kammuryōju* Sutra: The *Amitayurdhyana* Sutra
   The Sutra of Infinite Life
37. *Kegon* Sutra: The *Avatamsaka* Sutra
   The Flower Garland Sutra
38. *Kenkai Ron*: A Clarification of Precepts
39. *Kongōbei Ron*: Also *Kompei Ron*
   The Diamond Scalpel Treatise
40. *Kongōchō* Sutra: The *Vajrashekhara* Sutra
   The Diamond Crown Sutra
41. *Konkōmyō* Sutra: The *Suvarnaprabhasa* Sutra
   The Golden Light Sutra
42. Lotus Sutra: *Myōhō-renge-kyō*
   The *Saddharmapundarika* Sutra
43. *Maka Shikan*: Great Concentration and Insight
44. *Maya* Sutra: The Mahamaya Sutra
45. *Mitsugon* Sutra: The *Ghanavyuha* Sutra
   The Sutra on Rebirth in the Pure Land
   of Mahavairochana
46. *Muryōgi* Sutra: The Sutra of Infinite Meaning
47. *Muryōju* Sutra: A Chinese version of the larger *Sukhava-
   tivyuha*
48. *Nikyō Ron*: Abbr. of *Ben Kemmitsu Nikyō Ron*
   A Comparison of Exoteric and Esoteric
   Buddhism
49. *Ninnō* Sutra: The Sutra of the Benevolent King
50. Nirvana Sutra: The *Mahaparinirvana* Sutra
51. *Ōjō Ron Chū*: A Commentary on the Treatise on Rebirth in the Pure Land
52. *Rokuharamitsu* Sutra: The *Sadparamita* Sutra
   The Sutra of the Six *Paramitas*
53. *Ryōga* Sutra: The Lankavatara Sutra
54. *Senchaku Shū*: The Sole Selection of Nembutsu

55. *Shakusen*: Abbr. of *Hokke Gengi Shakusen*
          Annotations on the Profound Meaning of the
          Lotus Sutra
56. *Shinjikan* Sutra: The *Hridayabhumidhyana* Sutra
              The Sutra on the Contemplation of the
          Mind
57. *Shōjōhōgyō* Sutra: The Sutra on the Practice of the Pure
          Law
58. *Shōman* Sutra: The Shrimala Sutra
59. *Shuryōgon* Sutra: The *Shuramgama* Sutra
60. *Soshitsuji* Sutra: The *Susiddhikara* Sutra
              The Sutra on the Accomplishment of
          Perfection
61. *Tōshun*: A Commentary on the Words and Phrases of
          the Lotus Sutra
62. *Yakushi* Sutra: The *Bhaishajyaguru* Sutra
              The Sutra of the Buddha of Healing
63. *Yuga Ron*: Treatise on the Yogachara Practice

Glossary

Note: Buddhist terms, titles of documents and the names of figures in the sutras appear in Japanese unless otherwise indicated. Names of historical persons are given in their original language, with the exception of those Indian scholars who made their home in China.

Aeon: (Skt kalpa) Extremely long period of time. Sutras and treatises differ in their definitions. Aeons fall into two major categories, those of measurable and those of immeasurable duration. There are three kinds of measurable aeons: minor, medium and major. One explanation says that a minor aeon is approximately sixteen million years long. According to the treatise *Kusha Ron* (Skt Abhidharma-kośa-śāstra), a world goes through four stages: formation, continuance, decline and disintegration. Each of these four stages lasts for twenty minor aeons and is equal to one medium aeon. Finally, one complete cycle equals a major aeon. Immeasurable aeons are described in several ways. For example, an aeon has been said to be longer than the time required to wear away a cube of stone, 18 km on each side, if one brushes it with a piece of cloth once every hundred years. According to another explanation, an aeon is longer than the time needed to remove all the poppy seeds stored in a castle the same size as

329

the stone mentioned above, if one takes away one seed every hundred years.

Agon sutras: (Skt Āgama-sūtra) Generic term for all Hinayana sutras. T'ien-t'ai classified Shakyamuni's teachings into five periods, according to the order of preaching. The *Agon* sutras belong to the second period. *See also* Five periods.

Ajatashatru: (Jap Ajase) Son of King Bimbisara of Magadha, India. Incited by Devadatta, he killed his father, a follower of Shakyamuni Buddha, and ascended the throne to become the most influential ruler of his time. Later he contracted a terrible disease and, in remorse for his evil acts, converted to Buddhism and supported the First Buddhist Council.

Amida Buddha: (Skt Amitāyus, "Infinite Life," or Amitābha, "Infinite Light") Buddha of the Pure Land in the western region of the universe. According to the *Muryōju* Sutra, many aeons ago a bodhisattva named Hōzō (Skt Dharmakara) wished to create his own Buddha land and made forty-eight vows concerning his bodhisattva practice. After practicing austerities for many aeons, he became Amida Buddha, and it is said that his Pure Land was realized. Amida is the Buddha worshiped by the Jōdo sect.

Ananda: (Jap Anan) One of Shakyamuni's ten major disciples. He was a cousin of the Buddha and also the younger brother of Devadatta. He accompanied Shakyamuni wherever he went and as a result heard more of his teachings than any other disciple. In addition, he was renowned for his excellent memory. This talent allowed him to play a central part in compiling the sutras at the First Buddhist Council.

Anger: (Jap *shura*) Fourth of the Ten Worlds. In this state, one is conscious of self and driven by the competitive spirit to dominate, but cannot grasp things as they are and therefore tramples on the dignity of others. *See also* Ten Worlds.

Animality: (Jap *chikushō*) Third of the Ten Worlds. This is the state in which one follows the pull of desires and instincts, and turns totally toward self-preservation and immediate profit, lacking the wisdom of self-control. *See also* Ten Worlds.

Anryūgyō: *See* Four [Great] Bodhisattvas.

Arhat: (Jap *arakan*) Highest state of Hinayana enlightenment in which all delusions and desires are eradicated. Also indicates those who are in this state.

Aryasinha: (Jap Shishi-sonja) The last of Shakyamuni's twenty-four successors, who appeared in India in the sixth century. His efforts to propagate Buddhism led to his execution by Dammira, a king who destroyed many Buddhist temples and murdered scores of priests.

Ashoka (r. 268–232 B.C.): Third ruler of the Indian Maurya dynasty, also the first king to unify India. He began as a tyrant but later regretted his cruelty and renounced war, basing his rule upon Buddhist mercy. India prospered under his reign. While supporting the compilation of the sutras and the spread of Buddhism, Ashoka also professed religious tolerance and established what we now call "freedom of religion." One of his well-known achievements was a series of edicts proclaiming that people should act in a universal spirit of equality and mercy. These edicts were carved on stones and pillars throughout his domain so that all people might read and practice them. He convened a council to compile the Buddha's teachings and dispatched learned priests throughout India and also to Syria, Egypt, Ceylon and other countries to propagate Buddhism.

Ashura: (Skt asura) In Indian mythology, devils who fight continually with the god Taishaku. In terms of the Ten Worlds, ashura represents the world of Anger.

Ashvaghosha: (Jap Memyō) Second-century Buddhist philosopher of the kingdom of Shravasti, India. At first he criticized Buddhism but was later refuted by Punyayasha (or Parshva) and converted. He led many people to the Buddha's teachings by the high literary quality of his writings.

Bekkyō: Literally, specific teaching. *See* Eight teachings.

Bodhisattva: (Jap *bosatsu*) Ninth of the Ten Worlds. Life-condition characterized by compassion, in which one dedicates himself to others' happiness. Also indicates one who seeks enlightenment for himself and for others. *See also* Ten Worlds.

Bodhisattvas of the Earth: (Jap *jiyu no bosatsu*) Innumerable bodhisattvas who appeared in the *Yujutsu* (15th) chapter of the Lotus Sutra and pledged to propagate the Mystic Law in the Latter Day. They alone are charged with this mission. In the strictest sense, Nichiren Daishonin alone is the incarnation of the Bodhisattvas of the Earth, but in a broader sense they signify those who chant and propagate Nam-myoho-renge-kyo.

Bonten: (Skt Brahmadeva) With Taishaku, one of the principal Buddhist gods. He is said to live in the realm of form above Mount Sumeru and rule the *saha* world.

Brahma-heaven: The first and lowest of the four *dhyana* heavens in the world of form. In this heaven is the palace of Brahmadeva (Bonten), who was considered to be supreme among the gods.

Brahmanism: Religion of ancient India. Earliest phase of Hinduism, rooted in the Vedic tradition. Brahman doctrine provided the rationale for the old Indian caste system.

Buddhahood: (Jap *butsu*) Highest of the Ten Worlds. This state is reached when one has the wisdom to realize the essence of his own life, that it breathes in perfect harmony with the rhythm of the universe and continues to exist from the infinite past to the eternal future. Buddhahood is an ideal condition that one experiences in the depths of his life as he continues to act with benevolence in everyday life. Buddhahood appears in daily life as the actions of a bodhisattva. *See also* Ten Worlds.

Buddha land: The place where a Buddha dwells. Since Buddhism views the environment as part of oneself, it is often used to refer to the absolute happiness that Buddhas enjoy and does not necessarily indicate a state of paradise or land removed from mortal sufferings.

Buddhist gods: (Jap *shoten zenjin*) Also heavenly beings and benevolent deities. Traditionally means gods in the universe who assembled to listen to Shakyamuni teach the Lotus Sutra and vowed to guard its devotees, but more properly is understood to mean the powers of protection inherent in natural phenomena of the universe and in the individual, which are activated by one's Buddhist practice.

Ceremony in the air: One of the three assemblies described in the Lotus Sutra. The description extends from the *Hōtō* (11th) chapter to the *Zokurui* (22nd) chapter. In the *Yujutsu* (15th) chapter, the Bodhisattvas of the Earth make their appearance; the essential teaching (*hommon*) begins here. In the *Juryō* (16th) chapter, Shakyamuni clarifies his original enlightenment in the remote past of *gohyaku-jintengō*. In the *Jinriki* (21st) chapter, he transfers the sutra to the Bodhisattvas of the Earth led by Bodhisattva Jōgyō, entrusting them with the mission of propagating it in the Latter Day of the Law. From the viewpoint of Nichiren Daishonin's Buddhism, the ceremony in the air signifies the real aspect of the Gohonzon of the Three Great Secret Laws.

Chang-an (561–632):   (Jap Shōan) Legitimate successor to T'ien-t'ai. He recorded T'ien-t'ai's lectures which were later compiled as the *Hokke Gengi*, *Hokke Mongu* and *Maka Shikan*. His own works are the *Nehangyō-sho* (Commentary on the Nirvana Sutra) and the *Nehan Gengi* (Profound Meaning of the Nirvana Sutra).

Chin-kang-chih (671–741):   (Jap Kongōchi; Skt Vajrabodhi) The fifth patriarch of the esoteric Shingon sect. He was a Buddhist scholar from India who became a disciple of Nagabodhi and studied esoteric teachings for seven years. In 720, he journeyed to China and won the respect of Emperor

Hsüan-tsung. He translated many sutras into Chinese. Pu-k'ung was one of his disciples.

Chishō (814–891):   The fifth successor of Enryaku-ji temple, the head temple of the Tendai sect. His name was Enchin. Chishō Daishi is a posthumous name and title. In 853 he went to China and studied the T'ien-t'ai and esoteric doctrines. After his return to Japan, he often preached esoteric Buddhism and asserted its superiority over the T'ien-t'ai doctrine. In 868 he became the chief priest of Enryaku-ji temple.

Daichido Ron: (Skt Mahāprajñāpāramitopadeśa), attributed to Nagarjuna, and translated into Chinese by Kumarajiva (344–409). It is a hundred-volume commentary on the *Mahaprajnaparamita* Sutra.

Daimoku: (1) Title of a sutra, in particular, the title of the Lotus Sutra, *Myōhō-renge-kyō*. (2) The invocation of Nam-myoho-renge-kyo, one of the Three Great Secret Laws.

Dainichi Buddha: (Skt Mahāvairocana) The Buddha said to have expounded esoteric Buddhism. The Shingon sect holds that all other Buddhas and bodhisattvas are born of Dainichi Buddha and that he is superior to every other Buddha, including Shakyamuni. He is viewed by Shingon as the idealization of the truth of the universe and makes no physical appearance in this world.

Daishonin: Title given to the Buddha of the Latter Day of the Law who appeared to save all mankind. *Dai* literally means great or supreme, and *shonin* literally means saint, but carries the connotation of Buddha. The title implies that Nichiren is the original Buddha and not a great bodhisattva as claimed by other Nichiren sects.

Daitsū Buddha: Also Daitsūchishō Buddha (Skt Mahābhi-jñājñānābhibhū). According to the *Kejōyu* (seventh) chapter of the Lotus Sutra, he was a king who attained enlightenment in the remote past of *sanzen-jintengō* and expounded the Lotus Sutra at the request of his sixteen sons. Later all of them spread the Lotus Sutra as bodhisattvas. The sixteenth son was in time reborn in India as Shakyamuni.

Devadatta: Cousin of Shakyamuni Buddha, who first followed him but later became his enemy out of jealousy. He was so arrogant that he sought to kill the Buddha and usurp his position. He committed three of the five cardinal sins by (1) destroying the unity of the Buddha's disciples and luring away five hundred of Shakyamuni's followers; (2) attempting to murder Shakyamuni by dropping a boulder on him from atop a cliff, causing the Buddha's foot to bleed; and (3) beating to death a Buddhist nun called Utpalavarna when she reproached him for his evil acts. Because of these sins he is said to have fallen into hell alive. However, in the *Devadatta* (12th) chapter of the Lotus Sutra, Shakyamuni revealed that in some past existence he himself had practiced Buddhism under a hermit named Ashi (Skt Asita) and that this hermit was Devadatta. He then predicted that Devadatta would attain enlightenment in the future—the first scriptural instance of a totally evil person reaching Buddhahood.

Devil of the Sixth Heaven: (Jap Dairokuten no Ma-ō) Most powerful of the devils, who dwells in the highest of the six realms of the world of desire. He works to prevent believers from practicing Buddhism and delights in sapping the life force of others. The Daishonin interprets this devil as a manifestation of the fundamental darkness (*q.v.*) inherent in life.

Dragon King's daughter: (Jap Ryūnyo; Skt Nāgakanyā) Daughter of one of the eight great dragon kings said to dwell in a palace at the bottom of the sea. Historically it seems that "dragon" was the symbol of a coastal tribe. According to the *Devadatta* (12th) chapter of the Lotus Sutra, she began to seek enlightenment when she heard Bodhisattva Monju preach the Lotus Sutra in her father's palace. Later, upon hearing Shakyamuni's sermon at Eagle Peak, she immediately attained enlightenment. The pre-Lotus Sutra teachings held that women could not attain Buddhahood and that even men had to practice austerities for a great many aeons in order to do so. Such ideas were refuted by the example of the Dragon King's daughter.

Eagle Peak: (Jap Ryōjusen; Skt Grdhrakūta) Mountain located to the northeast of Rajagriha, the capital of Magadha in ancient India. This was the place where Shakyamuni expounded the Lotus Sutra. In English it is often called Vulture Peak. Also symbolizes the Buddha land or the condition of Buddhahood.

Ehō: The objective world, or one's environment. Buddhism teaches that oneself and one's environment are inseparable, since both are manifestations of Myoho-renge-kyo. *See also* Shōhō.

Eight teachings: One system by which T'ien-t'ai classified Shakyamuni's sutras. The eight teachings are subdivided into two groups: four teachings of doctrine (*kehō*) and four teachings of method (*kegi*). The first is a division by content and the second, by method of teaching. The four teachings of doctrine are: (1) *Zōkyō*, which corresponds to the Hinayana teachings. These teachings stress precepts to control earthly desires. (2) *Tsūgyō*, lower provisional Mahayana teachings aimed at those in the states of Learning, Realization and Bodhisattva. The concept of *kū* is introduced at this stage. (3) *Bekkyō*, a higher level of provisional Mahayana taught exclusively for bodhisattvas. The three truths (*santai*) (*q.v.*) were first revealed in these teachings. (4) *Engyō*, or true Mahayana. The name translates literally as "round teaching," round meaning full or perfect. *Engyō*, or perfect teaching, indicates the Lotus Sutra, Shakyamuni's highest teaching, which places all the others in perspective and reveals that all people have the potential for Buddhahood.

The four teachings of method are: (1) *Ton*, meaning

"abrupt." Indicates those teachings expounded by Shakyamuni without giving his disciples preparatory knowledge. An example is the *Kegon* Sutra, the first teaching he expounded after his enlightenment at Buddh Gaya. (2) *Zen*, or "gradual." Teachings Shakyamuni expounded to his disciples in progressive levels so they could grow to understand higher doctrines. (3) *Himitsu*, or "secret." Teachings from which everybody, unknowingly, received a different benefit according to his capacity. (4) *Fujō*, or "non-fixed." Teachings from which everybody knowingly received a different ("non-fixed") benefit.

Emanations of the Buddha: Manifestations of a true Buddha, who divides his body and appears in various lands to save the people. The true Buddha in this case is a reference to Shakyamuni used often in the Daishonin's writings.

Emma: (Skt Yamarāja) King said to pass judgment on the dead. In Buddhism, he is the lord of hell who judges and punishes those who have fallen into his domain. He is a symbolic figure representing the strictness of the causal law.

Engaku: (Skt pratyekabuddha) Realization, eighth of the Ten Worlds. Also indicates a person who seeks to attain enlightenment without a teacher—for example, in a world where there is no Buddha—by observing and pondering natural phenomena.

Engyō: *See* Eight teachings; Perfect teaching.

Esoteric teachings: Teachings attributed by the Shingon sect to Dainichi Buddha. They are called esoteric because they are said to contain in their depths Dainichi Buddha's true enlightenment, which is beyond the understanding of ordinary people. The esoteric teachings were brought by Kōbō (*q.v.*) from China to Japan and were later incorporated into the Tendai sect. *See also* Exoteric teachings.

Essential teaching: (Jap *hommon*) Latter fourteen chapters of the Lotus Sutra. T'ien-t'ai divided the Lotus Sutra into two parts to clarify its structure. In the latter half, specifically in the *Juryō* (16th) chapter, Shakyamuni revealed that he had first attained enlightenment not in this life but in the remote past of *gohyaku-jintengō*. It is called the essential teaching because, in contrast to the theoretical teaching which discusses Buddhahood abstractly, it presents Shakyamuni's actual experience of realizing the true entity of life. *See also* Theoretical teaching.

Exoteric teachings: Those teachings which were revealed explicitly, in contrast to the esoteric teachings. The Shingon sect defined Shakyamuni Buddha's teachings as exoteric and Dainichi Buddha's teachings as esoteric. *See also* Esoteric teachings.

Fa-tao (1086–1147): (Jap Hōdō) Chinese priest who remonstrated with Emperor Hui-tsung of the Sung dynasty when the emperor supported Taoism and attempted to reorganize the order of Buddhist priests. Later he was exiled to Tao-chou, a place south of the Yangtze River.

Fifth five-hundred-year period: Last of the five five-hundred-year periods after the Buddha's decease, which corresponds to the beginning of the Latter Day of the Law. According to the *Daijuku* Sutra, this period is one of struggle and strife in which Shakyamuni's Buddhism will perish.

Fifty-two stages of bodhisattva practice: Fifty-two ranks through which a bodhisattva progresses toward Buddhahood. They are described in the *Bosatsu Yōraku Hongō* Sutra. The fifty-two consist of ten stages of faith, ten stages of security, ten stages of practice, ten stages of devotion, ten stages of development, *tōgaku* (stage almost equal to enlightenment) and *myōkaku* (enlightenment).

Five cardinal sins: In Buddhism, the five most serious offenses. Explanations vary according to different sutras and treatises. The most common version of the five sins is: (1) killing one's father; (2) killing one's mother; (3) killing an arhat; (4) injuring a Buddha; and (5) causing disunity among believers.

Five impurities: (1) Impurity of the age caused by war, natural disasters, etc.; (2) impurity of thought, or illusions, caused by confusion in the realm of philosophy and religion; (3) impurity of desires, or ugly tendencies such as greed, anger and stupidity; (4) impurity of the people, weakened both physically and spiritually by impurities of thought and desire; and (5) impurity of life itself. The *Hōben* (second) chapter of the Lotus Sutra states that the Buddha appears in an evil world that is defiled by the five impurities.

Five periods: T'ien-t'ai's classification of Shakyamuni's teachings according to the order of preaching. The five periods are: (1) the Kegon period, in which Shakyamuni expounded his first teachings after attaining enlightenment; (2) the Agon period, in which the Hinayana teachings were expounded; (3) the Hōdō period, in which Shakyamuni refuted his disciples' attachment to the Hinayana teachings and directed them toward provisional Mahayana teachings such as those taught in the *Amida*, *Dainichi* and Vimalakirti sutras; (4) the Hannya period, in which Shakyamuni taught a higher level of provisional Mahayana and revealed the doctrine of *kū*; and (5) the Hokke-Nehan period, an eight-year interval in which Shakyamuni expounded the Lotus Sutra, fully revealing his enlightenment and the truth of life. On the last day of his life he restated the important principles of the Lotus in the Nirvana Sutra. T'ien-t'ai asserted that the Hokke-Nehan period represents the Buddha's highest teaching.

Five practices: Five kinds of practice described in the *Hosshi* (10th) chapter of the Lotus Sutra. They are to embrace, read, recite, teach and transcribe the Lotus Sutra.

Five types of vision: (1) The physical eyes, or eyes of common mortals, which distinguish color and form; (2) the heavenly eyes which can see things even in the darkness and distance; (3) the eyes of wisdom or the ability of people in the two vehicles to discern principles at work within changing phenomena; (4) the Dharma eyes, or eyes of the Law, by which bodhisattvas see all phenomena from the viewpoint of Buddhism; (5) the eyes of the Buddha which see the true nature of life, spanning past, present and future and penetrating the essence of all things and phenomena in the universe.

Five vehicles: The worlds of Humanity, Heaven, Learning, Realization and Bodhisattva. Many people in Shakyamuni's time were under the misapprehension that the supreme purpose of life lay in one of these worlds.

Former Day of the Law: (Jap *shōhō*) First millennium after Shakyamuni's death. This period saw the spread of Hinayana, and later, provisional Mahayana Buddhism.

Four [Great] Bodhisattvas: Jōgyō (Skt Viśiṣṭacāritra), Muhengyō (Anantacāritra), Jyōgyō (Viśuddhacāritra) and Anryūgyō (Supratiṣṭhitacāritra). The leaders of the Bodhisattvas of the Earth described in the *Yujutsu* (15th) chapter of the Lotus Sutra. They signify respectively the four noble qualities of life: true self, eternity, purity and happiness.

Four evil paths: The first four of the Ten Worlds—Hell, Hunger, Animality and Anger. The worlds of suffering which people undergo because of their evil karma.

Four Heavenly Kings: Jikokuten (Skt Dhṛtarāstra), Kōmokuten (Virūpāksa), Bishamonten (Vaiśravana) and Zōchōten (Virūdaka), lords of the four heavens, said to live halfway down the four slopes of Mount Sumeru. Their respective functions are to protect the world, to discern evil and punish those who commit it, to listen to the sutras and protect the place of practice, and to relieve people of their sufferings. In the *Dharani* (26th) chapter of the Lotus Sutra, they pledged to protect those who embrace the sutra.

Four kinds of believers: (Jap *shishu*) Sometimes called the four kinds of people. Priests, nuns, laymen and laywomen.

Four noble worlds: The highest four of the Ten Worlds—Learning, Realization, Bodhisattva and Buddhahood. The states in which one makes efforts to transcend the uncertainty of the six lower worlds by realizing the eternal essence of life

GLOSSARY 341

within. In contrast to the six lower worlds, in which one is governed by his environment, these four noble worlds are established through one's own efforts.

Fourteen slanders: Fourteen types of slander against Buddhism described in the *Hiyu* (third) chapter of the Lotus Sutra: (1) arrogance toward Buddhism; (2) negligence in Buddhist practice; (3) arbitrary, egotistical judgment of Buddhist teachings; (4) shallow, self-satisfied understanding; (5) adherence to earthly desires; (6) lack of a seeking spirit; (7) lack of faith; (8) disgust toward Buddhism; (9) mistaken doubt; (10) vilification of Buddhism; (11) contempt for Buddhist believers; (12) hatred toward believers; (13) jealousy toward believers; and (14) grudges against believers. The first ten are slanders against the Law and the latter four are slanders against those who embrace the Law.

Four wheel-turning kings: Ideal rulers appointed by Heaven to govern the four continents surrounding Mount Sumeru. They are so called because they rule the world by turning the wheels of the law they are given by the gods on their coronation. These wheels are of four kinds: gold, silver, copper and iron. The Gold-wheel-turning King rules all four continents; the Silver-wheel-turning King, the eastern, western, and southern continents; the Copper-wheel-turning King, the eastern and southern continents; and the Iron-wheel-turning King, the southern continent.

Fugen: (Skt Samantabhadra) With Monju (Mañjuśri), one of the leaders of the bodhisattvas of the theoretical teaching. He represents the faculties of reason and learning. In the *Fugen* (28th) chapter of the Lotus Sutra, he made a vow to protect the Lotus Sutra and its believers.

Fugen Sutra: "Sutra of Meditation on Bodhisattva Fugen," a one-volume sutra believed to have been preached three months before Shakyamuni's passing. Since this sutra is a continuation of the *Fugen* (28th) chapter of the Lotus Sutra, T'ien-t'ai regarded it as the conclusion of the Lotus Sutra.

Fukyō: (Skt Sadāparibhūta) Bodhisattva who appears in the
   Fukyō (20th) chapter of the Lotus Sutra. After the death of
   Ionnō Buddha in the remote past, he propagated a teaching
   expressed in twenty-four characters and showed respect
   toward all people for their innate Buddha nature. People
   ridiculed and attacked him with staves and stones, but he
   continued to practice in this way. Those who slandered him
   fell into hell, but after expiating their slander, they were
   reborn with Fukyō and were saved by practicing his teaching. Fukyō literally means never to despise.

Fundamental darkness: (Jap *gampon no mumyō*) Also translated as primal ignorance. Blindness to the true nature of
   one's life. Fundamental darkness is regarded as the source of
   all other illusions and earthly desires.

Gods of the sun and the moon: Deifications of the sun and the
   moon. In Buddhism, they are regarded as Buddhist gods
   who protect the votaries of the Lotus Sutra.

Gohonzon: Object of worship in Nichiren Daishonin's Buddhism. The Gohonzon is the physical manifestation of the
   ultimate law of life which is one with the life of the original
   Buddha. Nichiren Daishonin established the Gohonzon to
   enable all people to manifest their inherent Buddha nature.

Gohyaku-jintengō: Immeasurably distant time in the past
   when Shakyamuni first attained enlightenment. This period
   is described in the *Juryō* (16th) chapter of the Lotus Sutra.
   Not until the essential teaching of the Lotus Sutra was expounded did Shakyamuni reveal that his enlightenment
   had originally taken place long before *sanzen-jintengō* when
   he appeared as the son of Daitsū Buddha. *Gohyaku-jintengō* is
   explained in the *Juryō* chapter as follows: "Suppose there is
   one who reduces five hundred, thousand, ten thousand,
   hundred thousand, nayuta (10^{12}), asōgi (10^{51}) major world
   systems into particles of dust, and then takes them all toward
   the east, dropping one particle each time he traverses five

hundred, thousand, ten thousand, hundred thousand, nayuta, asōgi worlds. Suppose that he continues traveling eastward in this way, until he has finished dropping all the particles. . . . Suppose all these worlds, whether they received a particle or not, are once more reduced to dust. Let one particle represent one aeon. Then the time which has passed since I attained Buddhahood surpasses this by one hundred, thousand, ten thousand, hundred thousand, nayuta, asōgi aeons."

Gosho: The individual and collective writings of Nichiren Daishonin, generally divided into letters of personal encouragement, treatises on Buddhism and recorded oral teachings. *Go* is an honorific prefix and *sho* means writing(s).

Great Teacher: (Jap Daishi) Honorific title awarded to priests of eminence by the Imperial court, usually posthumously. In 866 Saichō was given the posthumous name Dengyō Daishi (the Great Teacher Dengyō) and Kūkai, that of Kōbō Daishi. These are the first instances of the use of the honorific title Daishi (Great Teacher) in Japan.

Guketsu: The abbreviation of *Maka Shikan Bugyōden Guketsu*. Miao-lo's annotations on the *Maka Shikan* (Great Concentration and Insight).

Hachiman: Originally revered as a god of harvest and later honored as a god of war. In the late twelfth century, the founder of the Kamakura shogunate erected a shrine to Hachiman, and worship of this deity thereafter became popular throughout Japan. He is often called [Great] Bodhisattva Hachiman. In Buddhism, he is regarded as one of the gods who protect the votary of the Lotus Sutra.

Hannya sutras: Higher provisional Mahayana sutras belonging to the fourth of the five periods of Shakyamuni's teachings. The concept of *kū* was first revealed in these sutras. *See also* Five periods.

Heaven: *See* Rapture.

Hell: (Jap *jigoku*) First and lowest of the Ten Worlds. State of life marked by suffering and despair, in which one is governed by the impulse to destroy both himself and others. *See also* Ten Worlds.

Hell of incessant suffering: (Skt avīci) The worst of the eight hot hells. A state of suffering without relief which those who commit the five cardinal sins or slander Buddhism are said to undergo.

Hinayana: Literally, the "lesser vehicle." One of the two major streams of Buddhism. About a century after Shakyamuni's death, schisms began to form within the Sangha or community of monks, which subsequently divided into two major schools. The conservatives held strictly to doctrine and practice as originally formulated; this was the Theravada school, later termed Hinayana by Mahayana Buddhists. The other, a more liberal group, interpreted doctrine with greater freedom and stressed the importance of teaching the masses. This was the Mahasanghika school, whose emphasis on altruism is said to have initiated the new movement of Mahayana Buddhism. Believers in Hinayana hold that the Buddhist believer works out his own salvation by faithful adherence to the way demonstrated by the Buddha. Hinayana Buddhism spread mainly to Ceylon, Burma, Thailand, Cambodia, Laos and other parts of Southeast Asia. *See also* Agon sutras.

Hōben chapter: "Expedient Means." The second chapter of the Lotus Sutra and key chapter of the theoretical teaching. In this chapter, Shakyamuni explains that all Buddhas appear in the world solely for the purpose of enabling all people to attain Buddhahood. The pre-Lotus Sutra teachings set forth three goals of life—the states of Learning, Realization and Bodhisattva. However, in the *Hōben* chapter Shakyamuni states that these three vehicles were simply expedients used to lead people to the supreme vehicle of Buddhahood, which is the goal of Buddhist practice. Preceding the revelation of Buddhahood as the ultimate goal of life, the Buddha sets forth the Ten Factors as the theoretical basis for this revelation. Shakyamuni makes clear that all phenomena in the universe comprise these Ten Factors, which are common to all states of life from Hell to Buddhahood. The supposedly insurmountable barrier between the nine worlds of common mortals and Buddhahood is thus removed. The message of the *Hōben* chapter is that Buddhahood is not separate from the nine worlds but exists within the lives of ordinary people.

Hōdō sutras: Lower provisional Mahayana sutras belonging to the third of the five periods of Shakyamuni's teachings. In these sutras Shakyamuni refuted his disciples' attachment to Hinayana and led them toward higher teachings. *See also* Five periods.

Hokke Gengi: "Profound Meaning of the Lotus Sutra," one of T'ien-t'ai's three major works. It gives a detailed explanation of the profound meaning of the title of the Lotus Sutra, *Myōhō-renge-kyō*.

Hokke Mongu: "Words and Phrases of the Lotus Sutra," one of T'ien-t'ai's three major works. In this commentary, he divided the Lotus Sutra into two parts, theoretical and essential teachings, and gave a correct and profound interpretation of its sentences and phrases.

Hokke-Nehan sutras: Shakyamuni's highest teachings, expounded during the last eight years of his life. Includes the Lotus Sutra and the Nirvana Sutra. *See also* Five periods.

Hōnen (1133–1212):   Founder of the Jōdo (Pure Land) sect in Japan. He first studied the Tendai doctrine but later embraced the teaching of the Chinese Pure Land sect. In 1175 he established this as a separate sect in Japan and urged people to discard all the Buddha's teachings except the three sutras on which the Jōdo sect is based.

Hsüan-tsang (or Hsüan-chuang) (602–664):   (Jap Genjō) Chinese priest of the T'ang dynasty and founder of the Fa-hsiang (Hossō) sect, also a noted translator of Buddhist scriptures and an authority on India. He traveled west in 629 and spent sixteen years in India collecting sutras. In 645 he returned to China with many Sanskrit texts and images of the Buddha. He translated 1,330 fascicles into Chinese and wrote the *Record of the Western Regions*, an extensive record of his travels to India.

Humanity: *See* Tranquillity.

Hunger: (Jap *gaki*) Second of the Ten Worlds. This life-condition is dominated by insatiable selfish desires for wealth, fame, or pleasure, etc. *See also* Ten Worlds.

Ichinen sanzen: Principle that every life-moment (*ichinen*) possesses all three thousand (*sanzen*) possible worlds. *Ichinen* indicates the life-essence, and *sanzen*, the phenomena it manifests. This system of thought was developed by T'ien-t'ai on the basis of the Lotus Sutra. At each moment, life experiences one of ten conditions, i.e., the Ten Worlds. Each of these worlds possesses the potential for all ten within itself, thus making one hundred possible worlds. Each of these hundred worlds possesses the Ten Factors, thus becoming one thousand worlds. Finally, each of these worlds possesses the three realms of existence, thus equaling three thousand worlds. These three realms of existence multiplied by the thousand worlds equal three thousand possible conditions of life.

Itai dōshin: Unity of people with a common cause. *Itai* (literally, different bodies) points to the need for many different personalities and abilities in achieving a given purpose. *Dōshin* (same mind) indicates the importance of uniting in the same spirit or upholding a common ideal in order to be successful. In the Daishonin's Buddhism, *itai dōshin* means that people advance together to achieve their common goal of *kōsen-rufu* in the same spirit as Nichiren Daishonin, while at the same time respecting each other's individuality, situation and character, and developing their own potential.

Jigage: Verse section which concludes the *Juryō* (16th) chapter of the Lotus Sutra. The *jigage* is so called because the verse (*ge*) section begins with the phrase *ji ga toku butsu rai* (literally, "since I attained Buddhahood"). The *jigage* restates in verse form the eternity of the Buddha's original enlightenment revealed in the foregoing part of the same chapter.

Jikaku (794–864):   Third chief priest of Enryaku-ji, head temple of the Tendai sect in Japan. In 838 he journeyed to China where he studied both T'ien-t'ai's teachings and esoteric Buddhism. In 847 he returned to Japan and in 854 became chief priest of the Tendai sect. However, he was later influenced by the esoteric teachings and asserted that the *Dainichi* Sutra, the basis of esoteric Shingon, was superior to the Lotus Sutra. This created serious confusion within the Tendai sect.

Jōdo sect: Jōdo literally means "pure land." A sect based upon the worship of Amida Buddha which spread widely in Japan shortly before Nichiren Daishonin's birth. *See* Nembutsu.

Jōgyō: Leader of the Bodhisattvas of the Earth who appeared in the *Yujutsu* (15th) chapter of the Lotus Sutra and vowed to propagate Myoho-renge-kyo in the Latter Day of the Law. Shakyamuni transferred all his teachings to Bodhisattva Jōgyō in the *Jinriki* (21st) chapter. The Gosho says that Nichiren Daishonin is "carrying out the work of Bodhisattva Jōgyō" to indicate that he is propagating the essence of the Lotus Sutra. *See also* Four [Great] Bodhisattvas.

Jōzō and Jōgen: (Skt Vimalagarbha and Vimalanetra) Two sons of King Myōshōgon (Śubhavyūha) who are described in the *Myōshōgonnō* (27th) chapter of the Lotus Sutra. Their mother was Lady Jōtoku (Vimaladattā). They were taught the Lotus Sutra by a Buddha named Unraionnō, and exhorted their mother to go to see him. The mother urged them to take their father, a follower of Brahmanism, as well. They talked to him about discarding his attachment to Brahmanism and converting to the Buddha's teachings. At their mother's request, they displayed mystic powers to their father and caused him to thirst for Buddhism. Later, all of them attained enlightenment.

Juryō chapter: "Life Span of the Tathagata." The 16th chapter of the Lotus Sutra, key chapter of the essential teaching. Shakyamuni reveals here that he first attained enlightenment not in this lifetime, but in the remote past of *gohyaku-jintengō*, and that ever since then he has been in the mundane world, teaching the Law. In other words, a Buddha is himself a common mortal endowed with the nine worlds. The *Juryō* chapter discusses Shakyamuni's Buddhahood in terms of its cause, effect and land. By citing his own actual experience of attaining Buddhahood, he demonstrates that it is possible for all other human beings to do the same.

Jyōgyō: *See* Four [Great] Bodhisattvas.

Kakutoku: Priest who appears with King Utoku in the Nirvana Sutra. A considerable time after the death of the Buddha called Kangi Zōyaku Nyorai (literally, Joy Increasing Buddha), Buddhism was about to perish. Kakutoku tried to protect the orthodox Buddhist teachings and was harshly persecuted by many misguided priests and their followers. King Utoku fought against these slanderous people to protect Kakutoku and died in the battle. It is said that because of their devotion to Buddhism, King Utoku was reborn as Shakyamuni Buddha and Priest Kakutoku as Kashyapa Buddha.

Kalpa: *See* Aeon.

Kannon: (Skt Avalokiteśvara) Bodhisattva who appears in the *Fumon* (25th) chapter of the Lotus Sutra. According to the sutra, he assumes thirty-three different forms to save the people. In the *Kammuryōju* Sutra he and Bodhisattva Seishi (Mahāsthāma-prāpta) appear as the attendants of Amida Buddha.

Katyayana: (Jap Kasennen) One of the ten major disciples of the Buddha. He was born to a Brahman family in South India. He was regarded as a skilled debater, and known as foremost in the analysis and exegesis of the Buddha's teaching.

Kegon sect: (Chi Hua-yen-tsung) Sect based upon the *Kegon* Sutra. The sect was founded by Tu-shun (557–640) during the early period of the T'ang dynasty in China. The Japanese Kegon sect was founded by Sim-sang (Jap Shinjō, d. 742), a priest from Korea.

Kegon Sutra: (Skt Avataṃsaka-sūtra) Compilation of the teachings Shakyamuni expounded during the first three weeks following his enlightenment at Buddh Gaya. First of the five periods. Kegon represents a very high level of teaching, second only to the Lotus Sutra. Shakyamuni began his lifetime of teaching with this profound doctrine, setting forth the bodhisattva practice in order to awaken his audience to the depth of Buddhism.

Kishimojin: (Skt Hārītī) Female demon. She had five hundred (some sources say one thousand or ten thousand) children, including the ten daughters who appear in the *Dharani* (26th) chapter of the Lotus Sutra. Because she is said to have fed her children the babies of others, she symbolizes the selfish nature of a mother who protects her own child but cares nothing for other children. However, in the *Dharani* chapter, she and her daughters pledged to safeguard the votaries of the Lotus Sutra.

Kōbō (774–835): Founder of the Shingon sect in Japan. Also known as Kūkai. Kōbō Daishi was his posthumous name and title. He was ordained in 793 at the age of twenty and went to China in 804, where he studied the doctrines and rituals of esoteric Buddhism. He returned to Japan in 806 and devoted himself to the propagation of Shingon, asserting the supremacy of the *Dainichi* Sutra over all others.

Kōsen-rufu: Literally means to teach and spread [Buddhism] widely. Also, to secure lasting peace and happiness for all mankind through the worldwide propagation of Buddhism. The term *kōsen-rufu* appears in the *Yakuō* (23rd) chapter of the Lotus Sutra.

Kū: (Skt śūnya or śūnyatā) A state of latency or potential, the qualitative or spiritual realm of life which cannot be defined in terms of either existence or nonexistence.

Kuon ganjo: Time without beginning. Also Buddhahood or enlightenment which inherently exists in human beings. When used as the "Buddha of *kuon ganjo*," it means the original Buddha who has been enlightened from the time without beginning.

Kyō and chi: *Kyō* means "objective reality or truth," and *chi*, "the subjective wisdom to grasp the truth." In the Lotus Sutra, *kyō* indicates the objective truth that all things, living or nonliving, are entities of the Mystic Law. *Kyō* also indicates the objective reality of Buddhahood within one's own life. *Chi* means the Buddha's wisdom to grasp the truth. The fusion of *kyō* and *chi* (*kyōchi myōgō*) means the attainment of Buddhahood, realizing that one is a Buddha himself. In practical terms, *kyō* means the Gohonzon and *chi*, our faith in the Gohonzon. To believe in and chant to the Gohonzon is the only way to attain Buddhahood in the Latter Day.

Latter Day of the Law: (Jap *mappō*) Period beginning two thousand years after Shakyamuni's death, when his teachings lose their power and the original Buddha makes his advent to lead all people to enlightenment.

Learned Doctor: (Jap *sanzō*) Honorific title given to those who are well versed in the three divisions of the Buddhist scriptures (Jap *sanzō*, Skt tripitaka). The three divisions are sutras, which contain the Buddha's teachings; vinayas, which set forth the precepts; and shastras, which contain various commentaries on Buddhist doctrines.

Learning: (Jap *shōmon*; Skt *śrāvaka*) Seventh of the Ten Worlds. This is a condition experienced when one seeks the truth through the teachings or experience of others. *See also* Ten Worlds; Men of Learning.

Lotus Sutra: (Jap *Hokekyō*) (1) Shakyamuni's ultimate teaching, expounded during the last eight years of his life. It is generally divided into twenty-eight chapters, the most important of which are the *Hōben* (2nd) and *Juryō* (16th) chapters. In the former, Shakyamuni taught that the Buddha nature is inherent in common mortals, and in the latter, he revealed his original attainment of Buddhahood. (2) Highest Buddhist teaching of a particular age. In the Latter Day it means Nam-myoho-renge-kyo or the Gohonzon of the Three Great Secret Laws. Nichiren Daishonin often used the words "Lotus Sutra" in his writings to indicate Nam-myoho-renge-kyo.

Mahakashyapa: (Jap Kashō) One of Shakyamuni's ten major disciples. He was born to a Brahman family, encountered Shakyamuni in Magadha and became his disciple. He was known as the foremost in ascetic practice (*dhūta*) to purify the mind and body. After Shakyamuni's death, Mahakashyapa, as chief of the order, presided over the First Great Council for compiling the sutras. He then propagated Hinayana teachings for two decades as the first of Shakyamuni's twenty-four successors. He died at Mount Kukutapada in Magadha after transferring the teachings to Ananda.

Mahayana: Literally, the "greater vehicle." One of the two major streams of Buddhism. "Vehicle" indicates a teaching or means to carry people to enlightenment. The Mahayana teachings are so called because they are not only concerned with individual salvation but stress the importance of leading all people to enlightenment. The Mahayana movement is said to have begun around the beginning of the Christian era; it subsequently spread to Central Asia, China, Korea and Japan. *See also* Hinayana.

Maka Shikan: "Great Concentration and Insight," one of T'ien-t'ai's three major works, compiled by his disciple, Chang-an. It elucidates the principle of *ichinen sanzen* (*q.v.*), the core of the Lotus Sutra.

Mandala: Literally, cluster of blessings. In Nichiren Shoshu Buddhism, mandala indicates the Gohonzon because it embodies all the practices and resulting virtues of all the Buddhas in the universe.

Maudgalyayana: (Jap Mokuren) One of Shakyamuni's ten major disciples. He was born to a Brahman family and was a close friend of Shariputra from childhood. Originally a student of Brahmanism, he grew dissatisfied with its philosophy and became a disciple of the skeptic Sanjaya Belatthiputta, leader of one of six new philosophical movements. Again he grew disenchanted and became a disciple of Shakyamuni. He is said to have been particularly skilled in occult practices.

Men of incorrigible disbelief: (Jap *issendai*, Skt icchantika) Those who, being unreceptive to Buddhism, have no prospect of attaining enlightenment.

Men of Learning: (Jap *shōmon*, Skt śrāvaka) Literally, those who listen to the Buddha's teachings, i.e., Buddhist disciples. In the Hinayana school it denoted aspirations for arhatship, the ideal state according to the early sutras. Learning is one of the Ten Worlds.

Miao-lo (711–782):   (Jap Myōraku) Ninth patriarch of the T'ien-t'ai sect in China. He is revered as the restorer of the sect and wrote profound commentaries on T'ien-t'ai's three major works, thus contributing to the theoretical clarification of his teachings. Miao-lo's principal commentaries are the *Hokke Gengi Shakusen*, *Hokke Mongu Ki* and *Maka Shikan Bugyōden Guketsu*.

Middle Day of the Law: (Jap *zōhō*) Second millennium after Shakyamuni's death. During this period, Mahayana Buddhism spread beyond India to China, Korea and Japan. Buddhism was firmly established in society but gradually became ritualized and no longer met the people's needs.

Middle Way: (Jap *chūdō*) Ultimate reality which gives rise to all phenomena. In Nichiren Daishonin's Buddhism, the law of Nam-myoho-renge-kyo.

Miroku: (Skt Maitreya) Bodhisattva born to a Brahman family in southern India who became Shakyamuni's disciple. He passed away before Shakyamuni. According to the *Miroku Jōshō* Sutra, he was reborn in the Tushita Heaven, and the *Bosatsu Shotai* Sutra predicted that he would reappear in this world 5,670 million years after the Buddha's death to teach the Law. Bodhisattva Miroku's persistent questions induced Shakyamuni to expound the *Juryō* chapter at the ceremony of the Lotus Sutra.

Monju: (Skt Mañjuśrī) Leader of the bodhisattvas of the theoretical teaching. He represents the virtue of wisdom.

Muhengyō: *See* Four [Great] Bodhisattvas.

Muryōgi Sutra: "Sutra of Infinite Meaning," introductory teaching to the Lotus Sutra. Shakyamuni explains in this sutra that all principles and meanings (*muryōgi*) derive from one Law, and implies that this Law will be revealed in the Lotus Sutra. He proceeds to state that for the past forty years he had not yet revealed the complete truth. In the final analysis, he expounded the provisional teachings solely in order to lead people to the Lotus Sutra.

Mutual possession of the Ten Worlds: (Jap *jikkai gogu*) Principle that each of the Ten Worlds has the potential for all ten within itself. The chief implications of this principle are that one can change his fundamental life-condition and that common mortals of the nine worlds inherently possess the potential for Buddhahood.

Myoho-renge-kyo: (1) Title of Shakyamuni's Lotus Sutra. (2) True entity of life, the law of Nam-myoho-renge-kyo.

Myōjisoku: The second of the six stages (*rokusoku*) on the way to enlightenment expounded by T'ien-t'ai. At this stage one understands in principle that he has the Buddha nature and that all phenomena are manifestations of the Law. It may also be called the stage at which one first takes faith in Buddhism. Since the Daishonin teaches that "embracing the Gohonzon is in itself enlightenment," there are no intermediary stages in the practice of his teaching. In other words, the stage of *myōjisoku* leads directly to Buddhahood.

Mystic Law: (Jap *myōhō*) Ultimate law of life and the universe, the law of Nam-myoho-renge-kyo.

Nagarjuna: (Jap Ryūju) Major Indian philosopher of Mahayana Buddhism in the third century. Born to a Brahman family, he at first mastered Hinayana Buddhism but later devoted himself to the study and propagation of Mahayana Buddhism. He authored many treatises on Mahayana Buddhism such as the *Chū Ron* (Skt Mādhyamika-śāstra) and the *Daichido Ron* (Mahāprajñāpāramitopadeśa). These made a significant contribution to the development of Buddhist philosophy.

Nam-myoho-renge-kyo: Name of the original Buddha. Also, the invocation of Nichiren Daishonin's Buddhism, one of the Three Great Secret Laws. Nichiren Daishonin defines the fundamental principle of the universe as Nam-myoho-renge-kyo. Briefly *nam* or *namu* derives from Sanskrit and means dedication, specifically to integrate one's life with the eternal truth of Myoho-renge-kyo. *Myōhō* means mystic law. *Myō* indicates the essential nature of life, and *hō*, its phenomenal manifestations. *Renge* means lotus flower; it symbolizes the simultaneity of cause and effect and also the emergence of the Buddha nature from within the lives of common mortals. *Kyō* indicates the teachings of a Buddha, or in a broader sense, all universal activity. *See* Myoho-renge-kyo.

Nembutsu: Generally, to worship Amida Buddha and recite his name (Namu Amidabutsu). Nembutsu is the practice of the Jōdo (Pure Land) sect which preaches that by reciting the Buddha's name one can ascend to the Pure Land of Amida Buddha after death. In China, this teaching was advocated by such priests as Hui-yüan (Jap Eon, 334–416) and Shan-tao (Zendō, 613–681). It is based upon the *Muryōju* (the larger Sukhāvatīvyūha), *Kammuryōju* (Amitāyurdhyāna) and *Amida* (the smaller Sukhāvatīvyūha) sutras. *See also* Hōnen.

Nichiren Daishonin (1222–1282): Founder of Nichiren Shoshu. Born as a fisherman's son, he was called Zennichimaro. He went to Seichō-ji temple in his home province of Awa to study Buddhism in 1233. Shortly after his tonsure at sixteen, he took the name of Renchō and went to Kamakura for further studies. After returning from Kamakura, he traveled to Kyoto and Nara, the old centers of traditional Buddhism in Japan, where he mastered all the sutras and literature of Buddhism. In 1253, returning to Seichō-ji, Renchō adopted the name Nichiren (Sun-Lotus) when he advocated "Nam-myoho-renge-kyo" for the first time. He declared the establishment of a new Buddhism. In 1279 he inscribed the Dai-Gohonzon for the peace and happiness of all mankind. He died three years later. *See* "The Life of Nichiren Daishonin" in the Introduction of *The Major Writings of Nichiren Daishonin*, vol. 1.

Nikkō Shonin (1246–1333): Successor to Nichiren Daishonin, and the Daishonin's most loyal disciple. He was converted to the Daishonin's teaching while studying Buddhism in 1258 at Jissō-ji temple, where the Daishonin was doing research in the temple library in preparation for writing the "Risshō Ankoku Ron." On accepting him as a disciple, Nichiren

Daishonin renamed him Nikkō. Nikkō Shonin shared the Daishonin's exile at Izu and Sado, and he converted the lord of the Minobu area, allowing the Daishonin to go into retreat there. He was twice named by the Daishonin as his successor, once in a document written at Minobu and again in a document written just before Nichiren Daishonin's death at the home of Ikegami Munenaka. Nikkō Shonin subsequently established the temple that later became the Head Temple, Taiseki-ji, at the foot of Mount Fuji.

Nine consciousnesses: (Jap *kushiki*) Classification of the spiritual functions of perception. The first five consciousnesses are the perceptions of the five senses: sight, hearing, smell, taste and touch. The sixth consciousness enables one to integrate the perceptions of the five senses and form judgments about them. The seventh or *manas*-consciousness is the realm of abstract thought, reason, awareness of self, etc. The eighth consciousness is called *alaya*, meaning repository, an unconscious realm where impressions or karmic effects are stored and new mental actions, or internal causes, originate. The ninth consciousness is called *amala*, meaning immaculate. Unlike the eighth consciousness, which may produce causes for either good or evil, the ninth consciousness is free from all karmic impurity. It corresponds to one's eternal Buddha nature or essential self.

Nine great persecutions: Attempts to kill or discredit Shakyamuni. For example, Devadatta tried to crush him by dropping a boulder from atop a cliff, and King Ajatashatru attempted to kill him by stampeding wild elephants.

Nine worlds: The nine conditions from Hell to Bodhisattva, often contrasted with the world of Buddhahood to indicate deluded states of life. *See also* Ten Worlds.

Nirvana: In the Hinayana sutras, to attain enlightenment by extinguishing earthly desires and escaping the cycle of birth and death. But since desire is a function of life, one cannot

destroy desire without destroying himself. Hence the Maha-
yanists condemned Hinayana as the teaching of "annihilating
one's consciousness and reducing his body to ashes." The
Lotus Sutra explains that since all phenomena reveal the true
entity, enlightenment is to be found within the realities of
life in this world. On the basis of this concept, Nichiren
Daishonin taught that one who taps his Buddha nature by
chanting Nam-myoho-renge-kyo can transform earthly desires into enlightenment (*bonnō soku bodai*) and change the
sufferings of life and death into nirvana (*shōji soku nehan*).
Nirvana in the Daishonin's Buddhism means an enlightened
condition of life in the real world, based on faith in the
Gohonzon.

Nirvana Sutra: (Jap Nehan-gyō) Teaching expounded by
Shakyamuni on the last day of his life, reconfirming the
major principles of the Lotus Sutra. The Nirvana Sutra belongs to the category of true Mahayana but is inferior to
the Lotus Sutra. *See also* Five periods.

One-eyed turtle: According to Buddhist legend, a one-eyed,
limbless turtle dwells on the ocean floor. His back is icy cold
and his belly is burning hot. His sole desire is to climb up on
a piece of floating sandalwood and cool his stomach in a
hollow of the wood while exposing his back to the warm
sunlight. However, he can only float to the surface once
every thousand years, and even then he rarely encounters a
piece of sandalwood. And even when he does, being one-
eyed, he cannot easily judge which way the wood is drifting,
and even if he can, his lack of limbs makes it difficult for him
to climb onto it. This story symbolizes the difficulty of
encountering the true teaching of Buddhism.

Perfect teaching: (Jap *engyō*) Last of Shakyamuni's four
teachings of doctrine as classified by T'ien-t'ai. The teaching

which completely clarifies the inseparable relationship of all phenomena and enables all people to attain enlightenment. *See also* Eight teachings.

Pratyekabuddha: *See* Engaku.

Provisional Buddha: (Jap *shakubutsu*) A Buddha who does not reveal his eternal nature but appears as a being bound by time and space. In terms of the Lotus Sutra, Shakyamuni is regarded as a provisional Buddha before he revealed his true identity in the 16th chapter of the Lotus Sutra and as the original Buddha after that chapter. Nichiren Daishonin is regarded as the original Buddha because he revealed the ultimate law of life and the universe. In this sense, Shakyamuni is not regarded as the original Buddha, as he only indicated the Law in the Lotus Sutra but did not clearly reveal it. *See also* True Buddha.

Provisional Mahayana: All Mahayana teachings expounded prior to the Lotus Sutra. They are called "provisional" because Shakyamuni used them as a means to elevate his disciples' understanding to a point where they could comprehend the Lotus Sutra.

Provisional teachings: All pre-Lotus Sutra teachings. T'ien-t'ai of China divided Shakyamuni's teachings into two categories: provisional and true. The provisional teachings, which include both Hinayana and provisional Mahayana, were expounded during the first forty-two years after Shakyamuni's enlightenment. He taught these doctrines according to the people's capacity in order to lead them toward an understanding of his true teachings, which he expounded in the Lotus Sutra.

Pu-k'ung (705–774):   (Jap Fukū, Skt Amoghavajra) The sixth patriarch in the lineage of the esoteric Shingon sect. He was born in North India and came to China in 720 with his master Chin-kang-chih (*q.v.*), whom he assisted in the translation of sutras. He strongly advocated the esoteric teachings.

Pure Land: Land of bliss where the Buddha dwells. Pro-

visional teachings held that the pure land was remote from
the mundane world, but the Daishonin's Buddhism teaches
that it is wherever one devotes himself to the practice and
propagation of the Mystic Law.

Pure Law: The true teaching of a Buddha. The Pure Law
indicates all of Shakyamuni's teachings, especially the Lotus
Sutra.

Purna: (Jap Furuna) One of Shakyamuni's ten major disciples. He was noted as the foremost in eloquence. Born to a
rich Brahman family, he practiced austerities in the Snow
Mountains (Himalayas) and attained a kind of enlightenment. Thereafter, when he heard that Shakyamuni had
attained Buddhahood, he became the Buddha's disciple.

Rahula: (Jap Ragora) Shakyamuni's son. Rahula followed
his father in renouncing the world and became one of the
Buddha's ten major disciples. Under the guidance of Shariputra, he devoted himself to inconspicuous yet thorough
observance of the precepts and was known as "foremost in
inconspicuous practice."

Rapture: (Jap ten) Also called Heaven. Sixth of the Ten
Worlds. State of joy or satisfaction which one feels upon
release from suffering, fulfillment of desire or completion of
a goal. See also Ten Worlds.

Realization: (Jap engaku, Skt pratyekabuddha) Eighth of the
Ten Worlds. This is the state in which one consciously
attempts to realize the ultimate truth of life through one's
own observations of phenomena. See also Ten Worlds.

Rissho Ankoku Ron: "On Securing the Peace of the Land
through the Propagation of True Buddhism," treatise written in 1260 by Nichiren Daishonin and submitted to the
retired regent, Hojo Tokiyori. This document, in the form
of a dialogue between host and guest, clarifies the basic
principles for securing world peace. It explains that misleading beliefs create suffering, while faith in the Mystic Law will

enable society to become peaceful and prosperous. In this treatise, the Daishonin also refuted the errors of the Nembutsu sect and predicted both internal strife and foreign invasion if the government continued its patronage of heretical sects.

Ritsu sect: Buddhist sect based on the rules of discipline set forth in the sutras. This sect is divided into several schools. Representative is the Nan-shan (Jap Nanzan) school founded in China by Tao-hsüan (Dōsen, 596–667) which teaches that strict observance of precepts is the only way to Buddhahood. In 754, Chien-chen (Ganjin, 688–763) introduced this teaching to Japan and founded the Ritsu sect. In the Kamakura era, this sect incorporated the prayers of the esoteric Shingon sect and the invocation of the Jōdo sect in order to attract more adherents.

River of three crossings: An imaginary river which, in Buddhist tradition, the dead must cross on the seventh day after death. It has three points of crossing with different depths—shallow, deep and very deep. Everyone must cross it at one of these three points according to the offenses he committed in his lifetime. Those who did the most evil must cross at the deepest point.

Ryōkan (1217–1303): Gokuraku-ji Ryōkan, a priest of the Ritsu sect. At the age of seventeen he renounced secular life and studied Buddhism in Nara under Eison, who was a priest of the Ritsu sect. In 1261 he went to Kamakura, where Hōjō Tokiyori, the fifth regent of the Kamakura government, had founded Kōsen-ji temple. Ryōkan was named the first chief priest of the temple. Later he was appointed first chief priest of Gokuraku-ji by Hōjō Nagatoki, who had restored the temple. He also won Hōjō Shigetoki's favor and came to wield political influence. In addition, he generously engaged in civic works, although citizens complained about the exorbitant tolls on the roads and bridges financed by

Ryōkan. He persecuted the Daishonin and his disciples, both openly and covertly.

Saha world: The mundane world in which Shakyamuni Buddha preached the law. *Saha* means to endure. The *saha* world is this real world, full of sufferings, which people must endure to survive.

Sanzen-jintengō: An immensely long period of time. Refers to the distant past when Shakyamuni was the sixteenth son of Daitsū Buddha (*q.v.*) and preached the Lotus Sutra to people who were later reborn with him in India as his disciples. The *Kejōyu* (seventh) chapter of the Lotus Sutra describes the duration of *sanzen-jintengō* as follows: Suppose someone reduces a major world system (all the stars and planets of a galaxy) to dust and then travels eastward, bearing with him the entire mass of dust particles. When he has passed a thousand worlds, he drops one particle. When he has passed another thousand worlds, he drops a second particle. He continues traveling eastward in this manner until he finally disposes of the entire mass. Then all the worlds he has passed, whether they received a dust particle or not, are also reduced to dust. Each particle signifies one aeon (approximately sixteen million years); the length of time corresponding to the total number of those particles of dust is called *sanzen-jintengō*. *See also* Gohyaku-jintengō.

Sea of suffering: In Buddhism the sufferings caused by the endless cycle of birth and death are often compared to a great ocean which is difficult to cross.

Sessen Dōji: Shakyamuni in a previous lifetime. His story is described in the 14th volume of the Nirvana Sutra as follows: A youth called Sessen Dōji was living in the Snow Mountains (Himalayas), practicing austerities in pursuit of enlightenment. The god Taishaku decided to test his faith. He appeared before Sessen Dōji in the form of a demon and recited half a verse from a Buddhist teaching: "All is changeable, nothing is constant. This is the law of birth and death." Certain that this verse contained the truth which he was seeking, Sessen Dōji beseeched the demon to tell him the second half. The demon agreed but demanded the boy's flesh and blood in payment. Sessen Dōji gladly consented and the demon taught him the latter half of the verse: "Extinguishing the cycle of birth and death, one enters the joy of nirvana." Sessen Dōji scrawled this teaching on the nearby rocks and trees in order to transmit it to others. Then he leapt into the demon's mouth. Instantaneously, the demon changed back into Taishaku and praised the young man for his dedication. Sessen Dōji symbolizes the fact that practicing in a spirit of total commitment will lead to Buddhahood.

Seven disasters: *See* Three calamities and seven disasters.

Seven sects to the north and the three sects to the south: The major Buddhist sects of China in T'ien-t'ai's day, located to the north and south of the Yangtze River. Each of these sects upheld a different Buddhist teaching and dogmatically opposed the others. The Great Teacher T'ien-t'ai defeated them in debate and proved the superiority of the Lotus Sutra over all those sects.

Shakubuku: Propagating Buddhism by refuting another's erroneous or prejudiced ideas and leading him to the correct Buddhist teachings. This method is commonly used in the Latter Day of the Law and among people with misconceptions about Buddhism. *See also* Shōju.

Shakyamuni: The historical Buddha who lived about 3,000 years ago in India. *Shakya* was the name of his tribe, and *muni* means "sage." He was born to King Shuddhodana and Queen Maya and was named Siddhartha. His mother is thought to have died soon after giving birth to him, and he was raised by his aunt Mahaprajapati. As heir to the throne, he was instructed in both civil and military arts but was also inclined to meditation. He married Yashodhara, who bore him a son named Rahula. But, even though surrounded by luxury, he could not dispel from his mind a deep desire to solve the questions of birth, old age, sickness and death. Finally, at the age of nineteen (twenty-nine according to some sources) he renounced his claim to the throne and embarked upon a religious life.

He studied under one Brahman sage and then another but was dissatisfied with the fruits of their disciplines and eventually resolved to practice religious austerities alone. He observed these austerities more diligently than any other ascetic, reducing himself to a state of emaciation, until he finally realized that such practices would lead, not to enlightenment, but to death. He seated himself beneath a pipal or Bodhi tree in Buddh Gaya, sank into profound meditation and there achieved enlightenment. He is said to have been thirty at the time.

He left the forest and set out for the Deer Park in Benares where he preached his first sermon to five men who had formerly accompanied him in his ascetic practice. Then he journeyed to Magadha where he converted King Bimbisara, who donated the Bamboo Grove Monastery to the new Buddhist Order. Over a period of time, Shakyamuni attracted renowned disciples such as Shariputra, Maudgalyayana and Mahakashyapa. He later converted many others: his cousins, Ananda and Aniruddha; his son, Rahula; his father, Shuddhodana; his aunt, Mahaprajapati; his wife, Yashodhara; the king of Koshala; and Sudatta, who donated the Jetavana Monastery.

He taught all sorts of people, irrespective of their status, passing on his enlightenment to as many as possible. He lived for fifty years after reaching enlightenment at Buddh Gaya, and the teachings he expounded during this period were so numerous that they later came to be called the "eighty thousand teachings." He passed away at the age of eighty.

Shan-wu-wei (637–735): (Jap Zemmui; Skt Śubhākarasiṃha) Founder of the esoteric Shingon sect in China. He was born a prince in Udyana, India, and ascended the throne at thirteen, but abdicated and entered the priesthood because of his brother's jealousy. He studied esoteric Buddhism under Dharmagupta of the Nalanda Monastery. In 716 he came to China and engaged in translation of the sutras, including the *Dainichi* and *Soshitsuji* sutras. He was the first to introduce the esoteric teachings to China.

Shariputra: (Jap Sharihotsu) One of Shakyamuni's ten major disciples, known as the "foremost in wisdom." He was born in Magadha and was at first a follower of Sanjaya, one of the six non-Buddhist teachers. One day Shariputra happened to meet Ashvajit, a disciple of Shakyamuni, who taught him about the law of cause and effect. So impressed was Shariputra by the profundity of this doctrine and by Ashvajit's noble bearing that he joined the Buddhist Order. He later attained enlightenment when he heard the revelation in the *Hōben* (second) chapter of the Lotus Sutra that all phenomena are manifestations of the true entity of life.

Shibi: (Skt Śibi) The name of Shakyamuni in a past existence. One day the god Bishu disguised himself as a dove and Taishaku changed into a hawk in order to test King Shibi's faith. The dove was being pursued by the hawk and flew into King Shibi's robes for protection. In order to save the dove, Shibi sacrificed himself, offering his flesh to the starving hawk.

Shingon sect: Sect which upholds the esoteric teachings. The word *shingon* corresponds to the Sanskrit *mantra* (secret word, mystic syllable). This sect bases its doctrine on the *Dainichi* and *Kongōchō* sutras. In the eighth century Chinkang-chih (*q.v.*), Shan-wu-wei (*q.v.*) and Pu-k'ung (*q.v.*) came from India to Ch'ang-an, then the capital of China, bringing with them the esoteric teachings. In 804 the Japanese scholar Kūkai (Kōbō, *q.v.*) journeyed to Ch'ang-an and studied this teaching under Hui-kuo (Jap Keika), a disciple of Pu-k'ung. On returning to Japan, he established the Shingon sect there. In 816 he constructed Kongōbu-ji temple atop Mount Kōya and in 823 was given Tō-ji temple by the Imperial court. The Shingon sect engages in the practice of esoteric rituals. *See also* Dainichi Buddha; Esoteric teachings.

Shōhō: One's self, or subjective world. Buddhism teaches that the self and the environment are inseparable, because both are manifestations of Myoho-renge-kyo. *See also* Ehō.

Shōju: Propagating Buddhism without refuting misconceptions, gradually leading others to the supreme Buddhist teachings. *Shōju* was generally employed in the Former and Middle Days of the Law but is also used in the Latter Day among those who have no knowledge of, or prejudices against, Buddhism. *Shōju* also means to seek Buddhism, rather than to propagate it actively. *See also* Shakubuku.

Shōmon: (Skt śrāvaka) *See* Men of Learning.

Six difficult and nine easy acts: Comparisons expounded in the *Hōtō* (11th) chapter of the Lotus Sutra to teach people how difficult it would be to meet and embrace the Lotus Sutra during the Latter Day of the Law. The six difficult acts are to propagate the Lotus Sutra widely, to copy it, to recite it, to teach it to even one person, to hear of the Lotus Sutra and inquire about its meaning, and to maintain faith in the Lotus Sutra during the Latter Day of the Law. The nine easy acts include such feats as walking through fire carrying a load of dry grass on one's back without being burned, or kicking a major world into another corner of the universe with one's toe. These comparisons emphasize the need for endurance in the practice of true Buddhism. Although the nine easy acts appear impossible, they are nonetheless easy when compared with the difficulty of propagating the Lotus Sutra in the Latter Day of the Law.

Six non-Buddhist teachers: The six most influential thinkers in central India in the lifetime of Shakyamuni. They openly broke with the old Vedic tradition and challenged Brahman authority in the Indian social order. Though their doctrines differed considerably, they all rejected established moral standards and in consequence developed somewhat nihilistic schools of thought. They are Makkhali Gosala, Purana Kassapa, Ajita Kesakambalin, Pakudha Kacchayana, Sanjaya Velatthiputta, and Nigantha Nataputta.

Six paramitas: Six practices for bodhisattvas of Mahayana Buddhism. *Paramita* (Skt) means to cross from the shore of delusion to the shore of enlightenment. The six *paramitas* are the offering of alms, the observance of precepts, forbearance, assiduousness, meditation and the obtaining of wisdom.

Six paths: The first six of the Ten Worlds—Hell, Hunger, Animality, Anger, Humanity (or Tranquillity) and Heaven (or Rapture). The six paths indicate a state of delusion or suffering. They are contrasted to the four noble worlds— Learning, Realization, Bodhisattva and Buddhahood.

Six [Nara] sects: Sects which prospered in Nara, the Japanese capital during the Nara period (710–784). They are the Kusha, Jōjitsu, Sanron, Ritsu, Hossō and Kegon sects.

Subhuti: (Jap Shubodai) One of Shakyamuni's ten major disciples. He is said to have been a nephew of Sudatta, who donated the Jetavana Monastery to Shakyamuni. He was regarded as foremost in understanding the doctrine of *kū*. The *Juki* (sixth) chapter of the Lotus Sutra prophesied his enlightenment.

Sumeru, Mount: In ancient Indian cosmology, the highest of all mountains which stands at the center of the world. The Indians believed that the world is divided into four continents with Mount Sumeru in the middle. To the south of this mountain lies the continent called Jambudvipa (Jap *ichiembudai*) on which Buddhism spreads.

Sun Goddess: (Jap Tenshō Daijin or Amaterasu Ōmikami) A goddess in Japanese mythology, also regarded as one of the protectors of Buddhism. According to the oldest extant histories, the *Kojiki* (Record of Ancient Matters) and the *Nihon Shoki* (Chronicles of Japan), this goddess is the central deity and also the progenitor of the Imperial clan. She is also thought to be responsible for agricultural fertility.

Supreme vehicle: The teaching or means which leads all people to enlightenment. Sometimes called the "one supreme vehicle," indicating that the teaching which leads to Buddhahood is one and one alone. In Shakyamuni's teachings, the Lotus Sutra is the supreme vehicle. Before the Lotus Sutra, the three provisional vehicles of Learning, Realization and Bodhisattva remained paramount goals. In the Lotus Sutra, Shakyamuni refuted his disciples' attachment to these three as goals in themselves and revealed that the sole purpose of Buddhist practice is to attain Buddhahood through the supreme vehicle. In Nichiren Daishonin's Buddhism, the supreme vehicle is the Gohonzon.

Tahō Buddha: (Skt Prabhūtaratna-tathāgata) Buddha who appeared within the Treasure Tower at the ceremony in the air to lend credence to Shakyamuni's teachings in the Lotus Sutra. According to the *Hōtō* (11th) chapter of the Lotus Sutra, he lived in the land of Treasure Purity in an eastern part of the universe. While still engaged in bodhisattva practice, he pledged that, after he attained Buddhahood, he would appear in the Treasure Tower and attest to the validity of the Lotus Sutra wherever anyone might teach it. *See also* Ceremony in the air.

Taishaku: (Skt Śakra devānām Indra) One of the main tutelary gods of Buddhism, together with Bonten. He was originally the god of thunder and was adopted as a protective deity of Buddhism. Supported by the Four Heavenly Kings, he governs the thirty-three realms of heaven. He transformed himself into various forms to test Shakyamuni in his bodhisattva practice, but after Shakyamuni's enlightenment, he pledged to protect Buddhism. He appeared at the ceremony of the Lotus Sutra with twenty thousand retainers.

Tathagata: (Jap *nyorai*) One of the ten honorable titles of the Buddha. One who comprehends the true entity of life.

Tendai sect: T'ien-t'ai Buddhism in Japan as established by Dengyō in the early ninth century. *See also* Dengyō.

Ten directions: The eight points of the compass as well as up and down. Indicates the spatial dimension. "All Buddhas of the ten directions" means all Buddhas throughout the universe.

Ten factors: (Jap *jūnyoze*) Principle clarifying life's entity and functions. The Ten Factors are common to all life in any of the Ten Worlds. The first three factors are the appearance (*nyozesō*), nature (*nyozeshō*) and entity (*nyozetai*) of life. These three correspond, respectively, to life's physical aspects, spiritual aspects, and the entity which gives rise to and sustains both. The next six are power (*nyozeriki*), influence (*nyozesa*), internal cause (*nyozein*), relation (*nyozeen*), latent effect (*nyozeka*) and manifest effect (*nyozehō*)—all of which can be understood as functions of life. Lastly the principle which maintains them all in perfect harmony is called consistency from beginning to end (*nyozehommatsukukyōtō*).

Ten Goddesses: (Jap *Jūrasetsu-nyo*) Ten daughters of Kishimojin (*q.v.*), a female demon. In the *Dharani* (26th) chapter of the Lotus Sutra, this mother and her daughters pledged to protect the votaries of the Lotus Sutra.

Ten Worlds: (Jap *jikkai*) Ten states of life that are manifest in both physical and spiritual aspects of all human activities. They are Hell (Jap *jigoku*), Hunger (*gaki*), Animality (*chikushō*), Anger (*shura*), Humanity or Tranquillity (*nin*), Heaven or Rapture (*ten*), Learning (*shōmon*), Realization (*engaku*), Bodhisattva (*bosatsu*) and Buddhahood (*butsu*). All ten are eternally inherent in life and emerge in response to one's interaction with his environment.

Theoretical teaching: (Jap *shakumon*) Former half of the twenty-eight-chapter Lotus Sutra. The core of the theoretical teaching is revealed in the *Hōben* (second) chapter, which proclaims that all phenomena are manifestations of the true entity of life, and that Buddha wisdom is innate in all human beings. On the basis of this principle, it further reveals that the three goals of Learning, Realization and Bodhisattva are provisional and that the purpose of the Buddha's advent is to lead all people to Buddhahood.

Three calamities and seven disasters: (Jap *sansai shichinan*) Calamities described in various sutras. There are two categories of three calamities—minor and major. The minor ones are high grain prices or inflation (especially that caused by famine), warfare and pestilence. The major ones are disasters caused by fire, wind and water when the end of the world comes. The seven disasters differ according to the sutras. The *Yakushi* Sutra defines them as pestilence, foreign invasion, internal strife, extraordinary changes in the heavens, solar and lunar eclipses, unseasonable storms and typhoons, and unseasonable droughts.

Three evil paths: The three lowest of the Ten Worlds—Hell, Hunger and Animality. *See* Ten Worlds.

Three existences: Past, present and future. Three aspects of the eternity of life, linked inseparably by the law of cause and effect. Indicates the dimension of time. "Throughout the three existences" means throughout eternity.

Threefold world: The world of unenlightened men who dwell among the six paths. According to Vasubandhu's *Kusha Ron*, this world is divided into three: (1) the world of desires; (2) the world of form, where the inhabitants are free from desires but still bound by some kinds of material restrictions; (3) the world of spirit or formlessness, where one is beyond the restrictions of desire and matter.

Three Great Secret Laws: The core of Nichiren Daishonin's

Buddhism. (1) The true object of worship, the Dai-Gohonzon which Nichiren Daishonin inscribed on October 12, 1279; (2) the invocation of the daimoku, that is, the chanting of Nam-myoho-renge-kyo both for oneself and others; and (3) the high sanctuary, the *kaidan* which should be built in a place of magnificent beauty and insure the preservation of the Dai-Gohonzon.

Three groups of Shakyamuni's disciples: Also called the three groups of men of Learning. The men of Learning whose enlightenment was prophesied in the first half of the Lotus Sutra. Shakyamuni revealed in the theoretical teaching that the purpose of human life is not to attain the state of Learning, Realization or Bodhisattva, but to attain Buddhahood. However, his disciples differed in their capacity to understand this teaching. Shariputra was the first to understand, upon hearing it explained theoretically in the *Hōben* (second) chapter. He constitutes the first group. The *Hiyu* (third) chapter predicts his enlightenment. Maudgalyayana, Mahakashyapa, Katyayana and Subhuti understood the Buddha's teaching through the parable related in the *Hiyu* chapter. These disciples form the second group, whose enlightenment is predicted in the *Juki* (sixth) chapter. Purna, Ananda, Rahula and others, who finally understood the Buddha's teaching by hearing about their relationship with Shakyamuni since the remote past of *sanzen-jintengō* as explained in the *Kejōyu* (seventh) chapter, comprise the third group.

Three illusions: T'ien-t'ai divided illusions into three main categories. (1) Illusions of thought and desire. The former are distorted views of life, of which T'ien-t'ai said there were eighty-eight types. The latter include such base inclinations as covetousness, anger, ignorance and arrogance. These illusions, he said, cause people to suffer in the six paths. (2) Illusions preventing bodhisattvas from saving others. These occur when a bodhisattva lacks understanding of the teachings he must learn to save all men. (3) The forty-two fundamental illusions which prevent a bodhisattva from attaining enlightenment, the last and most serious one being fundamental darkness (*gampon no mumyō*).

Three obstacles and four devils: (Jap *sanshō shima*) Various obstacles to the practice of Buddhism. The three obstacles are: (1) *bonnō-shō*: obstacles due to the three poisons—greed, anger and stupidity; (2) *gō-shō*: obstacles due to karma created by committing the five cardinal sins. *Gō-shō* also means opposition from one's wife and children; (3) *hō-shō*: obstacles due to painful retribution caused by actions in the three evil paths—Hell, Hunger and Animality. *Hō-shō* also refers to obstacles caused by one's superiors (sovereign, parents, etc.).

The four devils are: (1) *bonnō-ma*: obstructions arising from the three poisons (*q.v.*); (2) *on-ma*: the obstacle of the five components—form, perception, conception, volition and consciousness. The human body and mind come into existence through the temporary combination of these five components, and they cause many kinds of sufferings; (3) *shima*: the obstacle of death, which ends one's practice of Buddhism, or the untimely death of a believer which provokes doubts in others; (4) *tenji-ma*: obstruction by the Devil of the Sixth Heaven (*q.v.*). This obstruction occurs in the form of oppression by men of influence and power and is the most difficult of all to conquer.

Three poisons: (Jap *sandoku*) Greed, anger and stupidity— the fundamental evils inherent in life which give rise to human suffering.

Three powerful enemies: (Jap *sanrui no gōteki*) Three types of people described in the *Kanji* (13th) chapter of the Lotus Sutra who will persecute those who propagate the sutra in the evil age after the Buddha's passing. They are: (1) lay people ignorant of Buddhism who denounce the votaries of the Lotus Sutra and attack them with swords or staves; (2)

arrogant and cunning priests who slander the votaries; and
(3) those priests who enjoy the respect of the general public
and who, in fear of losing fame or profit, induce the
authorities to persecute the votaries of the Lotus Sutra.

Three properties: (Jap *sanjin*) The property of the Law (*hos-shin*), the property of wisdom (*hōshin*) and the property of
action (*ōjin*). *Hosshin* is the truth of a Buddha's life; *hōshin* is
the wisdom to perceive the truth; while *ōjin* is the merciful
actions of a Buddha to save people and the physical body
which manifests the Buddha's life in this world for that
purpose. Before the Lotus Sutra these three were explained
as three different Buddhas, but in the Lotus Sutra they were
shown to be the three properties of a single Buddha.

Three realms of existence: (Jap *sanseken*) Also three principles
of individualization. (1) The five components of life (*go'on-seken*)—form, perception, conception, volition and con-sciousness. (2) The realm of living beings (*shujō-seken*). (3)
The realm of the environment of living beings (*kokudo-seken*). *See also* Ichinen sanzen.

Three teachings: Teachings expounded before the Lotus
Sutra. Indicates *zōkyō, tsūgyō* and *bekkyō*, the first three of the
four teachings of doctrine. *See* Eight teachings.

Three thousand conditions: (Jap *sanzen*) All phenomena in
the universe, or all possible conditions of life. *See* Ichinen
sanzen.

Three treasures: (Jap *sampō*) The Buddha, the Law and the
Priesthood. The Buddha is one awakened to the truth of life
who possesses the three virtues of sovereign, teacher and
parent. The Law is the teaching expounded by the Buddha
revealing his own enlightenment. The Priesthood indicates
the Buddha's disciples who inherit and transmit the Law to
future generations. Explanations of the three treasures differ
according to the time and the sect of Buddhism. In Nichiren
Shoshu, "the Buddha" indicates the original Buddha, Nichi-ren Daishonin; "the Law" is the Dai-Gohonzon, the object

of worship; and "the Priesthood" is specifically Nikkō Shonin, who succeeded Nichiren Daishonin, and more broadly indicates the successive high priests.

Three truths: (Jap *santai*) Also called the three perceptions of existence. These truths are temporary form (*ketai*), nature or potential (*kūtai*) and entity (*chūtai*). Temporary form indicates the physical or material aspects of life, nature indicates spiritual or qualitative aspects, and entity, the eternal and unchanging life-essence which is neither physical nor spiritual but manifests itself as both.

Three vehicles: The states of Learning, Realization and Bodhisattva. Also, the provisional teachings expounded for people in these three states. In his provisional teachings Shakyamuni encouraged his disciples to aspire to the three vehicles as goals in themselves, but in the Lotus Sutra he refuted these states as final aims and taught that they were simply means to lead people to the ultimate purpose of life, attaining Buddhahood.

Three virtues: (Jap *santoku*) The virtues of sovereign, teacher and parent which the Buddha possesses. The virtue of sovereign means the power to protect the people. The virtue of teacher means the wisdom to lead them to enlightenment. The virtue of parent indicates the compassion to save them from unhappiness.

T'ien-t'ai (538–597): Another name for Chih-i. Founder of the T'ien-t'ai sect who expounded the doctrine of *ichinen sanzen*. He classified all Shakyamuni's sutras into five periods and eight teachings according to their order, content and method of preaching, demonstrating that the Lotus Sutra is the highest of all. His profound studies of the Lotus Sutra were compiled in three major works: the *Hokke Gengi*, *Hokke Mongu* and *Maka Shikan*. It was in the *Maka Shikan* that he revealed the theory of *ichinen sanzen*. *See also* Ichinen sanzen; Five periods; Eight teachings.

Tranquillity: (Jap *nin*) Also called Humanity, fifth of the Ten

Worlds. Life-condition in which one controls his desires and impulses with reason, exercises good judgment and lives in harmony with his surroundings. *See also* Ten Worlds.

Treasure Tower: (Jap *hōtō*) Tower of Tahō Buddha which appeared in the *Hōtō* (11th) chapter of the Lotus Sutra. The Treasure Tower is adorned with seven kinds of precious substances including gold and silver. In Nichiren Daishonin's Buddhism it indicates Nam-myoho-renge-kyo and also the lives of those who worship the Gohonzon.

True Buddha: (Jap *hombutsu*) The Buddha who revealed his true identity. By this terminology Nichiren Daishonin refers to two Buddhas: Shakyamuni who attained enlightenment at the time of *gohyaku-jintengō* and himself, the Buddha of *kuon ganjo*. In the latter sense, the expression "original Buddha" is also often used.

True Mahayana: The Lotus Sutra. Mahayana teachings are divided into two categories—provisional and true. Provisional Mahayana was expounded only as a means to lead people gradually to the Lotus Sutra. True Mahayana is so called because it fully reveals the Buddha's enlightenment.

Tsūgyō: *See* Eight teachings.

Twenty-four successors: The successors of Shakyamuni Buddha who appeared in the Former Day of the Law and propagated the Buddha's teachings. They are listed in an account entitled *Fuhōzō Innenden* (The History of the Buddha's Successors). The twenty-four successors are: (1) Mahakashyapa, (2) Ananda, (3) Madhyantika, (4) Shanakavasa, (5) Upagupta, (6) Dhritaka, (7) Mikkaka, (8) Buddhananda, (9) Buddhamitra, (10) Parshva, (11) Punyayasha, (12) Ashvaghosha, (13) Kapimala, (14) Nagarjuna, (15) Kanadeva, (16) Rahulata, (17) Samghanandi, (18) Samghayashas, (19) Kumarata, (20) Jayata, (21) Vasubandhu, (22) Manorhita, (23) Haklena, and (24) Aryasinha.

Two vehicles: (Jap *nijō*) The two kinds of teachings expounded for people of Learning and people of Realization respectively. *Nijō* also means men of Learning and Realization, but the translations in this book employ the terms "men of *shōmon* and *engaku*" or "men of the two vehicles." *See also* Shōmon and Engaku.

Vasubandhu: (Jap Tenjin or Seshin) Fifth-century Buddhist scholar of northern India. He originally studied Hinayana and wrote the *Kusha Ron* (Skt Abhidharma-kośa-śāstra). At first he criticized Mahayana but was later converted by his elder brother Asanga, and wrote many treatises clarifying the Mahayana teachings.

Votary of the Lotus Sutra: One who propagates the Lotus Sutra and practices Buddhism in exact accordance with its teachings. In the Middle Day of the Law, T'ien-t'ai and Dengyō practiced as votaries of the Lotus Sutra. In the Latter Day of the Law, the term "votary of the Lotus Sutra" refers specifically to Nichiren Daishonin and in a more general sense to those who embrace the Law of Nam-myoho-renge-kyo and devote themselves to its propagation.

Yakuō: (Skt Bhaisajya-rāja) Bodhisattva who serves people by providing them with medicine to cure their physical and spiritual diseases.

Yakushi Buddha: (Skt Bhaisajya-guru) Lord of the Emerald World in the eastern part of the universe. As a bodhisattva he vowed to cure the diseases of all people.

Zen sect: Buddhist sect based on the idea that enlightenment is attained by meditation. Zen generally denies the sutras, maintaining that the Buddha's enlightenment is not transmitted by the Buddhist scriptures but transferred from mind to mind.

Zōkyō: *See* Eight teachings.